Contemporary Debates on Terrorism

Contemporary Debates on Terrorism is an innovative new textbook, addressing a number of key issues in contemporary terrorism studies from both 'traditional' and 'critical' perspectives.

In recent years the terrorism studies field has grown significantly, with an increasing number of scholars beginning to debate the complex dynamics underlying this category of violence. Within the broader field, there are many identifiable controversies and issues that divide scholarly opinion, a number of which are discussed in this text:

- theoretical issues, such as the definition of terrorism and state terrorism;
- substantive issues, including the threat posed by al-Qaeda and the utility of different responses to terrorism;
- ethical issues, encompassing the torture of terrorist suspects and targeted assassination.

The format of the volume involves a leading scholar taking a particular position on the controversy, followed by an opposing or alternative viewpoint written by another contributor. In addition to the pedagogic value of allowing students to read opposing arguments in one place, the volume will also be important for providing an overview of the state of the field and its key lines of debate.

Contemporary Debates on Terrorism will be essential reading for all students of terrorism and political violence, critical terrorism studies, security studies and IR in general.

Richard Jackson is Professor in International Politics at Aberystwyth University. He is the Founding Editor of the Routledge journal *Critical Studies on Terrorism*, the convenor of the British International Studies Association (BISA) Critical Studies on Terrorism Working Group (CSTWG), and Editor of the Routledge Critical Terrorism Studies series. He is the author/editor of four books on terrorism and conflict issues.

Samuel Justin Sinclair is Assistant Professor of Psychology at Harvard Medical School, and Director of Research at the Massachusetts General Hospital's Psychological Evaluation and Research Laboratory (PEaRL). He is also Founder and Co-Editor-in-Chief of the peer-refereed journal *Behavioral Sciences of Terrorism and Political Aggression*. He is the author/editor of two books.

Contemporary
Debates on Terrorism

**Edited by Richard Jackson
and Samuel Justin Sinclair**

Routledge
Taylor & Francis Group

LONDON AND NEW YORK

First published 2012
by Routledge
2 Park Square, Milton Park, Abingdon, Oxon, OX14 4RN

Simultaneously published in the USA and Canada
by Routledge
711 Third Avenue, New York, NY 10017

Routledge is an imprint of the Taylor & Francis Group, an informa business

British Library Cataloguing in Publication Data
A catalogue record for this book is available from the British Library

Library of Congress Cataloging-in-Publication Data
Contemporary debates on terrorism / edited by Richard Jackson and Samuel Justin Sinclair.
p. cm.
Includes bibliographical references and index.
1. Terrorism. 2. Terrorism–Prevention. I. Jackson, Richard, 1966– II. Sinclair, Samuel J., 1975–
HV6431.C6528 2012
363.325–dc23
2011032277

ISBN13: 978–0–415–59115–7 (hbk)
ISBN13: 978–0–415–59116–4 (pbk)
ISBN13: 978–0–203–13535–8 (ebk)

Typeset in Baskerville by
Keystroke, Station Road, Codsall, Wolverhampton

MIX
Paper from
responsible sources
FSC   FSC® C004839
www.fsc.org

Printed and bound in Great Britain by
TJ International Ltd, Padstow, Cornwall

Dedication

Richard Jackson: This book is dedicated to my supervisor, colleague and friend, Professor Jacob Bercovitch (1946–2011).

Samuel Justin Sinclair: This book is dedicated to my mentor, colleague and, most importantly, my friend, Dr Mark Alan Blais.

Contents

Acknowledgements   xi
The editors   xiii
Notes on contributors   xv

Introduction: contemporary debates on terrorism   1
Richard Jackson and Samuel Justin Sinclair

PART I
Definition of terrorism   9

**1 Is terrorism still a useful analytical term or should it be
abandoned?**   11

YES: The utility of the concept of terrorism   11
Paul Wilkinson

NO: A landscape of meaning: constructing understandings of   17
political violence from the broken paradigm of 'terrorism'
Dominic Bryan

Discussion questions   24
Further readings   25

PART II
Categories of terrorism   27

2 Is there a 'new terrorism' in existence today?   29

YES: The 'new terrorism' or the 'newness' of context and change   29
Alejandra Bolanos

NO: The fallacy of the new terrorism thesis   35
Isabelle Duyvesteyn and Leena Malkki

Discussion questions   42
Further readings   42

3 Can states be terrorists?   **43**

YES: State terror: the theoretical and practical utilities and
implications of a contested concept   43
Michael Stohl

NO: State terrorism: who needs it?   50
Colin Wight

Discussion questions   57
Further readings   57

PART III
The terrorism threat   **59**

4 Is terrorism a serious threat to international and
national security?   **61**

YES: The continuing threat to state security   61
James Lutz and Brenda Lutz

NO: Why terrorism is a much smaller threat than you think   66
Ian S. Lustick

Discussion questions   74
Further readings   75

5 Is WMD terrorism a likely prospect in the future?   **76**

YES: WMD terrorism: a potential threat to international security   76
Natividad Carpintero-Santamaría

NO: WMD terrorism: the prospects   84
John Mueller

Discussion questions   89
Further readings   89

6 Does al-Qaeda continue to pose a serious international
threat?   **90**

YES: The enduring al-Qaeda threat: a network perspective   90
Jeffrey B. Cozzens and Magnus Ranstorp

NO: Al-Qaeda: a diminishing threat   97
Lee Jarvis

Discussion questions   103
Further readings   103

PART IV
The causes of terrorism   **105**

7 Is terrorism the result of root causes such as poverty and exclusion?   **107**

YES: Do structural factors explain terrorism?   107
Dipak K. Gupta

NO: Poverty and exclusion are not the root causes of terrorism   113
L. Rowell Huesmann and Graham R. Huesmann

Discussion questions   119
Further readings   120

8 Is religious extremism a major cause of terrorism?   **121**

YES: Religious extremism as a major cause of terrorism   121
Amanda Munroe and Fathali M. Moghaddam

NO: 'Religious terrorism' as ideology   127
Jeff Goodwin

Discussion questions   134
Further readings   134

PART V
Dealing with terrorism   **135**

9 Are counterterrorism frameworks based on suppression and military force effective in responding to terrorism?   **137**

YES: The use of force to combat terrorism   137
Boaz Ganor

NO: Wars of terror – learning the lessons of failure   143
Paul Rogers

Discussion questions   150
Further readings   150

10 Is the use of coercive interrogation or torture permissible and effective as a counterterrorism method?   **152**

YES: The truth about American state interrogation techniques, torture and the ticking time-bomb terrorist   152
Jeffrey Addicott

NO: Why torture is wrong   159
Robert Brecher

Discussion questions   165
Further readings   165

11 Is the targeted assassination of terrorist suspects an effective response to terrorism?   **166**

YES: A viable and vital policy option   166
Stephanie Carvin

NO: The case against targeted assassination   173
Andrew Silke

Discussion questions   180
Further readings   180

12 Have global efforts to reduce terrorism and political violence been effective in the past decade?   **181**

YES: 'Looking for a needle in a stack of needles'   181
Mark Cochrane

NO: 'Using a sledgehammer to crack a nut'   187
Rachel Monaghan

Discussion questions   193
Further readings   193

References   195
Index   215

Acknowledgements

This book would not have been possible without the generous and dedicated involvement of the eminent group of professionals who contributed chapters to it. We are extremely grateful to them for their grace and patience in dealing with our demands and requirements, and for their time and thoughtfulness in helping us assemble what we view to be an important body of work. In particular, we are very grateful to those contributors who came in at the last minute and wrote excellent chapters under immense time pressures. You know who you are, and so do we.

We are also grateful to Andrew Humphrys at Routledge who was crucial in developing the project in the first place, and who encouraged us to persevere at critical points along the way. The book would not have happened without his involvement. In fact, all the staff at Routledge have shown genuine skill and professionalism during the project, and we are thankful to have such a wonderful publication team.

We would also like to express our appreciation and gratitude to our respective academic institutions for the encouragement and support they have shown us in this project. Specifically, Richard Jackson would like to thank the Department of International Politics at Aberystwyth University, Wales. Much of the work for this volume was completed during a generous university sabbatical. Samuel Justin Sinclair would also like to thank Dr Mark Blais and his friends and colleagues at the Massachusetts General Hospital and Harvard Medical School, particularly those working within the Psychological Evaluation and Research Laboratory (*The PEaRL*). We both feel very lucky to have such a strong and supportive group of colleagues with whom to engage in what we see as important work.

We are especially grateful to Michelle Jackson who gave generously of her time and read every line and spent hours checking all aspects to try to help make it the best manuscript it could be. Her support, both personal and professional, has been immensely important to the success of this venture. Of course, any remaining errors are the sole responsibility of the editors.

Finally, we want to express our sadness at the death of Paul Wilkinson who passed away during the final production of this volume. We are honoured and privileged that we are able to publish his chapter as the first substantive piece of the book. Paul Wilkinson was a true giant in the field of terrorism studies and leaves a lasting intellectual legacy. One of its original founders, he was highly influential in the field's development and growth to the position it occupies today, and he continued to be active in terrorism research up to his death. We are immensely grateful to have been able to work with him, even briefly, and we want to express our deepest condolences to his family, friends and colleagues.

Richard Jackson	Samuel Justin Sinclair
Aberystwyth, Wales, UK	Boston, Massachusetts, USA

The editors

Richard Jackson is Professor of International Politics, Aberystwyth University, UK. He is Editor-in-Chief of the journal *Critical Studies on Terrorism* and the editor of the Routledge Critical Terrorism Studies series. He is the author or editor of several books on terrorism and conflict resolution, including: *Contemporary State Terrorism: Theory and Cases* (Routledge, 2010, co-edited with Scott Poynting and Eamon Murphy); *Conflict Resolution in the Twenty-first Century: Principles, Methods and Approaches* (Michigan University Press, 2009, co-authored with Jacob Bercovitch); *Critical Terrorism Studies: A New Research Agenda* (Routledge, 2009, co-edited with Marie Breen Smyth and Jeroen Gunning); and *Writing the War on Terrorism: Language, Politics and Counterterrorism* (Manchester University Press, 2005). He blogs regularly on terrorism, war and peace at: http://richardjacksonterrorismblog.wordpress.com/.

Samuel Justin Sinclair is an Assistant Professor at Harvard Medical School and Director of Research at The Massachusetts General Hospital's Psychological Evaluation and Research Laboratory (*The PEaRL*). He is also Founder and Past-President of the Society for Terrorism Research (STR), and Founder and Co-Editor-in-Chief of the peer-refereed journal, *Behavioral Sciences of Terrorism and Political Aggression*. He is also co-author of the forthcoming book, *A Psychology of Fear: Understanding the 'Terror' in Terrorism* (Oxford University Press, forthcoming 2012). Additionally, he has published numerous papers in the areas of terrorism, aggression, violence, psychological assessment and psychometrics, and continues to have active research programs in these areas. Dr. Sinclair is also the developer of the *Terrorism Catastrophizing Scale* (TCS), a psychological assessment tool measuring anticipatory fears about terrorism. He is also a past recipient of the Association for Threat Assessment Professional's (ATAP) Dr Chris Hatcher Memorial Scholarship Award (2007).

Notes on contributors

Jeffrey Addicott is Distinguished Professor of Law and Director of the Center for Terrorism Law, St. Mary's University School of Law. He holds a B.A. (with honors), University of Maryland; J.D.; University of Alabama School of Law LL.M.; The Judge Advocate General's Legal Center and School; LL.M. (1992) and S.J.D. (1994), University of Virginia School of Law. He served for twenty years in the US Army and was the senior legal adviser to the US Special Forces. His latest book is *Terrorism Law: Materials, Cases, and Comments* (Lawyers and Judges Publishing Co. 2011). This chapter was prepared under the auspices of the Center for Terrorism Law located at St. Mary's University School of Law, San Antonio, Texas.

Alejandra Bolanos is an Associate Professor and Head of the International Security Studies Department at the College of International Security Affairs, National Defense University in Washington, DC. She received a Masters of Arts in Law and Diplomacy and her Ph.D. from The Fletcher School of Law and Diplomacy. As a fellow and analyst, Dr. Bolanos has held positions at Singapore's Institute of Defence and Strategic Studies, the International Centre for Political Violence and Terrorism Research (ICPVTR) at the SITE Intelligence Group, and at the Center for Strategic International Studies (CSIS) in Washington DC. She has worked with private and non-profit organizations on products linked to the overall transformation of warfare as it relates to the ongoing synergy between social movements, violent non-state actors, information technologies, and religio-political ideologies.

Robert Brecher is Professor of Moral Philosophy at the University of Brighton, UK, and Director of its Centre for Applied Philosophy, Politics and Ethics. He has published over 60 articles in moral theory, applied ethics and politics, healthcare and medical ethics, sexual politics, terrorism and the politics of higher education. His latest book, *Torture and the Ticking Bomb* (Wiley-Blackwell, 2007) is the first book-length rebuttal of calls to legalize interrogational torture. Currently, he is working on a theory of morality as practical reason, building on his earlier book, *Getting What You Want? A Critique of Liberal Morality* (Routledge, 1997). A past president of the Association for Legal and Social Philosophy, he is also on the Board of a number of academic journals.

Dominic Bryan is Director of the Institute of Irish Studies at Queens University, Belfast, the Chair of Diversity Challenges, and the former Chair of Democratic Dialogue, Ireland's first think tank. He is an anthropologist researching political rituals, commemoration, public space and identity in Northern Ireland. In 2001/2, he was a part of the Clio Group that evaluated government funding to victims groups in Northern Ireland. He is a member of the Living Memorial subgroup of Healing Through Remembering, and is part of a number of research projects examining processes of commemoration. He has also worked with the Northern Ireland Human Rights Commission and the Northern Ireland Community Relations Council.

Natividad Carpintero-Santamaría is Professor at the Polytechnic University of Madrid (Spain), General Secretary of the Institute of Nuclear Fusion, diploma in High Studies of Defence and collaborator in the field of CBRN threats at the Air Force Warfare Center and at the Center for National Defence Studies. She is the author of *The Atom Bomb: The Human Factor during Second World War* (Ediciones Díaz de Santos, 2007) and co-editor of *Inertial Confinement Nuclear Fusion: A Historical Approach by its Pioneers* (Foxwell & Davies, 2007). She has lectured in Latin America, the Middle East, the former Soviet Union, and the United States, and has co-organized eight international conferences as general secretary. In 1991, she received the Alfonso XIII Award from the National Academy of Sciences and the first prize for her Ph.D. thesis in 1994. She has been awarded the Air Force White Cross for Aeronautical Merit and is a corresponding member of the European Academy of Sciences.

Stephanie Carvin is a Lecturer in the Department of Politics and International Relations, Royal Holloway University of London. She is the author of *Prisoners of America's Wars: From the Early Republic to Guantanamo* (Columbia/Hurst: 2010), and has published in the *Journal of Conflict and Security Law*, and *International Studies Perspectives*. She holds a Ph.D. in International Relations from the London School of Economics, and blogs on international law, human security and the 'War on Terror' at http://duckofminerva.blogspot.com.

Mark Cochrane is a former Police Officer with over 28 years of experience in the Police Service of Northern Ireland (PSNI) and the Royal Ulster Constabulary George Cross (RUC GC). For over 20 years, he was employed in national security intelligence work and, prior to his retirement, was the officer in charge of counterterrorism training in the PSNI. He is a former recipient of a Fulbright Police Fellowship that was spent with the FBI in New York. Currently a self-employed intelligence and training consultant, he is engaged in work with a number of agencies, in addition to teaching part-time at the University of Ulster and lecturing at US academic institutions.

Jeffrey B. Cozzens is President of White Mountain Research, an international affairs firm specializing in counterterrorism research and advising. He served previously as Religious Extremism Advisor at the Army Directed Studies Office, and has researched Islamist movements and terrorism since 1995.

Isabelle Duyvesteyn is Associate Professor at the Department of History of International Relations at Utrecht University in the Netherlands. She completed a Ph.D. in War Studies at King's College London, and has worked at the Netherlands Institute of International Affairs and the Netherlands Defence Academy. Her research interests include problems of war and peace and the history of terrorism and insurgency. Her work has been published in, among others, *Civil Wars*, *Security Studies* and *Small Wars and Insurgencies*.

Boaz Ganor is the Deputy Dean of the Lauder School of Government, Diplomacy and Strategy, and the Founder and Executive Director of the International Institute for Counter-Terrorism (ICT). He is the founder and President of the International Academic Counter-Terrorism Community (ICTAC). In 2008–2010, Dr. Ganor served as a Koret Distinguished Visiting Fellow at the Hoover Institution, Stanford University. He is also a member of the International Advisory Council of the International Centre for Political

Violence and Terrorism Research, and the co-founder of the International Centre for the Study of Radicalization and Political Violence (ICSR), and was a Senior Fellow at The Memorial Institute for Prevention of Terrorism (MIPT), Oklahoma City, USA. Dr. Ganor is a member of the International Advisory Team of the Manhattan Institute (CTCT) to the New York Police Department (NYPD). In addition, he has served as an advisor on counterterrorism to several Israeli ministries and the Israeli National Security Council.

Jeff Goodwin is Professor of Sociology at New York University, where he has taught since 1991. His writings have focused on social movements, revolutions and political violence. He is currently finishing a book titled *Choosing Terror*. His book *No Other Way Out: States and Revolutionary Movements, 1945–1991* (Cambridge, 2001) won the Outstanding Book Prize of the Collective Behavior and Social Movements Section of the American Sociological Association (ASA). He is the co-editor, with James M. Jasper, of *Contention in Context* (Stanford, 2012), *The Social Movements Reader*, 2nd edn (Wiley-Blackwell, 2009), *Rethinking Social Movements* (Rowman & Littlefield, 2004), and *Passionate Politics: Emotions and Social Movements* (University of Chicago, 2001), also co-edited with Francesca Polletta.

Dipak K. Gupta is Professor Emeritus and Distinguished Professor in Political Science at San Diego State University. He is the author of, among many other books, *Understanding Terrorism and Political Violence: The Life Cycle of Birth, Growth, Transformation and Demise* (Routledge, 2008).

Graham R. Huesmann is a Clinical Fellow in Epilepsy and a Research Fellow in Neurology at Harvard Medical School and Massachusetts General Hospital. He received his BS at the University of Oregon in 1993, and his M.D. and Ph.D. in Neuroscience from the University of Illinois in 2007. Since 2007, he has been on the staff of Harvard Medical School and Massachusetts General Hospital where he completed his neurology residency in 2011. His prior research has focused on the role of caspase-3 in memory trace capture, the regulation of this enzyme in normal brains and the role of genetic and functional mutations in Alzheimer's and autism. His work has been funded by an NRSA and an R25 grant from NINDS.

L. Rowell Huesmann is the Amos N. Tversky Collegiate Professor of Psychology and Communication Studies and Director of the Research Center for Group Dynamics at the University of Michigan's Institute for Social Research. He is also editor of the journal *Aggressive Behavior* and past-president of the *International Society for Research on Aggression*. He was the recipient in 2005 of the American Psychological Association's award for Distinguished Lifetime Contributions to Media Psychology. Currently, he is a member of the National Academy's Institute of Medicine's Forum on Global Violence Prevention. His research and writing over the past 40 years has focused on the psychological foundations of aggressive and violent behavior. He received his BS at the University of Michigan in 1964 and his Ph.D. at Carnegie-Mellon University in 1969. Prior to joining the faculty at Michigan in 1992, he was an Assistant and Associate Professor of Psychology at Yale University and Professor of Psychology and chair of the psychology department at the University of Illinois at Chicago.

Lee Jarvis is Lecturer in the Department of Political and Cultural Studies at Swansea University, UK. He is author of *Times of Terror: Discourse, Temporality and the War on Terror* (Palgrave, 2009) and co-author (with Richard Jackson, Jeroen Gunning and Marie Breen Smyth) of *Terrorism: A Critical Introduction* (Palgrave, 2011). His work on terrorism and counterterrorism has been published in *Security Dialogue, Contemporary Politics, Critical Studies* *on Terrorism* and *Journal of War and Culture Studies*. His most recent project (with Michael Lister) is the ESRC-funded *Anti-terrorism, Citizenship and Security in the UK*, a qualitative investigation of public attitudes towards counterterrorism powers within the United Kingdom.

Ian S. Lustick is the Bess W. Heyman Professor of Political Science at the University of Pennsylvania, USA. He is the author of *Trapped in the War on Terror* (University of Pennsylvania Press, 2006) and numerous books and articles on various aspects of the Arab-Israeli conflict, Middle East politics and American foreign policy. He is a pioneer in the development of analytic and preductive models integrating social service theory and computational singulation. Professor Lustick worked as a Middle East analyst in the State Department's Bureau of Intelligence and Research from 1979 to 1980.

James and Brenda Lutz Currently Professor and Chair of Political Science at Indiana University-Purdue University, James M. Lutz received his Ph.D. from the University of Texas. Dr Brenda J. Lutz received her Ph.D. from the University of Dundee and is presently a Research Associate at the Decision Science and Theory Institute at Indiana University-Purdue University. They have collaborated on two editions of *Global Terrorism* (Routledge, 2004 and 2008), and *Terrorism: Origins and Evolution* (Palgrave, 2005), *Terrorism in America* (Palgrave, 2007), and *Terrorism: The Basics* (Routledge, 2011). They have also compiled a four-volume collection of articles and chapters, *Global Terrorism* (Sage, 2008) and co-authored a dozen articles or chapters dealing with terrorism and political violence.

Leena Malkki is a university teacher at the Network for European Studies at the University of Helsinki, Finland. Her Ph.D. thesis examined how and why the terrorist campaigns of the Rode Jeugd and the Symbionese Liberation Army declined. Her publications include *Terrorismin monet kasvot* (Many Faces of Terrorism), co-authored with Jukka Paastela *et al.* (WSOY Oppimateriaalit, 2007). Her work has been published in, among others, *Terrorism and Political Violence* and *Critical Studies on Terrorism*.

Fathali M. Moghaddam is Professor, Department of Psychology, and Director, Conflict Resolution Program, Department of Government, Georgetown University. His research interests include intergroup conflict and the psychology of globalization, dictatorship and terrorism. His most recent books include *The New Global Insecurity* (Praeger Security International, 2010) and *Words of Conflict, Words of War* (with Rom Harré, Praeger, 2010). He is currently writing a book on *The Psychology of Dictatorship* to be published by APA Press. More about his research can be found at: fathalimoghaddam.com.

Rachel Monaghan is Senior Lecturer in Criminology at the University of Ulster, Northern Ireland. Her Ph.D. was from the University of Reading, England and examined the phenomenon of single-issue terrorism. She has been researching paramilitary violence in Northern Ireland for the past 13 years. Her publications include *Informal Justice in Divided Societies* (with Colin Knox) published by Palgrave Macmillan in 2002, and she has published articles in *The Journal of Conflict Studies*, *Terrorism and Political Violence* and *Studies in Conflict and Terrorism*.

John Mueller is Woody Hayes Chair of National Security Studies at the Mershon Center at Ohio State University in the United States. He is the author of a dozen books, including *Retreat from Doomsday* (Basic Books, 1989), *Capitalism, Democracy, and Ralph's Pretty Good Grocery* (Princeton University Press, 1999), *The Remnants of War* (Cornell University Press, 2004), *Overblown* (Free Press, 2006), *Atomic Obsession* (Oxford University Press, 2010), *War and Ideas*

(Routledge, 2011), and (with Mark Stewart), *Terror, Security, and Money: Balancing the Risks, Costs, and Benefits of Homeland Security* (Oxford University Press, 2011). He is a member of the American Academy of Arts and Sciences, has been a John Simon Guggenheim Fellow, and has received grants from the National Science Foundation and the National Endowment for the Humanities. In 2009, he received the International Studies Association's Susan Strange Award recognizing 'a person whose singular intellect, assertiveness, and insight most challenge conventional wisdom and intellectual and organizational complacency in the international studies community'.

Amanda Munroe is a Master's candidate in the Conflict Resolution Program, Department of Government, Georgetown University. Her current research focuses on intercultural integration and sport as a tool for peace education.

Magnus Ranstorp is Research Director of the Center for Asymmetric Threat Studies at the Swedish National Defence College, and a Member of EU Expert Groups on (Violent) Radicalisation. He has 20 years of experience in research on counterterrorism issues and testified at the 9/11 Commission hearing.

Paul Rogers is Professor of Peace Studies at Bradford University, UK, and is a consultant to the Oxford Research Group, an independent UK think tank. The most recent of his 26 books are *Global Security and the War on Terror: Elite Security and the Illusion of Control* (Routledge, 2007) and the third edition of *Losing Control: Global Security in the 21st Century* (Pluto Press, 2010).

Andrew Silke is the Director for Terrorism Studies at the University of East London where he also holds a Chair in Criminology. He is widely recognized as an expert on the psychology of terrorism in particular, and has over 100 publications on subjects dealing with terrorism and counterterrorism. Professor Silke serves by invitation on the United Nations Roster of Terrorism Experts and the European Commission's European Network of Experts on Radicalisation. He has provided invited briefings on terrorism-related issues to Select Committees of the UK House of Commons and was appointed in 2009 as a Specialist Advisor to the House of Commons Communities and Local Government Committee for its inquiry into the UK Government's programme for preventing violent extremism. In 2010, he gave invited oral testimony before the Canadian Special Senate Committee on Anti-terrorism. His most recent book is *The Psychology of Counter-Terrorism* (Routledge, 2011).

Michael Stohl is a Professor in the Department of Communication and the Department of Political Science at the University of California, Santa Barbara. He is the author of four books and more than one hundred journal articles and book chapters, and the editor of eleven other volumes. His most recent books are *Crime and Terrorism*, co-authored with Peter Grabosky (SAGE Publications, 2010) and *Fragile States: Violence and the Failure of Intervention* (Polity Press, 2011, co-authored with Lothar Brock, Hans-Henrik Holm and George Sorensen). His article (co-authored with Cynthia Stohl) 'Networks of terror: theoretical assumptions and pragmatic consequences', published in *Communication Theory* in 2007, won both the International Communication Association best published article of the year and the National Communication Association best published article in Organizational Communication awards. In 2010, he was awarded the International Communication Association Public Policy Research Award for his work on Human Rights and State Terrorism.

Colin Wight is a Professor of International Relations at the University of Sydney. He has previously taught at Aberystwyth University, the University of Sheffield and the University of Exeter. His research focuses on the philosophy of social science, social theory and international relations theory. Selected publications include *Scientific Realism and International Relations* (edited with Jonathan Joseph, Routledge, 2010), *Agents, Structures and International Relations: Politics as Ontology* (Cambridge, 2006) and *Realism, Philosophy and Social Science* (co-authored with Kathryn Dean, John Roberts and Jonathan Joseph, Palgrave, 2006). He has published in *International Studies Quarterly*, *Political Studies*, *Millennium* and the *European Journal of International Relations*. He is also currently the Editor in Chief of the *European Journal of International Relations*. He is currently writing a book titled *Terrorism, Violence and the State*.

Paul Wilkinson was Emeritus Professor of International Relations and Chairman of the Advisory Board of the Centre for the Study of Terrorism and Political Violence at St Andrews University, Scotland. His most recent publications include *International Relations: A Very Short Introduction* (Oxford University Press, 2007), *Homeland Security in the UK: Future Preparedness for Terrorist Attack Since 9/11* (Routledge, 2007) and *Terrorism Versus Democracy: The Liberal State Response* (Routledge, 3rd edn, 2011).

Introduction

Contemporary debates on terrorism

Richard Jackson and Samuel Justin Sinclair

Introduction

It seems hard to believe now, but there was a time before 11 September, 2001 when terrorism was a fairly minor concern of public policy, academia and popular culture. In those days, following the period of cold war rivalry, policy-makers were more concerned with issues like the illegal drug trade, nuclear proliferation, rogue states, civil war and humanitarian crises. Unbelievable as it may seem, there were few laws specifically designed to deal with terrorism and only a handful of fairly small agencies devoted to its control. In academia, Terrorism Studies was a minor sub-field within International Relations, with a few select scholars devoted to its study; a very small number of universities offered courses of study in it and doctoral research in terrorism was considered by many to be a questionable career choice. Culturally, in the days before 9/11, there were few Hollywood films, television shows, popular novels, video games, comics, plays, songs or comedy routines which took terrorists or terrorism as a central theme, and the topic was only periodically discussed in the mainstream news media.

It is safe to say that this zeitgeist has changed greatly over the last decade. Today we live in a terrorism-saturated world. Not only is terrorism a major concern of domestic and international policy with truly vast resources invested in it, but the lives of virtually every person on the planet have been altered in some way by new laws and measures designed to combat it (Jackson *et al.*, 2011). These new anti-terrorism measures affect air travel, health care systems, political decision-making, attendance at university, banking and other economic systems, internet usage, immigration, policing practices and a great many other areas of social and political life. At a minimum, almost every major university in the world teaches classes on terrorism, while at the other end of the continuum are comprehensive degree programmes up to the doctoral level that offer advanced curriculum and training within this domain. Hundreds of millions, if not billions of dollars are invested every year in academic and applied research into terrorism; dozens of new specialized research centres and networks have been established; new scholarly journals have been launched; and there are literally thousands of terrorism scholars and 'experts'. As a consequence, it has been estimated that a new book with terrorism in its title is published every six hours in the English language (Silke, 2008: 28). In popular culture, terrorism is rarely out of the news, and new movies, TV shows, novels, plays, Internet websites, jokes, songs, comedy routines, sermons and other cultural products which deal with it are released every day.

However, despite the rapid growth of terrorism as a subject of academic study and public concern in the past decade, there is still a great deal that we do not know about the phenomenon and its effects, and there are many areas of controversy and dispute between terrorism scholars and experts. One of the main purposes of this volume therefore, in amongst this veritable deluge of information and material, is to provide an accessible discussion of what we believe are 12 key questions which in many ways define the core debates and controversies within the Terrorism Studies field today. The questions we have identified touch on all the important subjects of terrorism research – how it should be defined and understood as a concept, its main types or categories, the nature of the threat it poses, its origins and causes and how it should be dealt with and managed over time. The chapters in this volume represent the latest thinking about these core questions, and as such, they provide a kind of snapshot or distillation of what we know about terrorism today, what we are still unsure of and where the key lines of debate – and thus future research – lie.

These questions are important for both analytical and normative reasons, because the answers have profound implications for both how to approach the study of terrorism, and advise policy-makers in terms of prevention, response and overall management. For example, the question of whether states can also be terrorists (Question 3) will affect both the kinds of data we gather on terrorist incidents and the approaches we take to understanding the causes of terrorism, and the kinds of policies we recommend for ending its use. Moreover, the question of whether terrorism is caused by religious extremism or root causes like poverty and exclusion (Questions 7 and 8) will greatly affect the kinds of variables we examine and the solutions we suggest to prevent terrorism's emergence. Similarly, the answer to the question of whether force-based responses to terrorism are effective (Question 9) will affect the efforts scholars put into studying non-violent counterterrorism measures and the kinds of policies recommended to practitioners. In other words, wrestling with the questions posed in this volume goes to the very heart of how to approach the subject of terrorism and how to respond to it as a society. Importantly, the fact that there are opposing viewpoints on all these questions alerts us to the limits of our current knowledge and the need for continuing systematic and rigorous research.

Aims and approach

The volume has a number of important aims. First, it aims to provide an overview of the key questions and debates of the terrorism field at this moment in history. We do not claim that these are the only controversies currently taking place among terrorism scholars, simply that they seem to be the most important and pressing at this time. As such, the volume provides an important overview of the broader field and the kinds of research currently taking place in it. A second aim is to bring together in one place a group of leading terrorism scholars to debate these key questions with each other. In other words, the volume provides a central forum in which the world's experts can present their views on questions of great importance to their subject. Finally, the volume aims to provide a useful tool for teaching students and interested readers about the nature, threat, causes and solutions to terrorism. Using counterposed arguments can, we believe, be a powerful way of encouraging critical thinking and argumentation skills. We are convinced that such skills are crucial for making real progress in our attempt to understand the complexities of modern terrorism.

The format and approach we have adopted is very straightforward: in each case, a leading scholar taking a particular position on a given question, followed by an opposing or alternative viewpoint written by another leading scholar. With a clear and forceful articulation of each side of the argument, the reader is then able to evaluate the relative merits of each set of arguments and make up their own mind. Supplementing the arguments on each side of the controversy, we have provided a follow-up set of discussion questions and recommended readings.

Overview of the volume

The volume is divided into five main sections which correspond broadly to the main areas of research in terrorism: (1) the definition of terrorism; (2) categories or types of terrorism; (3) the terrorism threat; (4) the causes of terrorism; and (5) responses to terrorism. Within each of these areas, we have identified a number of key questions for our expert contributors to debate. Below, we provide a brief overview of the central questions and the main arguments made in the debates.

In Part I, Definition of terrorism, the first question posed is: *1 Is terrorism still a useful analytical term or should it be abandoned?* Paul Wilkinson takes the affirmative position. He begins by noting that the term 'terrorism' is more than just an analytical concept, it is a generic concept covering a range of phenomena which is now indispensable for political discourse and scholarly debate. He goes on to argue that there is sufficient consensus on the meaning of terrorism and it can be clearly distinguished from other forms of political violence. Moreover, the potential for misuse does not automatically disqualify it. Few would doubt that 9/11 and the actions of al-Qaeda amounted to terrorism, for example. Dominic Bryan follows with an outline of the negative argument. He begins by explaining how the labeling of particular acts of political violence, whether as terrorism, war or crime, for example, occurs in complex fields of meaning, culture, conflict and power. He argues that there is no consensus on the definition of terrorism, and as a concept, it is too simplistic and compromised to be of real use in the study of political violence.

In Part II, Categories of terrorism, we pose two important questions, the first of which is: *2 Is there a 'new terrorism' in existence today?* Alejandra Bolanos takes the affirmative position on this question. She demonstrates how since the 1990s at least, terrorists have shown a greater willingness to cause mass casualties and to use weapons of mass destruction, they have more often been motivated by religious ideology rather than political goals, and they have organized as decentralized networks with global reach and global ambitions. She argues that, in combination with the changes in the international context, the characteristics of terrorism have evolved and we can therefore cautiously describe them as 'new' forms of terrorism. Isabelle Duyvesteyn and Leena Malkki put forward the negative argument. They begin by noting that there may be political and self-interested reasons for promoting the 'new terrorism' argument, before going on to argue that all the features which supposedly characterise 'new terrorism', such as its network structure, its global scope, new weapons, religious goals and intent to cause mass casualties, have been present in terrorism for more than 100 years. They do not deny that new features have been manifested, but they argue that these are complex and insufficient to warrant the category of 'new terrorism'.

A second important question regarding the way we construct the categories of terrorism is: *3 Can states be terrorists?* Michael Stohl answers in the affirmative. He begins by outlining how the term 'terrorism' was first used to describe state violence and argues that early scholars of terrorism had no problem using the term to describe both state reigns of terror and non-state oppositional violence. He argues for an act-based definition of terrorism rather than an actor-based definition, before showing how state violence is not always legitimate and how it is possible to distinguish between state terrorism and other forms of state violence like repression and oppression. He ends by suggesting that scholars can learn a great deal about insurgent terrorism by studying state terrorism. Colin Wight responds to the question in the negative. He argues that scholars have to take into account the fact that most people understand terrorism as a non-state form of violence, and challenging this perspective would therefore require sound theoretical and empirical reasons. He suggests that there is little to be gained analytically or normatively by considering certain forms of state violence under the confused label of 'terrorism', especially as proponents of the concept define it so broadly that virtually all state actions would fall under it. He suggests that we cannot conflate terror with terrorism, and just because there are similarities in acts of violence committed by state and non-state actors, it is wrong to assume that they have the same intentions.

In Part III, The terrorism threat, the first question to be debated is: *4 Is terrorism a serious threat to international and national security?* James Lutz and Brenda Lutz respond in the affirmative, demonstrating how terrorism, often in combination with other forms of violence, has undermined the security of states in a wide variety of ways, both historically and in the present day. They argue that ignoring terrorism or not taking it seriously can often result in it seriously threatening the security of the state later on, and there is always the possibility of terrorists becoming more sophisticated and deadly in the future. Ian S. Lustick takes the negative position on this question. He begins by noting the very small risk that terrorism poses statistically and the absence of any serious terrorist attacks on US soil in the past decade. He suggests that the real question to be answered is why people have consistently exaggerated fears of the terrorism threat. The answers, he argues, lie in media sensationalism, political manipulation, vested interests in the largesse of counterterrorism and aspects of human psychology. He ends with an impassioned plea for a more reasoned assessment and response to terrorism.

A second related question about the terrorist threat is: *5 Is WMD terrorism a likely prospect in the future?* Natividad Carpintero-Santamaría answers in the affirmative, describing some of the many recorded incidents and attacks involving WMD, and pointing out the widespread availability of deadly materials, the spread of information on the Internet about how to weaponize them for attacks and the vulnerabilities of modern societies to such attacks. She argues that while some forms of WMD terrorism are more likely than others, there are many groups that have the mindset to contemplate their usage, while others have clearly stated their desire to do so. John Mueller takes the negative position, arguing that the record of terrorists engaging in WMD attacks provides little cause for concern, and that there are many myths about how destructive WMD weapons can actually be in any case. He demonstrates how difficult it really is to use these kinds of weapons effectively, and how their use would in fact be counterproductive to the terrorist's goals. He suggests that the available evidence, even for groups like al-Qaeda, is that terrorists are much more likely to stick with tried and trusted conventional methods of attack.

The final question we ask about the nature of the terrorist threat is: *6 Does al-Qaeda continue to pose a serious international threat?* Jeffrey B. Cozzens and Magnus Ranstorp answer in the affirmative. They argue that al-Qaeda (AQ) remains a functional network with real capabilities, adaptability, structures of continuity, the ability to reproduce itself in the face of external pressure and a list of tangible achievements. They show how the Internet has been crucial for giving the AQ network global reach and enhanced ability to facilitate activities. Consequently, they suggest that AQ remains a potent threat to the West, not least because of its ability to attack in unexpected ways. Lee Jarvis makes the negative argument. He argues that the organization has been severely weakened following the deaths and capture of so many of its core leadership, including Osama bin Laden, in the years after 9/11, the loss of a state base from which to conduct operations, a series of internal divisions within the organization itself and shrinking support from allied groups and the wider Islamic world due to its continued attacks on civilians and Muslims. He suggests that the pathetic record of recent attacks by self-motivated amateurs in recent years is indicative of the weakened state that AQ now finds itself in and its limited ability to threaten the West.

In Part IV, The causes of terrorism, the first important question we pose is: *7 Is terrorism the result of root causes such as poverty and exclusion?* Dipak K. Gupta takes the affirmative position. After dismissing the suggestion that terrorists are mad, and carefully assessing the empirical evidence, Gupta demonstrates how structural inequalities and imbalances are a necessary cause of political violence. He argues that the missing variable in the often muddled picture of terrorism's causes is the key role played by leaders and 'political entrepreneurs' who can harness and channel the grievances generated by structural conditions like poverty, exclusion and lack of democracy. L. Rowell Huesmann and Graham R. Huesmann adopt the negative position. They argue that environmental factors like poverty and exclusion should not be considered root causes, as they are neither necessary nor sufficient for causing violent behaviour in individuals. Rather, they suggest that the causes of violence in particular cases lie in a complex convergence of situational precipitating factors such as exposure to violence, and predisposing psychological factors that have developed over time, such as perceptions of relative deprivation, post-traumatic stress disorder and neurobiological changes.

A second important question about the causes of terrorism is: *8 Is religious extremism a major cause of terrorism?* Amanda Munroe and Fathali M. Moghaddam make the affirmative argument. Rejecting a simple linear causality between religion and terrorism, they argue instead that processes of 'fractured globalization' have faced many identity groups with 'sudden contact' with out-groups and the threat of evolutionary extinction. This, they argue, puts tremendous pressure on religious fundamentalist movements and causes aggression within individual members, often leading to violent resistance or terrorism. The recent violent actions of Islamic fundamentalists therefore can be understood as a reaction to the threat of extinction by the structural forces of modern globalization, in much the same way as Native Americans historically responded violently to settler encroachment. Jeff Goodwin takes the negative position. He argues that while religion has been used to explain more recent trends in terrorism, it does not by itself provide sufficient explanation for why organizations and states engage in terrorist tactics. He further suggests that simplifying terrorism in this way may mask the complex array of factors that reinforce this type of violence, while also serving important ideological functions for those who support this line of thinking.

In Part V, Dealing with terrorism, the first question we pose is: *9 Are counterterrorism frameworks based on suppression and military force effective in responding to terrorism?* Boaz Ganor responds with an affirmative argument. He argues that the proactive use of force is both a legitimate and effective response to terrorism, because it can severely disrupt and degrade the capabilities of terrorist organizations, thereby preventing further attacks. He suggests that democratic states have a responsibility to respond forcefully to the threat of terrorism against their citizens, and the serious threat posed by suicide terrorism in particular, makes proactive force a necessity. Nonetheless, states must carefully calculate the costs and benefits of force-based counterterrorism operations and always conduct them within the limits imposed by humanitarian law. In contrast, Paul Rogers takes the negative viewpoint on how effective the use of military force, rather than law-based approaches can be as a response to terrorism. Examining the course and major consequences of the global war on terror which was a major military response to the 9/11 attacks, he argues that the use of military force has elevated the status of the terrorists and played into their hands. It has also failed to stop the growth and spread of al-Qaeda, and has had a number of long-term deleterious consequences for Iraq, Afghanistan, Pakistan and elsewhere, which may take decades to overcome. The record of using force in other contexts like India, Russia, Sri Lanka and Israel, has been similarly limited.

A second important question about the appropriate response to terrorism is: *10 Is the use of coercive interrogation or torture permissible and effective as a counterterrorism method?* Jeffrey Addicott takes the affirmative position on this question. He begins by setting out the clear difference between torture which is always illegal, and lesser forms of coercive interrogation which may be permissible, especially in cases of unlawful enemy combatants. Demonstrating that the US has never officially authorized the use of torture, he argues that torture does nonetheless work in some instances, as recognized by the US military and the Israeli Supreme Court, among others. In the case of a 'ticking bomb scenario', and given the threat posed by terrorism today, torture might be the lesser evil and justified under the necessity defence. He disagrees with the argument that legal torture warrants should be enacted, though. Robert Brecher takes the negative position. He focuses on the so-called 'ticking bomb scenario' and argues that it is very unhelpful for making political decisions because it is unlikely that the authorities can be certain that the suspect knows the information required, that time is running out or that torture is necessary to obtain the information. He argues that no systematic empirical studies have demonstrated that torture works effectively, and that in any case, the consequences of legalizing torture would be much worse for society in the long run than not torturing suspects and risking terrorist bombs, not least because it would require trained torturers and torture involves being willing to destroy an individual's humanity.

A third question in this area is: *11 Is the targeted assassination of terrorist suspects an effective response to terrorism?* Stephanie Carvin takes the affirmative response. Starting from the position that current definitions of targeted killing are problematic and that the available evidence is inconclusive at best, and noting that it is an imperfect strategy, she nonetheless argues that it can be both effective and legitimate. She shows how it can have a range of positive effects, including disrupting terrorist activities and saving lives, and that it can also be a legitimate form of self-defence for states facing an implacable foe. Andrew Silke adopts the negative argument. He looks at the empirical evidence on the effects of targeted assassination on future terrorist attacks and argues that it has never been shown to reduce the number of subsequent terrorist attacks. This, he argues, can be demonstrated by a close analysis of cases like Israel, Northern Ireland, Spain, Afghanistan and elsewhere. In part, this is because terrorist groups expect such attacks and prepare for them accordingly. He suggests that targeted assassination therefore fails as an evidence-based policy and should be eschewed in favor of more proven measures.

Our final question for this area, and the question which rounds out the volume as a whole, is *12 Have global efforts to reduce terrorism and political violence been effective in the past decade?* Mark Cochrane takes the affirmative position. He argues that the response to 9/11 was largely determined by the complex threat posed by the new forms of terrorism and the necessity to protect and reassure the public. Noting that terrorists only have to be successful once, while the state must be successful every time, he suggests that critics have failed to recognize the successes of counterterrorism since then, including the closure of terrorist bases in Afghanistan, the disruption to al-Qaeda, the prevention of another 9/11-like attack, the degradation of terrorist capabilities and opportunities, the enactment of a host of new security measures and laws, greater cooperation and coordination between counterterrorism agencies, and public involvement in counterterrorism programmes and measures. Rachel Monaghan adopts the negative position. She examines both hard-line and soft-line counterterrorism approaches which have been adopted since 9/11 and argues that they have had little effect in reducing terrorism internationally or reducing the number of terrorist attacks and plots by home-grown terrorists. Moreover, she argues that the costs of these measures have been excessive, including the deaths of thousands of innocent civilians and soldiers in Iraq and Afghanistan, the abuse of prisoners, the widespread resentment caused by harsh measures among Muslims and the undermining of international human rights law. She suggests that these actions have actually encouraged terrorist groups and may have created new cycles of violence.

An important caveat

The arguments presented in each chapter have been deliberately made in unambiguous terms in order to draw out their most salient aspects. That is, as editors, we asked each contributor to make the strongest case possible for the side of the argument they were asked to present. It is crucial however, that the reader understands that this is purely an analytical and pedagogic approach designed to help draw clear lines of debate and set up opposing viewpoints which the reader can then individually evaluate. It is not necessarily an indication of the authors' views and should not be automatically interpreted as such. In reality, very few scholars hold such black-and-white opposed viewpoints. Most often, they can appreciate a variety of sides to a controversial issue and they consequently hold to a much more nuanced personal position than the arguments presented here. In particular, we would stress that on the most controversial questions, such as whether coercive interrogation or targeted killing should be adopted, or what role root causes play in generating terrorism, for example, the authors making the positive argument should not be taken as advocates of a particular position, nor should they be attributed as personally holding to a particular standpoint. In all cases, the contributors to the volume were asked to make a strong case for a position for the purposes set out for the volume and not because they were seen as exemplars of any particular viewpoint. This is a crucial fact to keep in mind while reading the following chapters.

Conclusion

There are some important lessons and observations to be drawn from the chapters presented in this volume, not least that our understanding of terrorism is still at a nascent stage. This is clear from the very fundamental and basic debates we are still having about exactly what terrorism is, how it should be understood and what kind of threat it poses, among others. In part, this is because with its origins in the early 1970s and its rapid expansion after 9/11, it is still a relatively young field of research (see Gordon, 2010; Ranstorp, 2006). Acknowledging the uncertain state of our knowledge should induce caution towards any attempts to assert categorical knowledge of terrorism, and in particular, any claims that particular counter-terrorism measures will be successful in controlling it.

We must also acknowledge that the terrorism field, like most other academic fields, is made up of different viewpoints, assumptions and theoretical approaches to the subject. In part this is because, like the contributors to this volume, the study of terrorism attracts scholars from a multiplicity of different disciplines and research traditions, from international relations and security studies, to psychology, history, philosophy, criminology, economics, law and many others. This diversity is to be welcomed, as different perspectives and approaches can provide new ways of looking at core questions and new arguments to consider. As a case in point, the editors of this volume originally met in Belfast, Northern Ireland several years ago at an inter-disciplinary conference on terrorism and political aggression, and over a glass of wine we debated the significance of the terrorism threat, our views reflecting, at least in part, the very different professional backgrounds from which we hail (i.e., political science and clinical psychology).

Finally, it seems clear from the contributions to this volume that the terrorism field is currently in its most dynamic, exciting stage of development, and there are numerous avenues and questions waiting to be explored further. We hope that this volume will inspire its readers to pursue some of the questions, topics and controversies touched upon here.

Part I
Definition of terrorism

1   Is terrorism still a useful analytical term or should it be abandoned?

YES: The utility of the concept of terrorism

Paul Wilkinson

Introduction

I should make it clear at the outset that when I was invited to contribute to the debates in this volume it was to write on the utility of the concept of terrorism. I note that the editors wished to change this to 'the analytical concept' of terrorism. I intend to stick to the original agreed title because 'terrorism' is much broader than an analytical concept: it is a *generic* concept covering a wide range of phenomena. Of course, academic specialists use it as an analytical tool, but it also has important political, philosophical, psychological, historical, ethical and legal dimensions, which need to be considered.

It is also important to observe that those scholars who say they wish to abandon the concept of terrorism nevertheless continue to use it in their articles and books. This is because the term is well established in popular discourse, and in the literature of a number of academic disciplines, and those who wish to abolish the concept have been unable to find a suitable alternative. For many who read this brief essay, I realize I am preaching to the converted. Hence, I shall direct my observations to giving examples of the utility of the concept of terrorism and to showing that the oft-repeated objections to the concept are, on closer examination, unsustainable.

The generic concept

There is a perfectly clear and concise definition of terrorism in the *Oxford English Reference Dictionary* (revised second edition): 'the systematic use of violence and intimidation to coerce a government or community, esp. into acceding to specific political demands' (Pearsall and Trumble 2006). The term 'systematic' in this definition is clearly designed to stress that terrorism is an activity deliberately carried out by its perpetrators. Natural disasters such as earthquakes, volcanic eruptions and hurricanes can undoubtedly cause terror among the people caught up in them, but terrorism is a result of human intention. It is a special type of violence, not a synonym for political violence in general. It is the use and credible threat of extreme violence to create a climate of fear to intimidate a wider target than the immediate victims of the terrorist attacks. Non-state terrorism involves attacks on civilian, symbolic and random targets, most frequently using improvised explosive devices (IEDs), and is usually, though not exclusively, aimed at bringing about political change. Regime or state terrorism is used to intimidate the civilian population into submission. State-sponsored terrorism occurs when a regime hires a group to silence or intimidate exiled dissidents or to create a climate of fear in a state designated as an 'enemy' by the regime.

Throughout history, it has been regimes with an overwhelming preponderance of coercive power which have been the most deadly perpetrators of terrorism on a mass scale. They habitually use their secret police and armed forces both as instruments of internal repression and social control and as a weapon of external aggression. Regime/state terrorism did not disappear with the ending of the Cold War. Many regimes continue to use torture and extra-judicial killing. In the Arab Spring of 2011 there were numerous examples of peaceful protesters being shot dead in the streets where they were demonstrating. In Libya, the Gaddafi regime, a major perpetrator of state-sponsored terrorism in the 1970s and 1980s, deployed its heavily armed military against civilian protesters in an attempt to terrorize them into submission. Sadly, there is a long way to go before we see an acceptance of the values of the rule of law, democracy and human rights throughout the international system.

Since the end of the Second World War, Western Europe has experienced many acts of terrorism, for example, in Spain, Italy, Germany and France, as well as in the United Kingdom, unaccompanied by an insurgency or wider war. Historically, however, terrorism has often been used as an auxiliary weapon in a wider armed conflict or as the stock-in-trade of repressive regimes. The central point is that the generic concept of terrorism can be distinguished from closely related concepts such as insurgency, war and repression. As will be made clear in the following section on typology, terrorism covers a wide range of phenomena, which have been experienced in many countries not only in the contemporary world, but also throughout history.

The concept of terrorism is often misused, as when it is employed as a synonym for political violence in general. It is also frequently used loosely and inconsistently. However, this is a fate shared by many political concepts, but concepts are not responsible for the way in which they are misused. If we banned all political concepts that are often misused, we would soon be bereft of the means of political discourse.

An oft-repeated objection to the concept of terrorism is that it is 'value-laden' and hence not 'scientific'. In this respect, it shares the same problem as other key political concepts, such as 'imperialism', 'racism' and 'democracy'. None of these concepts is value-neutral, and all have at times been exploited as instruments of propaganda; yet when properly used they are indispensable for political discourse. There is a sufficiently widely shared acceptance of the core meaning of such concepts for them to play a central role in international political and social scientific debate. In 1988, Alex P. Schmid and his colleagues published impressive evidence of the extent to which the international community of social scientists who studied conflict had accepted a consensus definition of terrorism (Schmid and Jongman 1988). It is also important to note that a whole body of international conventions and agreements dealing with the prevention, suppression and punishment of acts of terrorism has developed over the past 40 years. There is near-universal acceptance of the terminology used to describe the form of behavior to be prohibited and prevented. Why should we be 'value-neutral' about terrorism? Try explaining why terrorism is not a crime to those who have lost loved ones in a suicide bombing.

History of the concept

Our modern words 'terror', 'terrorize', terrible' and 'terrorism', are derived from the Latin verbs *terrere*, to tremble or to cause to tremble, and *deterrere*, to frighten from. The word *terror* also came to mean the action or quality of causing dread. Etymologists claim that the English terms 'terrorism', 'terrorist' and 'terrorize' did not come into general use in English until the equivalent French words had taken on a special significance during the French Revolution. The revolutionary regime's Reign of Terror was initiated by the extreme Jacobins as an instrument of control, not only to kill known supporters of the *Ancien Regime*, members of the nobility and the clergy, but also to eliminate those individuals who were branded as enemies of the revolution. The Law of Suspects was introduced to enable the regime to imprison anyone merely on suspicion of involvement in treasonous plots.

As Alex Schmid notes (Schmid 1997):

> The term *terrorism* spread fast throughout Europe, into Russia, and even into India. As it spread, the word changed its meaning. By the late nineteenth century the term *terrorist*, originally used for those who made unjust mass arrests in the name of the state, became more strongly associated with anti-state violence. The violent French and Russian anarchists of the 1880s and 1890s were the main groups responsible for this shift in meaning.

However, by the mid-twentieth century, there was a big revival of interest, mainly among political scientists and historians, in regime terror. This work was engendered by the emergence of the Nazi and Soviet regimes, both of which used the weapon of terror on a massive scale. Those critics who claim that terrorism studies scholars have ignored regime/state terror are ignoring many modern classics (see Conquest 1968; Arendt 1967–68; Dallin and Breslauer 1970; Bullock 1962; Broszat 1981). As the literature on state use of terror makes clear, there are key attributes in common with terrorism by non-state actors: it is always arbitrary, unpredictable and indiscriminate in its effects. Its perpetrators are not susceptible to the appeals of law or reason. Ultimately, the terror is turned on the revolutionary followers themselves, as Robespierre, Trotsky and many others found to their cost.

In the late twentieth century, academic attention swung back to research into the use of terror by non-state actors and the particular problems experienced by liberal democracies faced with terrorist attacks on their citizens, and governmental and commercial targets at home and abroad. The renewed interest in non-state terrorism was of course greatly intensified by the rise of al-Qaeda, its devastating 9/11 attacks on the US and its continuing international campaign of terrorism aimed at causing mass casualties, typically using co-ordinated no-warning suicide bombings. It is worth noting that the United Nations and almost every government and national public in the world has had no hesitation in describing the attacks by al-Qaeda and its affiliates as terrorism. For the vast majority of the public in countries that have experienced attacks by al-Qaeda and its network, it would seem absurd to be told that they must abandon the concept of terrorism. Are they to pretend that terrorism does not exist, or that people caught up in such atrocities do not experience any fear? However, there is ample evidence that in the early decades of the twenty-first century, we face difficult challenges from both terrorism by non-state actors and regimes.

The ending of the Cold War contains another important lesson with positive implications for the future of international relations: the 'revolution' in the communist world, which had gathered pace with such speed in the 1980s and early 1990s was in truth 'velvet', that is to say (with the exception of Romania), the revolution was peaceful and was carried out without any recourse to violence by anti-communist opposition or armed intervention on their behalf by outside powers. Hence, the really good news is that despite decades of state repression and terror, the desire for democratic freedoms and human rights could not be extinguished. The velvet revolution revealed that even powerful modern states using the full repertoire of techniques of totalitarian control and backed up by terror are not invincible. The collapse of the former Soviet Union and the start of the Arab Awakening in 2011 have shown that oppressive dictatorships can be toppled by the determined will of the people seeking democratic change.

But, of course, it would be, to say the least, premature to assume that the demise of communist rule in the former Soviet Union and Eastern Europe means the end of state terror. For example, in the Far East the phenomenon of the one-party regime depending extensively on its own security apparatus for internal control is an ever-present reality. The Chinese People's Republic is notorious throughout the world for its ruthless suppression of the students' pro-democracy movement in the Tiananmen Square massacre of 1989, and its continued crackdown both against pro-democracy activists and against ethno-religious separatism in Tibet and Singkiang. China's neighbor, North Korea, is a true Cold War dinosaur, a totalitarian state complete with personality cult and one of the most repressive systems of internal control in the world.

However, terror is not a weapon exclusive to communist one-party states. There are numerous military regimes and other forms of dictatorship where the use of terror for internal control is routine. One of the clearest indicators that a regime of terror is operating is a high level of torture – the archetypal form of state terror. It has been estimated that in 1995 torture and/or other cruel, inhuman or degrading treatment or punishment existed in 151 out of the 185 member states of the UN (Schmid and Jongman 1997). But torture is widespread or commonly used only in around a third of these countries. For example, it has been employed extensively in countries such as Iraq and Syria in the Middle East, Burundi, Rwanda and Zaire in Africa, in Myanmar and Indonesia in Asia, and in Serbia and Chechnya in Europe – all countries that have suffered high levels of both regime and factional terror.

It is of course no accident that such countries have frequently experienced both regime and sub-state terror and the horrors of civil war. Very often, it is repressive terror of the regime which provokes a campaign of counterterror, or vice versa. It is also no accident that regimes which routinely use terror as a weapon of domestic policy also have a tendency to employ it as a tool of foreign policy. Hence, state sponsorship of terrorist clients operating abroad is likely to remain a feature of the international system as long as regimes of state terror exist. A further paradox is that the sharp reduction in the number of states actively involved in giving sponsorship, safe haven and other forms of support, makes the role of the remaining state sponsors all the more critical to the survival of their terrorist group clients.

However, while there are some effective multilateral measures that can be taken to discourage and reduce state sponsorship of terrorism as a weapon of intervention in foreign states, the international community generally, and the major democracies in combination, have precious little power to influence those regimes that are inflicting major human rights violations on their own populations by waging state terror. For most states, almost certainly including the majority of liberal democracies, the international norms of non-intervention in the internal affairs of other states are a highly convenient rationale for restricting themselves to expressions of humanitarian concern, condemnatory resolutions at the UN and perhaps support for international economic sanctions against the offending regime.

However, in the 1990s, there were signs that in particularly egregious cases of mass terror, as in the cases of the plight of the Kurds in northern Iraq, the 'ethnic cleansing' or genocide in Bosnia, the genocide in Rwanda and Burundi and the Serbs' campaign of massive ethnic cleansing against ethnic Albanians in Kosovo, the international community may be persuaded to override the norms of non-intervention and to make strenuous efforts to bring those guilty of crimes against humanity and war crimes before an international tribunal. This is already happening in the cases of the former Yugoslavia, Rwanda and Burundi. The UN Security Council Resolution 1973 passed in March 2011 allowing international action to protect Libya's civilian population against the Gaddafi regime's efforts to slaughter them is further evidence of this trend. Regime terror poses huge challenges not only to those in the international community seeking to defend human rights, but also to scholars engaged in a serious analysis of terrorism.

Typology

Every terrorist movement and regime has its own particular aims, beliefs and modus operandi. It would be foolish to try to apply a 'one size fits all' theory of how and why each variety of terrorism arose, why terrorism was chosen as a weapon, what the organizers of the terrorism hoped to achieve, to what extent their terrorist strategy and tactics were effective in securing their stated aims and their wider impact on national/international politics and society. At the most basic level, how do terrorist regimes and movements recruit, train and deploy operatives who carry out the orders of their terrorist chiefs?

Terrorism, as explained earlier, is a generic concept encompassing a wide range of phenomena. Hence, specialists in the study of terrorism have found it essential to develop typologies as an analytical tool. The most obvious distinctions to be made are between regime terror and terror used by non-state actors, and between *internal and domestic terrorism* confined to attacks within a specific nation-state, and *international terrorism* which affects the nationals, civil aviation, shipping, diplomatic facilities and commercial enterprises of more than one sovereign state. In the analysis of terrorist groups, scholars have found it helpful to classify on the basis of their general political orientation. *Ethno-separatist terrorists* are those seeking to win national independence for a specific ethnic group. *Ideological terrorists* are campaigning to replace a particular national government with a system of rule in accord with a political ideology of the extreme left (e.g., neo-Marxism) or an ideology of the extreme right (e.g., neo-Facism). *Religio-political terrorist groups* are those which combine extreme religious beliefs with an extreme political agenda (e.g., al-Qaeda and its affiliates). *Single-issue terrorists* are those extremists prepared to use extreme violence to further a particular cause such as opposition to abortion (e.g., Army of God) or to alleged abuse of animal rights (e.g., Animal Liberation Front).

Regimes of terror depend on a secret police *apparat* whose members are trained in methods of torture, forced confessions and denunciation, as well as methods of murder. In order to inculcate conformity to the regime, dictatorships often resort to brainwashing and censorship (e.g., North Korea). In some cases (e.g., Nazi Germany), the regime turns on entire ethnic groups, religious minorities and social classes (e.g., the Soviet Union and the Pol Pot regime in Cambodia) who become its victims. Legal experts have subjected anti-terrorism measures at national and international levels to intensive scrutiny. It would clearly be absurd to claim that political scientists and historians should monopolize terrorism studies!

Objections to the concept

One of the frequently voiced objections to the concept of terrorism is the tired old cliché 'one man's terrorist is another man's freedom fighter'. Those who use this well-worn cliché commit the logical fallacy of the excluded middle. Serious students of the history of terrorism know that many groups which have used the weapon of terrorism have ardently proclaimed that they have been fighting for freedom (the Russian and French anarchists, the IRA, ETA and the Tamil Tigers, to name but a few). Militants and their supporters may believe that their political aim is sufficient expiation for the crime of blowing up their innocent fellow citizens, but terrorism is terrorism whatever the group or regime ideology or diktat used to justify it. Many who commit acts of terrorism like to style themselves as liberation fighters, holy warriors, or, in some cases, as guerrillas. But people can give themselves these labels while continuing to commit terrorism. For propaganda purposes, of course, it is more convenient and flattering to describe yourself as a 'fighter', a 'soldier' or a 'warrior'.

This brings us to another frequent objection to the concept of terrorism, that is, the claim we should avoid using the term because it will be seen as insulting by those who are engaged in terrorism or who support such activities! This objection overlooks the fact that many terrorist groups, past and present, such as the Russian and French anarchists in the nineteenth century (Butterworth 2010) and al-Qaeda today, proudly boast of waging a terrorist campaign, because they are ardent believers in the value and efficacy of terrorism as a method of struggle (Kepel and Milelli 2008). More important, however, is the point that we should not abandon concepts simply because some of the people they are applied to believe they are pejorative. Should lawyers and criminologists abandon concepts such as 'crime', 'murder', 'rape' and the like for fear of upsetting the criminals? Should we ban terms such as 'serial murderer' and 'war criminal'? Surely not! There are clearly well understood criteria for judging whether such terms are being used appropriately. The same is true of the concept of 'terrorism' and 'terrorist' and we should be honest and consistent in our use of these concepts. To duck out of using them is to be guilty of a kind of intellectual appeasement.

It is important to be aware that some academics have been opposed to the development of terrorism studies, not because they reject the concept of terrorism, but because they believe that somehow those who study such subjects must be, at worst, manipulated by governments and crime-fighting agencies, or, at best, must have compromised their academic objectivity and independence. Any student reading the academic literature on terrorism will conclude that this is a complete caricature: the leading scholarly journals and books are full of strong criticisms of misguided and counterproductive responses to terrorism by governments; for example, note the strong criticisms of governments on the grounds that they have failed to respect human rights and the rule of law (Ranstorp and Wilkinson 2008; Bingham 2010; Schmid 1997).

Alex P. Schmid, a leading scholar in terrorism studies, has concluded:

> When scholars look at terrorism, the distance they can keep from the conflict should allow them a more objective perspective. Academics should pursue an intellectual, but not a moral, neutrality between terrorists and victims for 'the purpose of investigation'. The academic culture of curiosity, skepticism and methodical inquiry can lead to a more independent, non-partisan assessment than is usually possible elsewhere.

Conclusion

It is to be hoped that members of the 'critical terrorism studies' group stop arguing for the abandonment of the concept of terrorism and turn their efforts to the wide array of projects of empirical and historical research which would make a significant addition to our knowledge and understanding of non-state terrorism and regime terrorism, and the responses of states and international organizations, public opinion, the media, legal systems and the business sector. There remains a clear need for major in-depth case studies of terrorist movements and campaigns in particular countries. Context is all in the study of political violence in all its forms. Unless we can begin to understand the specific political, social, economic and cultural background to a terrorist conflict and the personalities and ideas of its leading figures, we will not have the knowledge to begin to understand the underlying causes and etiology of a particular conflict and its wider implications. It is a serious mistake to underestimate or neglect the value of historical scholarship, biographical and other key sources of qualitative research.

Similarly, there is a great need for detailed case studies of regime terrorism and state-sponsored terrorism, its operatives, structures and processes and its impact on societies and on international relations. As in the study of non-state terrorism, proper attention needs to be given to qualitative as well and quantitative research methods. Major work is needed to identify the key determinants of 'success' or 'failure' in campaigns of terrorism, and in the efforts of many nations and the international community to prevent, or at least reduce terrorism.

The above lists only a small part of the research agenda for serious terrorism studies research. As stated at the beginning of this chapter, terrorism has important psychological, legal and ethical dimensions, and much valuable work has been done in all these aspects. However, it is certain that scholars working in these various disciplines would all agree that there is much more work to be done on terrorism by specialists in their particular field, just as there is a rich field of future research for historians, political scientists and international relations specialists. Terrorism is a multidisciplinary, sometimes interdisciplinary, research subject. It is hard to see what would be gained by trying to pretend that it does not exist.

NO: A landscape of meaning: constructing understandings of political violence from the broken paradigm of 'terrorism'

Dominic Bryan

Introduction

Few acts of political violence have been more meaning-*full* than those of the pilots of the planes that flew into the World Trade Center, the Pentagon and the Pennsylvanian earth on 11 September 2001. It was meaningful for those that committed the acts, and then for the thousands of victims' families and friends and billions of witnesses. But it also provided millions of images communicated as the terrible day progressed (in almost slow motion), and the billions of images communicated and reused in the months and years that followed as political consequences unfolded. 9/11 was to be cited in countless political contexts, driving governments' policies and legislation around the world, sometimes leading to further acts of violence and wars with many more victims than on that terrible day. And, of course, millions of dollars of funding have been provided for terrorism studies because of 9/11. It certainly ranks with the dropping of the first atomic bomb or the assassination of Archduke Ferdinand, sparking the First World War, as an act of violence with multiple consequences and interpretive resonances. Indeed, because of the spectacular and public natures of what took place, more than the significant number of people that died, it is difficult to keep the 9/11 events in perspective.

How then should we approach an analysis of this event? Surprisingly, we do not have to. It was done almost immediately. Once the second plane hit the tower and any possibility that it could be a freak accident could be dismissed, this was an act of 'terrorism'. The event was labeled with a highly pejorative term and thrown into a category of violent acts or threats so broad and multifaceted that it is shared with the French republican revolutionaries of 1793, the Lehi group (or Stern gang) in Palestine in 1940, Nelson Mandela, communist insurgents in Nepal, the anarchists demonstrating in Chicago in 1886, the Irish Republican Army (IRA), and Gavrilo Princip, killer of Archduke Ferdinand, June 1914.

The pejorative use of 'terrorism' can be seen everywhere. Even the much-used phrase, 'one person's terrorist is another's freedom fighter', accepts that the term 'terrorism' is negative, not value-free. Sitting in Hanoi airport, I read in the *Viet Nam News* 'Bahrain charges protestors as terrorists' (9 May 2011 p. 12), the label attached to so many the state does not like. And that is right at the heart of the problem with the use of this category. As Jackson (2005: 59–91) argues, the terrorists are always depicted as 'the others', the bad guys, and that 'other' is dehumanized:

> 'Hun', 'japs', gooks', 'rag-heads' and 'skinnies' are the means by which fellow human beings – who are also husbands, sons, brothers, friends – are discursively transformed into a hateful and loathsome 'other' who can be killed and abused without remorse or regret. The term 'terrorist' is simply the latest manifestation of this discursive process – today's 'terrorists' are the new 'gooks'.
>
> (Jackson 2005: 60)

Can we use such a problematic term as a category in academic research?

I want to argue that we need to stop using the category of 'terrorism' when we analyse political violence. Instead, I want to place at the heart of academic research on violence the need to understand the meanings, motivations and relationships of power in which acts of violence take place. It is my contention that in using the label 'terrorist' or 'terrorism', we immediately make assumptions about the acts of violence, as well as their reception by victims, witnesses and the wider society. And of course, we differentiate those acts of violence labeled terrorism from those acts of violence that are not given that label, thus sometimes excluding reasonable comparisons.

Anthropology and studying violence in Northern Ireland

My own personal background has a bearing on the argument I wish to make. As a social anthropologist, I have spent 20 years studying the transformation of conflict in Northern Ireland. My research on public space, particularly around parades and the use of flags, has led me to explore threats of violence and displays by groups identified as 'terrorist' in United Kingdom legislation. In that work, I have not only spoken to and interviewed people commonly labeled 'terrorists', I have worked with some of them in conflict transformation projects.

Central to the task of social anthropology is to comprehend the human condition by attempting to understand the cultural context within which people act. Put simply, we are interested in the world-views of the people with whom we are conducting research. For most anthropologists, having attempted an understanding of particular social actions from the perspective of those taking part, we might then make a second order analysis of that activity, an analysis that can be in contradiction to those who took part in the social action, but nevertheless should account for their views. We do not need to accept the views of the people we study, but we do need to understand them.

Let me look very briefly at the range of violent acts in Northern Ireland to see how useful the category of 'terrorism' is. In what was termed 'the Troubles', from 1969 to 1998 paramilitary groups, particularly the Irish Republican Army (IRA), used strategies incorporating violence. Strategies included a 'suicidal' hunger strike to resist the policies of prison officers and the state, defending 'their communities' through punishment beatings of children involved in activities seen as socially unacceptable, killing police officers and British soldiers, assassinating judges and politicians, and planting car bombs in public areas likely to kill members of the public and members of the security forces and economically impair Northern Ireland (see English, 2003). At the same time, the Ulster Volunteer Force (UVF) and Ulster Defence Association (UDA), pro-state, but illegal, loyalist paramilitary groups used strategies of violence to attack republicans, nationalists and Catholics, sometimes with the tacit or specific support of the forces of the British state (Taylor 1999). Meanwhile, the British state utilized its armed forces, often with substantial force, to suppress these groups with strategies including illegal forms of interrogation, shoot-to-kill policies and stop and search tactics using emergency legislation (Ní Aoláin 2000). There are also symbolic displays of violence through parades, demonstrations, murals and flags which carry images of weapons, soldiers, historical battles, as well as the colors of contemporary paramilitary groups (Jarman 1997). Undoubtedly, some of these acts and threats of violence by state and non-state actors engendered fear that on occasion could be described as terror; but some of those same acts could also engender a sense of safety. To say the least, to place some of these activities under the rubric of 'terrorism' is unhelpful in terms of developing an understanding of what is taking place. The violence existed in a complex political and historical context, in a landscape of meaning.

Anton Blok, in an insightful essay, has identified the tendency to understand violence in terms of a utilitarian 'rational' means and ends relationship, but conversely that violence is also frequently seen as 'senseless' and devoid of meaning (Blok 2000: 24). This, he argues, avoids the difficult job of understanding the meanings attached to violence:

> The pacification of society and its acceptance as 'natural' lie at the basis of both scholarly and popular accounts of violence: if focused on the actual use of violence at all, the emphasis falls on the instrumental, most obvious act of violence. The cultural dimensions of violence – its idiom, discourse and meaning – receive less attention.
>
> (Blok 2000: 23)

The complex layers of meaning that surround 9/11 or the violence that erupted in parts of Northern Ireland need to be explored without making assumptions. For example, in 1971 groups of men in Protestant working class areas gathered to defend their residential areas from the perceived threat from the IRA and under the impression that the police and British

Army were not doing enough. These 'defence associations' eventually formed themselves into a populist movement known as the Ulster Defence Association (UDA). This organization, under the name Ulster Freedom Fighters (UFF), then carried out a range of types of violence, including some of the most indiscriminate mass killings of the Troubles (Crawford 2003). The UDA, however, produced some of the more enlightened political documents in the 1970s and 1980s. Although the UFF was proscribed as a terrorist organization by the UK government, the UDA did not come under terrorism legislation until 1992. How do we therefore understand this organization, let alone the range of violent acts it perpetrated?

Labeling the terrorist

Social scientists have long understood the practice of labeling. Howard Becker, in his landmark work on the sociology of deviance, provided the basis for what is now known as labeling theory:

> Social groups create deviance by making rules whose infraction constitutes deviance, and by applying those rules to particular people and labeling them as an outsider. From this point of view, deviance is not a quality of the act the person commits, but rather a consequence of the application by others of rules and sanctions to an offender.
>
> (Becker 1963: 9)

In our case, the act of violence is defined as terrorist not because of an analysis of the act, but because a particular group are labeled as terrorist. Put simply, almost any act that al-Qaeda commits is defined as a terrorist act, because the group is now defined as terrorist. Conversely, the dropping of the atomic bomb on Hiroshima, an act calculated to terrify, is not an act of terrorism because we choose to define the US Air Force as engaged in an act of war. Crucially, this defining process takes place within a web of power relationships whereby those with more power are able to define the acts of those with less power.

Labeling becomes more pernicious in times of social unrest, or in what Stanley Cohen has described as 'a moral panic'. This is a period of time when the fundamental values of society appear to be under attack: 'a condition, episode, person or group of persons [who] become defined as a threat to societal values and interests' (Cohen 1972/1987: 9). Once there is broad acceptance in society that there is a threat, there tends to be hostility towards the out-group and a disproportionate reaction to the problem. 9/11 provided just such a moral panic. George W. Bush, the leader of the most powerful state in the world, declared a 'war against terrorism' and in that context, repressive policies came thick and fast, and wars were declared that had little or no relationship to the original act (Mueller 2006).

Academic inquiry was not going to be oblivious to the new environment. Millions of dollars were directed through US military and State agencies to combat the new threat. Gupta observed that the 'number of books with "terrorism" in their title published in the six and a half years since 2001 was more than ten times the total number of publications for the past six decades' (Gupta 2008: 2). Although, as I will show, there is not even a minimal consensus on how to define terrorism, the number of academics working on political violence, very often driven by public funding, increased exponentially.

Across the globe, over many years, political violence from non-state actors had offered a potential threat. The 1970s was punctuated with the activity of the Red Brigade, the Palestinian Liberation Organisation, the Baader-Meinhof gang or Red Army Faction, the IRA and the Euskadi Ta Askatasuna (ETA), to name a few. Given that the Soviet Union could have had a potential interest in funding such groups, the threat was not insignificant. But whilst American citizens overseas were frequently targets, the US homeland was not. The post-9/11 era however, created a period of panic that, for example, led directly to war in Afghanistan and has seen US spending on defense maintained, despite the end of the Cold War. In the new context, 'terrorism' replaced the Soviet Union or 'the reds', as the politically stated significant external threat, even though any cursory risk assessment would suggest that levels of threat to the US compared to the Cold War are low. In this context, the way terrorism becomes defined by academics, as well as official institutions, is important.

Definitions of terrorism

There are an enormous range of attempts to define terrorism, reflecting just how difficult such a definition is (see for example, Townsend 2002; Hoffman 1998/2006; Wilkinson 2001/ 2006/2011; Gupta 2008; English 2009; Jackson 2011). Richard Jackson has made a case for retaining the category of 'terrorism' for particular types of political violence. Under the rubric of 'Critical Terrorism Studies', he puts forward a succinct and informed 'strategy for advancing a "persuasive definition" of terrorism', in order to find a convergence around a clearly defined concept (Jackson 2011: 118–119). Whilst agreeing with much of his analysis, I am not persuaded that the paradigm of 'terrorism' can be usefully rescued. I am, as hc puts it, a rejectionist (Jackson 2011: 117). To explain why, let me now look at what seem to me to be the five basic elements of a definition of terrorism so that I can show why the multiple attempts at creating a workable category, in my view, fail.

First, a key element of an act of violence defined as terrorist is that it is politically motivated. This in itself of course is not very distinguishing. If we take the broadest definition of politics as being activities relating to relationships of power, then even acts of violence that relate simply to the person, such as armed robbery, assault or rape have, in the broadest sense, a political dimension. If we narrow our definition of politics to what might be called big 'P' politics, the regulation of power between groups, then we can exclude some acts of violence, although feminists might reasonably argue that this should still include rape. But even within this narrowed category, we still have all violence contained within war. Even if we exclude legally constituted wars, many types of violent acts create problems for a definition. Violence connected with football matches is not normally described as terrorism, yet it is highly symbolic, has non-combatants as potential targets, and is non-state. To take another example, robberies of white-owned farms by poor black people in Zimbabwe and South Africa have often had levels of violence that are clearly political, and a level of organization. Yet these also have not normally been described as acts of terrorism.

Closely related to the political nature of the violent act is the second element of a definition of terrorism, namely, that the act has a highly symbolic or communicative component. Jackson stresses that 'it is communication to an audience which is the important element of terrorist violence, not necessarily publicity' (Jackson 2011). In other words, the objective of the act is not limited to achieving a narrow strategic outcome as one might find in war when armed forces are attempting to take control of territory or destroy the enemy's ability to inflict damage. Yet nearly all acts of violence have communicative aspects to them: the dropping of the atomic bomb at Hiroshima was designed to be communicative. Capital punishment is designed as a highly symbolic act. On the other hand, organizations defined as terrorist may well undertake acts that have the limited strategic objectives that a national army (which some would argue they are) might have in a legally constituted war.

The third and possibly more popularly understood aspect of terrorism is that it targets civilians, non-combatants or those who are innocent. This, of course, is part of the symbolic message and the communication of terror. However, it does not appear in some of the academic attempts at definition (see for example English 2009: 24; Hoffman 1998/2006: 40; Jackson 2011). The reasons for this quickly become obvious. Defining what is a military target and what is not is highly problematic. For example, the Pentagon, a target on 9/11, could be described as the most powerful military institution in the world. It is interesting that a few years later the US State Department, clearly struggling with this element of a definition, suggested the following aspect of a definition of terrorism:

> For purposes of this definition the term non combatant is interpreted to include, in addition to civilians, military personnel who at the time of the incident are unarmed and/or not on duty . . . We also consider as acts of terrorism attack on military installa-tions or on armed military personnel when a state of hostilities does not exist at the site.
>
> (United States Department of State 2004: xii)

In other words, under this definition, terrorism is any violent political act where the United States has not defined a state of war. And yet, of course, civilians and non-combatants are routinely killed in attacks defined as war or as acts of defence. In recent years, these victims have come to be known as 'collateral damage'. This produces the strangest of outcomes. The tens of thousands of Cambodian civilians who died when the US bombed that country during Operation Menu in 1969 are therefore not deemed victims of terrorism, whereas the military personal in the Pentagon, or the police officer and soldiers in Northern Ireland, are deemed victims of terrorism.

The defining of the status of military and civilian personnel is closely connected to the fourth element of a definition: is a legal designated war taking place? Townsend suggests that, 'the essence of terrorism . . . is surely the negation of combat' (Townsend 2002: 7). Under international law, there is a right to conduct war. This, of course, is one of the reasons that the use of force in the 2003 Iraq war was so hotly debated at the United Nations. But there are a number of major problems with this part of a definition. It tends to assume that those groups that are powerful enough to influence international bodies become arbiters of what is and is not the legitimate use of violence. Israel, frequently with US backing, stridently defends the right to use force to defend itself. In a high-profile example in 2010, Israeli forces boarded a ship, in international waters, bound for the Gaza strip, an area of land that under international law does not belong to Israel, and killed nine people on the boat, apparently in self-defense (United Nations Human Rights Council 2010). There are arguments for and against the legal legitimacy of what took place, but my point is that it is difficult to define. And of course, states are also involved in countless acts of violence in attempts to subvert political processes in other countries – and all of this occurs before you define acts of violence within a civil war or acts of nationalist resistance. In other words, the status of armed conflicts are always highly problematic. The IRA, ANC and the PLO all believed they were fighting legitimate wars for freedom. The classic question of legitimacy remains: were they terrorists or freedom fighters? The struggle for a legal definition of terrorism (see Saul 2008) is, of course, a different practice than that to find a definition that works for academic research.

The fifth element of a definition is, I think, the most important. What the vast majority of those involved in the study of terrorism are interested in are the acts of political violence perpetrated by non-state actors. They are interested in the strategies and techniques which non-state groups utilize in order to make political gains in a given sphere. Groups which have relatively few resources available to them often need to resort to methods that give them a sense of presence out of proportion to their numbers, and asserts them to increase their political leverage. Specific and comparative studies into this are, of course, quite legitimate, and indeed, important. But here lies the fundamental problem. If we label these acts with the pejorative term 'terrorism', we are making an immediate judgment about the legitimacy and meaning of the violence or threat of violence. The model is thus pro-state, whatever the nature of the state. And if that was not problematic enough, it, by definition, means that the state does not use the same strategies, or if they do then we will not label them in the same way. As such, some writers on terrorism include state and non-state violence in their definitions (English 2009: 24), thus creating an enormous category which makes comparative studies very difficult, whilst others are determined to maintain the focus on non-state actors and in doing so, reproduce a labeling of the violence that essentially legitimizes the state (see Hoffman 2006: 40). Why do the range of violent strategies used by these non-state actors need to be labeled in such a way?

Lastly, in defining terrorism we can take the word literally. It is violence which is about terror. But of course, a vast range of violence can induce terror. The US-led attack on Iraq in 2003 was entitled 'shock and awe'. It was designed to induce such a level of power that the enemy would surrender. Townsend argues that this psychological outcome of violence has been part of strategic bombing since the Second World War (Townsend 2002: 6–7). And yet at the other end of the spectrum, whilst many of the acts of violence defined as terrorism are undoubtedly terrifying for those caught up in it, can we really argue that the wider population are *terrified*? Worried, horrified, even scared . . . but terrified? Any possibility of collapsing the meaning of the word terrorism to a definition based on the intended psychological outcome of the act is clearly not plausible.

Conclusion

As for identifying objective criteria for identifying terrorism activity, common sense indicates that the general public in most countries in the world can recognise terrorism when they see campaigns of bombing, suicide bombings, shooting attacks, hostage-takings, hijackings and threats of such action, especially when so many of these are deliberately aimed at civilians.

(Wilkinson 2001/2006/2011: 1)

As academic researchers, we are absolutely interested in what Wilkinson describes as 'common sense'. But the idea that some global general public shares that common sense understanding of a variety of acts of violence is surely wrong. Such a 'common' understanding does not even exist amongst the general public in Northern Ireland. And we cannot base comparative academic research, let alone empirical and quantitative research, on such a general understanding.

The problems with finding a useable definition of terrorism are overwhelming. When you read what many academics have to say on the issue, I think you can tell that they know this. The better works invariably struggle in the first chapter to come up with a definition. Many of those chapters point out all of the problems I have discussed above. Then, to my mind, they inexplicably carry on using the term. Why might that be? Possibly the most under-standable reason is that put forward by Jackson, who argues that academia needs to critically engage with policy-makers, politicians and the general public, and to do this we need to utilize the terms that are dominant in the public arena (2005, 2011). Thus, Jackson has called for

'Critical Terrorism Studies' and hopes that there will be 'convergence around a clearly defined concept' (Jackson, 2011). Such a strategy of engagement is required, but the costs of conforming to the terrorism paradigm are great. We are sustaining a paradigm that has no academic validity and is highly pejorative. To put it another way, once we know that the world is round, there is no point pretending that it is flat just for the sake of academic engagement.

There is a further problem with maintaining the term 'terrorism' and it is one that many of those that use it would find ironic. There can be no doubt that the use of the term contains a moral valuation; that is part of the term's power and why it is used as a labeling device. So a vast range of acts of violence are reduced to one moral category, and no matter what the justification of the violence, it gains a pejorative label. Even more damaging, it thus provides that state with justifications for introducing often significant mechanisms to restrict freedom (Bryan, Kelly and Templer 2011). The 'war on terror' has proved an environment that has legitimized torture, imprisonment without legal justification, significant restrictions on freedom of assembly and immense force delivered to those people and places accused of harboring terrorists. Many times, as in Northern Ireland in the 1970s, these types of policies proved to be massively counterproductive and surely delayed political solutions.

A vast amount of money and resources has been directed at the problem of terrorism, out of all proportion to the problem (Mueller 2006). In the academy, where resources are at a premium, the temptation to conform to a particularly well-funded paradigm is great. If my argument is correct, not only has much money been wasted on empirical work of little worth, but that work, in sustaining a broken paradigm, makes difficult solutions to political problems even harder to find. We simply sustain the 'flat earth' policies. Responsible academic engagement must involve a critique of the paradigm and the development of new models with which to understand the use of violence by non-state actors (Bryan, Kelly and Templer 2011).

So what should a dynamic critical research strategy exploring the use of political violence by non-state actors look like? As I outlined at the start, the key is that such work seeks to understand the world-view and motivations of those conducting and threatening violence, and this must be done within the context of power relationships predominantly provided by the State. As part of this, there is already much useful work understanding how the discourse of terrorism is sustained, as well as how and why the labeling process takes place (see Jackson 2005). Examining networks, relationships and ideologies is part of this strategy. An engagement with policy-makers and politicians is critical, but it cannot be at the cost of the research rigor provided by a clearly designed and defined research process. Careful comparative analysis is important, but it must be culturally sensitive. Research should include an analysis of risk which provides a more balanced and proportional response to political violence. Ultimately, research must take into account the local context, the landscape of meaning and the diversity of power within this landscape.

Discussion questions

1 What elements do you believe are sufficient to define an act of violence as 'terrorism'?
2 Is it possible to identify the key features which distinguish terrorism from other forms of political violence?
3 Terrorism is a crime according to both international law and the national laws of many nation states. Is this a sensible and legitimate application of the concept of terrorism?
4 Has the definition of 'terrorism' changed over time?
5 Why do certain acts of violence get labeled as 'terrorist' whilst others do not?

6   Does the fact that the concept of terrorism is frequently misused or employed as a propaganda weapon mean that it should be abandoned?
7   If the concept of 'terrorism' were to be abolished what alternative should replace it?
8   Can we describe George W. Bush's war against terrorism as a *moral panic*?
9   How can we research what any particular act of violence means?

Further readings

Bryan, D., Kelly, L., and Templer, S., 2011. 'The Failed Paradigm of "Terrorism"', *Behavioral Sciences of Terrorism and Political Aggression*, 3(2): 80–96.

Crenshaw, M., ed., 1995. *Terrorism in Context*, University Park, PA: Pennsylvania State University Press.

Laqueur, W., 2003. 'Postmodern Terrorism', in Kegley, Jr., C., ed., *The New Global Terrorism Characteristics, Causes, Controls*, Upper Saddle River, NJ: Prentice Hall.

Mueller, J., 2006. *Overblown: How Politicians and the Terrorism Industry Inflate National Security Threats, and Why We Believe Them*, New York: Free Press.

Schmid, A., ed., 2011. *The Routledge Handbook of Terrorism Research*, London and New York: Routledge.

Schmid, A., and Jongman A., 1988. *Political Terrorism: A New Guide to Actors, Authors, Concepts, Data Bases, Theories and Literature*, Amsterdam: SWIDOC.

Townsend, C., 2002. *Terrorism: A Very Short Introduction*, Oxford: Oxford University Press.

Wilkinson, P., 2003. 'Why Modern Terrorism? Differentiating Types and Distinguishing Ideological Motivations', in Kegley, Jr., C., ed., *The New Global Terrorism: Characteristics, Causes, Controls*, Upper Saddle River, NJ: Prentice Hall.

Part II
Categories of terrorism

2 Is there a 'new terrorism' in existence today?

YES: The 'new terrorism' or the 'newness' of context and change

Alejandra Bolanos

Introduction

The objective of this chapter is to inform the reader about one side of the 'old' versus 'new terrorism' debate, namely, the thesis that favors the existence of a 'new terrorism.' To accomplish this, we will begin by setting some parameters that can help refine what is meant by these two words, namely, 'new' and 'terrorism.' The chapter will then revisit the broader and more prevalent observations that have been put forth by the proponents of the new terrorism thesis. Following this review, the chapter will offer a brief overview of the counter-arguments in the debate. It will conclude with a few additional insights related to *change* and *context* that might help understand why certain aspects of contemporary terrorism can be cautiously labeled as new.

Prior to delving further into the new terrorism thesis, it is first necessary to try to set parameters for what is meant by these two words. Beginning with the concept of terrorism, a necessary evil and almost a cliché for anyone writing about this subject is to openly concede that there is no widely accepted definition of the term (see Weinberg, Pedahzur and Hirsch-Hoefler, 2004). Amidst all of its meanings and disputed attributes, other efforts in this book focus on examining whether the word itself remains a viable concept that can be used in the analysis and description of specific forms of violence. Shying away from trying to solve these definitional issues, this chapter observes one parameter, specifically, that terrorism is here described as a violent approach adopted by armed non-state actors.

While the political, expressive and emotive nature of terrorism has prompted hundreds of definitions, the seemingly innocuous word 'new' also has more than one meaning. The term can be used to refer to something that did not exist before. It may also describe something that, although in existence, was not known to us – something experienced or discovered for the first time. We also use this word to convey more subtle or elaborate meanings, all of which are mentioned in the *Oxford English Dictionary*. For example, new might be contrasted with something old, emphasizing the (small or large) differences between them. Interestingly, the dictionary explains that new can also be used to refer to a resumption or repetition of some previous act or thing or to allude to something resurgent.

The new terrorism: its time frame and defining characteristics

Before exploring the arguments within the new terrorism thesis, it is important to identify certain time frames. In other words, when were the new terrorism arguments put forth, and what do these arguments have to say about the period of time that points to the beginning of, or marks the difference between, the old and the new terrorism? In the past, more than one observer has referred to *The New Terrorism* and to novel aspects of this historically prevalent phenomenon (Harris, 1983; Gutteridge, 1986). However, the arguments that inform the most current debate date from the 1990s and can be subdivided into those put forth before 2001 and those that were either produced or revised in the aftermath of 9/11. For the most part, this literature identifies the beginning of the new terrorism and its trends as more evidently taking place in the post-Cold War environment and reaching a peak with the advent of the twenty-first century.

Many of these discussions were originally prompted by several terrorism incidents that took place in the 1990s, including the 1993 World Trade Center attack in New York, the 1995 sarin subway attack in Tokyo, the 1995 Alfred P. Murrah Federal Building bombing in Oklahoma City, the 1996 Khobar Towers bombing in Saudi Arabia, and the 1998 U.S. Embassy bombings in Kenya and Tanzania. In the area of international terrorism, the September 11, 2001 attacks were perceived to be the devastating result of the newly developing trends and al-Qaeda as the epitome of a 'new terrorist' organization. It should also be noted that several authors who focus on religiously inspired terrorism (as part of the new terrorism phenomenon) trace its incipient stages to the 1980s and to some of the events described by Rapoport as setting the stage for the fourth or religious wave of terrorism (Rapoport, 2003). The Iranian Revolution and the Soviet occupation of Afghanistan are listed as some of these precedents.

Having determined the period of time assigned to the emergence of the new terrorism, the next task is to name its defining characteristics. In other words, what are those trends or elements that make terrorism new? The first characteristic that is most commonly ascribed to the new terrorism is its increasing lethality. This notion seems not to need further discussion if one focuses on the number of fatalities that resulted from the September 11, 2001 attacks. However, most authors agree that the increasing lethality trend began in the 1980s and continued throughout the 1990s (Mockaitis, 2007; Lesser *et al.*, 1999). Those in favor of the new terrorism proposition have pointed at several reasons for this upward trend.

One of the most prevalent explanations offered is the growing importance of religious motivation amongst terrorist groups (Hoffman, 1998/2006). In fact, religion – as the key motivator for several terrorist organizations – is considered as a second defining characteristic of the new terrorism. Among the organizations and individuals who have been religiously inspired to adopt terrorist violence, those who espouse a radical interpretation of Islam are predominantly singled out. However, the relevance of millenarian, cultic, and extreme-right Christian groups is also underscored. According to some authors (Gurr and Cole, 2002/2005), the proliferation and significance of religiously motivated terrorist groups is notable in the period of time commonly assigned to the emergence of the new terrorism. Evidence of this claim is supported by trends that refer to the percentage of religiously inspired groups in relation to the total number of terrorist organizations. This literature indicates that numbers grew from less than 4 percent in 1980 to 42 percent by the mid-1990s (Lesser *et al.*, 1999).

The correlation between religiously inspired groups and the increasing lethality of their attacks follows a specific logic (Jurgensmeyer, 2003). According to this logic, due to their religious worldview, the new terrorist organizations have extremely broad and diffuse goals.

In some cases, the sacred nature of these goals makes them appear as unbound, at least in comparison with specifically defined and politically driven objectives. For example, consider the difference between the Japanese group Aum Shirikyo's apocalyptic goals aptly illustrated by the book title, *Destroying the world to save it* (Lifton, 1999), and the more specific aims of previous organizations motivated by anti-colonial objectives attainable through national independence or self-determination. More specifically, according to the new terrorism perspective, religion is also said to affect the use of violence by making it more indiscriminate. In other words, the sacralization of violence is often accompanied by the demonization or dehumanization of 'the other.' The other, the enemy category, is thus extended to widespread segments of the population who are deemed unbelievers, uninitiated, or apostates. As such, they become viable targets. In this case, the new terrorist organizations will not limit the use of force by directing it exclusively against specific authorities or political figures. Instead, the unlimited targets will include entire populations. This view has led some authors to believe that the well-known aphorism that argues that terrorists want 'a lot of people watching, but not a lot of people dead' (Jenkins, 1975), is not applicable to the new forms of terror. A few authors have gone as far as to conclude that the new terrorism objectives are 'not to influence, but to kill, and in large numbers' (Benjamin and Simon, 2000a).

Two additional reasons commonly ascribed to the increased lethality of the new terrorism are the desensitization of audiences, and the availability of, and the proclivity to use, methods of mass destruction and/or disruption, namely, chemical, biological, radiological and nuclear (CBRN) weapons. Some argue that the increasing desensitization of audiences caused by media trends have forced terrorists to become more violent and 'spectacular' (Neumann, 2009). According to this argument, the constant and increasing portrayal of gruesome and cruel spectacles on television and other mass communication outlets has made people less responsive to shocking depictions. This, in turn, has forced terrorists to magnify the terrorizing effect by increasing the lethality of their attacks. As for the use of CBRN weapons, new terrorism proponents point to the fact that certain groups are now willing to employ these unconventional and destructive means (Laqueur, 1999/2001). A frequently cited example is the case of the separatist (and religiously inspired) Chechen rebels' use of non-fissionable radiological devices during the 1990s (Graham, 2005). The same authors point not only at the increasing willingness to employ these kinds of weapons, but also at the relatively successful attempt to develop them, including al-Qaeda's CBRN programs and the successful development and use of nerve gases by the Japanese Aum. Thus, the new terrorism thesis argues that these groups do not require the sponsorship of a state for acquiring CBRN weapons (Benjamin and Simon, 2000b). While state sponsorship may continue to play a role in aiding the new terrorist organizations, emphasis is given to the fact that many of the latter do not act as proxies of the state and can grow, amass strategic strength and survive without a country's active financial backing or central oversight.

The lack of central oversight is one of the core organizational traits attributed to the new terrorist organizations. The last of the key defining characteristics of the new terrorism is the emphasis on a decentralized organizational architecture. The main proponents of this thesis raise several important points (Arquilla, Ronfeldt, and Zanini, 1999). First, they argue that a growing number of terrorist organizations, perhaps best exemplified by al-Qaeda and its numerous affiliates, are adopting networked and diffuse structures in contrast to the discrete and hierarchical arrangement of the 'older' organizations. As just mentioned, command and control of the 'new' groups is said to be decentralized and not observant of the top-bottom approach of their more traditional counterparts. According to these authors, the network configuration is aided in part by the communicative power of the information revolution. The ability to communicate intent and guidance to greater audiences, at larger distances, also leads to an increasing number of amateur recruits, who are ready to join the cause and engage in violence without ever receiving orders or guidance from a face-to-face encounter with the terrorist leadership (Tucker, 2001).

The structure of the new and networked entities is also conducive to dispersion and thus to greater international reach. Some observe that a single new terrorist network can have operational and logistical presence in several continents. When this fact is considered in conjunction with the aforementioned ideological breadth and unbound strategic goals, authors implicitly argue that contemporary groups like al-Qaeda are unprecedented because of their global aims, coverage, structure and means (Shultz, 2008).

The counterarguments

As mentioned earlier, there are at least two sides to this debate. On the one hand, there are the new terrorism proponents who substantiate their claims with the propositions of increased and indiscriminate lethality, caused by the preponderance of religious motivation, the accompanying warning of CBRN propensities, the absence of state patrons, and the adoption of networked, loosely knit and far-reaching (global) organizational structures as characteristics that define the new terrorist groups. On the other side of the debate, there are several scholars who have either questioned or argued against the new terrorism thesis. For the most part, they have done so with one premise in mind: that most of the new terrorism proponents have used the adjective 'new' in order to refer to a terrorism that did not exist before or to allude to aspects of it that were not known to us – something that holds true for some, but not all new terrorism proponents.

The one sub-proposition that is agreed upon by the majority of scholars within these two camps is the increasing lethality of contemporary terrorism. Beyond this, there is little agreement on the causes of the lethality trend. Furthermore, those who question the new terrorism thesis have also put forth several counter-arguments to underscore the message that most of what is deemed as new was there in the past and had been discussed in previous literature.

First, several counter-arguments on the issue of religious motivation assert that this is not a new phenomenon by referring to ancient precedents such as the Judaic roots of the Zealot movement against the Romans or to religious elements found in twentieth-century nationalist organizations such as the National Organization of Cypriot Fighters (EOKA) or the National Liberation Front of Algeria (FLN) (Duyvesteyn, 2004). Other counter-arguments to the supposedly diffuse goals linked to the religious motivation of groups like al-Qaeda underscore the existence of specific political and strategic considerations of these contemporary groups.

Second, there is some agreement regarding the increasing availability of CBRN materials that could be accessed by violent non-state actors. However, counter-arguments on this sub-proposition include the use of some of these means by 'traditional' terrorists, such as the early 1990s use of chlorine gas by the Tamil Tigers and the use of cyanide by the Kurdistan Workers Party (Spencer, 2006). Questions are also put forth on whether the use of these means truly represents a serious departure from the traditional terrorist willingness to cause serious harm by conventional means.

Third, rebuttals on the absence of state sponsorship for the new terrorism mostly converge on the idea that while Afghanistan, Somalia, or Sudan might not actively dictate the activities of new groups like al-Qaeda and its affiliates, they still provide a form of passive support. There are also voices of caution about the fact that new terrorism funds could possibly be traced to sources close to certain regimes in South and Southwest Asia. Finally, as for the networked and far-reaching organizational structure of groups like al-Qaeda, those that disagree with the new terrorism thesis dismiss this argument by pointing at historical cases of traditional terrorist organizations whose configuration was also diffuse, cellular, and where cooperation between groups gave traditional terrorists an international presence. The most prevalent historical examples in support of this counter-argument are: first, the internal configuration of the Palestinian Liberation Organization (PLO) as a vast umbrella organization; second, Hezbollah's and the Irish Republican Army's (IRA) tendency to adopt cellular arrangements; and third, the prior existence of seemingly far-reaching networks represented by the cooperation between the PLO, the Japanese Red Army, the German Red Army Faction and the IRA. The intercontinental connections between many of these groups and the vast international appeal of older ideologies like Communism are often used to demystify recent claims about the global newness of terrorism.

Change and context: a cautious 'newness'?

It seems appropriate to conclude this chapter by revisiting the central question that has led to the aforementioned debate: Is there anything new about some of the contemporary instances of terrorism or have we seen it all before? Martha Crenshaw, the doyenne of terrorism studies, provides us with appropriate ways of framing answers to this question. First, while illuminating this debate, Crenshaw (2009: 135) posits, 'The point is not that there has been no change in terrorism [,] but that the changes that have occurred need to be precisely delineated.' If there is anything new about terrorism, it should be considered as a matter of changing degrees, of evolutionary differences, and not as a list of clear-cut findings or smoking guns pointing at unprecedented traits or innovations. Second, following the lesson provided by one of her seminal edited volumes, Crenshaw (1995) argues that our quest will be futile unless we consider *terrorism in context*. In other words, terrorism is highly dependent (contingent) on the setting from which it originates and within which it develops.

As mentioned earlier, many of those who disagree with the new terrorism proposition have primarily done so because they depart from the premise that the new terrorism proponents are speaking about fundamentally and intrinsically new characteristics of terrorism. I argue that, if we are to use the label new, we should do so cautiously and by echoing Crenshaw's two previously stated arguments. In other words, there are some things about terrorism that are different and several of these differences are being shaped by the current environment. First and foremost, contemporary terrorists are different because they are more lethal. Al-Qaeda took the lives of roughly 3,000 people in one day. In doing so, it came to be known as a strategic contender to the most powerful country in the world, a dispensation that, at least in the twentieth century, was exclusively assigned to other nation-states. One could hope to dismiss the 2001 events as a singularity. However, details of subsequent plots inspired by these attacks provide further evidence to substantiate the ongoing lethality trend and its devastating potentials (for example, the 2006 plan by British-born Islamist extremists in the UK to detonate explosive devices on board at least 10 intercontinental flights).

Second, terrorism is different because groups such as al-Qaeda (even if we take the more conservative approach while defining its organizational boundaries) *combine* several facets of the numerous twentieth-century groups referred to in the previous paragraphs. Al-Qaeda is motivated by politics (U.S. interventionism, Israeli occupation of Palestine, corruption of Middle Eastern regimes) *and* by religion (violence as the duty of believers to ensure that God's indivisible nature and sovereignty are observed in this world and guided by the strict interpretation and application of the divinely ordained scriptures). By appealing to political arguments and metaphysical justifications as it sees fit, it has managed to partially legitimize the use of discriminate violence against tribal leaders, renowned journalists, naval destroyers, as well as rather indiscriminate attacks on buses, trains, planes and weddings. Against these targets, locally and globally, al-Qaeda has employed a vast array of means that range from the dagger, the AK47 and the traditional bomb to rocket-propelled grenades, chlorine gas and idiosyncratic hybrids comprised of aircrafts, jet fuel and operatives willing to die in order to kill. On several occasions – just in case there were no journalists or anchors on hand – al-Qaeda members made sure to produce video recordings of their operations. They did so because this organization wants *both* more people watching and more people dead. Finally, al-Qaeda has not only managed to create a network of affiliates or provide an umbrella structure to several organizations, it has created an international brand name (for example, al-Qaeda in the Arabian Peninsula, formerly known as al-Qaeda in Saudi Arabia and al-Qaeda in Yemen; al-Qaeda in the Land of the Two Rivers or al-Qaeda in Iraq; al-Qaeda in the Islamic Maghreb; and the less verifiable al-Qaeda in Lebanon, al-Qaeda Organization in the Levant and Egypt, al-Qaeda in Europe, al-Qaeda Organization for Jihad in Sweden, etc.). All of this has taken place because of intrinsic and extrinsic factors during a 20-year evolution – roughly coterminous with the time frame of the debate in question.

Third, contemporary terrorists are different, because their context – driving externalities or extrinsic factors – is also different and in flux. Among other things, the current context is an international setting pervaded by interacting, opposing and still unleashing forces. These forces include integration, fragmentation, hyper-information/communication, isolation, and state fragility – commonly associated with the era of globalization, the information age and the post-Cold War order. Groups that employ terrorism have benefited from several factors within this context (see Hanlon, 2008), including the ability to travel and move goods in ways and at a scale that is relatively unprecedented. Increasingly, current organizations have found what is best described, not as state-sponsors, but as safe havens. These safe havens are fragile states (or parts thereof) where government oversight is lacking. They are sanctuaries where terrorists can plan and act with relative impunity, and from which they can launch operations against other nation-states. Finally, as mentioned earlier, the current context also provides terrorists with greater access to certain tools, including highly disruptive/destructive weapons as well as enhanced means of communication and access to information.

Conclusion

In 2011 certain means of communication, namely the Internet and mobile phone technology, are said to have played a role in the revolutions that swept parts of Africa and the Middle East – leading to regime changes in Egypt and Tunisia, UN Sanctions for Libya, and serious turmoil in Yemen, Syria and Bahrain. A different debate is underway on whether information technologies can be considered as a key component unleashing these changes or whether these new tools are simply accessories to conflict based on structural and long-standing regional problems. More research needs to be done to understand and measure the importance of information technologies in the transformation of social movements.

A few things are for certain: these technologies are new and they reach audiences, connect people, retrieve and transfer information on an unprecedented scale and with an unprecedented speed. Terrorist groups know this and have begun to try to maximize the opportunities provided by these new tools. For example, we know that al-Qaeda temporarily changed the location of some of its training camps from Tora Bora (Al Masada Camp), Kabul

(Al Ghuraba Camp), and Jalalabad (Al Farouq Camp), to different addresses – virtual ones: www.al-farouq.com/vb, www.alguraabah.co.uk, or www.alm2sda.net. Occasionally, one can detect online activity by individuals closely affiliated with terrorist organizations who – according to their own words – have a mission 'to implement and devise a strategy to exploit Facebook's advantages as distribution and network platforms' (SITE Intelligence Group, 2009). The degree to which these tools are going to fundamentally change terrorism and organized violence in the twenty-first century – if at all – is something that we need to explore in more depth.

In sum, we could play with the different meanings of the adjective 'new' and with all the definitions provided at the beginning of this chapter. Recalling that new has subtler meanings, including something 'resurgent' or something more or less 'different', and considering the reasons provided in the immediately preceding paragraphs, we could conclude that contemporary cases of terrorism deserve the qualifier 'new.' Yet I want to close this chapter by emphasizing that we will probably be better off by focusing on trying to understand terrorism, not by adding adjectives to it, but by carefully examining its subtle and not so subtle adaptations for what they are and within their current context. We will most certainly be more accurate in our understanding if we are properly acquainted with historical lessons and previous dynamics of terrorism. We may benefit by being honest about the limitations of our research and the motivations that drive us to entertain certain debates, because whether academics and analysts like it or not and whether they do so intentionally or not, their conclusions about the 'newness' or 'oldness' of terrorism might end up shaping more than the academic debate.

NO: The fallacy of the new terrorism thesis

Isabelle Duyvesteyn and Leena Malkki

Introduction

Since the mid-1990s, it has been popular to view terrorism as substantially different from everything that went on before. The Oklahoma City bombing and the sarin gas attacks on the Tokyo subway in 1995 had proven, according to several notable experts, that terrorism had crossed a new boundary (see Simon and Benjamin, 2000). This was again confirmed by the 9/11 attacks (Laqueur, 2001, 2003; Tucker, 2001). The use of information technology, weapons of mass destruction, the desire to kill as many people as possible and the religious and vague goals of the perpetrators were, among others, deemed to hail a new era. The claims of innovation in terrorism practices did not stand alone. There have been debates in adjacent academic fields such as war studies and counter-insurgency, where similar claims about newness have also surfaced (van Creveld, 1991; Kaldor, 1999; Duyvesteyn and Angstrom, 2005; Kilcullen, 2010; MacKinlay, 2009). In particular, the latter field of study currently witnesses an interesting debate about whether the transnational nature of insurgency is truly a constitutive and new feature (see Jones and Smith, 2010).

The new terrorism argument has been particularly popular among policy circles in Washington (Copeland, 2000). Its popularity has declined a little in the past few years, but it still appears now and then in publications (Kurtulus, 2011). One cannot help but suspect that the popularity was linked to its two most important consequences. First, it would relieve scholars of the arduous task of a study of the rich history of terrorism. Second, it would mean more funding would have to be made available to dissect the new features and possible answers to the challenges of the new terrorists. This, of course, would be to the benefit of the research community. Indeed, the production of terrorism-related publications has augmented steeply. As Andrew Silke has calculated, every six hours a book is published in the English language about terrorism, leaving out articles and anything published in other languages (Silke, 2008: 28–29). Few of these studies on terrorism have taken a serious look at the history of the phenomenon, using historical description as an obligatory opening in many publications and then quickly moving on to a purely contemporary focus. The historical investigations that are worthwhile remain largely limited to single case studies and in-depth analyses of a handful of familiar Western cases, such as the Irish Republican Army (IRA), Euskadi ta Askatasuna (ETA) and the Red Army Faction (RAF).

The discussion about whether terrorism is new is complicated by the description and delimitation of the concept of terrorism. Without wanting to regurgitate the definitional debate, many studies into terrorism have started to incorporate what analytically needs to be distinguished as 'insurgency'. What has occurred in Iraq and Afghanistan should not be seen as terrorism per se. Within the context of these two civil wars, militant groups have applied terrorist tactics while pursuing a subversion and insurgent strategy against foreign occupying forces (Duyvesteyn and Fumerton, 2009). As a matter of fact, many scholars have overlooked the fact that during most of the twentieth century, terrorism has been used within the context of insurgency struggles in the non-Western world, which has traditionally witnessed the most armed conflict. A campaign in which terrorism is a strategy in its own right hardly occurs in the non-Western world. Factors that explain this phenomenon include, for example, the firm control most Western states manage to exert over their territory which precludes the safe havens or liberated zones that are the lifelines of many insurgency organizations. Other distinguishing criteria are targets (non-military versus military), organizational features (political front organizations and shadow states) or number of victims (see Duyvesteyn and Fumerton, 2009). Instead, the control of Western states makes the strategy of terrorism, relying on an avant-garde of activists living underground and committing acts of violence, more feasible as a way of advancing political agendas.

This chapter is intended to reflect on the arguments the new terrorism thinkers have brought forward in the debate. It aims to provide evidence to substantiate the argument that there is indeed nothing new under the sun. To be sure, the purpose of this chapter is not to argue that *nothing* has changed; quite the contrary. The main ideas on which this contribution rests are, first, as outlined, the idea that terrorism should be seen as a strategy; and, second, that terrorism is a social phenomenon. Social phenomena are dependent on, and products of, their social environment. It would have been highly surprising if terrorists had not adapted and started using the products of modern society and the fruits of globalization: the freely accessible ideas about alternative visions on life, action and effect made available through increased information technology. An entirely different question, however, is whether these changes warrant the term 'new terrorism' as a category and do indeed 'render much previous analysis of terrorism based on established groups obsolete' (Lesser *et al.*, 1999: 2).

The definition of 'new' that we use is:

> can signify that a phenomenon has not been witnessed before, such as the discovery of a
> new star in a far-away galaxy. Alternatively, the label 'new' can rightly be applied when

it concerns seen before phenomena but an unknown perspective or interpretation is developed, such as the theory of relativity or the idea that the earth is round.

(Duyvesteyn, 2004)

Terrorism: old and new

Contemporary terrorism, it is claimed, is new due to five main characteristics. These will be elaborated and dissected in turn.

Organisation

First, it is argued that the organizational structure of terrorist groups has developed from hierarchical organizations to fluid network organizations. That is, while traditional terrorist organizations such as the IRA and the RAF operated largely as hierarchical organizations with a top leadership directing cadres below, the new terrorists are said to operate in a loose network structure. More recently, it has been argued that the current operating mechanism is a 'leaderless jihad' (Sageman, 2008). Furthermore, lone wolf terrorism perpetrated by individuals who have self-radicalized has been added as a supposedly new feature of the practice of terrorism.

These ideas, however, are too simplistic to describe a complex and variegated reality. First, the traditional terrorists also used network structures. Anarchism, one of the most important sources of terrorist violence in the nineteenth century, was by definition organized as a loose network (Bach Jensen, 2004). In more recent history, the PLO and Hezbollah have operated fundamentally as networks with only rudimentary central control (Tucker, 2001: 3–4).

The organizational format that terrorist groups adopt is often a function of the environment, and importantly, the counter-measures the state enacts against it. For example, the IRA, as its name implies, used to be organized according to an army model, with regiments and brigades. This structure allowed the British to relatively easily infiltrate the organization. As a consequence of the counter-measures, the IRA adapted its structure to become more immune to infiltration. This could also be argued for the case of Israeli counter-measures against the PLO and Hezbollah, such as the decapitation strategy which robbed these organizations of their leadership. This necessitated organizational changes, which were a result of state action rather than a wilful or conscious choice of these groups. Similar developments have inspired the idea of leaderless resistance among the American far right (Beam, 1992; Kaplan, 1997). We can also witness this development in several currently active groups which have become increasingly fluid and intangible to such an extent that some experts prefer to describe al-Qaeda as an ideology rather than an organization.

It may also be that there is a tendency to assume that groups in the past have been more tightly and rigidly organized than they actually were because of the way the groups described themselves. Terrorist groups have often presented themselves as small armies, consisting of different units, having their own rules and military ranks for their members. While this corresponded with the way the groups would have liked to be, it did not necessarily reflect reality. The Symbionese Liberation Army, a radical leftist group which was active in California in 1973–1974, is an extreme example of this. It had the entire blueprint drafted for an armed revolutionary federation, complete with codes of war and military ranks. In reality, this 'army' consisted of a dozen members who lived together (Malkki, 2010).

The individuals participating in today's networks are argued to constitute a virtual community, which is supposed not to have existed before. The experts claiming this overlook the fact that 'imagined communities' were a crucial factor in the rise of nationalism in the nineteenth century. It is not a new phenomenon in the realm of terrorist movements either. Such imagined communities existed within the European and American leftist groups of the 1970s. While some of them were more internationally oriented than others, their worldview and strategy was strongly based on the idea that they were part of a revolutionary movement against capitalism and imperialism, with national liberation struggles in the Third World presenting the frontline of this struggle (Malkki, 2011).

Another related claim is that the role of the media has changed substantially and that this has changed the organizational parameters of terrorist activity considerably (Norris, Kern and Just, 2003). Now, the terrorist movements are no longer dependent on the conventional media, but instead the Internet serves as the main conduit for terrorist messages and recruitment. Furthermore, the Internet has allegedly opened whole new avenues for inter-action across boundaries and with minimal risk of getting caught. It is true that the medium has changed; the Internet is an important channel for communication and distribution of information in many fields of life, and again, terrorism is a product of society. However, one has to be careful not to overestimate the benefits that the recent changes have brought to terrorist movements. While the possibilities for virtual communication may have been extended, the real life communication and building of underground movements seems to have become exceedingly difficult in the West. Online communication is not without its difficulties; it does leave traces and building trust and alliances with the sole means of digital communication is risky (Innes, 2007).

Lone wolf terrorism cannot be seen as a fundamentally new organizational aspect of terrorism either (Stewart and Burton, 2008). There are many examples historically where individuals without any clear organizational structures behind them were responsible for terrorist acts (Spaaij, 2010). The nineteenth-century anarchists are again an important example, as is the decade-long struggle of the FBI to try to find the UNA bomber, Ted Kaczinsky (Chase, 2004). Lone wolfs are of all ages, and this claim that new terrorism is primarily per-petrated by amateurs and self-radicalizers might again be linked to the effect of the state's counter-measures.

Scope

A second argument is that terrorist actors have shifted from a purely national and territorial focus to a transnational and non-territorial focus in their operations. The central claim here is that traditional terrorist organizations have operated largely within one national territory with a national focus and agenda. New terrorist organizations, on the contrary, no longer limit themselves to addressing a national audience and a national agenda; instead, they operate on a worldwide scale and pursue an international agenda.

This argument overlooks important features of traditional terrorist organizations. First, the national and territorial focus does apply mainly to those terrorist organizations focusing on decolonization and nationalism, such as the campaign by the Front de Libération Nationale (FLN) in Algeria and the IRA in Northern Ireland. However, even these organizations operated internationally with significant support bases in France and the United States, respectively. Terrorist groups pursuing left-wing agendas had, of course, a variety of Marxist ideals, which shared a common vision that was not limited to national states or to territory, but instead focused on a worldwide revolutionary struggle.

Second, these older terrorist groups possessed important transnational links themselves. Traditional terrorists practiced international exchange and cooperation, within the limits of what was feasible at the time. In the nineteenth century, there was an international anarchist movement whereby individuals would travel to several countries and circulate within anarchist circles. In more recent times, there were strong links between Marxist-inspired groups around the world, including those involved in terrorism. To give some examples of the transnational contacts in the 1970s, several European activists traveled to China where they met other like-minded activists from other countries. The Weather Underground key members, for example, met with representatives of the Vietnamese people. While these contacts involved primarily information exchange, there were also more substantial contacts. It is well known that many German and Dutch left-wing radicals followed guerrilla training organized by Palestinian groupings in Jordan and South Yemen. There were allegedly also logistical support networks between the German Red Army Faction and the Dutch radicals (Malkki, 2010). Joint operations by people of different citizenship is not a novelty: the group that executed the OPEC attack in Vienna in 1975 serves as an example, as does the so-called Euro-terrorism of the mid-1980s, which was an attempt by the left-wing terrorist movements to combine forces.

In other words, not only were the traditional terrorist organizations more transnational and non-territorial than has often been allowed for, but the so-called 'new' organizations are in fact more focused on national and territorial aspects than is frequently acknowledged. First, the al-Qaeda ideology explicitly strives for the unification of all states with a majority of Muslims, stretching from North Africa to South East Asia, realizing the partly territorial ideal of a Caliphate. Second, an important agenda point is the removal of Western influence from the land of the three holy places and the ridding of the Middle East of regimes that are corrupted by the West. Third, the state is still seen as the most important vehicle for realizing these theocratic ideals. This can among others be witnessed in the co-opting of Sudan and Afghanistan as staging bases for the al-Qaeda struggle. Recently, the tribal regions of Pakistan and Yemen seem to have taken over this function.

Aims

A third argument about the new terrorism is that the aims of the actors have moved from political agendas to a religious focus. Traditional terrorist movements are considered to have espoused nationalist or left-wing ideologies. This has recently shifted to religious inspiration and therefore the label 'new' has been applied (Ranstorp, 1996; Juergensmeyer, 2001). These arguments are in themselves highly contentious, because they imply mono-causality, which is of course a fallacy. Detailed case study analysis reveals that most terrorist organizations have multiple, overlapping and highly changeable goals. Notwithstanding this serious shortcoming, two questions are in order here: to what extent can the traditional terrorist organizations be considered non-religious or secular; and to what extent are the new terrorist organizations inspired by religion?

First, traditional terrorist movements were hardly non-religious or purely secular. Some examples include the IRA with an almost exclusive Catholic following, Irgun which was exclusively Jewish, and EOKA in Cyprus with a Greek Orthodox membership. In pre-modern times, as argued by David Rapoport (1984: 658), the most prevalent justification for terrorism was in fact religion. Second, the new terrorist organizations are also influenced by secular and more mundane considerations. We have already argued that national and territorial issues play a key role for new terrorist organizations; having a long-term religiously inspired goal does not exclude the possibility of having short-term political objectives (Sedgwick, 2004). Important examples are the nationalist agendas of Hamas and Hezbollah (see Gunning, 2007).

An entirely different question is what kind of sociological/socio-psychological significance this alleged shift in objectives has. It has often been claimed that the religious motive makes the terrorist movement behave and think along different lines. The religious terrorists are arguably engaged in a 'cosmic war' (Juergensmeyer, 2001). However, it should be noted that religious movements do not have a monopoly on apocalyptic or utopian thinking. Jeremy Varon, for example, argues that the RAF and the Weather Underground had an apocalyptic dimension, including the idea that existing society is corrupt and must be destroyed and that this would make the emergence of something new and better possible. This thought, in its turn, made it possible for these groups to 'take their violence out of the realm of political calculation' and see it as a struggle between good and evil (Varon, 2008: 35–37).

Methods

A fourth argument regarding new terrorism is that the means with which terrorist attacks are carried out are shifting from conventional explosives to weapons of mass destruction. The most important instrument used to carry out a terrorist attack remains the bomb; in particular, the car bomb enjoys unprecedented popularity (Hoffman, 2001). Paradoxically, the most important instrument before the advent of dynamite, the nitroglycerine bomb, has been enjoying a small renaissance. The substance was used mostly because of a lack of alternatives but is notorious because of its instability.

Weapons of mass destruction, or to be more precise, so-called NBCR (nuclear, biological, chemical and radiological) weapons, and the risks of them falling into the hands of terrorist organizations, have received a lot of attention from academics, think tanks and the popular press. Almost 20 percent of the literature on terrorism focuses on weapons of mass destruction (Lum, Kennedy and Sherley, 2006a: 493). The fear of WMD falling into the hands of terrorists has been discussed for a very long time: 'warnings about the possibility that small groups, terrorists and errant states could fabricate nuclear weapons have been repeatedly uttered at least since 1947' (Mueller, 2005: 489; Jenkins, 1975, 1985). However, there are only two confirmed examples of the use of such weapons with potential for mass destruction: the sarin gas attack by the Aum Shinrikyo sect in the Tokyo underground in 1995, and the anthrax letters sent in the aftermath of 11 September 2001 attacks in the United States. Although they were highly threatening, two examples hardly constitute a trend.

Even if the terrorists were looking at causing more destruction than before, it does not mean that the use of weapons of mass destruction would be imminent. Noteworthy is the observation of John V. Parachini that those who wish to inflict mass casualties, especially those with some level of professionalism, have tended to opt for conventional means, presumably because of the unpredictability that unavoidably comes with using the so-called NBCR material (Parachini, 2001).

The discussion also suffers from terminological imprecision. The term 'weapons of mass destruction' seems to increasingly relate more to the effect of mass casualties rather than the composition of the specific weapon used. To talk about NBCR weapons (and even less NBCR material as such) as weapons of mass destruction is hardly more precise, because they are not always weapons of mass destruction by their effect. The influence of the non-proliferation think tanks, so prominent during the Cold War period and still in existence today, can be felt in this area.

Means

Finally, it is argued that the means used by terrorists have changed in the effect they seek, from small-scale bomb attacks and airplane hijacking to mass casualty attacks. This contention is based on two false premises. First, small arms can have large-scale effects. Even small explosives can produce large numbers of victims. Carried out with a truck load of conventional explosives, the 1983 attack on a United States barracks in Lebanon, which cost the lives of over 200 American marines, was at the time described as beyond all boundaries (Fisk, 1990). Also a conventional bomb attack in Omagh, carried out with a truck load of conventional explosives in 1998 managed to kill 28, the largest number in one incident of Northern Irish terrorism (Dingley, 2001).

Second, mass casualties are not a recent phenomenon. It is a consistent feature of discussions about terrorism to describe the effect as boundless and inhuman. This applies to the nineteenth century as much as today (Miller, 1995: 31). Scholars have found time and again that the number of victims per terrorist attack is on the increase since the start of the 1980s (Hoffman, 1998: 94, 201). This trend does not coincide with the supposed development of the new terrorism since the mid-1990s. Furthermore, it has been argued that the choice of targets of the new terrorists is increasingly indiscriminate. It is true that the last decade of the nineteenth century has been described as the decade of political murder with attacks focusing on individuals, in particular heads of state. However, both the old and the new terrorists seek highly specific and individual targets, as well as more symbolic and general targets. The plots to kill President Bush and the detonation of bombs on the Madrid and London public transport systems could purportedly have had the same effect.

What seems to be overlooked in many of these claims is the so-called law of diminishing returns, whereby every subsequent attack has to strike harder in order to attain the same effect (Laqueur, 2001: 108). The shift from highly specific to more indiscriminate targeting may also occur because security arrangements have made it increasingly difficult to target high-level politicians and public figures. This is called the substitution effect, which plays a major role in terrorism (Arce and Sandler, 2005; Enders and Sandler, 2005). Statistical studies have indicated that the 'war on terror' has already given rise to shifts in types of attacks, namely, less sophisticated bombings and shifts from American targets to Western allies, as seen in the London, Madrid and Bali bombings (Enders and Sandler, 2005; Rosendorf and Sandler, 2004).

Observations and conclusions

What is truly new in the field of terrorism is the huge impetus scholarship has received since 2001. While not all of it is top quality, substantial progress has been made in our understanding of terrorism and its related phenomena (Pape, 2009). The key question is whether the combination of the developments examined above deserves the label 'new'? The trends brought up by new terrorism thinkers may exist in some form, but they do not form such dramatic developments as is suggested, and therefore do not add up to a phenomenon we might call 'new terrorism'. The trends are not as intertwined as the argument tends to portray. While Aum Shinrikyo was fascinated with weapons of mass destruction, the organizational form it adopted was decidedly hierarchical and did not take the flat, diffuse network shape. Furthermore, Hamas, an example of an allegedly religiously motivated movement active today, does not share the main characteristics and aspirations ascribed to the new terrorism thesis (Gunning, 2007).

Instead, we are dealing with a series of developments that have not affected the phenomenon of terrorism as a concept and as a strategy in any uniform or universal manner (see for example, Neumann, 2009). These developments reinforce the need to refine our understanding of terrorism. This contribution has attempted to show that when taking a much needed and closer look at the history of terrorism, there is nothing that suggests that we are dealing with an entirely new phenomenon that makes all previous research on terrorism redundant. The realities of terrorism remain more complex than the policy-makers would like to have it, but refusing to pay attention to historical parallels and diversity in terrorist movements may lead to grave misjudgements and wasted resources.

Discussion questions

1 What are some of the 'new' features of terrorism?
2 Is religion a new and dominant feature of terrorism?
3 If the motivations and choices of the 'new terrorist' groups are based on religious belief and appear broad and diffuse, does this mean that they are irrational?
4 What are some of the intrinsic or extrinsic factors that can cause transformations among terrorist organizations?
5 What are some of the current trends and elements of terrorism that can lead to future challenges for nation-states and for the international community?
6 Do the detractors and proponents of the new terrorism thesis agree on anything? Why?
7 What can history teach us about the evolution and nature of terrorism?
8 Are fears of terrorists using nuclear weapons justified?
9 To what extent does terrorism derive its power from the law of diminishing returns and the substitution effect?
10 What are some of the academic and political implications of arguing that there is a new terrorism in existence?

Further readings

Crenshaw, M., ed., 1995. *Terrorism in Context*, University Park, Pennsylvania, PA: Pennsylvania State University Press.
Duyvesteyn, I., 2004. 'How New is the New Terrorism', *Studies in Conflict and Terrorism*, 27(5): 439–454.
Hanlon, Q., 2008. 'Globalization and the Transformation of Armed Groups', in Horowitz, J., ed., *Armed Groups*, Newport, RI: US Naval War College.
Lesser, I., Arquilla, J., Ronfeldt, D., Hoffman, B., Zanini, M., and Jenkins, B., 1999, *Countering the New Terrorism*, Santa Monica, CA: The Rand Corporation.
Neumann, P., 2009. *Old and New Terrorism*, Cambridge, UK: Polity.
Rapoport, D., 1984. 'Fear and Trembling; Terrorism in Three Religious Traditions', *American Political Science Review*, 78(3): 658–677.
Rapoport, D., 2004. 'The Four Waves of Modern Terrorism', in Cronin, A., and Ludes, J., eds, *Attacking Terrorism: Elements of a Grand Strategy*, Washington, DC: Georgetown University Press.
Sedgwick, M., 2007. 'Inspiration and the Origins of Global Waves of Terrorism', *Studies in Conflict and Terrorism*, 30: 97–112.

3   Can states be terrorists?

YES: State terror: the theoretical and practical utilities and implications of a contested concept

Michael Stohl

Introduction

> If the basis of a popular government in peacetime is virtue, its basis in a time of revolution is virtue and terror – virtue, without which terror would be barbaric; and terror, without which virtue would be impotent . . . Terror is nothing other than justice, prompt, severe, inflexible.
>
> (Robespierre, 1794)

In this chapter, I will confront the question 'can states be terrorists?' in the affirmative. I also will address the main arguments put forth by those who argue the negative. In addition to explaining why and how states can be terrorists, this also requires an explanation of how certain forms of state violence amount to terrorism. Finally, I will examine the negative implications of excluding states from the study of terrorism, both for confronting reality and for assisting our understanding of non-state political actors' decisions to employ terrorism.

The etymology of terrorism

The term 'terrorism' entered the English language in the aftermath of *La Terreur* (The Reign of Terror) to refer to the revolutionary state's systematic use of violence against French citizens. The term 'terrorist' was applied to Robespierre, Saint Just and others of the committee of Public Safety (Kropotkin, 1927; Bienvenu, 1970: 228–230). The French word for terror itself had ancient roots. It was derived from the Latin verb *terrere*, which meant 'to frighten'. The term was applied to the *terror cimbricus*, as a panic and state of emergency in Rome in response to the approach of warriors of the Cimbri tribe in 105 BC. The Romans employed the specter of terror themselves as a core component of their power in the aftermath of conquest, as a response to slave uprisings and rebellion and towards criminals through the use of crucifixion, which was intended not only as a punishment of the victim but as a message to the audience that bore witness. The concept itself had an ancient lineage and the use of terror was common amongst rulers before the creation of the Roman Empire. Aristotle reflected on the use of terror by tyrants in his *Politics*, for example:

> The three aims of the tyrant are, one, the humiliation of his subjects; he knows that a mean-spirited man will not conspire against anybody; two, the creation of mistrust among them; for a tyrant is not to be overthrown until men begin to have confidence in one another – and this is the reason why tyrants are at war with the good; they are under the idea that their power is endangered by them, not only because they will not be ruled despotically, but also because they are too loyal to one another and to other men, and do not inform against one another or against other men – three, the tyrant desires that all his subjects shall be incapable of action, for no one attempts what is impossible and they will not attempt to overthrow a tyranny if they are powerless.
>
> (Aristotle, 2000: 227)

The questions of whether the state can be a terrorist, or if the concept of state terror is a useful concept, are relatively new. In fact, discussions of the state as terrorist and the implications of state terror have been the subject of many of the twentieth century's most significant scholars of political violence and the state. These studies of state terror provided some of the finest analytic work on terrorism and how and why it works within the political process. These works included Hannah Arendt's *The origins of totalitarianism* (1968), Robert Conquest's *The great terror* (1968), Barrington Moore's *Terror and progress – USSR* (1966), E. V. Walter's *Terror and resistance* (1969), and A. Dallin and G. Breslauer's *Political terror in communist systems* (1970). Much of this work came in response to the historical reality of the rise of what were called the totalitarian states – the Soviet Union, Nazi Germany, Fascist Italy and the People's Republic of China. Scholars observed, for example, three phases in the Bolshevik regime's terror. First, terror was employed against counterrevolutionaries in the immediate aftermath of the Revolution and the end of the First World War. Secondly, the terror was directed against the wealthy peasants (kulaks) during the 1920s and 1930s. Finally, as had been the case in the French Revolution, state terror was increasingly used against party members and state administrators who became victims of the very regime that they had helped create. In the end, as Khrushchev's 1956 denunciation of Stalin indicated (Khrushchev, 1956), within the Soviet Union no one would ever be above suspicion and thus every Soviet citizen perceived themselves a potential victim of state terror. The result, as Duvall and Stohl (1983: 242) have argued, was that fear lingers long after the violent periods and the extremes of state terror. In its earliest phase, this terror was justified by one of its most famous later victims:

> The degree of ferocity of the struggle depends on a series of internal and international circumstances. The more ferocious and dangerous is the resistance of the class enemy who have been overthrown, the more inevitably does the system of repression take the form of a system of terror.
>
> (Trotsky, 1920: 55)

However, despite this long history and knowledge of the utility of the act and threat of violence to coerce and intimidate, as well as the etymological roots of the word 'terrorism' and its original association in English as a concept with the 'reign of terror' of the French revolutionary regime of Robespierre, many contemporary scholars who consider themselves experts on 'terrorism' refuse to consider the violence perpetrated by the state against its own population or those of states beyond their borders as terrorism, reserving the term instead for use only for those challenging the state. Some have even argued that the two are so dissimilar as to be two different concepts: 'I cannot help but feel that state terrorism is actually a rhinoceros which has strayed close to our terrorism elephant. So while there are similarities between the two, they are ultimately two different creatures' (Silke, 1996: 22).

This transition in scholarly attention can be traced primarily to the dramatic rise of Palestinian terrorism in the latter part of the 1960s which, taking part in the aftermath of the colonial uprisings in places such as Kenya, Algeria and Vietnam in the 1940s–1960s, focused new attention on the problem of state security. In the beginning of this transition, as insurgent terrorism reemerged as an international problem and attracted greater public attention, scholars such as Thornton (1966) saw no need to discard the concept of state terrorism, but rather distinguished between agitational terrorism and enforcement terrorism, reserving the former for terrorism against the state and the latter for terrorism by the state. Thus, as Teichman (1989: 508) argues, there are clear etymological and historical arguments for the concept of state terror:

> I suggest we show respect for the past, and for etymology, by allowing that there are three species of terrorism, corresponding to the three main phases in the history of the word. These are state terrorism, or reigns of terror, terrorism which consists solely in the assassination of specifically chosen victims, and modern terrorism, which roughly speaking is usually but not invariably a kind of violent nationalistic rebellion carried out in a variety of ways.

Conceptualizing terrorism

Before engaging the argument of contemporary scholars who deny that there is such a thing as state terror and that the state cannot be referred to as terrorist, it is useful to discuss the political choices that are involved in developing a useful social science definition of terrorism, as well as the implications of these choices for discussing state terrorism. As we shall see, one can declare that there is no state terrorism by simply defining it out of existence, as has often been the case when the defining actor represents the state within international fora or the legislative branch. Such an approach is political rather than conceptual. The same process is employed to label the terrorist of which one approves as 'freedom fighters', and those that one does not as 'terrorists'. There is no firm conceptual ground to do so, however.

Terrorism, as a social science concept, is an act that describes a particular relationship among perpetrator(s), victim(s) and audience(s). While there is much disagreement within the scholarly community as to the exact definition of terrorism – see, among many others, Schmid (2009/2011) who has catalogued more than 200 definitions of terrorism used in the social science and policy literature – many of these definitions attempt to 'refine' the concept so that it applies only to certain actors and circumstances. When one reviews the definitions that Schmid identifies, it is clear that there is significant agreement that a definition of terrorism should include the following components: 'There is an **act** in which the perpetrator **intentionally** employs **violence** (or its threat) to instill **fear** (terror) in a **victim** and the **audience** of the act or threat.'

You will notice that these core items in bold do not include terms which limit the perpetrators or the victims to particular 'classes' of persons, either 'subnational agents' or 'non-combatants', as does the definition found in Title 22 of the United States Code, Section 2656f(d):

> The term 'terrorism' means premeditated, politically motivated violence perpetrated against noncombatant targets by subnational groups or clandestine agents, usually intended to influence an audience.
>
> (United States Department of State, 2011)

Much of the same limitations are built into the argument by Wight (2009: 102), who suggests that at a minimum, the following elements are required for a definition of terrorism:

- It is a form of violent political communication
- It is always illegitimate violence
- It involves the deliberate targeting of non-state actors and institutions
- The victims are not the intended recipients of the political message.

While both the US code and the Wight formulations include violence, victims, audience and intentionality (even if the words chosen are different), they also include restrictions on who the targets and perpetrators may be. The limit on perpetrators clearly is intended to limit the act of terrorism to actors who oppose the state. The limit on targets has had the unintended effect of preventing the single most deadly act of terrorism against the United States before September 11, the first major suicide bombing in which Hezbollah targeted United States and French Marines in Lebanon and killed 299 servicemen in their barracks, as being listed as terrorism – unless the marines were redefined as non-combatants because they were sleeping in their barracks and not in the 'ready' position.

I would propose an actor-neutral definition of terrorism: *Terrorism is the purposeful act or the threat of the act of violence to create fear and/or compliant behavior in a victim and/or audience of the act or threat.* This definition focuses upon the act or threat of the act of violence and the victim and audience to whom it is directed (see Stohl, 1988 for further discussion of the implications). It is crucial to understand that the victims of the violent act must be distinguished from the multiple targets of the act, that is, the audience(s) of that violence. Further, this definition focuses on behavior, is neutral as to the perpetrator(s) of the act and does not differentiate among perpetrators who are in-groups or out-groups, state or non-state actors, or legitimate or illegitimate governments who are wielders of the violence. In addition, this definition also helps to distinguish terrorism from other forms of political violence (whether by state or non-state actors). Not all acts of state violence are terrorism. It is important to emphasize that in terrorism the violence, threatened or perpetrated, has purposes broader than simply physical harm to a victim. In the most extreme form of mass killing, when the state engages in a policy of genocide by attempting to eliminate an entire identity group (Tutsis in Rwanda, Jews and the Roma across Europe by the Nazis), the murder of the victims is the end in itself. The perpetrators do not pursue their killing to influence a wider audience; likewise when a state engages in 'ethnic cleansing', as occurred during the wars that followed the breakup of the Yugoslav state.

However, in terrorism, the audience of the act or threat of violence is more important than the immediate victim; hence, the oft cited Chinese maxim, 'Kill one, frighten 10,000', attributed to Sun-Tzu. This is the case when terrorists can secure media coverage of their acts, or in cases of particularly nasty terrorists acts such as kneecapping where the victim is maimed for life and by being left to walk about becomes an advertisement of the danger posed by the terrorist (state or non-state), and thus reaches a far wider audience than solely through the physical act of maiming. This is not to say that terrorists are always open about their activity or that they seek mediated publicity. They are not. Campaigns of murder, both covert and overt, are all too well known, from the victims of Stalin's 'terror' mentioned above to 'los desaparecidos' (the disappeared) of the authoritarian regimes of the 1970s and 1980s in Latin America, where the disappearance, in addition to eliminating particular persons on the political left, was calculated to send a message (despite the state pretending not to be involved in the disappearance) to the potential opposition about the dangers of doing so. Studies have indicated that the particular historic and socio-cultural context and the strength of the state heavily influence the choice of covert versus overt behavior (Duvall and Stohl, 1983).

Thus, when we consider acts of terrorism we need to recognize that the actions are denoted by three key elements which correspond quite directly to those enumerated by Walter (1969). First, threatened or perpetrated violence is directed at some victim. Second, the violent actor intends for violence to induce terror in witnesses (mediated or unmediated) who are generally distinct from the victim – the victim is instrumental. Third, the violent actor intends or expects that the terrorized witnesses will effectuate a desired outcome, either directly (in which case the witness is the target) or indirectly (in which case the witnesses and the target are distinct – the witness is also instrumental). The process of political terrorism may thus be characterized as consisting of three component parts: the act or threat of violence, the emotional reaction to such an act or threat, and the social effects resultant from the acts and reaction. The state as a political actor clearly has participated in the terrorism process, and as many have argued, with far greater effect than insurgents (see Stohl, 1979; Blakeley, 2009; Jackson *et al.*, 2011).

Objections to the notion of state terrorism

As indicated above, there are those who argue that the State cannot be a terrorist and that state terrorism is not a meaningful concept. Wight, for example, argues that the state is:

> the organisation that (successfully) claims a monopoly on the legitimate use of physical force within a given territory . . . If part of any definition of terrorism includes the notion of 'illegitimate force' then the concept of 'state terrorism' is a contradiction in terms. Doubtless those that want to preserve the commitment to state terrorism will object. But I believe that the Weberian dictum is an essential part of the modern state and that terrorism always involves illegitimate violence carried out by non-state actors. So there can be no such thing as state terrorism.
>
> (Wight, 2009: 101)

The observant reader will note that Wight (as indicated above) has slipped in what I have argued above are two non-essential components for a definition of the act of terrorism – legitimacy and non-state actors. In Weber's formulation, he argues that 'the state is a relation of men dominating men, a relation supported by means of legitimate (i.e. considered to be legitimate) violence' (Weber, 1958: 78). For many, the meaning of 'legitimate' in this context is subject to controversy. To some, it has normative meaning – that the state should monop- olize force; to others, it has positive meaning – that the people accept the 'legitimacy' of the state monopoly. Even though violence by legitimate states tends to be considered well within the legitimate practices of the state (and hence not terrorist in nature), it is important to note, as Crelinsten (1987) has argued:

> the legitimacy and power of the state tend to cloak any overt forms of its violence in different guises, such as arrests instead of abduction, imprisonment instead of

hostage-taking, execution instead of murder and coercive diplomacy instead of blackmail.

(Crelinsten, 1987: 440)

However, these language substitutions constitute the power of framing, not the legitimacy of actions. Thus, not all actions by a legitimate government and state are in themselves legitimate simply because the state (or its officials) commits them. Rather, as Claridge argues:

> When a state uses violence as a means of *coercing* society, rather than defending it, it initiates an abuse of the '*monopoly of the legitimate use of physical force*'; and if a state institutes a policy of *elimination* of entire sections of its own (or another) society it is clearly behaving in an unacceptable and illegitimate manner – beyond the limits of its sovereignty.
>
> (Claridge, 1996: 48, original emphasis)

State actors do in fact violate the laws of the state and are frequently held accountable by the judicial system for those acts. Judges, executive or administrative officials and legislators are impeached or prosecuted in democratic systems when they are found guilty of such violations of the law. Their actions are not considered legitimate (or legal) simply because they hold a state office. In the specific example of the use of violence, officers of the law can be prosecuted for their excessive or unauthorized use of force. There are also numerous examples of members of the police and security forces employing violent 'extrajudicial' means, either as 'private' citizens, and/or with the full connivance of the authorities of the state to accomplish political ends for which 'normal' mechanisms are conceived of as either too slow or cumbersome. For example, in the 1980s, Prime Minister Gonzalez of Spain employed various extrajudicial means against the Basques, including the GAL (Anti-Terrorist Liberation Groups) with the justification that 'Democracy is defended in the sewers as well as the salons' (Woodworth, 2001: 235). Many additional examples may be found in Stohl (1979).

Wight further argues that the special status of the state as the holder of the monopoly of violence imposes other obligations on those who proffer a concept of state terrorism:

> Moreover, it is incumbent on those keen to defend the notion of 'state terrorism' to provide an account of why a particular form of state activity is terrorism and not another form of violence, and they do not seem to have fared too well in this respect so far.
>
> (Wight, 2009: 102)

I agree that it is important to delimit the concept of state terrorism and not to confuse it with any violence committed by the state or other misuses of state power. However, we should first confront the misuse of power by the state. As Gurr (1986: 49) argues:

> State terror should be judged not in the absolute but against some standard. Normatively, the standard might be that of international law (which at present condemns genocide but not state terrorism), or the domestic laws of the state in question, or the laws of culturally similar states, or some not-yet-codified conception of global human rights.

Next, we should distinguish different means by which the power of the state may be employed to manipulate and coerce a population. A starting point is the introduction of the concept of *oppression* to describe the situation where social and economic privileges are denied to whole classes of people, regardless of whether or not they oppose the authorities; and *repression* as the use of coercion or the threat of coercion against opponents or potential opponents in order to prevent or weaken their capability to oppose the authorities and their policies (Bissell *et al.*, 1978: 9). Whereas the manipulation of violence is the core mechanism of terrorism, oppression and repression, while relying on the power of the state, are not defined by violence. They rely instead on the structures of power to enforce obedience to rule (regardless of the 'legitimacy' of rule). In the midst of the consolidation of the Soviet State, Leon Trotsky in his reply to Karl Kautsky, an Austrian socialist opposed to the state terror employed by the Bolsheviks against their opposition, echoing Robespierre above, both defended the use of terror and distinguished it from repression exactly on this basis of the use of violence and indicating that it was a subset of that repression when used by the state:

> The degree of ferocity of the struggle depends on a series of internal and international circumstances. The more ferocious and dangerous is the resistance of the class enemy who have been overthrown, the more inevitably does the system of repression take the form of a system of terror.
>
> (Trotsky, 1920: 55)

Oppression, repression and terrorism may thus be concurrent and coordinated policies and actions, but they are nonetheless different phenomena and should be distinguished. In the case of state activities, it is useful to see terrorism as the most delimited of the phenomena reliant on the manipulation of violence to influence the wider audience, whereas oppression determines the political arena within which repression and terrorism often transpire. It is also important to recognize, as the justifications provided by Robespierre and Trotsky remind us that, 'In reality, most terrorism occurs in the context of wider political and social struggles in which the use of terrorism is one strategy among other more routine forms of contentious action' (Tilly, 2004: 6), and we should not be surprised therefore that its use is not reserved for only one class of political actor, those that challenge the state, to employ. Thus, not surprisingly, I agree with Jackson (2009: 13):

> As such, there is no deontological reason which precludes an actor – state or non-state – from engaging in acts of terrorism as part of a broader political strategy. In research terms, to suggest that when agents representing a state engage in the very same actions as non-state actors, such as when they blow up civilian airliners (the Lockerbie bombing) or a protest ship (the *Rainbow Warrior* bombing) or plant a series of bombs in public places (the Lavon affair), it automatically ceases to be terrorism is illogical and analytically unworkable.

There is a further reason for not concluding, as did Silke, that state terrorism and non-state terrorism are a rhinoceros and an elephant. As indicated above, much of the finest analytic work by scholars on the problem of terrorism and the decisions of terrorists were directed at state terrorism and state terrorists. Contemporary scholars of terrorism who ignore this work deny themselves a wealth of insight. Further, as Maxwell Taylor (1988: 40) wrote:

> A consideration of state terrorism allows us to examine the problem [of insurgency terrorism] from a different and rather less familiar perspective. In doing so we will see more clearly some of the considerations inherent in the term. We will also, and more importantly, develop a more sophisticated notion of the nature of terrorism. By 'peeling' away the complications arising out of our everyday view of terrorism as the activity of a secret or underground society, we can better come to look at terrorism as a process, and attempt to identify the particular kind of acts that characterise it.

Conclusion

In the preceding, we have confronted the question 'can states be terrorists?' in the affirmative and have established the etymological, historical and contemporary existence of state terrorism. We have seen that the questions of whether the state can be terrorist or if the concept of state terror is a useful concept are relatively new and that the state as terrorist and the implications of state terror were the subject of many of the twentieth century's most significant scholars of political violence and the state. We have addressed the main arguments put forth by those who argue the negative and in addition to explaining why and how states can be terrorists, we have explored how only certain forms of state violence should be defined as terrorism and separated from the many other means by which the state can invoke its power.

In short, we have established that states as actors commit acts of terrorism. To deny the existence of state terrorism as a concept ignores significant scholarship and creates further impediment to understanding the context, conditions and implications of the decision calculus of all political actors who engage in the instrumental use of violence and the manipulation of audiences and the political process. As Teichman (1989: 510) argues:

> quite apart from historical considerations, we have to acknowledge that governments often do things, both to their own people, and against enemies in peace and war, which share the features of the worst types of revolutionary terrorism . . . The only problem for philosophy here is a not very interesting sorites question: how many killings and unjust imprisonments etc. constitute a reign of terror?

NO: State terrorism: who needs it?

Colin Wight

Introduction

The explosion of research into terrorism post-9/11 was an understandable reaction to events that have undoubtedly shaped global politics. Prior to 9/11, terrorism was a relatively narrow field of study that crossed many academic disciplinary borders. Within International Relations (IR), interest in terrorism was dependent upon whether the phenomenon (however defined) was at the forefront of public consciousness. Hence, when major acts of terrorism were perpetrated, interest in the subject grew; when terrorism played less of a role in public debate the subject drifted back to the margins of disciplinary concerns. Logically, the lack of interest in terrorism makes intuitive sense for IR scholars, because terrorism has never represented a major threat to either the security of the international system or the security of individual states (Laqueur, 2001; Chaliand and Blin, 2007). Even state-sponsored terrorism (Byman, 2005/2007; Cline and Alexander, 1986) was largely viewed as a minor instrument of state policy that had little impact on the development of the international system.

The supposed minor role of terrorism in terms of international political outcomes also helps (in part) to explain why few IR theories attempt to incorporate the phenomenon. After all, something so marginal as terrorism does not require theorising. Another explanation for the lack of theoretical work on terrorism is its particularity. It is extremely difficult, if not impossible, to theorise a phenomenon that is so dependent on contextual changes.

The place of terrorism, both in the public consciousness and IR, was to change radically after 9/11 and the tragic events of that day served to bring terrorism back to the forefront of political and academic awareness. Writing in 2008, Andrew Silke claimed that 'the five years since 9/11 have probably seen more books published on terrorism than appeared in the previous 50 years. Currently, one new book on terrorism is being published every six hours' (Silke, 2008: 28). However, the increase in 'research' outputs does not seem to have produced better accounts of the phenomenon. In fact, many of those working on the subject seem to be disdainful of the research produced by their colleagues. According to Carlyle A. Thayer (2009), terrorism studies is the 'dismal science'; a view echoed by Schmid and Jongman, who suggest that research into terrorism is 'not research-based in any rigorous sense; instead it is often too narrative, condemnatory, and prescriptive' (Schmid and Jongman, 1988: 179).

Post-9/11 new scholars entering the field have attempted to reconfigure the research potential of terrorism studies. Much of the best work in this area goes under the rubric of critical terrorism studies (CTS) and these approaches have played a major role in facilitating a better understanding of the subject. One important area that has been integral to the development of CTS is the relationship between terrorism and the state. Terrorism can only be understood through a structural explanatory logic that sees the state and terrorism as inextricably linked. Yet CTS has focused its attention less on the structural relationship between the state and terrorism and much more on the problematic concept of 'state terrorism'. The concern with state terrorism is not new (see, for example, Chomsky, 1991; George, 1991; Goodin, 2006; Stohl and Lopez, 1984, 1986). Yet in revisiting the issue of state terrorism, CTS has provided an unnecessary complication that acts as a barrier to the achievement of its main strategic aims. In effect, the critique of traditional terrorism studies at the core of CTS has suffered because in being focused on the confused concept of 'state terrorism', it is not clear that the two approaches are addressing the same object domain.

The problem with the concept of state terrorism

There are three broad arguments to consider in this context. First, there is a problem derived from the nature of social scientific enquiry itself: when natural scientists define their objects of enquiry they do not need to take into account how the objects understand their own situations. In the social sciences, on the other hand, the practices of the actors we study are embedded within self-understandings that draw on concepts that the social sciences are trying to explain. Hence, the social scientists' account of the phenomena under study have to, in some ways, map onto the understandings of the actors involved in the study. Or, as Conor Gearty has put it, the meaning of terrorism 'is moulded by government, the media and in popular usage, not by academic departments' (Gearty, 1991: 6).

Second, despite the vast literature that has emerged post-9/11, there is still no consensus surrounding a definition of the term. Moreover, when combined with the concept of the state, we have a complex composite concept that defies appropriate theoretical specification in anything approaching a 'scientific' sense – however this term is understood. Third, is a strategic/political/ethical argument: in short, the admirable critical imperatives that drive CTS are not best served through an expansion of the concept of terrorism to include 'state terrorism'.

In this chapter, I will address the conceptual problems first and then deal with the political/strategic/ethical issues. In terms of the conceptual discussion, I will base my analysis around the work of Richard Jackson (2008) and Ruth Blakeley (2009), both of whom advance some of the strongest arguments in favour of the concept of 'state terrorism'.

Before moving on to discuss the problematic nature of terrorism and its associated definition, I need to address the broader question of the ontology – or nature – of the social world. All academic subjects need to define their objects of enquiry. Without such a definition, researchers cannot be sure they are researching the same object. In the social sciences it is generally accepted that the concepts actors possess must play an integral role in social scientific accounts of their practices. Thus, when analysing terrorism, for example, part of the specification of that object are the beliefs and concepts of the actors involved in the practice (broadly conceived). By this, I do not just mean the concepts and beliefs of the terrorists themselves (setting aside for a moment the definitional problems with the term). Rather, because terrorism is a public political practice, we have to include in our accounts what lay actors and publics think terrorism is. We do not have to give these lay accounts precedence, and it may well be that a social scientific account corrects the lay accounts of terrorism in fundamental ways. After all, we have no reason to assume that the actors involved in a given practice will always understand the totality of that practice, and politicians and the media cannot be given sole authority to use a term in any way they desire.

However, even when a correction of a given actors' set of beliefs around a phenomena is required, it can only take place through an engagement with those concepts. In terms of terrorism, the consensus of public discourse treats the issue as related primarily to non-state actors. Now, assuming for a moment that these public understandings of terrorism are flawed, then any academic account that attempts to correct them has to be able to demonstrate why these accounts are so prevalent, as well as explaining how more expansive views are relevant. In short, the social scientist has to demonstrate why the lay actors' accounts are wrong. Social scientists simply cannot say that these actors have it wrong and begin using terms commonly used in public discourse in a fundamentally different way from that used by the actors. In the context of 'state terrorism', this can only be achieved through sustained engagement with the problematic concepts of the state and terrorism. Thus far, terrorism studies have not satisfactorily resolved the definitional issue of terrorism, let alone the issue of state terrorism.

Object specification is a necessary starting point for any form of scientific enquiry. Without it, we could not know what the object we purport to study was. In terrorism studies, this is a deeply contested domain. This is what is known as the 'definitional problem'. Both Jackson and Blakeley accept this is a major problem and both authors argue that a sustained analysis of 'state terrorism' has been missing from terrorism studies (Jackson, 2008; Blakeley, 2009); in effect, the 'definitional problem', however solved, has to be broad enough to encompass what Jackson and Blakeley call state terrorism. Of course, this claim only makes sense if we can talk meaningfully about something such as state terrorism. Hence, in order for Jackson and Blakeley to show how the analysis of state terrorism is absent from terrorism studies, they will need to arrive at a definition of terrorism broad enough to encompass those activities conducted by states that they consider to be state terrorism. It is easy enough to see the problem here. Both Jackson and Blakeley begin with a set of state practices they find problematic and then adjust the definition of terrorism in such a way that those state practices can fall under the new definition of terrorism; in effect, they begin from the assumption that there is such a thing as state terrorism and adjust the definition of terrorism to accommodate it. Not all of the state practices that Jackson and Blakeley want to bring under the label of state terrorism are in fact dealt with comprehensively in the literature, they are simply not referred to as forms of terrorism; and given the problems surrounding the definition of terrorism, not without good reason.

Blakeley accepts this, arguing that work on repression, ethnic cleansing, genocide and authoritarianism, is prevalent in the discipline and cognate areas (see for example, Gareau, 2004; Marchak, 1999). Yet despite the existence of this and other literatures dealing with state violence, both still ask why such political violence is not studied as state terrorism? Of course, one could reverse this and ask just what we gain by dealing with such violence as state terrorism? Indeed, if such literature is widely available what do we gain by encompassing it under the confused rubric of terrorism? Yet, following Robert E. Goodin (2006) Jackson and Blakeley are effectively asking: why is it that similar acts of violence (such as a bomb on a plane) are treated as terrorism when planted by non-state agents but something else when planted by state agents?

Now this implies that the act itself and not (also) the intentions and aims of the actors are the sole determinant of how the act is understood. This is a very behaviourist account of social action. Consider the following counter arguments. Imagine two human subjects who die after being administered lethal injections. Have both subjects been murdered? How could we tell? Both acts are identical, but we simply lack sufficient information about both cases to make a judgement. One of the subjects, for example, could have been inadvertently administered an incorrect drug. One could have been a prisoner subject to a lethal injection. In both cases to treat them as murder is to mis-describe them. Likewise, consider two humans having limbs removed. Are both being tortured, or is one being tortured and the other subject to a life-saving amputation? The act (the removal of the limb) is the same, but does the same description fit both acts? The same can be said about the bomb example; it only makes sense to compare the two acts as one and the same if we already assume some important details are the same in both instances; details we do not actually have. So were the state agents acting with, or without, the authority of the state? Were the people on the plane civilians, military personnel or perhaps even fanatics of some kind or other intent on flying the plane into a shopping centre, or some other public space? Surely, if it was the latter and state agents had exploded a bomb on the plane to protect national security, then would this not still be considered terrorism?

To say that there is a similarity between two acts is not the same as saying they are identical. The ethical and political motives of Jackson and Blakeley are admirable: it is just the tactic that is confused. Both are concerned to demonstrate how the violence perpetrated by states is worse than that perpetrated by non-state actors. On this I agree, but argue that nothing is gained, apart from analytical confusion, through discussing such violence as terrorism.

So just what is state terrorism for Jackson and Blakeley? Both conflate terror with terrorism. Jackson, for example, argues that there is within the literature on terrorism virtually no mention or discussion of 'Western state terrorism, the terror of strategic bombing, the terror of democratic state torture' and so on (Jackson, 2008: 7). Likewise, Blakeley approvingly cites Eugene Victor Walter's (1969) problematic definition of terrorism, which is centrally concerned with the use of violence to spread terror. Now, it is clear that terror is not the same thing as terrorism, and Walter's definition of terrorism demonstrates why the two need to be distinguished. According to Walter, terrorism involves three key features: first is threatened or perpetuated violence directed at a victim; second is a violent actor that intends the use of violence to induce terror in some witness who is distinct from the victim (in other words the victim is a means not an end); and third, the violent actor intends or expects that the terrorised witnesses to the violence will alter their behaviour (Walter, 1969).

The problems with this definition are clear. First, it makes no mention of terrorism as a distinctly *political* practice. Walter's definition could equally well apply to criminal gangs or many other aspects of social practice; a father perhaps, who controls his family by the selective use of violence and threats of violence. Likewise, a director of horror movies instrumentally uses their actors to install terror and fear into their audience. We would not normally call horror movies examples of terrorism, and rightly so. Nor would we typically describe the violence enacted by criminal gangs to control either their own members or populations they interact with as terrorism. In this respect, the 'ism' matters, and not all social practices that involve terror are terrorism. This point can be illustrated if one looks at the historical development and practice of the nation state.

The history of the development of the modern state can be understood as a long process of appropriation and accumulation (of territory, peoples and resources) achieved through the use of violence, fear and terror; a process that had winners and losers. Noting the place of violence in the development of the modern state allows us to situate what many consider to be the defining element of the state – the Weberian idea that it is that organisation that (successfully) claims a monopoly on the legitimate use of physical force within a given territory. Understood this way, terrorism and other forms of non-state violence can be interpreted as reactions to this process and rejections of the claim to state legitimacy.

Contemporary state theory has tended to focus attention on the consensual aspect of state power. Whilst broadly acceptable, particularly in the context of highly developed modern states, we should never forget that ultimately state control rests on the potential use of violence. And this potentiality rests on the terror of the possibility of violence. A classic example here would be the justice system, which exists not only to punish offenders, but also to send a signal to the population at large that offenders will be punished. Thus, states can legitimately be considered as terror machines (Goodin, 2006; Perdue, 1999) and everything states do ultimately rests on the potentiality of force – a potentiality that is demonstrated through the daily exercises of state power.

Most developed states now have their populations so under control that state violence against them is an aberration, not the norm. Nonetheless, it is the potentiality of state violence that underpins this control, and where such control breaks down, state violence will follow. To say that the state exercises a claim on the monopoly of the use of legitimate violence does not mean that all exercises of that violence are legitimate, or morally acceptable. Equally, to say that terrorist violence (as I define it) is by definition illegitimate does not mean that other forms of non-state violence are necessarily illegitimate. The state's theoretical claim on the monopoly of the legitimate use of violence is precisely that; a claim. And in terms of specific states, the right of those to exercise this claim has been historically constituted through violence. Some groups objecting to that state may have legitimate claims against it, which if not resolvable through non-violent means, might have a legitimate resort to violence.

The problem with the conflation of terror and terrorism is that just about every aspect of state practice would be an act of terrorism on this account. And indeed, this is how Jackson and Blakeley seem to treat it. Thus, according to Jackson, 'if we define terrorism as the threat or use of violence against one group of people in order to terrify or intimidate another group of people as a means of preventing or changing their political practice', then all sorts of state practices come under the rubric of terrorism (Jackson, 2008: 8). Jackson is quite explicit about this, arguing that:

> state doctrines and practices of 'nuclear deterrence', 'coercive diplomacy', 'constructive engagement', sanctions and certain peace settlements involving making pacts with groups who have engaged in widespread use of terror, can also constitute state terrorism.
> (Jackson, 2008: 10)

I fail to see what we gain here apart from analytical confusion. If all of these state practices can be considered terrorism, then it is difficult to see what cannot.

Blakeley's analysis has the same problem. According to Blakeley state terrorism involves the following four key elements (Blakeley, 2009: 30):

1. A deliberate act of violence against individuals that the state has a duty to protect, or a threat of such an act if a climate of fear has already been established through preceding acts of state violence;
2. The act must be perpetrated by actors on behalf of or in conjunction with the state, including paramilitaries and private security agents;
3. The act or threat of violence is intended to induce extreme fear in some target observers who identify with that victim; and
4. The target audience is forced to consider changing their behaviour in some way.

There are various problems with this definition. First, it seems strange that Blakeley would claim that state terrorism always involves violence against individuals that the state has a duty to protect. Many of the examples of state terrorism that she provides are actually acts perpetrated by states against individuals who are not citizens of the state committing the act (torture, for example, or extraordinary rendition), in which case, the state concerned has no duty to protect them. This aspect of Blakeley's definition seems to imply that states can only be involved in state terrorism against their own citizens. She attempts to correct this by arguing that if a state has prisoners of war it has an obligation to protect them; but even this qualification does not help extraordinary rendition (where it is doubtful that those being held are prisoners of war) or the terrorising of publics of other states. After all, states are typically considered to have a duty to protect only their own citizens and not the citizens of other states. Points three and four run up against the same problem as that faced by Jackson; they seem to imply that everything the state does is state terrorism, or at least is potentially so.

What is particularly puzzling about Blakeley's discussion is that she accepts that it is counter-productive to define state terrorism in relation to domestic law, because when states violate such laws they normally justify themselves in terms of some emergency powers. Blakeley attempts to get around this problem by arguing that state terrorism can be examined in relation to international norms and laws, specifically those concerned with human rights (Blakeley, 2009: 31). This seems to me wholly correct, but I fail to see why a violation of human rights or international norms needs to be described as state terrorism, particularly since state terrorism has not been codified in international law whereas the violation of human rights has. Hence, Blakeley argues that 'it is deemed illegal and inhuman when non-state actors commit those that [acts Blakeley considers to be terrorism] and it is no more humane if the perpetrator is a state' (Blakeley, 2009: 33). Well of course it is no more humane to say that the state has committed the act, but it adds nothing to the moral judgement of such acts to call them terrorism.

A related problem with Blakeley's discussion of state terrorism concerns the level of secrecy that states may exhibit in relation to their activities. Terrorism is normally considered to be a public demonstration that symbolically spreads fear around a larger population for political ends; it is a form of political communication. Blakeley argues that secrecy is not such a problem in relation to state terrorism, because even in those incidents when states 'do all they can to avoid their actions being exposed, they are nevertheless seeking publicity among a particular, albeit small, audience' (Blakeley, 2009: 33). It is difficult to see how Blakeley can substantiate this claim. If states deny outright that they have been involved in a particular act, how can Blakeley, or anyone else, know that the state is attempting, and intentionally so, to spread fear? This is not to say that we should always believe everything that the state says it does or does not do, but it does mean that determining this cannot rest on the claims of a few that see the exercise of state power and conspiracy everywhere.

In fact, when Blakeley discusses the forms of state terrorism it is difficult to see what activity would not come under this definition and indeed her list is quite exhaustive. To name but a few: disappearances, illegal detention, torture, assassinations, intelligence gathering, kidnap, interrogation, torture, bombing campaigns, the killing of enemy combatants that had been disarmed, the legal targeting of civilians, other humiliating and degrading treatment, extraordinary rendition and so on. Blakeley goes further, arguing that even if the intention was not the explicit intimidation of a target audience beyond the victim, states can still be accused of state terrorism if fear emerges in some audience (although not a target audience, for a target implies intention); terrorism by accident, presumably. So, for example, if a state is testing new airborne weapons and some audience observes the testing and decides that aliens are about to invade, and that audience spreads such fear among the general population then the state, having spread fear, however inadvertently, is, for Blakeley, guilty of state terrorism.

The problems with all of this should again be clear. Blakeley extends the definition of terrorism to all forms of political activity, even those that do not involve intentional violence. This is the main problem with the use of the term state terrorism; it begins to look like every state activity is, or potentially can be, a form of state terrorism. I do not doubt, or deny, that states engage in activities intended to spread fear and terror among populations. Often the target audience of such state activity will be the citizens of that state themselves and often they are citizens of another state. Yes, such state actions are morally reprehensible and should be challenged and rejected whenever possible. What I do not accept is that we need to call this terrorism and nor do I understand what we gain in doing so. And here is the crucial political, ethical and strategic motive for denying the concept of state terrorism.

Conclusion

Since 9/11, the international system has been wracked by a so-called 'war on terror'. In the name of this war on terror, major wars have been instigated, nations illegally invaded and countless humans killed. These include both state actors and non-state actors. Alongside this, civil and human rights have been abused and wide-ranging legislation introduced at the global and domestic level to control more and more aspects of human behaviour. Those involved in the more radical edge of terrorism studies have decided that the best way to deal with these abuses of state power is to point to some moral equivalence and to claim that this all amounts to state terrorism. The net effect of this, however, is to produce an 'inflationary' account of terrorism; there is no moral equivalence and what states have done, and continue to do, far exceeds the suffering inflicted by terrorists.

Yet the irony of this is that it seems to suggest that terrorism is more prevalent in the international system than it actually is. Terrorism, when equated with terror, is everywhere. This simply plays into the hands of states who can legitimately claim that since terrorism is everywhere, then we need more and more action against it, and thus the spiral continues. Terrorism, whilst terrible in its effects on those individuals who come into contact with it, is not a major security threat to individual states or the international system. On a restrictive (deflationary) definition of terrorism, actual deaths by such acts are few and far between. Certainly, they are horrific, but on a relative scale they do not come close to enacting destruction on the scale of poverty, child malnutrition, state neglect, or disease, or the unacceptable use of state power, to name but a few. On a 'deflationary' account of terrorism, the resources wasted on a war on terror are both obscene and meaningless. Nothing high-lights just how ridiculous the inflated understanding of terrorism has become so much as the recent attempt by members of the US government to label Wikileaks founder, Julian Assange, a terrorist. Perhaps, in the face of such insanity, we should just stop using the term altogether. Yet this is not possible. Why?

As already argued the concepts and understandings held by actors engaged in the practices we examine are an integral aspect of what any good social science should study. We cannot possibly understand these practices without taking these concepts into account. Of course, we do not have to accept them, but in order to reject them we would need good sound empirical, moral and theoretical reasons to do so. In relation to terrorism, I cannot see any such reasons. What most people mean when they refer to terrorism are forms of non-state violence, and those that confuse the issue of 'state terror' with terrorism need to defend their accounts by providing more theoretically nuanced versions of both the state and terrorism.

Discussion questions

1   Why is there such great reluctance within the contemporary scholarly community to recognize and study state terrorism? Are the roots of this reluctance conceptual or political?
2   What difference might there be between the victim's and the audience's perspectives on the debate about the existence of state terrorism?
3   Is the concept of 'state terrorism' theoretically coherent?
4   How can the concept of state terrorism be reconciled with the state's monopoly on violence?
5   Does referring to the use of state terror as 'terrorism' add anything useful to the moral judgement of the act?
6   Can the study of state terrorism tell us anything about the use of terrorism by non-state actors?
7   What are the key differences in the means by which states and insurgents employ terrorism?
8   Should terrorism only be known as a 'weapon of the weak'?
9   Are there any situations in which state terrorism could be justified?
10 Can the use of state terror be adequately dealt with under international law relating to human rights and other international norms?

Further readings

Becker, T., 2006. *Terrorism and the State: Rethinking the Rules of State Responsibility*, Oxford: Hart Publishing.
Blakeley, R., 2009. *State Terrorism and NeoLiberalism*, New York: Routledge.
Goodin, R., 2006. *What's Wrong with Terrorism?*, Cambridge: Polity.
Jackson, R., 2008. 'The Ghosts of State Terror: Knowledge, Politics and Terrorism Studies', *Critical Studies on Terrorism*, 1(3): 377–392.
Primoratz, I., ed., 2004. *Terrorism: The Philosophical Issues*, Basingstoke: Palgrave.
Stohl, M., and Lopez, G., eds, 1984. *The State as Terrorist: The Dynamics of Governmental Violence and Repression*, Westport, CT: Greenwood Press.
Stohl, M., and Lopez, eds, 1986. *Government Violence and Repression: An Agenda for Research*, Westport, CT: Greenwood Press.
Wight, C., 2009. 'Theorising Terrorism: The State, Structure and History', *International Relations*, 23: 99–106.

Part III
The terrorism threat

4 Is terrorism a serious threat to international and national security?

YES: The continuing threat to state security

James Lutz and Brenda Lutz

Introduction

Governments have frequently argued that terrorism constitutes a grave threat to national security. In some cases, that belief is based on the idea that terrorism never works in accomplishing the objectives of the groups practicing it (Abrams, 2006). Others have suggested that terrorist actions that threaten the national security of a specific country or even more broadly, overall international security, have been exaggerated (Mueller, 2006). While governments and/or some political leaders may have had domestic political reasons to emphasize such threats, terrorists do constitute a very real danger for many states. The level of danger can be seen in the fact that the security of countries has been undermined in the past, and that changes have occurred because of the level of threat that has existed. Even if dangers to state security in the past were limited, it is possible that threats from terrorism can become greater in the future. Finally, it is important to recognize that if terrorism were to be ignored, it could become a much greater threat or problem than it currently is. Thus, while terrorism may not currently be a major threat in some countries, failure to deal with the potential threat of terrorism could result in more significant dangers in the future.

Terrorist challenges that worked

The suggestion that terrorist activities cannot threaten state security ignores at least some cases where it has led to changes in the structure of states. Fascist groups in Europe after World War I were able to use terror and violence, combined with other political methods, to help undermine governments. The Fascists in Italy and the Nazis in Germany were among the political movements that were able to combine terrorism and other tactics to assume power in their countries (Wilkinson, 1977: 22). Fascist or conservative movements in other countries that relied on similar tactics contributed to changes in governments and policies in a number of countries. Anti-colonial campaigns relying on terrorism (and other forms of protest and political violence) have resulted in independence. The French left Algeria, and the British left Cyprus and Palestine. In the case of Cyprus and Algeria, terrorism was combined with guerrilla attacks, but the campaign by Jewish settlers in Palestine relied solely on terrorism to convince the British to evacuate the territory. While the British and the French could have persisted in all these cases in maintaining control, the cost of continuing to rule the colonies outweighed the perceived benefits. The nature of colonial situations is one reason why these successful challenges have been considered special cases (Cronin, 2009: 82–85; Hoffman, 1998/2006). The change in control of the territory from a colonial power to indigenous elites would clearly constitute a successful challenge to state security.

More recently, the Tamil Tigers in Sri Lanka came close to victory in their quarter of a century struggle that would have challenged the territorial integrity of the country. While the Tamil insurgency has been defeated (at least for the moment), the struggle was a long and costly one for all the inhabitants of the islands. The initial attacks by the Tamil insurgents relied heavily on terrorism, but the violence escalated to guerrilla attacks and then to what amounted to full-scale civil war. Iraq and Afghanistan have faced similar campaigns which illustrate that terrorism can destabilize a country. The Iraqi government is currently dealing with threats to national unity from different groups, and the future of the state is uncertain. The combined attacks by global jihadists, Sunni militants, Shia groups and a variety of nationalist organizations have been effective so far in preventing the successful establishment of a working government (Tan, 2006: 166). The situation in Afghanistan is similar, and the future of that state and its government is also quite uncertain. The situation in Yemen suggests the dangers that terrorism can hold for weaker governments. Not only has al-Qaeda in the Arabian Peninsula launched attacks against the United States and the West in general, including the attempt by a Nigerian to blow up a plane landing in Detroit on Christmas day, 2009, and packages containing bombs sent in 2010, it also has helped to destabilize the government of Yemen. The problems that the Russian government has faced in Chechnya and the northern Caucasus in general have clearly threatened the security of the entire region, and the continued violence could pose problems in the future. Violence from right-wing and left-wing groups in Turkey led to the deaths of tens of thousands and threatened the stability of the country and economic and social progress (Sayari and Hoffman, 1994). Terrorism combined with insurgencies has threatened the very existence of African countries such as Liberia, Sierra Leone and the Congo (Zaire). These countries are still trying to re-establish functioning governments for the citizens of their countries. Similarly, the terrorism campaign by secular groups in Iran against the new Islamic Republic weakened the new government while it was trying to establish itself and made it more vulnerable to the invasion from Iraq in 1980 (Green, 1995: 579–580).

It can be argued that the Tamil Tigers, the nationalists in Algeria and Cyprus, the Chechens in Russia, groups in African countries and the insurgents in Iraq and Afghanistan were only successful in threatening the security of the state when the violent techniques extended beyond the use of terrorist tactics (Cronin, 2009: 81; Lutz and Lutz, 2011: 136–138). While the increase in the threat level resulted from the escalation of violence, the initial use of terrorism was an important early step in the process of challenging governments in power. The fact that terrorism was only a first step to set the stage for greater threats does not mitigate the danger that terrorism represented to state security. Fascist groups did not escalate to guerrilla warfare, but relied on other techniques to supplement the violence in the streets. The situation in Palestine during the period of the British Mandate, however, did not escalate to different types of violence. Similarly, the situation in Yemen has not yet reached the stage of guerrilla attacks or civil war (by groups involved in terrorism). Thus, escalation to more violent techniques has not been essential for threats to state security.

The threatening effects of terrorism for state security can also be seen in both India and Pakistan. India has faced a serious challenge to its control of Kashmir due to Muslim insurgents and terrorists. The problems in this province have had implications for the rest of India, as indicated by the 2008 Christmas attacks in Mumbai which were launched by groups involved in the struggle for Kashmir and continuing tensions between Muslims and Hindus in India. Attacks by terrorists have not yet destabilized the Indian state, but they have been costly for the country because the government has been forced to expend significant military and security resources in order to maintain a semblance of control in the disputed province. The concentration of military and security resources in Kashmir has had other consequences. Because of the focus on Kashmir, the Indian government has had difficulties in controlling other dissident groups. Leftist rebels (the Naxalites) have become increasingly active in West Bengal and surrounding provinces (Lutz and Lutz, 2011: 128–130). Tribal groups in Assam region have been able to operate against migrant groups and government officials in the northeast of the country. There was also the major uprising in the past in the Punjab province by the Sikhs, which led to the assassination of Prime Minister Indira Gandhi. There have also been outbreaks of communal violence in which Hindus have targeted Muslims, or less frequently Muslims have targeted Hindus, which have become more difficult to control (Oommen, 2005). Terrorism from a variety of sources has affected India, and the multiethnic and multilingual nature of the state makes secession or breakup a possibility. The terrorism in Kashmir, combined with terrorism and political violence by other groups, has increased the possibility that the Indian state may not survive. If India should collapse or separate into a number of states in the future, terrorism will have played a role.

In the twenty-first century, there has obviously been a clear and present danger that threatens Pakistan from a combination of terrorism and insurgency. The attacks by the Taliban and groups allied with the Taliban against the national government threaten Pakistan's stability. Conflicts among Sunni and Shia populations in Pakistan also present significant dangers to the relatively weak central government. The threat of instability in Pakistan is of even greater concern, of course, because Pakistan is a nuclear power (as is India). Should the central government collapse, it is possible that nuclear weapons could fall into the hands of terrorist groups. However unlikely this possibility might be, it would represent a major increase in threat levels to the national security of a number of countries. The unrest in Pakistan has already had some negative effects on state security of its neighbors. The Pakistani government has been unable to control some regions of its own territory effectively – the Federally Administered Tribal Areas, among others – and it appears that the government cannot afford to crack down on militants active in Kashmir or launching other attacks in India. It has also not been effective in controlling groups that support dissidents in Afghanistan because such policies would be unpopular with portions of its own population. Faced with threats to national stability and security the government cannot afford to alienate more domestic sectors. A government already weakened by terrorism and insurgency cannot afford the risk of increased public discontent.

Limited terrorist success

Even in cases where outright terrorism has not succeeded, the presence of terrorist activities has changed the nature of states. Changes in policies and programs could then result in situations in which the security of the state may be compromised in the future. Terrorists in Colombia or Lebanon were not successful in taking control of the government or dismantling the state, but they did significantly undermine state security. The weakened security situation in Lebanon in turn provided opportunities for a variety of organizations to threaten the security of neighboring states. The IRA in Northern Ireland was threatening enough to convince the British government to enter into discussions about the future of Northern Ireland (Alonso, 2001: 142). Similarly, the campaign by the Basque nationalists of ETA led to the Spanish government granting much greater autonomy for the region (Shabad and Ramo, 1995: 468). After many years of violence, the Palestinians were finally able to enter into a dialogue with Israel that resulted in the negotiation of the Oslo Accords and the creation of the Palestinian Authority. While the future of any Palestinian state still remains uncertain, the threat to continued, unchallenged Israeli control of the West Bank and Gaza Strip was sufficient to bring about negotiations between the two sides and that has at least created the potential for a change of status.

There is one other situation in which governments may fear for national security. Some states have not acted against terrorist groups that use their territory for activities out of fear that their country may become targets (Lutz and Lutz, 2011: 85). Although this threat does not directly change the security of the state that follows such a permissive attitude, it does indirectly contribute to insecurity in other countries, and it suggests that some governments themselves see that a major threat to their security is present in the form of terrorist organizations.

Future threats

One of the major threats facing any number of countries is the fear that terrorists will acquire and use weapons of mass destruction. While the potential threat of the use of such weapons may be unlikely, at least by terrorists, it still remains a possibility. The attempt by Aum Shinrikyo in Japan to use sarin nerve gas indicates the potentially destabilizing nature of such weapons. The attacks were at a busy time and concentrated in subway stations that government workers used to get to their offices (Tucker, 1996: 167). If the attacks had been more deadly, as intended, the government would have been seriously disrupted, although the Japanese government probably would have survived. Technological changes may affect the likelihood that weapons designed to cause mass casualties will be used. Even though it is possible that technological change may make it easier to detect and defeat terrorist groups, it is also possible that new technologies may provide new opportunities for terrorist groups willing to use such weapons to inflict major casualties. Access to biological, chemical, or radiological materials and the knowledge of how to use them could and will likely expand. Increasingly technological societies also face the danger of increased vulnerability from these weapons or other types of sophisticated attacks. Disruptions of transport infrastructures, communication networks, or utility systems could cause serious harm. Power blackouts could paralyze more modern societies, or even less modern ones. Leftist dissidents in El Salvador in the 1980s were quite successful in causing such blackouts in order to embarrass the government and as one part of a much broader effort to undermine the economy (Beckett, 2001: 205).

Terrorism can threaten the security of a state in other ways. There have been significant increases in costs for governments and the private sector as they have attempted to provide the necessary security for buildings, personnel and the general public. Much of the resources that have been diverted towards security are less productive than are many other types of investments by governments or the private sector. Money spent on physical security, counterterrorism policies and agencies and efforts to deal with foreign sources of terror cannot be spent on education, infrastructure, health care or an increased investment in factories and jobs by the private sector. Developing countries facing terrorist threats are forced to divert scarce resources from these types of activities towards defense measures. More advanced countries, such as the United States, Russia, the United Kingdom and West European states, have expended funds for military and police activities to combat terrorism that have drawn resources away from other types of investments and expenditures. This diversion of resources will inevitably have an adverse effect on national economies and could thereby weaken state security in the future.

Terrorism can also affect state security over the longer term by changing the nature of the political systems that are in place. Many democratic states have become less concerned with civil liberties as they have attempted to face the challenges of terrorist organizations. In dealing with violence in Northern Ireland, the United Kingdom practiced longer periods of interrogation, preventative detention and the use of Diplock Courts. The United States has begun to use wiretaps and searches more frequently than in the past, with decreased supervision by the courts (Lutz and Lutz, 2011: 112–113; Nacos, 2008/2011: 214–217). States that had been moving toward more open, democratic systems have reversed course when faced with the prospect of terrorist violence. For example, Russia may not have made the transition to a true democracy after the breakup of the Soviet Union, but the problems in Chechnya made the reversion to a more authoritarian government seem necessary and easier to accept by many politicians and citizens. The movement away from greater participation and more popular input in countries that face such threats could ultimately affect state security in the future by stimulating unrest or leading to more dissidents. Even if the original groups that organized the attacks have disappeared from the scene, the earlier violence and the response to it could have a long-term impact on the security of a state. Although the political system survives, the movement away from more participation could be considered a change for the worse that slows down the eventual adoption of more equitable and participatory political systems.

There is one final threat, which in a way is more of a theoretical one in most cases, but which can occur with states that are under greater pressure from terrorist groups. Terrorism is not likely to be a threat to the survival of a large number of states when governments take the necessary steps to defeat it. Despite the fact that some terrorist groups are ultimately successful, most terrorist groups are quickly defeated by governments (Cronin, 2009: 10–11). Those that last longer may mount a major challenge, but, like the Tamil Tigers, most will still be defeated in the end. If states do nothing to deal with terrorism, however, then the threat becomes much more real, and ultimately state security might be significantly undermined, just as public health would be threatened if governments chose to never provide medical vaccines for the public. The Shining Path movement in Peru became as dangerous as it did because the government of Peru was oblivious to the danger it represented in the countryside and let it gain support (Barnhurst, 1991: 82). Had the authorities acted more quickly, the eventual threat to the state would have been much less, and it would not have taken as long for the government to deal with the violence that resulted. The fact that governments find it necessary to deal with terrorist groups indicates that such violent activities can be a threat to the security of a country.

Conclusion

There is little doubt that terrorism can challenge the security of a state under the right circumstances. While there may not be a large number of modern examples of terrorism successfully taking over a state or leading to its dissolution, they do exist. In other cases, terrorism played an important role in setting the stage for successful insurgencies that have led to governmental changes or to other types of important events such as occurred with the fascist movements in the 1920s. At the very least, all countries threatened by terrorism have had to divert resources to deal with the resulting problems, which in turn led to greater economic difficulties. In addition, a reduction in civil liberties may indirectly result in situations in which the public eventually reacts negatively to government activities and the state is weakened as a consequence. Of course, if terrorist activity is ignored by a state, it can eventually become a major threat that can undermine the security of a state. As a consequence, terrorist groups have to be treated as if they are dangerous, since they cannot be ignored indefinitely.

What used to be Yugoslavia can serve as an example of how terrorism, often combined with other factors, can threaten state security. After the formation of Yugoslavia at the end of World War I, the new state faced internal dissent from Croats, Albanians and Macedonians unhappy with the domination of the state by the Serb elite. There were a variety of terrorist attacks by different groups against the state and retaliation by the government in some cases. The end result was a weakened state torn by dissension. When German and Italian troops invaded in 1941, the Yugoslav resistance collapsed, in part because of inadequate preparation and in part because many elements of the multiethnic state were unwilling to fight for the Serb leadership. Yugoslavia was reestablished after World War II, but faced continuing dissent from Croats who launched occasional terrorist attacks. Albanians in Kosovo were unhappy with domination by Serbs in the autonomous region. When Yugoslavia was in the midst of a transition from the old system to a more open political regime, the previous strains in the country erupted. Croatia, Slovenia and Macedonia broke away. Bosnia and Herzegovina was finally able to separate. Montenegro and then Kosovo became independent. Yugoslavia is gone, and the pressures from terrorism and unrest in general that began in the 1920s and which continued in later years helped to set the stage for the dissolution of Yugoslavia. Bosnia and Macedonia have also experienced terrorist attacks and violence that threatened their security after they became independent. Clearly, terrorism can, and has, threatened the security of Yugoslavia and its successors.

NO: Why terrorism is a much smaller threat than you think

Ian S. Lustick

Introduction

We can all agree that terrorists threaten the United States. But how serious is that threat? We can begin by considering the leading causes of death (apart from old age and the diseases of old age) as serious threats (see Mueller, 2006). The leading non-violent cause of death in the United States is traffic accidents – 385,601 fatalities between 1999 and 2007. Unintentional poisonings comes in second with 177,973 fatalities in that same time period, followed by unintentional falls – 156,906 fatalities. The leading cause of violent death is suicide, with 273,162 fatalities between 1999 and 2007 including 152,056 firearm suicides. Next is homicide with 150,878 fatalities including 106,125 firearm homicides. The total for deaths in the United States caused by terrorism is exactly the number killed on 9/11 and no more: 2,973. As a first approximation, it is reasonable to consider traffic accidents, suicides, accidental poisonings and homicides as serious threats to Americans. Comparing the dimensions of these threats to Americans with these data suggests that as threats they are on the order of 50–130 times more serious than terrorism. It is difficult to imagine that a threat that has a record of inflicting 50 to 130 times less damage than a 'serious' threat should also be considered serious. The same point can be made in another way. If we do classify terrorism as a 'serious threat,' then we have to come up with vastly different terms to describe traffic accidents, accidental poisonings, suicides and homicides. For if terrorism is a 'serious threat,' then threats 50 or 100 times greater would need to be considered as 'cataclysmic' or perhaps 'immensely cataclysmic.'

In fact, we do not need to engage in such silliness. All we need do is recognize that terrorism is a threat that requires a response; just not a particularly serious threat. Once that is understood, we can proceed to the obvious question. If it is not a serious threat, why do Americans believe it is? And why does the country spend hundreds of billions of dollars a year, and sacrifice values, lives and the precious attention of its leaders, to 'counter' this relatively non-serious threat?

One important fact we can glean from data on hundreds of thousands of murders, suicides, acts of arson and other violent crime in the US is that despite the success our law enforcement agencies have in deterring criminals and incarcerating perpetrators, we are threatened by massive numbers of violent people. That means that if many terrorists were present in the United States they would have little difficulty, despite the 'War on Terror,' in killing Americans. Again, this strongly suggests that the scale of the threat is much lower than is generally believed. For over the last 20 years, only three attacks classified by the FBI as terrorism have occurred in the United States – the 1993 bombing of the World Trade Center by Ramzi Yousef, the 1995 bombing of the Oklahoma City Federal Building by Timothy McVeigh and the 9/11 attacks in 2001 by al-Qaeda.

Based on these simple observations, it would appear that although terrorism may be a problem in the United States, Europe, and in other developed countries, and although there can be no guarantee against our worst fears being realized, both evidence and logic suggest that the threat is not so serious that it should distract us from a plenitude of larger problems and opportunities. Still, most of us feel impelled to imagine the possibility of 'another 9/11' and yearn for an impossible guarantee that it cannot happen again. This yearning makes it difficult to appreciate the enormous distance between what 'cannot possibly happen' and what 'is likely to happen.' How are we to decide how seriously to consider a threat that may indeed materialize, which could not be definitely prevented no matter how many resources were devoted to the task, and which cannot be demonstrated to be likely enough to outweigh certain and potent threats from which we may be distracted by the phantom of a terrorism threat that may be, in relative terms, almost negligible? This is an exceedingly difficult question. Great care, professional assessment of evidence and the exclusion of narrow political agendas are all required when seeking an answer. Above all, we must not respond from the 'gut,' with visceral feelings of fear, panic, fury, or revenge. We just cannot afford it.

Yet that is more or less how the United States did respond to 9/11, with a 'War on Terror' created to serve narrow political agendas, drawing its power from fear and fury rather than sober analysis, and fashioned by politicians, not professionals. In an extraordinarily revealing episode, Department of Homeland Security Secretary, Michael Chertoff, announced at the beginning of the summer of 2007 that he had a 'gut feeling' that over the near term there was an increased chance of an al-Qaeda terrorist attack in the United States (*New York Times*, July 11, 2007). No such attack occurred. But we have learned from the first Homeland Security Department Secretary, Tom Ridge, that political imperatives, including the desire to keep the American public distracted from other issues and focused on the politically useful topic of terrorism, lay behind a pattern of official government declarations to go into high states of alert against what were repeatedly declared to be a heightened threat of an imminent terrorist attack (MSNBC, August 20, 2009; Chossudovsky, 2005).

This evidence alone should make it obvious that when it comes to terrorism, 'gut instincts,' 'common sense,' or political passions, are not reliable bases for sound judgments. To move toward a more sensible assessment of the terrorism threat, we must first appreciate just how distorted are American public perceptions. For what is even more remarkable than the virtual absence of terrorism in the United States over the last decade, is the stubborn belief most Americans have that the threat of it is extremely serious.

The perception of threat

One reason for the public's exaggerated impression of the terrorism threat is associated with how zealously and extensively we fund the apparatus for discovering it, and how incentivized the news media, law enforcement officials and politicians have been to inflate the image of its dangers. This tendency to see as much as possible as if it were terrorism, or a sign of the possibility of terrorism, is why a substantial majority of the terrorism cases developed by the police and the FBI are rejected by district attorneys as too weak to secure indictments. Law enforcement agents are so anxious to produce suspects for terrorism indictments that the vast majority of the cases they develop pertain to people guilty of no offense whatsoever. Indeed, federal prosecutors refused to seek indictments for 67 percent of all terrorism cases brought to them by investigative agencies from 2005 to 2009 (Transactional Records Clearing House, September 28, 2009).

My point is that the flood of suggestions for indictments coming from law enforcement agencies and the thousands of individuals detained and questioned do not reflect a rising tide of terrorism threats, but rather an enormously expanded budgetary base for those departments within state, local and federal law enforcement agencies charged with finding terrorists:

> As the *Washington Post* put it, high profile prosecutions result from a carefully scripted routine the FBI has been perfecting since the September 2001 terror attacks. Sting operations, choreographed by FBI and Justice Department officials in Washington, have included plots against skyscrapers in Dallas, Texas, Washington subways, a Chicago nightclub and New York's John F. Kennedy International Airport.
>
> (CBSNEWS, November 30, 2010)

Hence it is that in almost all terrorist prosecutions, the defendants argue that they were entrapped by law-enforcement authorities who, via paid informants, provided not only the plan for the attack and the resources to carry it out but also the encouragement necessary to overcome doubts or misgivings on the part of the targets of the investigation.

In other words, although the public assumes that an arrest reflects a judgment about a danger that existed to the public, the reality is that whether an individual is brought to trial for terrorism in the United States is not determined by the seriousness of the crime committed or the threat posed, but by prosecutors judging that their juries will reject the potent arguments they know the accused will make of having been entrapped. Nor does the development of cases or decisions to investigate 'persons of interest' reflect specific concerns about a possible threat. Rather, under the doctrine of 'pre-emptive prosecution,' the FBI and other law-enforcement agencies seek targets of opportunity – individuals who can be portrayed as threats with the help of paid informers and knowledge of private remarks indicating sympathy, association, or identification with extreme Islamist views (Korotzer, 2010; Waldman, 2006).

The operation of this system does not just waste the attention of our legal system and disrupt or even destroy the lives of innocent people. It also shapes public opinion. The resulting distortions and nearly hysterical fears of terrorism influence decision-makers. This produces needless wars, dangerous suspensions of civil liberties and the diversion of rivers of funding from social welfare and infrastructure to an effort that is better understood, not as a 'War on Terror', but a campaign to foster fears of terrorism.

The overall approach to terrorism adopted by the Bush Administration, and reflected and operationalized by the law enforcement and prosecutorial practices described above, is often referred to as the 'One Percent Doctrine.' That phrase is the title of a book by award-winning journalist, Ron Suskind, who reported the views of Vice-President Cheney that when it came to terrorism, that is, to the possibility of low probability but high-impact events, the US government should act without respect to evidence of a threat, only its possibility or imaginability. Thus, even if there is only a one percent suspicion of a major terrorist threat, that one-out-of-a-hundred possibility should be treated, for purposes of action by the US government, as a certainty. As Suskind pointed out, the one-percent doctrine conferred on the Bush administration 'vast, creative prerogatives', 'to do what they want, when they want to, for whatever reason they decide', and to '*create whatever reality was convenient*' (Kakutani, 2006). In 2003, this doctrine led many Americans to support a catastrophic war in Iraq to destroy non-existent weapons of mass destruction under the illusion that a 'mushroom-cloud' over Manhattan would thereby be prevented. That same doctrine, guiding counterterrorism efforts in the United States and producing sensationalist news coverage of plots largely manufactured by the government itself, continues to produce enormously exaggerated public perceptions of the terrorist threats faced by our society.

Since 9/11, the expectations of Americans regarding the likelihood of terrorist attacks in the United States have been the subject of numerous polls. One survey posed the following question 15 times between October 2001 and October 2010: 'How worried are you that there will soon be another terrorist attack in the U.S.?' (Pew Research Center, 2010). The average percentage of Americans answering that they were very worried or somewhat worried was 63 percent. The lowest reading was 5 percent, registered soon after the American-led invasion of Iraq which the United States Government characterized (inaccurately) as a major victory in the War on Terror. In other words, for ten years a significant majority of Americans – up to three-quarters in some periods – have been worried that an attack would occur 'soon.' Another series of polls asked a question, not about how worried Americans are about an attack that might take place 'soon', but how 'likely' they believed an attack to be 'over the next few weeks.' Given this short time horizon, we would of course expect the judgments of likelihood to be lower, and they are. This question was asked nine times between August 2006 and May 2010. On average, 40 percent of Americans indicated they believed that 'further acts of terrorism in the United States over the next several weeks' were either 'very likely' or 'somewhat likely.' The most recent figure, for May 2010, was 55 percent, indicating that in the spring of 2010 a majority of Americans expected a terrorist attack within the next few weeks.

The role of the media

What accounts for the fact that more than 50 million Americans have been wrong virtually every month or week since 2010 about the seriousness of the terrorism threat? One key factor is imbalance in media coverage. For example, the initial coverage of an arrest of a terrorist suspect is invariably dominated by blood-curdling images of what could have occurred, of what might have been the intent of the terrorists, of how vulnerable our country is to such destruction, and to the question of whether or not law enforcement acted soon enough or not to apprehend the suspects and prevent the disaster. As time goes on, the coverage diminishes rapidly, so that only a miniscule proportion of those citizens who were terrified to learn of the plot and its horrifying purposes come to understand that, in the vast majority of cases, those plots were fantasies that had no prospect of being carried out, or were actually concocted by the government as part of schemes to arrange for persons under surveillance to incriminate themselves.

The contribution of media coverage to the exaggerated general belief in the extent of the terrorist threat springs as well from its sensationalism. As a typical example, consider the report 'The Edge of Disaster' (Lustick, 2008: 1–2). Based on former Bush administration official Stephen Flynn's book by that title, the segment dramatized the horrors of various imaginable terrorist attacks in the United States. The segment was updated and rebroadcast repeatedly on CNN for at least five subsequent months. A version of the show, 'We Were Warned: The Edge of Disaster,' was also advertised by CNN as available free of charge for schools to record and present in classes (grades 7 through college) with the following come-on:

> America's food supply, our ports, our power systems: Are they vulnerable to terror? Anderson Cooper investigates whether the government is ignoring vulnerabilities at home – and whether we're prepared for the next natural or human-made disaster.
>
> (CNN, 2007)

Truly terrifying dramatizations of some of the horrors terrorists might imaginably inflict on America drive home the point of the documentary. One portion of the script, describing a terrorist attack on a Philadelphia sports stadium, reads as follows:

> As the first pitch rockets towards home plate, none of the 45,000 inside has any idea of the terrible turn their lives are about to take. That's because terrorists not far away are moving forward on a plot to turn this stadium into both a spectacular political statement and a mass grave.

> Two trucks wind their way through the streets of South Philly, but strangely their destination isn't the stadium. It's the sprawling oil refinery just two miles away . . . as the first truck crashes into the refinery gates. The driver sets off a bomb, killing himself and anyone who might be nearby. The blast blows a hole in the gate big enough for the second truck to drive through.

> The second truck is a huge tanker filled with gasoline. When it crashes into a tank, the driver sets off another bomb. Louder than thunder, it brings a momentary hush to the Phillies game two miles away. Fans have no way of knowing a catastrophe is only beginning.

> That's because inside this refinery there's a dangerous chemical called hydrofluoric acid, and it's the terrorists' lethal weapon. When it spills, it creates a poisonous vapor, an invisible toxic cloud the wind will carry for miles.

As the toxic plume engulfs nearby south Philly neighborhoods, windows broken by the explosions expose people inside their homes. They are the first outside the plant to die ... Fans rush for the exits. But even if they move quickly, many have nowhere to go. Instantly, the parking lot is gridlocked. Traffic on the surrounding streets crawls, and then just stops. Tens of thousands are trapped trying to get away.

Next, immeasurable horror and agony as it reaches the stadium. Thousands begin to choke, convulse and die.

A steady diet of this kind of reporting and dramatization has hugely inflated American estimates of the terrorism threat, not only in relation to the actual scale of the terrorism threat, but also in comparison to media coverage of other, much more serious problems. For example, in early May 2010, Faisal Shahzad bungled an attempt to explode a small bomb in Times Square. Although in this case the perpetrator turned out to be an unrepentant and zealous supporter of violent Jihad, the contraption discovered in the SUV parked near Times Square was incapable of exploding. Nevertheless, despite the absence of an actual bomb, of casualties, or of significant disruption to the life of the city, media coverage of this incident was extensive and hysterical. In fact, the public's exposure to news about this non-disaster greatly exceeded what it read or saw in the media about a series of other, real, catastrophes that were simultaneously affecting the United States. Whereas the failed terrorist attempt was the focus of 25 percent of all news coverage in early May, the number two story – the disastrous state of the economy, including a scary one-day drop of 1000 points in the Dow – received only 13 percent of the coverage. Massive flooding in the Southeast that killed 31 people and laid waste to the city of Nashville received a mere 4 percent (Jurkowitz, 2010).

Remarkably, however, the public does not view the media as exaggerating the threat; quite the opposite. In a September 2010 poll, Americans were asked whether news reports are 'making the threat of terrorism in the US seem worse than it really is, seem better that it really is, or are reports showing the situation about the way it really is?' Although 44 percent said prevailing news reports were an accurate measure of the threat, 28 percent answered that the threat was really worse than reported, compared to only 17 percent who believed the press was exaggerating the threat.

The politics of threat inflation

Many factors beyond media coverage mold collective assessments of the seriousness of the terrorism threat to the United States. These include the calculated distortions offered by politicians to discredit opponents. This technique, of scoring points by accusing opponents of being 'soft on terror' or having a 'pre-9/11 mentality,' has been used by both Republicans and Democrats. While the use of this argument by Republicans is well known, in particular in the use of the supposed threat of terror from Iraq to justify the invasion of that country, a vivid example of Democratic use of this technique was the wave of criticism of the Bush administration's decision to allow a company based in the Arab principality of Dubai to handle port operations in some American cities (a task commonly assigned to companies based in foreign countries such as Singapore and China). Despite the absence of any professional evidence that this decision would pose security dangers, Democratic Party leaders unleashed a torrent of criticism against the President. In the face of attacks claiming that the administration's policy showed its weakness and incapacity with respect to a terrorism threat much larger and more dangerous than it was prepared to imagine, the President reversed his decision. Thus do politicians help create distorted assessments of terrorism. The larger effect of these distortions is an environment such that any government agency, company, think tank, professional association, or university that has wanted more funding or more contracts has been encouraged if not forced to exaggerate the scale of the terrorist threat *and* to exaggerate its capacity, if given enough funding or fat enough contracts, to help counter that threat (Lustick, 2006; Mueller, 2006).

The psychology of threat assessment

Apart from the political, economic, cultural and media-related sources of distortion in the estimates Americans make about the seriousness of the terrorism threat, there are deeper explanations. Fundamental aspects of human psychology make it almost inevitable that unless we take highly self-conscious and scientifically rigorous methods to restrain ourselves, we will inevitably exaggerate the scale of a threat such as terrorism. For example, in 2002 Daniel Kahneman won the Nobel Prize in Economics for work done with Amos Tversky on what is known as prospect theory – a vastly influential understanding of how human brains process information in distinctive ways that systematically distort judgments. One of the key patterns humans display, under the general heading of 'negativity dominance,' is to very greatly exaggerate the importance of information that might signal a risk of loss or damage and to minimize information about possible gains or achievements. Another feature of some threats that make them seem much more dangerous than they really are, is the belief that someone is trying to do us harm. Social psychological research has shown that even though dangerous circumstances may pose much greater threats to humans than the malevolent actions of others, if malevolent intent is believed to be involved in a threat, estimates of the likely danger those threats pose is much more likely to be exaggerated (Burns and Slovic, 2006).

Another powerful psychological mechanism that has fueled our distorted image of the terrorism threat is associated with post-traumatic stress disorder. This syndrome appears quite commonly in soldiers, victims of crimes, witnesses to atrocities or catastrophes involving the threats of injury or death. Due to the immense media coverage of the 9/11 attacks, and the hundreds of times the collapse of the towers has been vividly displayed on television to tens of millions of Americans in all its dramatic and grisly detail, it is fair to expect that large numbers of Americans have suffered, and are still suffering from, the effects of this traumatization. Among the most prominent symptoms is a tendency to relive the event, to imagine it as much more likely or even certain to recur than it is, and to sense signs of its presence in situations that have no objective relationship to it.

Conclusion

For all these reasons – imbalanced and hysterical media coverage, political pandering, incentivization of terrorism discovery, huge economic opportunities associated with acting as if there is a serious terrorism threat and fundamental psychological predispositions – we can be virtually certain that whatever our 'natural' or uncritical assessment of the terrorism threat, it is exaggerated. And here, in fact, is the most serious threat associated with terrorism. Terrified as we have been, and powerful as we are, we must stand guard against tendencies to unleash our power against non-existent or minimally dangerous terrorist threats, while cutting resources from more significant problems and opportunities. Without a disciplined individual and collective commitment to avoid distortions in our view of terrorism, it is probably inevitable that we would do much more harm to ourselves by chasing phantoms than we would suffer if we largely ignored the threats that cause us so much anxiety.

In fact, that is exactly what has happened. Leaving aside the incalculable damage to American lives and values associated with War on Terror-related shifts of expenditures away from social welfare and infrastructure, or restrictions on privacy and civil liberties, let us consider just the War in Iraq. In 2002 and early 2003, professionals within the American military, the State Department, academia and the intelligence community agreed that Iraq's dictator Saddam Hussein had played no role in the 9/11 attacks and did not pose a terrorism threat to the United States. Still, politically powerful individuals and groups within the office of the Vice President, the Office of the Secretary of Defense, in Congress and in the larger political community, were able to exploit panic over WMD terrorism to launch an invasion of Iraq. As documented by studies of a key organizer of the campaign for the war, the Project for a New American Century, that invasion was designed to serve extravagant ideological and political interests, including the entrenchment of conservative Republican control of the White House and Congress for generations (Daalder and Lindsay, 2005; Lustick, 2006; Mann, 2004; Packer, 2005).

In the end, that invasion undermined, rather than advanced the fortunes of conservative politicians, but neither, as we know, did it destroy or even discover weapons of mass destruction or the capacities to build them. What that war has accomplished is the waste of nearly $3 trillion worth of American taxpayer money that could have been used to solve any number of urgent problems, including protection from the effects of the financial collapse suffered in 2008 (Bilmes and Stiglitz, 2008). More poignantly, the Iraq war, a war that could only have been launched because of the enormously exaggerated beliefs prevailing in our country about the imminent threat of terrorism, resulted in the death of 4750 US service men and women and the mutilation of 32,000 more. To this grisly toll must be added thousands of casualties suffered by coalition allies, the documented death of 100,000 Iraqi civilians, and an incalculable amount of damage to US prestige abroad, the effectiveness of our foreign policy and our ability to focus resources and attention on the struggle in Afghanistan and against al-Qaeda (http://icasualties.org/Iraq/USCasualtiesByState.aspx). Nearly 3,000 Americans died on 9/11. The economic cost to the country of those attacks is calculated in the tens of billions of dollars. Yet by any measure the damage done to the United States on September 11, 2001, was minor compared to the harm we have done to ourselves by our response.

'Pogo' was a bitingly funny, if low-key American comic strip created by Walt Kelly. It was syndicated in American newspapers from 1949 to 1973. The most famous line uttered by its main character, the 'everyman' possum, Pogo, is: 'We have met the enemy, and he is us.' When it comes to the War on Terror, Pogo could hardly have been more right. But that should not be surprising. In 2009, the American military budget was more than $650 billion. China came in second, but its military expenditures were not even one-sixth of ours. Indeed, the United States spent more on security than the combined amounts spent by the 18 countries with the next biggest military budgets (Wikipedia). Overall, the United States is so powerful – economically, politically and militarily – that the only thing in the world strong enough to really hurt us is – the United States. With these fundamental realities in mind, we must do everything we can to prevent the passions of our politics and the casual dispositions of public opinion to drive policies designed to protect us from the evils of terrorism.

We can make professional and sober judgments about the threats that face us, and we can, based on the vast information acquisition and analysis capabilities we have, fashion reasonable, sustainable policies toward the relatively minor danger that international terrorism poses. The most important threats are from nuclear or radiological weapons. Most of our counterterrorism effort should be directed to those threats. But those threats are best combatted through multilateral cooperation against the proliferation of materials used to make such weapons, along with foreign policies that reduce the possibility that states or non-state actors would find support among their constituencies for such outrages. Indeed, our government is strongly involved in such efforts; but, properly, most of these activities are hidden from public view. Most other policies designed to interdict or discover would-be terrorists can be implemented as a regular part of the same criminal law enforcement apparatus that protects us against organized crime. One measure that would help promote a proper perspective on the risk of terrorism would be a national insurance policy covering anyone or any family in the United States affected by an act of international terrorism. This kind of policy will also send a message to our adversaries that whatever damage might be done by terrorism, it can be and will be absorbed by a society much too large and strong to be seriously affected by acts of terrorism.

It is imperative that the public be discouraged from viewing the terrorist threat as more serious than it is. We have been told to think of counterterror policies as a 'war.' But the scale of the problem is far from that. Terrorism is in fact a tiny problem, certainly compared to the challenge we faced in World War II against Nazi Germany, or to the nuclear annihilation stalemate we endured with the Soviet Union during the Cold War. If the public imagines counterterror measures as a 'war,' that will signal that our policies will continue to be driven by nightmares rather than by analysis and reasoned risk assessment. Overall, if we refuse to distinguish between threats (including terrorism), and serious threats (which, excluding nuclear weapons, do not include terrorism), and if we define ourselves as 'at war' with the terrorists, then the terrorists will have succeeded. They will not defeat us with their own strength. But they can devastate us by using our own strength against us. That is what has happened. We must not permit it to continue.

Discussion questions

1 What are some of the ways in which terrorism can threaten the security of states?
2 Is the security of India and Pakistan threatened by the existence of terrorist organizations that have targeted them? How great is the threat to these states?
3 Why are some terrorist organizations successful in challenging the security of the state while other groups are not?
4 What are some of the dangers that states could potentially face if terrorism is not taken seriously?
5 What risk does terrorism pose to individual safety in statistical terms?
6 Why do people consistently exaggerate the risk of terrorism?
7 Local weather forecasters often exaggerate the size and likelihood of storms and blizzards threatening major metropolitan areas. Why? Does the same explanation suggest why the news media would tend to exaggerate the size and likelihood of terrorist threats?
8 If thousands of Americans die in workplace accidents every year for every American who dies as a result of a terrorist attack, does that mean that thousands of times more money should be spent on the prevention of workplace accidents than on combating terrorism?
9 Should there be a national insurance policy to compensate any victims of future acts of terrorism in the United States and their families?
10 The threat of terrorism for state security is likely to increase in the future. Do you agree or disagree with this statement? Why or why not?

Further readings

Abrams, M., 2006. 'Why Terrorism Does Not Work,' *International Security*, 31(2): 42–78.

Cronin, A., 2009. *How Terrorism Ends: Understanding the Decline and Demise of Terrorist Campaigns*, Princeton, NJ: Princeton University Press.

Gerges, F., 2005. *The Far Enemy: Why Jihad Went Global*, New York: Cambridge University Press.

Glassner, B., 1999. *The Culture of Fear*, New York: Basic Books.

Kydd, A., and Walter, B., 2006. 'The Strategies of Terrorism,' *International Security*, 31(1): 49–80.

Lustick, I., 2006. *Trapped in the War on Terror*, Philadelphia, PA: University of Pennsylvania Press.

Lutz, J., and Lutz, B., 2009. 'How Successful Is Terrorism?', *Forum on Public Policy*, September 2009, 1–22, available online at: http://forumonpublicpolicy.com/spring09papers/papers09spring.html.

Mueller, J., 2006. *Overblown: How Politicians and the Terrorism Industry Inflate National Security Threats, and Why We Believe Them*, New York: Free Press.

5 Is WMD terrorism a likely prospect in the future?

YES: WMD terrorism: a potential threat to international security

Natividad Carpintero-Santamaría

Introduction

The twenty-first century was inaugurated with a devastating terrorist attack, different from the idiosyncratic patterns of the twentieth century's tactical and local terrorism. In his first interview after the events of September 11, Osama bin Laden was asked: 'Can you justify the killing of innocent men in the light of Islamic teachings?' He answered: 'The September 11 attacks were not targeted at women and children. The real target was America's icons of military and economic power' (www.alquimmah.net). He meant this: al-Qaeda's goal was to cause a great deal of quantitative and qualitative damage.

After September 11, 2001, a wave of high-profile terrorist attacks struck worldwide, although not all of them were committed by al-Qaeda. London, Casablanca, Madrid, Bali, Bombay, Afghanistan, Russia, India, Pakistan, Uzbekistan, Iraq, Israel, Egypt, Algeria and Turkey, for example, were victims of both attacks and plots to unleash new attacks, some of which were calculated to cause spectacular numbers of casualties (such as the London Heathrow plot in 2006). These facts provide a new perspective on the threat that makes it necessary 'to understand the consequences of terrorism in complex terms' (Sinclair, 2010).

In the same interview, Osama bin Laden was asked the following question:

> 'Some Western media claim that you are trying to acquire chemical and nuclear weapons. How much truth is there in such reports?' He answered: 'I wish to declare that if America used chemical or nuclear weapons against us, then we may retort with chemical and nuclear weapons. We have the weapons as deterrent.'

Non-state actor incidents with chemical, biological, radiological and nuclear (CBRN) agents are not new. In the Database of Chemical, Biological and Nuclear Terrorist Incidents (Gurr and Cole, 2002/2005), 192 such incidents are reported. Seventy-six of these cases involve the threat or use of pathogens and/or toxins (1910 to 1999); 97 involve the threat or use of chemical weapons (1946 to 2000); and 20 involve the threat of using nuclear weapons and nuclear material (1974 to the 1990s). The perpetrators included individuals and organisations with the most diverse motivations including fanatic vindication, personal revenge, left and right wing terrorists, extremist cult groups and others.

By way of contrast, since 2001 a significant amount of information related to al-Qaeda's activities with weapons of mass destruction (WMD) – that is, chemical, biological, radiological and nuclear (CBRN) agents – has been published. The most recent compilation includes 83 incidents (1998 to 2007) from sources of varying reliability (McNermey and Rhodes, 2009). This information, along with empirical evidence of varying scope about the deliberate intention of terrorists using WMD, has led to the perception that a terrorist attack with CBRN agents is plausible. In Spain, in addition to having endured an incomprehensible and painful 30 years of ETA terrorism, there is also the troubling presence of Jihadist groups with in-house criminal capabilities.

The severity of WMD terrorism, its complexity and potentially devastating effects, lead us to formulate the following question: would terrorists go beyond the bounds of perpetrating conventional attacks and actually carry out the distressing possibility of an attack with CBRN agents? This matter has been assessed by experts from different perspectives and by divergent approaches. Some think that the threat is pressing, while others do not share this opinion. In this chapter, I assess the threat of WMD terrorism, and argue for caution and a balanced threat assessment.

Terrorist motivations to perpetrate a WMD attack

The evolution of terrorist practice demonstrates that an indiscriminate number of victims, higher degrees of lethality and graphic impact are intrinsic features of twenty-first century attacks, along with the invariable intentions to exert coercion to reach political goals and cause social destabilization (Table 5.1).

Motivations for terrorists to perpetrate a WMD attack have been analysed in several studies and most of them share the opinion that extremist fundamentalist groups match up with the profile of those that might seek mass casualties. Organizations or sects based on apocalyptic mysticism are also plausible WMD perpetrators. Research by the Center for Nonproliferation Studies at the Monterrey Institute of International Studies identified the following profile of potential WMD attackers: 'charismatic leadership, no external constituency, apocalyptic vision, loner or splinter group, sense of paranoia/grandiosity and preemptive aggression' (Bowman and Barel, 1999). Research by Ackerman (2009) establishes a wider spectrum of potential actors: 'Sunni jihadists, apocalyptic cult, Shi'i jihadists, idiosyncratic/mentally ill individuals, non-Islamic religious extremists, right-wing, left-wing, single-issue actor, ethno-nationalistic group, state (covert), state (over as warfare) criminal group and other'. Alexander (2010) indicates that 'it is conceivable that a highly motivated and desperate terrorist group with technological and financial assets will attempt to improve its bargaining leverage by resorting to mass destructive violence.'

Chemical terrorism: from Tokyo's paradigm to a non-negligible contingency

It is well known by terrorists that the impact on public opinion depends on the characteristics of their attacks and the nature of the weapons used. The activities of the Japanese cult, Aum Shinrikyo, were virtually unknown outside Japan until they gained international attention after their attack with sarin nerve gas on the Tokyo subway in 1995 (Velarde and Carpintero Santamaría, 2010). Although the attack revealed the technical incapability of Aum in their

Table 5.1 Parameters in WMD terrorism

Intended qualitative and quantitative damage	Objectives	Prevention, detection, response, mitigation of effects	Security/counterterrorism
Numerous dead and injured	Mass disruption	Risk assessment	Global partnerships
Different magnitude of destructiveness	Social and political destabilization	Interdisciplinary programmes	Implementing of international agreements/verification
Psychosocial/psychogenic effects: fear and panic		Resilience/contingency plans	Intelligence
Long-term and unpredictable health effects		Research and development (R&D)	Military response
High decontamination costs/high economic losses		New technologies	Law enforcement
Mass-media repercussion			

purpose of inflicting mass casualties, the unprecedented aggression of their attack was a blow to the logistics of an overwhelmed Japanese emergency response. Twenty-three per cent of the personnel at St. Luke International Hospital that assisted the victims and about 10 per cent of the fire department members involved in the emergency response suffered secondary exposure (Saito, 2010).

In the late 1990s, al-Qaeda established a chemical weapons project called Al-Zabadi. This project was headed by the Egyptian chemical engineer, Midhat Mursi al-Sayyid Umar (Jihadi nickname, Sheik Abu Khabab al Masri), who established his headquarters in Darunta Camps (Jalalabad) in Afghanistan. Evidence of al-Qaeda's interest in the acquisition of chemical agents was also found in the Afghan Tarnak Farms Training Camp in Kandahar and the Khalden Training Camp in Khost.

Security and intelligence forces have acknowledged the difficulty involved in developing reliable systems to decode, intercept and prevent the influx of handbooks and manuals that are channelled through the Internet containing instructions on how to build weapons. With respect to chemical agents or procedures for the production of toxic substances, one of the classics is a manual that in 19 pages gives a general description of formulae to produce, for example, home-made chemical poisons and poisonous drugs (see www.alqimmah.net/show thread.php?t=7078). Another publication about the production of a chemical dispersal device based on hydrogen cyanide has been circulating on the web since 2005. Originally written in Arabic, this chemical dispersal manual includes diagrams and instructions on how the device could be used as a 'weapon of mass disruption' (Salama, 2006). These constitute only a small part of the several available printed books related to the manufacturing of poisonous materials and possible delivery systems, with an emphasis on guerrilla applications.

The term *weapons of mass disruption* is applied to those weapons that are intended to cause chaos, panic and the highest level of disturbance at the target site. They would imply economic losses, prohibition to access the bomb explosion site until it could be decontaminated or cleaned up, high economic losses in surrounding commercial areas, the paralysis of quotidian activities in the zone and most importantly, an unknown number of casualties and a great number of people psychologically impacted.

Sarin (or GB) is the most efficient chemical agent for weapons due to its extreme lethality and rapid action. Sarin is a highly volatile gas that can evaporate from liquid to vapour state.

It is also a non-persistent gas that dissipates quickly and can kill either by inhalation or by skin/eye contact. If inhaled, six-tenths of a milligram to a milligram can be lethal within one to ten minutes.

Although chemical agents do not require sophisticated delivery systems (crop duster airplanes, commercial spray devices, or improvised explosive devices [IEDs] might be sufficient), the acquisition of war chemical agents for a large-scale attack by terrorists would be technically very difficult, if not impossible. Terrorist intentions and terrorist capabilities do not always coincide. However, it is plausible that, as in the case of Aum Shinrikyo, a resolute terrorist group with powerful resources could carry out an attack using toxic industrial chemicals (TICs). TICs are highly toxic chemical substances used for industrial applications throughout the world. Ammonia, hydrogen cyanide or chlorine are included in the official list of these substances that can be found both in chemical plants or during transport. With respect to their security, 'recent studies demonstrate convincingly that chlorine-containing facilities . . . may be infiltrated with ease and regularity by trespassers' (Brodsky, 2007). Fraudulent acquisition might also come from transnational crime organizations that might, in turn, steal or divert the chemical agents from state reservoirs. The confluence of crime organizations with terrorist groups has been proven in divisions such as drug-trafficking and weapons supply.

Research by Tucker (2006) points out that in 2004 it was reported that the insurgent Iraqi group, Al-Abud, was unsuccessfully trying to produce chemical agents, but according to the Iraq Survey Group, it was alarming 'how quickly and effectively the group [was able to] mobilize key resources and tap relevant expertise to develop a program for weaponizing CW agents.'

Bioterrorism: an insidious outlook

Biological threats are a more complex matter, due to the nature of the agents used in this weaponry. These agents include, but are not limited to, the following: (1) pathogen viruses such as smallpox, and high fever viruses (HFVs) such as Ebola and Marburg, that have varying modes of transmission (airborne inhalation, direct contact with the infected individuals, urine, and saliva); and (2) pathogen bacteria such as anthrax, cholera, botulism and plague. Viruses are more complicated to manipulate than bacteria and some of them, such as the HFVs, which appear 2 to 21 days after exposure, are not easy to diagnose rapidly due to the varied symptoms that infected persons present. Viruses can also infect a large number of individuals with a small number of particles. Some pathogens can cause tens to hundreds of thousands of victims (Alibek, 1999). The HFVs viruses, for which no antidote has been discovered to date, are especially threatening. The efficiency of a bio-weapon lies basically in its potential morbidity rate.

Although the illicit acquisition of highly lethal germs is a difficult operation, its potentiality should not be misjudged. One of the biggest concerns came from the lack of security at Soviet WMD facilities after the dissolution of the country in 1991. The instability of these facilities triggered international alarm. At that time, the theft, diversion, abandonment or loss of a chemical, biological or even tactical nuclear weapon was feared possible in the numerous CBRN installations in former Soviet closed cities.

Currently, political stabilization in the Russian Federation has distanced the spectrum of those incidents, but Russian scientists have acknowledged the need to improve their particular situation with respect to medical, biological and pharmaceutical facilities. As Morenkov (2002) noted, 'Many of them are in a difficult financial position and sit half empty, rented out to private firms. The laboratory facilities of such institutes and plants could potentially be used by bioterrorist groups to cultivate pathogenic viruses and microorganisms.'

Vulnerabilities might also be present in other countries. For example, it is argued that 'multiple specimens of anthrax spores, Ebola virus and other pathogens have over the past decade been reported missing from the U.S. Army Medical Research Institute of Infectious Diseases (USAMRIID)' (Pilch, 2006). The RMR-1029 anthrax spores used in the mail attacks in the United States in 2001 were diverted from this Institution (The United States Department of Justice, 2010). The following statement from the Commission on the Prevention of WMD Proliferation and Terrorism (2008) has produced controversy. Some analysts consider it alarmist, but others consider it realistic:

> Unless the world community acts decisively and with great urgency, it is more likely than not that a weapon of mass destruction will be used in a terrorist attack somewhere in the world by the end of 2013 . . . terrorists are more likely to be able to obtain and use a biological weapon than a nuclear weapon.
>
> (Gottron and Shea, 2010)

Although there are multiple methods, military and non-military, of aerosolizing biological agents for delivery, weaponizing biological agents is a complex task requiring different levels of technical skills and specialized equipment. For a tactical attack, however, a low-technology delivery system would suffice – such as mail letters or packages. A significant covert bioterrorist attack was carried out in the United States in 1984. Members of a sect called the Rajneeshees infected salad bars at several restaurants in The Dalles (Oregon) with *Salmonella* bacteria, resulting in 751 cases of salmonellosis. The intention of the perpetrators was to bias the process of the county political elections that year. Apart from those people who became infected, the attack caused large economic losses: 'Almost a third of the town's restaurants were implicated (ten in all). This was enough to basically shut down the economy of The Dalles; many of these restaurants would close forever' (Ryan and Glarum, 2008).

Biotechnological advances are one of the leading resources in the prevention and mitigation of bioterrorist threats. Advances in biochip research and on microbial forensics research (i.e., DNA-based methods) are being carried out for the analysis of bio-crime evidence. Also, new discoveries in bio-nanoscience are being applied to the development of devices for the detection of airborne pathogens.

Nuclear terrorism: a challenge for terrorists

The efficiency of CB agents is a function of several variables, including atmospheric pressure, temperature, humidity, local wind, sunlight, persistency and the like. In the case of chemical agents, efficiency can depend also on composition. In the case of biological agents, efficiency in a large attack might also depend on additional factors. However, nuclear agents decay independently of any medium and their efficiency depends fundamentally on the toxicity level of the radioisotope employed and, to a lesser extent, on the physical state in which they can be found (solid, liquid or gas).

Nuclear terrorism could be perpetrated using any of the following means. First, it could involve the use of crude or improvised nuclear devices (INDs), taking into consideration that once the terrorist group obtained the needed highly enriched uranium (HEU), a uranium IND would require a low technological capacity. A plutonium IND, however, would require a high technological capacity even though the terrorist group had the needed highly enriched plutonium (HEP). Second, it could involve radiological dispersion devices (RDDs), also known as *dirty or radioactive bombs*. Third, it could involve an attack on a nuclear power plant (Velarde and Carpintero-Santamaría, 2010).

Although the veracity of the information found on the Internet must be taken cautiously, '*An encyclopedia for the preparation of nuclear weapons*' was found in 2005 on the website Al-Firdaws, under the heading: 'The Nuclear Bomb of Jihad and the Way to Enrich Uranium' (Askenazi, 2005). According to wmdinsights: 'This posting may be worthy of attention because it reveals an increase in the understanding of nuclear technology by the Jihadi community' (www.wmd insights.com/I1/MEI-Al-Qaeda.htm). On the other hand, sophisticated steganographic techniques for encrypting information are used to send data, applications and information that enable users to interact without being traced.

As far as the potential use of an atomic bomb by terrorists is concerned the Weapons of Mass Destruction Commission (2006) has argued:

> For terrorists wishing to develop or acquire nuclear weapons, the greatest difficulty is to obtain weapons-usable fissile material. While there are reports that Pakistani nuclear scientists met with members of Al-Qa´ida, as far as is known terrorists have not acquired nuclear materials from existing nuclear-weapon arsenals.

> It is unlikely that terrorist groups today could develop and manage the substantial infrastructure that would be required to produce enriched uranium or plutonium for weapons. However, nuclear weapons and weapon materials could be stolen by terrorists either from storage or during transportation.

The abovementioned reports refer to former Pakistan Atomic Energy Commission scientists, Sultan Bahir-ud-Din Mahmood and Chaudiri Abdul Majeed, who met Osama bin Laden in 2000 (Albright and Hygins, 2003). The rest of the argument of the WMD Commission concerns the critical situation of Pakistan and its evolution under troubling social and political instability. This country has been struck by terrorist groups that, as of July 1, 2010, have killed 3719 citizens and injured 9464 in 257 suicide attacks (Usmani, 2010; Khan, 2010). This danger is potentially grave, as Pakistan has a substantial number of nuclear weapons. Although the precise number is unknown, we can say with a reasonable degree of certainty that they have somewhere in the range of 60 to 80 uranium nuclear warheads, the estimate taking into account the number and capacity of high enriching uranium (HEU) ultra-centrifuge operative plants in Pakistan (Velarde, 2011).

Although the precise storing sites of nuclear weapons are kept secret, it is known that the Pakistani nuclear complex is spread out in the northern area of the country. Taking into account that it is not geographically large, some analysts have expressed concern that ultra-centrifuge plants found at Sihala (experimental plant, 1979), Kahuta (1984) and Golra (1987) devoted to uranium enrichment might be relatively close to the North West Frontier Province (NWFP). Another concern is that the nuclear centres are not sufficiently far from the labyrinth of the Federally Administered Tribal Areas (FATA) bordering Afghanistan, namely, Bajaur, Khyber, Kurram, Mohmand, Orakzai, North Waziristan and South Waziristan Agencies.

As far as the safety and security of Pakistani nuclear weapons are concerned, Pakistani authorities and former president, General Pervez Musharraf, have often stated that Pakistani strategic assets are safe. The control of nuclear weapons are under the National Command Authority, the Strategic Plans Division and the Strategic Forces Command, and have traditionally been under the command of the military, which has priority for making decisions related to nuclear weapons strategy.

With regard to the nuclear weapons establishments, Pakistani defence officers have pointed out their sound protection, security implementation and control measures in terms of:

> Electronic surveillance and physical protection with armed soldiers [ten thousand member Security Force led by a two star General] . . . state-of-the art sensors guard against intruders. Employees are screened by vetting staff from its SPD security force and officials from its ISI intelligence service. Warheads, detonators and launch vehicles are stored separately to prevent them being seized together.
>
> (Pakistan Defence, 2009)

Another point made by Pakistani authorities is that access to nuclear codes depends on the electronic device PALs (Permissive Access Link), and its authentication requires more than one person.

Although it has been acknowledged that the security of the Pakistani nuclear arsenal is suitable for coping with security breaches, the growing instability of the country has set off international concern on what could happen in the following circumstances: a democratic take-over of power by a radical regime or a *coup d'état* by hostile forces; or an illicit transfer of fissile materials from insiders, or, much more difficult taking into account the PALs access codes, the diversion of a nuclear weapon to terrorist groups. All of the above should also be considered in the complex scenario of the permanent confrontation between Pakistan and India.

The question of insiders who could act in pursuit of ideological, religious, economic or sentimental reasons is seen as a potential risk when assessing the clandestine diversion of materials or components in CBRN facilities. With respect to the transfer of a nuclear weapon to terrorist groups, thus far no state actor has been proven to have taken such a hazardous step. It is a generally accepted opinion that any country that supplied terrorist groups with fissile material or even a nuclear bomb would suffer a potentially devastating response from other countries.

Radiological terrorism or dirty bombs: a major threat, a major risk

The full scope of nuclear terrorism encompasses not merely the potential use of an IND or the much more remote possibility of a nuclear bomb. A real threat includes that a terrorist group, either acting independently or acting as part of a bigger organization, could detonate a radiological dispersion device or dirty bomb. The danger is, 'detonating a dirty bomb creates an expanding radioactive cloud capable of blanketing large areas, such as multiple city blocks, primarily to cause panic and terror in the target population' (Sharon *et al.*, 2008). Dirty bombs are easily made, with a combination of chemical explosives (such as gunpowder, dynamite, semtex, or C-4) and the kind of radioactive material (ampoule, vial or depot) that is commonly found in hospitals, industries, food sterilization facilities and biochemical research centres. Both the efficiency of the dirty bomb and its radioactive contamination level depend on the chemical explosive used and the radiological toxicity of the material. The greater the amount of chemical explosives, the more effective the dispersion of radioactive material will be.

The toxicity of radioisotopes has been divided by the International Atomic Energy Agency (IAEA) into five different categories, from most to least toxic effects. Category 1 includes radioisotopes used in food sterilization, hospital materials, teletherapy (e.g., Co60 and Cs137) and thermoelectric generators (e.g., Sr90 and Pu238). Category 2 includes radioisotopes used for industrial gammagraphy and brachytherapy (e.g., Co60 and Ir192). Categories 3 to 5 include radioisotopes used in nuclear and biology laboratories, radioisotopes used in positron emission tomography (PET) and radioisotopes used as tracing molecules (e.g., C11, F18).

In total, 1562 confirmed incidents of illicit trafficking or smuggling of nuclear and radioactive materials occurred between 1995 and December 2008. Of those 1562 incidents, 336 involved unauthorized possession and related activities; 421 related to theft or loss; and 724 involved unauthorized activities and events (IAEA-ITDB Factsheet, 2009). However, these numbers do not include all actual incidents. This discrepancy is due to several factors: some countries are not IAEA party members and some governments are reluctant to give a full report of the number of cases due to concerns about national security (Carpintero-Santamaría, 2010).

The main purpose of a dirty bomb is to cause chaos, panic and traumatic and post-traumatic psychological-psychogenic effects in the population. In addition to these effects, terrorists might consider the economic losses and the costs of decontamination that would follow from this type of attack. It has been estimated that decontamination costs could be anywhere from 1 to 300 million euros per km^2 depending on the radioisotopes used.

Conclusion

The acquisition, production and dissemination of pathogen agents are not simple tasks, but they could be done if a resolute terrorist group with substantial resources had an adequate level of technical skills and equipment. The same could be applied to chemical agents. The biological harm associated with the explosion of an IND would be very high, but the probability of an IND terrorist attack is small. Several data involving specific incidents of nuclear materials smuggling have been accounted (Allison, 2004; IAEA 2009), but the smuggling of fissile material in quantities sufficient to make an IND has never been reported. The application of nuclear forensic analyses could determine the characterization and attribution of the nuclear material, whether captured intact or from post-explosion debris.

The probability that a terrorist group could explode a dirty bomb is unfortunately high, due to the accessibility of its components. However, the biological harm associated with such an event can be reduced by means of an adequate emergency response. Decontamination costs would however be very high. It is somewhat worrying that such bombs could be used by splinter terrorist cells acting on their own.

Although it would be very difficult for a terrorist group to carry out a large-scale chemical, biological or radiological agents attack, it would not be difficult for such a group to perpetrate a tactical act of aggression in order to produce casualties, horror, panic and chaos. Individuals perceive CBRN agents as an intangible threat which increases their degree of anxiety. The widespread psychological impact of such weapons makes them an attractive option to certain types of groups seeking to make a powerful media impact.

In short, the development of preparedness, training and resilience programmes is very necessary to counteract the risk of CBRN terrorism. The key to efficient prevention, early detection and response to such terrorism, lies in a multidisciplinary countering strategy (see Table 5.1).

NO: WMD terrorism: the prospects

John Mueller

Introduction

In 1996, one of terrorism studies' top gurus, Walter Laqueur (1996: 34), concluded that some terrorist groups 'almost certainly' will use weapons of mass destruction 'in the foreseeable future'. Presumably any future foreseeable in 1996 is now history and Laqueur's near 'certainty' has yet to occur.

Laqueur's prediction was presumably heavily informed by a tragic event a year earlier when the Japanese cult Aum Shinrikyo, set off deadly gas in a Tokyo subway station, killing twelve. But that group's experience can scarcely be much of an inspiration to other terrorist groups that might like to pursue WMD. Aum Shinrikyo was not under siege and had some 300 scientists in its employ, an estimated budget of $1 billion, a remote and secluded haven in which to set up shop and even a private uranium mine. After making dozens of mistakes in judgment, planning and execution in a quest for nuclear weapons, it turned to biological ones and reportedly tried at least nine times over five years to set them off by spraying pathogens from trucks and wafting them from rooftops, hoping fancifully to ignite an apocalyptic war. These efforts failed to create a single fatality. In fact, nobody even noticed that the attacks had taken place. The group then turned to the infamous chemical attack that, however terrible, did not succeed in inflicting anything that could credibly be called 'mass destruction' (Frost, 2005: 38–40; Gilmore Commission, 1999: 40–51; Rapoport, 1999; Tucker and Sands, 1999: 51).

The experience of September 11, 2001, ought, it would seem, to be taken to suggest that the scenario most to be feared is one in which terrorists are once again able, through skill, careful planning, suicidal dedication and great luck, to massively destroy with ordinary, extant devices. However, concerns about a terrorist WMD attack, and particularly about the potential to go atomic, escalated greatly after the 2001 attacks, even though the al-Qaeda terrorists used weapons no more sophisticated than box-cutters. Despite such anxieties, however, the Aum Shinrikyo experience retains its pertinence: terrorists are likely to continue to find that a WMD attack remains exceedingly difficult to pull off.

Atomic terrorism

The scariest concern, of course, is the thought of terrorists with an atomic device. In the United States, Defense Secretary Robert Gates claims that what keeps every senior government leader awake at night is 'the thought of a terrorist ending up with a weapon of mass destruction, especially nuclear' (Mueller, 2010: xi). And in a major speech on April 11, 2010, President Barack Obama held the atomic terrorist to be 'the single biggest threat to U.S. security'.

Alarms about the possibility that small groups could set off nuclear weapons have been repeatedly raised over the decades. In 1974, nuclear physicist Theodore Taylor proclaimed the problem to be 'immediate' and explained that it was 'simple' to build a bomb. At the time, he thought it was already too late to 'prevent the making of a few bombs, here and there, now and then', or 'in another ten or fifteen years, it will be too late' (McPhee, 1974: 7, 225). In

1995, Graham Allison warned that 'in the absence of a determined program of action, we have every reason to anticipate acts of nuclear terrorism against American targets before this decade is out'. Then, unabashed, he maintained in an influential 2004 book that 'on the current path, a nuclear terrorist attack on America in the decade ahead is more likely than not' (2004: 15). And on *60 Minutes* (CBS) on November 14, 2004, former CIA spook Michael Scheuer assured his rapt and uncritical interviewer that the explosion of a nuclear weapon or dirty bomb in the United States was 'probably a near thing'.

However, terrorist groups thus far seem to have exhibited only limited desire and even less progress in going atomic. This may be because, after brief exploration of the possible routes, they, unlike generations of alarmists, have discovered that the tremendous effort required is scarcely likely to be successful (see Frost, 2005; Jenkins, 2008; Mueller, 2010).

A common concern envisions a nuclear country palming off a bomb or two to friendly terrorists for delivery abroad. However, there would be too much risk, even for a country led by extremists, that the ultimate source of the weapon would be discovered before or after detonation, or that it would be exploded in a manner and on a target the donor would not approve – including on the donor itself. In addition, al-Qaeda is unlikely to be trusted by just about anyone: its explicit enemies list includes all Middle Eastern regimes, as well as the governments of India, Pakistan, Afghanistan and Russia (Bergen and Hoffman, 2010: 23).

Nor is it likely that a working nuclear device could be stolen and detonated. 'A theft', point out physicists Christoph Wirz and Emmanuel Egger, 'would involve many risks and great efforts in terms of personnel, finances, and organization', while safety and security systems on the weapons 'ensure that the successful use of a stolen weapon would be very unlikely' (2005: 502). Bombs can be kept disassembled with the component parts stored in separate high-security vaults, and things can be organized so that two people and multiple codes are required not only to use the bomb but also to store, maintain and deploy it. Moreover, stresses Stephen Younger, former research director at Los Alamos, few people know how to cause an unauthorized detonation of a nuclear weapon. Weapons designers know *how* a weapon works, he explains, but not the multiple signals necessary to set it off, and maintenance personnel are trained only in a limited set of functions (Younger, 2009: 153–154; see also Levi, 2007: 125).

Most analysts consider a terrorist group's most promising route would be to attempt to make a bomb using purloined fissile material – plutonium or highly enriched uranium. However, as the Gilmore Commission stresses, building and deploying a nuclear device presents 'Herculean challenges'. The process requires a lengthy sequence of steps, and if each is not fully met, the result is not simply a less powerful weapon, but one that can't produce any significant nuclear yield at all or can't be delivered (Gilmore Commission, 1999: 31).

First, the terrorists would need to steal or illicitly purchase the crucial plutonium or highly enriched uranium. This most likely would require the corruption of a host of greedy confederates, including brokers and money-transmitters, any one of whom could turn on them or, either out of guile or incompetence, furnish them with material that is useless (Levi, 2007: 29, 32–33). The theft would also likely trigger an international policing effort. Then, to manufacture a bomb, the terrorists would need to set up a large and well-equipped machine shop somewhere and populate it with a team of highly skilled scientists, technicians, machinists and managers. These people would have to be assembled and retained for the monumental task while no consequential suspicions are generated among friends, family and police about their sudden and lengthy absence from normal pursuits back home.

Wirz and Egger (2005: 501) conclude that fabricating a nuclear weapon 'could hardly be accomplished by a subnational group' because of 'the difficulty of acquiring the necessary expertise, the technical requirements (which in several fields verge on the unfeasible), the lack of available materials and the lack of experience in working with these'. Younger has made a similar argument, stressing the 'daunting problems associated with material purity, machining, and a host of other issues' and concluding that the notion that a terrorist group could fabricate an atomic bomb or device 'is far-fetched at best' (2009: 146).

The process of fabricating a nuclear weapon requires, then, the effective recruitment of people who at once have great technical skills and will remain completely devoted to the cause. In addition, a host of corrupted co-conspirators, many of them foreign, must remain utterly reliable, international and local security services must be kept perpetually in the dark and no curious locals, including criminal gangs, must get consequential wind of the project as they observe the constant coming and going of outside technicians over the months or even years it takes to pull off.

Finally, the resulting weapon, likely weighing a ton or more, would have to be moved to a target site in a manner that did not arouse suspicion. And then a skilled crew, presumably suicidal, would have to set off its improvised and untested nuclear device, hoping that the machine shop work has been perfect, that there were no significant shakeups in the treacherous process of transportation, and that the thing, after all this effort, doesn't prove to be a dud. The financial costs of the extended operation in its cumulating entirety could easily become monumental. There would be expensive equipment to buy, smuggle and set up, and people to pay – or pay off. Any criminals competent and capable enough to be an effective ally in the project, are likely as well to be not only smart enough to see boundless opportunities for extortion, but psychologically equipped by their profession to exploit them.

Terrorists with other 'weapons of mass destruction'

Chemical, biological and radiological weapons have commonly been bracketed with nuclear ones, particularly over the last two decades, into a category known as 'weapons of mass destruction', but the identification is highly questionable (Carus, 2006; Mueller and Mueller, 2009; Mueller, 2010: 11–15). Although they can inflict damage, most can scarcely do so on a large scale. Nonetheless, Indiana senator Richard Lugar considers that terrorists armed with weapons of mass destruction present an 'existential' threat to the United States (Fox News Sunday, June 15, 2003), or even, in columnist Charles Krauthammer's (2004) view, to 'civilization itself'.

Developing such weapons, however, requires overcoming several major technological hurdles. Among them: gaining access to specialized ingredients, acquiring equipment and know-how to produce and disperse the agents and creating an organization that can resist infiltration or early detection by law enforcement (Tucker and Sands, 1999: 50–51). And, as the Gilmore Commission has concluded, 'the effective dissemination or dispersal of these viruses and poisons still presents serious technological hurdles that greatly inhibit their effective use' (1999: 38).

Chemical arms accounted for less than one percent of the battle deaths in the First World War where they were used extensively (Mueller, 2010: 24). And they cannot kill masses of people except when used in large numbers in a concentrated area: Matthew Meselson (1991: 13) calculates that it would take fully a ton of nerve gas or five tons of mustard gas to produce heavy casualties among unprotected people in an open area one kilometer square, something that would require the concentrated delivery into a rather small area of about 300 heavy artillery shells or seven 500-pound bombs.

The potential for biological weapons to kill masses of people is higher, but for the most destructive results, they need to be dispersed in very low-altitude aerosol clouds. Moreover,

90 percent of the microorganisms are likely to die during the process of aerosolization, while their effectiveness could be reduced still further by sunlight, smog, humidity and temperature changes. Explosive methods of dispersion may destroy the organisms and, except for anthrax spores, long-term storage of lethal organisms in bombs or warheads is difficult. In the summary judgment of two careful analysts, delivering microbes and toxins over a wide area in the form most suitable for inflicting mass casualties – as an aerosol that could be inhaled – requires a delivery system of enormous sophistication, and even then, effective dispersal could easily be disrupted, as in the case of chemical weapons, by unfavorable environmental and meteorological conditions (Tucker and Sands, 1999: 51; see also Gilmore Commission, 1999: 25; Leitenberg, 2005).

Radiological weapons or 'dirty bombs', in which radioactive materials are sprayed over an area by a conventional explosion, are incapable of inflicting much immediate damage at all. In fact, it would be almost impossible to disperse radioactive material from a dirty bomb explosion so that victims would absorb a lethal dose before being able to leave the area, and it is likely that few, if any, in the target area would be killed directly, become ill, or even have a measurably increased risk of cancer, although the costs of disruption and cleanup could be considerable (Zimmerman and Loeb, 2004: 11; Allison, 2004: 8). Moreover, although a dirty bomb would be easier to assemble than a nuclear weapon, the construction and deployment of one is difficult and requires considerable skill (Levi and Kelly, 2002).

Terrorist progress, if any

Presumably in part because of such difficulties, the degree to which al-Qaeda or other notable terrorist groups have pursued, or even have much interest in, any sort of WMD may have been exaggerated. In 2003, UN Ambassador John Negroponte proclaimed there to be 'a high probability' that within two years al-Qaeda would attempt an attack using a nuclear or other weapon of mass destruction. However, analyst Anne Stenersen concludes after an exhaustive study of available materials that, although

> it is likely that al-Qaeda central has considered the option of using non-conventional weapons [there] is little evidence that such ideas ever developed into actual plans, or that they were given any kind of priority at the expense of more traditional types of terrorist attacks.
>
> (2008: 39; see also Mueller, 2010: chapter 14; Bergen, 2010)

Moreover the use of unconventional weapons can be counterproductive by turning off financial supporters, dividing the movement and eliciting major crackdowns.

Various sources suggest that there were radical elements in Osama bin Laden's entourage who were interested in pursuing weapons of mass destruction when the group was in Afghanistan in the 1990s. However, the same sources indicate that bin Laden had little interest in this and essentially sabotaged the idea by refusing to fund a WMD project, or even to initiate planning for it. Indeed, evidence from an al-Qaeda computer left behind in Afghanistan in 2001 when the group beat a hasty retreat indicates that only some $2,000–4,000 was earmarked for WMD research and that mainly for very crude work on chemical weapons. In comparison, notes Stenersen, the millennial terrorist group Aum Shinrikyo, appears to have invested $30 million in its sarin gas manufacturing program alone (Stenersen, 2008: 35–36).

Khalid Sheikh Mohammed, the apparent mastermind behind the 9/11 attacks, reportedly says that al-Qaeda's atom bomb efforts never went beyond searching the Internet. After the fall of the Taliban in 2001, technical experts from the CIA and the Department of Energy examined information uncovered in Afghanistan and came up with conclusions generally supportive of that assertion. They found no credible information that al-Qaeda had obtained fissile material or a nuclear weapon, and no evidence of 'any radioactive material suitable for weapons'. Physicist and weapons expert David Albright is more impressed with the evidence, but he concludes that any al-Qaeda atomic efforts were 'seriously disrupted' – indeed, 'nipped in the bud' – by the invasion of Afghanistan in 2001, and that after the invasion the 'chance of al-Qaeda detonating a nuclear explosive appears on reflection to be low' (Mueller, 2010: 206).

Rumors and reports that al-Qaeda managed to purchase an atomic bomb, or several, have been around now for over a decade. If any of these reports were true, one might think the terrorist group (or its supposed Chechen suppliers) would have tried to set one of those things off by now or that al-Qaeda would have left some trace of the weapons behind in Afghanistan after it made its very hasty exit in 2001.

Bin Laden pronounced on the nuclear weapons issue a few times, talking about an Islamic 'duty' or 'right' to obtain the weapons for defense. Some of these oft-quoted assertions can be seen as threatening, but as Louise Richardson concludes, 'statements claiming a right to possess nuclear weapons have been misinterpreted as expressing a determination to use them', feeding 'the exaggeration of the threat we face' (2006: 162).

The future

These conditions are unlikely to change radically in the future. The basic knowledge about the destructive potential of biological and chemical weapons goes back decades, even centuries in some respects, and governments have spent a great deal of money in an effort to make the weapons more effective. Yet the difficulties of controlling and dispersing chemical and biological substances seem to have persisted.

Moreover, most terrorism specialists (and alarmists) are now contending that any terrorism problem principally derives from rather small numbers of homegrown people, often isolated from each other, who fantasize about performing dire deeds and sometimes receive a bit of training and inspiration overseas. In 2010, two prominent terrorism analysts concluded that such local terrorists would only be able to carry out 'less sophisticated operations' in the United States, a 'trend' they somehow deemed to be 'worrisome' (Bergen and Hoffman, 2010: 32). And in 2011, top officials announced that the 'likelihood of a large-scale organized attack' had been reduced (Serrano, 2011; see also 'Biden: Major terror attack on U.S. unlikely', cnn.com, February 11, 2010). Going even further, public officials have also publicly concluded that the 'greatest concern' has now become the 'lone wolf' terrorist. However, as Max Abrahms (2011) has pointed out, 'lone wolves have carried out just two of the 1,900 most deadly terrorist incidents over the last four decades'. The situation seems scarcely different in Europe and other Western locations. Michael Kenney (2010b) finds that Islamic militants there are operationally unsophisticated, short on know-how, prone to make mistakes, poor at planning and limited in their capacity to learn.

In addition, the popular notion that the Internet can be effective in providing operational information seems to be severely flawed. Kenney (2010a) notes that it is filled with misinformation and error and that it is no substitute for direct, on-the-ground training and experience. Stenersen is similarly unimpressed: the Internet manuals she has looked at are filled with materials hastily assembled and 'randomly put together' and contain information that is often 'far-fetched' or 'utter nonsense' (Stenersen, 2009: 56; see also Stenersen, 2008).

Overall, terrorists seem to be heeding the advice found in a memo on an al-Qaeda laptop seized in Pakistan in 2004: 'Make use of that which is available [,] rather than waste valuable time becoming despondent over that which is not within your reach' (Whitlock, 2007). Or, as another put it, 'a hand grenade that explodes in one of New York's streets is better than a nuclear bomb capable of destroying half of New York that does not explode!' (Stenersen, 2009: 59). That is: Keep it simple, stupid. There hasn't even been much in the way of a gas bomb even in Iraq where the technology is hardly much of a secret – Saddam Hussein's government had extensively used chemical weapons 20 years earlier.

Because terrorism of a considerably destructive nature can be perpetrated by a very small number of people, or even by a single individual, the fact that terrorists are few in number and limited in competence does not mean there is no problem. However, the notion that such people could come up with effective weapons of mass destruction seems remote. There may be reason for concern, or at least, for interest and watchfulness. But alarm and hysteria (not to mention sleeplessness) over the terrorist WMD threat are hardly called for.

Discussion questions

1 What are WMD, exactly? Is it sensible to include in the category weapons that are incapable of inflicting massive destruction?
2 Taking into account the confluence in drug trafficking and weapons supply between transnational crime organizations and terrorist groups, would crime organizations help terrorists to acquire WMD agents or materials?
3 Is there a real risk of Pakistan being the source of a future WMD attack, perhaps by stolen nuclear weapons?
4 In the supposed case that a tactical nuclear bomb could be stolen while being transported, could a terrorist group actually make it explode?
5 Why have WMD been used so infrequently by terrorists?
6 What are the main risks to terrorists of using WMD? Why would they choose to use them over conventional weapons?
7 Are the fears that terrorists would use WMD fully justified?
8 Do the people promoting the WMD fear have ulterior motives or interests? How do we explain the obsession with WMD terrorism today?

Further readings

Allison, G., 2004. *Nuclear Terrorism: The Ultimate Preventable Catastrophe*, New York: Times Books.
Antonius, D., Brown, A., Walters, T., Martín Ramirez, J., and Sinclair, S., eds, 2010. *Interdisciplinary Analyses of Terrorism and Political Aggression*, Newcastle Upon Tyne, UK: Cambridge Scholars Publishing.
Apikyan, S., and Diamond, D., eds, 2006. *Countering Nuclear and Radiological Terrorism*, NATO Security through Sciences Series – B: Physics and Biophysics, Dordrecht, The Netherlands: Springer.
Howard, D., and Forest, J., eds, 2008. *Weapons of Mass Destruction and Terrorism*, New York: McGraw Hill.
Jenkins, B., 2008. *Will Terrorists Go Nuclear?* Amherst, NY: Prometheus.
Levi, M., 2007. *On Nuclear Terrorism*, Cambridge, MA: Harvard University Press.
Mueller, J., 2010. *Atomic Obsession: Nuclear Alarmism from Hiroshima to Al Qaeda*, New York: Oxford University Press.
Ryan, J., and Glarum J., 2008. *Biosecurity and Bioterrorism*, Burlington, MA: BH Elsevier.

6   Does al-Qaeda continue to pose a serious international threat?

YES: The enduring al-Qaeda threat: a network perspective

Jeffrey B. Cozzens and Magnus Ranstorp

Introduction

Any doubts concerning al-Qaeda's (AQ) strategic intent to threaten international security are shattered upon reading the US Senate Select Committee on Foreign Relations' (2009) report, '*Tora Bora Revisited*: How We Failed To Get Bin Laden And Why It Matters Today.' The document recounts a rendezvous on the outskirts of Kandahar in August 2001 when Usama Bin Laden (UBL) and Ayman al-Zawahiri met two Pakistani nuclear scientists to discuss AQ's interest in acquiring nuclear weapons. Similarly, al-Qaeda in the Arabian Peninsula's (AQAP) emir, Nasir al-Wahishi, told the organization's publication, *Inspire*, in July 2010, 'America's actions require us to wipe them out of the map completely. America is a cancer that needs to be removed along with the West.' However, words alone do not a viable threat network make.

A serious question remains in the minds of some concerning whether the AQ network – for our purposes, the Pakistan-based senior leadership of AQ and its fighters; AQAP and its activists; al-Qaeda in Iraq; and al-Qaeda in the Islamic Maghreb (AQIM) – remains a threat to international security. Marc Sageman, a prominent analyst of militant Islamist networks, termed AQ 'a mythical entity' (Sageman, in Blitz, 2010). Sageman's view strongly contrasts with that of Georgetown's Bruce Hoffman, who describes at great length AQ's 'new grand strategy,' 'newfound vitality' and 'networking strengths' in a 2010 *Washington Post* editorial (Hoffman, 2010).

This chapter explores whether the AQ network remains a threat to international security. While it does not wrestle with all facets of the Sageman–Hoffmann debate, it uses a framework grounded in network theory to focus on the question of whether AQ is advancing as a network, as Hoffman has argued (Hoffman, 2010). This method seems logical given the constant reference to AQ as a network in the terrorism literature, and because much of the publicly available evidence suggests that this depiction is accurate. In the end, we argue that AQ is hitting the necessary benchmarks to sustain itself as a network, and therefore remains a threat.

What do we mean by 'network'?

As described ad nauseum in the literature, the AQ Core and its regional affiliates possesses the hallmarks of a networked organization resting atop a broader violent movement (Ronfeldt, 2007). While depicting AQ's precise network form is not our central focus, our portrayal of AQ and its affiliates as an atomized network *that still retains* a modicum of formal structure is based on several key premises.

First, leadership and hierarchy matter within AQ organizations. Barbara Sude, a former CIA al-Qaeda specialist now with RAND, writes: 'al-Qaeda's hierarchical structure has allowed the group to systematically acquire and disburse its human and material resources for operational needs – and for rapid regrouping if necessary' (Sude, 2010). Usama bin Laden was widely viewed as both the leader of the AQ organization and archetypal jihadi warrior. Directions and guidance flow from the central UBL faction to the various affiliates, if in different ways at different times, and some guidance appears to be operational in nature (ibid.). Further, as senior AQ militant Abdullah Muhammad Fazul observed, the 'mother al-Qaeda' appoints experienced or extraordinary militants to specific roles and functional committees, and replacements are found when required (Fazul, 2009: 310).

Second, a modicum of bureaucracy exists within the AQ network and between affiliates. The regional AQ affiliates have their own leadership cadres that have sworn *bayat* (an oath of loyalty pledged to an emir) to UBL yet exercise authority within their respective organizations. The Harmony database maintained by the United States Military Academy at West Point contains evidence highlighting such systemization, even if information concerning the conduct of relations between AQ Core and peripheral factions remains opaque (see Felter and Fishman, 2007).

Third, individuals are often cognizant of 'joining' these more organized factions. Pledging an oath of fealty, receiving a salary, submitting to a specific course of training or designated role, committing often significant financial resources upon entry and so on, indicate *in toto* that the individual chooses to identify with an organizational schema, authority and objectives (Bergen, 2006: 424).

Undoubtedly the AQ network has been forced to adapt and fragment in often significant and sometimes unknowable ways in response to the barrage of pressure brought to bear by intelligence, law enforcement and militaries around the world. However, there is scant evidence that the AQ core group and its geographic affiliates have lost or abandoned these network functions and principles internally or between their constituent parts (Fazul, 2009: 310).

Metrics of formal network success and applicability

Summarizing and condensing a broad spectrum of the social science literature, a recent Iowa State University publication on business networks (Korsching *et al.*, 2004) argues that the following characteristics must be at least maintained in networked organizations to generate forward momentum: strength in numbers and scope to leverage mobilization; organizational identity, prestige and image; mutual assistance and reciprocity within the network; accomplishments; and continuity in operations. Indeed, the very characteristics that bolster network effectiveness provide a grounded analytical framework for assessing the continued threat from the AQ network to the international community. Indications of the AQ network's ability to hit these metrics are synonymous with its continued threat.

Using this framework, we ask: does the AQ network leverage its manpower and geographic scope to mobilize? Does it possess an organizational identity that enhances internal commitment? Do the constituent components of AQ work together to assist the network as a whole to combat common enemies? Has the AQ network accomplished anything for its rank and file? And does the AQ network tackle the problems of continuity of operations and member retention?

Mobilization patterns of AQ core and affiliates

In 2001, Arquilla and Ronfeldt advanced the so-called SPIN model, an adaptation of Luther Gerlach's earlier model of social movements, as a way to capture the complexity of AQ and to conceptualize its multilayered, interlocking components. In this model, AQ is a 'segmented, polycentric, ideologically integrated network (SPIN)' (Arquilla and Ronfeldt, 2001). The SPIN model captures the multilayered relationships between the core leadership of AQ and its multiple peripheries, and the mobilization of the broader jihadi movement a decade later. Accordingly, Gerlach's model advanced that:

> (I)t is segmentary in that it is composed of many diverse groups which grow and die, divide and fuse, proliferate and contract. It is polycentric in that it has multiple, often temporary, and sometimes competing leaders and centers of influence. It is networked, forming a loose, reticulate, integrated network with multiple linkages through travelers, overlapping membership, joint activities, common reading matter, and shared ideals and opponents.
>
> (Gerlach, 2001)

Ronfeldt would later argue that AQ resembles 'a global tribe waging segmented warfare,' where the tribal principles of respect, dignity, pride and honor are core components, consistently projected globally as an integral part of their ideology. As such, AQ and its affiliates revolve around 'a gripping sense of shared belonging, principles of fusion against an outside enemy, and a jihadist narrative so compelling that it amounts to both an ideology and a doctrine' (Ronfeldt, 2007).

It is evident that AQ's tribal characteristics have materialized in its global mobilization strategies, especially in its tripartite narrative. First, as Roger Hardy notes, it is a narrative of humiliation painted in primary colors: the West is at war with Islam, as evidenced by conflicts from Chechnya to Somalia. This dimension is further reinforced by metaphorical wars (for example, the Danish Muhammad drawings). Second, the narrative offers to transform humiliation into inevitable victory, and shame into honor – the core tenets of the *mujahideen's* heroic tale. Third, it provides a compelling moral shock designed to spur collective action through graphic evidence of atrocities against Muslims (Hardy, 2006). Collectively, AQ's narrative represents an ever-expanding global 'quilt' of Muslim grievances and conflicts that it skillfully adapts to tap into the hearts and minds of sympathizers and activists – a powerful mobilizing device.

The polymorphous SPIN structure of AQ and its affiliates and the durability of its narrative are buoyed by the Internet. It allows AQ to project strength, share doctrinal strategies and tactical advice; to survive pressures and fissures; and to adapt to circumstances. The Al-Qaeda core and its regional affiliates, with the exception of AQIM, have gradually adapted its online strategies to changing political circumstances and to appeal to an expanded recruitment base in the West. For example, AQ Core has finally called on the popular revolutionaries to rise up in the post-Mubarak period and establish an Islamic state when it was initially sidelined by popular protests in Tunisia, Egypt and elsewhere. As argued by Snow and Byrd, 'the success of al-Qaeda on the global scale may be partly attributable to the ability of its leaders to adapt the diagnostic and prognostic components of its master frame to local contexts' (Snow and Byrd, 2007).

Cyberspace has been the engine driving AQ's collective action frames, constituting its ever-innovating central nervous system (Ranstorp, 2007). Nowhere is this more evident than the translation of various online magazines into languages other than Arabic. AQAP's *Inspire* is an ultra-slick, readily digestible 'how-to-guide' designed for Western recruits – increasingly the target audience, both in terms of travel to join the global jihad and as a means to instigate attacks from within the West.

AQ's organizational identity

Does the AQ network possess an organizational identity that enhances internal commitment? One way to address this query is to sample a cross-section of literature and statements from varied AQ militants (see for example, al-Banna, 2010; and 'Hanif' in Yousafzai and Moreau, 2010). In so doing, the contours and critical themes of a consistent group culture and identity – a common in-group set of attitudes, values and beliefs that offer a mechanism for both action and contrast against an out-group – crystalize. Abu Ubayd al-Qirshi, a popular AQ-linked online commentator and UBL associate, advanced a particularly forceful articulation of the core dimensions of AQ's organization identity in 'The Impossible Becomes Possible':

> With the New York and Washington raids, al-Qa'ida established a model of a proud Islamic mentality. This outlook does not view anything as impossible. Al-Qa'ida embodies Islamic unity. Blood from all the countries of the Islamic community has mixed together in the jihad that al-Qa'ida leads with no distinction between Arab and non-Arab . . . This is a step on the road to Islamic unity and the destruction of the . . . colonialist treaties that have torn the body of the Islamic community apart . . . [W]ith absolute trust in God, a willingness to die in God's path, patience, and generosity of spirit . . . these qualities . . . undoubtedly lead to victory.
>
> (al-Qirshi, 2002)

Statements like al-Qirshi's point to a distinct, even catalytic, organizational identity and corresponding network culture. Prior research has outlined the key components of this 'culture of global jihad,' which is constantly reinforced online and framed by sources of perceived social and religious authority to bolster morale and win recruits (Cozzens, 2009b).

But does this identity positively impact the commitment of those within the network? Notwithstanding often discussed 'cracks' within this identity, perhaps thousands of individuals remain motivated to act, or are prepared to act, on its perceived merits (Moghadam and Fishman, 2010). One quantitative example is the 2007 West Point study of foreign fighters in Iraq. When immigrating to Iraq to fight, these were queried by AQI as to why they came to the country, or what duty they hoped to perform: 217 of the 389 who responded (56.3 percent) indicated a desire for martyrdom, whereas 166 projected their roles as 'fighter' (or something similar) (Felter and Fishman, 2007). Granted, not all of these qualify as AQ 'members,' but these figures nevertheless testify to the magnetism of jihadi culture. Paul Cruickshank quantified yet another dimension of this identity in his 2010 report, 'The Militant Pipeline,' which discusses the 21 'serious' post-9/11 plots in the West (Cruikshank, 2010).

Al-Qaeda's network components: working synergistically

Al-Qaeda is the ultimate expression of what Mary Kaldor calls the dark underside of globalization (Kaldor, 1999). Since its 1988 origin, AQ managed to grow in sheer numbers and gravitational pull, attracting thousands of dedicated cadres from the Middle East, South Asia and Southeast Asia that trained in camps in Afghanistan before deploying around the world. Despite the subsequent fall of the Taliban and near-fragmentation of AQ's core, it is remarkable that it has managed to maintain a polymorphous structure and affiliation with over 30 terrorist groups in different parts of the world (Reinares, 2009). However, perhaps its greatest achievement has been to holistically utilize the Internet as an instrument of not only propaganda and communication, but also to 'spread tactics, technical know-how, and strategy' (Benjamin and Simon, 2005).

The Internet has functioned as a platform for multilayered, global collaboration for AQ from which it has maintained secure communications, broadcast clarion calls to action and spread propaganda, acquired targets and collaboratively brainstormed tactics. The latter point is evidenced in the proliferation of IED knowledge, migrating initially from Chechnya to Iraq, and then to the Salafist Group of Combat and Preaching (GSPC) in Algeria. Often, advice to circumvent counter-IED techniques was shared and operationally implemented within 48 hours by AQI. As recounted by an AQ recruit in 2010, around 50–60 Arab trainers left Waziristan to travel to Afghanistan 'to make IEDs, suicide vests, and other bombs, and to train the local Taliban in bomb making techniques' (Yousafasi and Moreau, 2010). The fact that *Inspire* magazine provides encryption keys and encourages activists to communicate with AQAP is also indicative of the global reach the organization commands. Moreover, the case of the British Airways software engineer, Rajib Karim, illustrates AQ's remote orchestration of terrorist plots from afar (Dodd, 2011).

Al-Qaeda's collective accomplishments

Al-Qaeda has provided its rank-and-file with both tangible and intangible boons. While many of the perceived personal 'benefits' of jihad and martyrdom for jihadi activists are described elsewhere (Wiktorowicz and Kaltenthaler, 2006), there are multiple profits that extend to the collective level that should be considered in an assessment of network viability. These accomplishments function as a bonding agent, essential to safeguard the network's internal commitment, persistence and attractiveness.

Collectively, AQ has provided its activists with a number of tangible accomplishments. However, perhaps none resonate as profoundly as the 11 September attacks. The fact that 'Ground Zero' in New York City remains under construction testifies to the fact that AQ was able to project power at a scale once held as the sole domain of states. As polling data indicated in 2003, the attacks catalyzed deep admiration for AQ in corners of the majority Muslim world, even if this has since dwindled (Pew Center for the People and the Press, 2003). As al-Qirshi (2002) argues, the attacks demonstrated that the 'martyrdom operations' of a few were sufficient to accomplish what the Soviet Union had been unable to achieve during the Cold War. Moreover, they exposed the 'hypocrisy and the *tawagheet*' ('false gods') in the majority Muslim world, sparked a conflict that exposed 'Jewish and Crusader' ambitions in countries like Afghanistan and Iraq and revived the 'neglected obligation' of defending Muslims and their lands (al-Qirshi, 2002). We see evidence of these perceived benefits in the testimonies of individuals who became jihadi activists following 9/11 and subsequent coalition actions, and in fact, in direct video testimony from AQ itself in the weeks following the attack (Michael and Wahba, 2001).

Further, history tells us that we should not overlook AQ's ability to withstand a full frontal assault from coalition forces for a decade in the same area where the storied *mujahideen* confronted the Soviets. If the Arab Afghans' fight against the Soviets became the stuff of legends in jihadi circles, how could AQ's resiliency and survival in the face of a determined international coalition be seen as anything but an omen of divine favor and confirmation of their cause (Cozzens, 2009b)? Periodic operational highlights, from the 2005 London attacks to Humam al-Bawlawi's December 30, 2009 attack against US intelligence personnel at Camp Chapman – even if not on the scale of the 9/11 attacks – are thus conceived as mile markers on the road to inevitable victory (Brinkbäumer and Goetz, 2010). Moreover, it should be remembered that even failed plots such as the foiled bombing of air cargo flights originating from Yemen are spun as strategic and propaganda victories by AQ media outlets (Ibrahim, 2010).

Finally, AQ ideologues such as the late Yusuf al-Uyayree spare no effort to highlight the network's alternative metrics of victory (al-Uyayree, n. d.). These are designed to strengthen resolve for AQ's activists when progress on strategic objectives may appear stalled, and cement unity of purpose in combatting AQ's enemies (Cozzens, 2009a).

Continuity and retention

Many of the primary reasons why AQ has been able to maintain continuity of its operations and retain many of its members have been addressed. However, there are several key components of this argument that remain unexplored: the systematic replacement of its strategic commanders, and the impact of jihadi veterans on member retention.

First, it is evident that AQ's branches place a premium on replacing commanders and ideologues that are arrested or killed. This systematic replacement is well noted in Pakistan, where coalition attacks have heavily targeted militants within AQ Core's 'Directorate of Operations' (Bergman and Tiedemann, 2010). However, in a testament to the organization's apparent succession plan, these individuals have often been quickly replaced – sometimes with militants entirely off the radar screen of Western intelligence agencies (Sude, 2010). In fact, as Sude notes, individuals have been observed to pick up where their predecessors left off, and in some cases, execute attacks or advance plots that were in the planning stages before their tenure. The 2005 London transit bombings and 2006 UK-based plot to bomb airliners are cases-in-point. Planned by Abu Faraj al-Libi and Hamza Rabia, respectively, they were then organized and carried out (or attempted) by other senior planners (ibid.). Regardless, it is clear that AQ has a succession plan in place – a logical step for an organization that has institutionalized martyrdom.

Finally, the inspirational impact and promotion of AQ's jihadi combat veterans (sometimes called *ghazis* in the English language jihadi literature, meaning 'warrior' or 'raider') on retaining and attracting other militants cannot be overlooked. The British AQ militant behind the infamous 'Gas Limos' plot, Dhiren Barot, wrote: 'Simply interacting with *ghazis* . . . can help to alter one's outlook and influence oneself to procure a taste for this noble path in their blood, making it akin to their nature' (al-Hindi, 1999). The authors developed this point further in a 2010 publication on jihadist foreign fighters (Cilluffo, Cozzens and Ranstorp, 2010: 32). It is difficult to overlook the *ghazi* paradigm as a critical component of AQ's retention and mobilization strategy (Yousafzai and Moreau, 2010).

Conclusion: the contours of the enduring al-Qaeda threat

We have argued that AQ possesses all of the characteristics of a network built for survival. It leverages its manpower and geographic scope to mobilize, and fosters an organizational identity and culture that yields committed operatives. Its network components also work synergistically towards common goals. Further, beyond the personal benefits of martyrdom and jihad, AQ can claim collective tangible and intangible accomplishments. It also appears to maintain a systematic plan for key leader replacement, and promotes jihadi archetypes like the *ghazi* as a means to build depth in numbers. Based on the social science research concerned with network advancement, our brief assessment suggests that the AQ network is indeed viable. And if the AQ network is viable, it is logically a threat to the international community. But what form will the threat take?

First, let us be clear: most Western analysis struggles to accurately conceptualize other cultures, high-context societies or the nature of the threat from AQ. When speaking of AQ's future threat, different concepts of time and space are involved between the network and its enemies (us), and alternative perceptions reign concerning how war is made and how winning is understood (Ranstorp, 2008). These differences are compounded by the countless definitions of 'threat' that litter the security studies lexicon, and multiple, even competing strategic visions within AQ itself. Critical differences exist in societal, tactical and strategic thinking across cultures – and often between our understanding of AQ and the network's own self-conceptions. This paradigmatic contrast between the West and AQ has been described as 'functionalism' pitted against 'culturalism' (Cozzens, 2006).

Second, while difficult to pinpoint, the AQ threat will continue to shock and surprise, given the complexity of its internal dynamics, history of scalable wildcard operations and the tremendous difficulties inherent to predicting precise forms of such sudden, violent and often game-changing eruptions. Indeed, there are limits to inductive reasoning when considering the possibilities of large, sudden and unexpected shocks to the international system, what have been described variously as 'Black Swans' or 'Wild Cards' (Ranstorp, 2008; Taleb, 2007). US Army Major Nidal Hasan's shooting rampage is indicative of the sudden and unexpected nature of this threat, as are the often-surprising provocations that fuel it, such as the Danish Muhammad cartoons controversy.

Finally, despite the inherent difficulty of conceptualizing the holistic AQ threat, the international community can be assured that the future will consist not only of kinetic attacks, but also strikes designed to fray social and economic cohesion along pre-existing lines within targeted societies – especially during a time when Western intelligence and military resource are stretched thin. This AQ strategy already targets the United States and European Union countries, as is discussed at great length in the jihadi literature, and is being violently played out in 'fault-line' conflicts in places like Pakistan, Iraq and Somalia. Hoffman's erudite 2010 assessment in the *Washington Post* poignantly highlights this theme: 'Al-Qaeda's newfound vitality is the product of a fresh strategy that plays to its networking strength . . . In contrast to its plan on Sept. 11, which was to deliver a knock-out blow to the United States, al-Qaeda's leadership has now adopted a "death by a thousand cuts" approach' (Hoffman, 2010).

NO: Al-Qaeda: a diminishing threat

Lee Jarvis

Introduction

The emergence of al-Qaeda can be traced to the Soviet Union's invasion of Afghanistan in 1979. The brutal war that followed this invasion lasted for ten years, and saw tens of thousands of individuals from across the Muslim world arrive to assist the Afghan population (Bergen, 2002: 58). Although these 'Afghan Arabs', as they were known, played only a limited role in bringing about the superpower's eventual withdrawal (Burke, 2003: 58), their experience in this conflict laid the foundations for the creation of the most infamous of modern terrorist groups. Specifically, the war provided training and combat experience, a sense of camaraderie and solidarity between those fighting, an opportunity for sustained contact amongst individuals and groups inspired by similar jihadist ideals, and – perhaps most important of all – a belief in the potential of violence to resist and combat injustices.

Prominent amongst the beneficiaries of this experience were those who would later inspire and lead al-Qaeda. These included Osama bin Laden – a wealthy Saudi who had travelled to offer logistical and financial support; Ayman al-Zawahiri – the leader of Tanzim al-Jihad who sought a base from which to continue his efforts to overthrow Hosnik Mubarak's regime in Egypt (Gerges, 2005/2009: 94); and Abdullah Azzam – bin Laden's spiritual teacher until his assassination in 1989. Those who had fought the Soviet Union dispersed after the conflict's conclusion, with Osama bin Laden moving to Saudi Arabia and then Sudan. Indeed, it is only after his return to the Taliban-led Afghanistan in 1996 that we begin to see al-Qaeda as a concrete organization emerging. Although the organization's precise date of birth is debated (see Burke, 2003: 5; Gerges, 2005/2009: 55), bin Laden's 'Declaration of Jihad on the Americans Occupying the Country of the Two Sacred Places' in 1996 called explicitly for attacks on Americans and their allies (Bergen, 2002: 96–97).

Bin Laden's 1996 Declaration of Jihad, and his subsequent establishment of a World Islamic Front for Jihad against the Jews and the Crusaders, highlight the feature of al-Qaeda that most distinguishes this organization – and the threat it poses – from other Islamist groups. Specifically, this is its ambition – to target acts of violence against the 'far enemy' of the United States and its allies (Gerges, 2005/2009). This ambition is traceable to two factors. The first is a long list of grievances against the US (grievances shared by many outside of al-Qaeda), including the permanent stationing of American troops in Saudi Arabia after the first Gulf War, its continuing support for the state of Israel and its close ties with regimes deemed apostate or 'un-Islamic', such as Saudi Arabia. The second is a very particular understanding of jihad (or struggle) inspired by the writings of the radical Egyptian, Syed Qutb (Burke, 2003: 49–53). For al-Qaeda, jihad is understood as a core tenet of Islam, an individual rather than collective commitment for Muslims, a permanent rather than temporary condition, and an offensive rather than purely defensive duty (Gerges, 2005/2009). This marriage of religious interpretation and perceived political injustices was thus used to legitimize violence against American and other Western targets, including – controversially – civilian populations. The result was a spate of attacks, including the 1998 bombing of American embassies in Kenya and Tanzania that killed over 200 people; a suicide attack in 2000 on the *USS Cole* – an

American naval warship stationed in Yemen – that killed seventeen sailors; and the downing of four aircraft in Washington, New York and Pennsylvania on 11 September 2001 which killed almost 3,000 people. In the years since 9/11, further attacks either attributed to, or claimed by, the organization have occurred in a wide spread of countries including Indonesia, Iraq, Jordan, Tunisia, Turkey and the United Kingdom.

Given these motivations and history of past attacks, it might seem counter-intuitive to argue that al-Qaeda no longer poses a serious international threat. In this chapter, however, I will do precisely this. Specifically, I will point to developments in the strategic, political and public realms after 9/11 which have severely, perhaps fatally, reduced al-Qaeda's capacity to conduct acts of international terrorism. My task here, however, is complicated a little by two factors. The first relates to the difficulties of calculating threat or risk: an inherently subjective process that involves predicting future events (Jackson *et al.*, 2011: 128). The second relates to a lack of consensus over what precisely al-Qaeda now is (see Hellmich, 2011), an issue complicated by changes to the movement after 9/11 and the difficulties of securing reliable intelligence on its activities. To address these, I will argue that whether we approach al-Qaeda narrowly – as a 'hardcore' inner circle of bin Laden's former associates – or expansively – as a now-dispersed social movement sharing little more than a common ideology – the international threat it poses is far less profound than is often assumed. Indeed, I will suggest that recent efforts to counter the threat of al-Qaeda have proved as harmful as the organization itself in some cases.

Al-Qaeda central

The emergence of al-Qaeda as a political force, as I have noted, took place in the aftermath of the 1979–1989 conflict in Afghanistan. The attacks that followed this war leading up to, and including, 9/11 can all be linked directly to the inner circle of this organization led by bin Laden and his deputy, Ayman al-Zawahiri. Yet, the events of 11 September 2001 represented the climax *and* the beginning of the end for this core that has been described by Marc Sageman (2008: 31) as 'al-Qaeda Central'. As a coherent organization active in the plotting, training and financing of attacks, al-Qaeda and the threat that it poses has been severely weakened (Burke, 2003: 12–23; Sageman, 2008) by at least five developments in the years since those attacks.

In the first instance, the attacks of 11 September 2001 were met by a US-led global counterterrorism campaign of comparable scope and expenditure to the Cold War (Jackson *et al.*, 2011: 249–256). In contrast to earlier limited responses such as President Clinton's 1998 cruise missile strikes on Sudan and Afghanistan (Bergen, 2002: 122–129) this global 'war on terrorism' mobilized a vast range of military, diplomatic, legal and intelligence resources to confront what was widely viewed as a new, exceptional threat to the security of the US and its allies (Jackson, 2005; Jarvis, 2009). Central to this confrontation was a military assault on Afghanistan – al-Qaeda's then base – which commenced in October 2001. Successes in that initial military conflict ended the Taliban's control of much of Afghanistan, and proved even more destructive to their client, al-Qaeda (Byman, 2005: 215–218). In the first instance, a substantial number of the organization's most experienced and active individuals were captured or killed in the invasion and ensuing war (Sageman, 2008: 137). Almost half the senior leadership in Afghanistan may have been affected this way (Hoffman, 2003: 433), with similar losses inflicted more recently on Abu Musab al-Zarqawi's al-Qaeda in Iraq (Bergen *et al.*, 2011: 74); a group that formally allied with bin Laden in 2004 (Gerges, 2005/2009: 257–258). Although it is difficult to quantify the impact of these on the organization's working

– and some scholars believe this to be limited (see for example, Bergen *et al.*, 2011) – a considerable amount of al-Qaeda's expertise and experience was clearly lost in these military campaigns, providing a major setback for an organization that, 'numbered fewer than 5,000 fighters at its zenith in 2001' (Gerges, 2005/2009: 294). More important, however, for assessing the threat of al-Qaeda was the loss of Afghanistan as a sanctuary from which to recruit and train militants for future attacks. This loss of state support – and in particular a space from which to operate – has greatly reduced the group's organizational and logistical capabilities (Byman, 2003: 159; Byman, 2005: 217; Sageman, 2008: 126), and it has found itself pushed back now to the border region with Pakistan along with the remnants of the Taliban regime (see Gerges, 2005/2009: 307; Sageman, 2008: 128–138).

On 4 May 2011, the military dimension of the war on terrorism saw its most dramatic moment to date. A US Navy Seal operation at Osama bin Laden's compound in Abbottabad, Pakistan, culminated in the killing of al-Qaeda's leader, almost ten years after the 9/11 attacks. If the full consequences of this assassination are still difficult to predict, bin Laden's death may serve, in the short term, to inspire retaliatory attacks such as the 13 May attack on a military training centre in Pakistan. It may also, temporarily, encourage new recruits to al-Qaeda as has happened in the past in the aftermath of the 'targeted killing' of Palestinian leaders, for example (Cronin, 2009: 26–31). In the longer term, the removal of al-Qaeda's figurehead and founder may dramatically reduce its appeal amongst those potentially drawn to this movement. It may also contribute to a decline in the coherence of al-Qaeda, which is already viewed by many as little more now than a loose network of allied groups (see below). Moreover, the apparent seizure of considerable intelligence in the operation, and the potential loss of bin Laden's financial connections, may further reduce the threat al-Qaeda now poses, although the group has been able to recover and evolve following the loss of other high-profile figures.

Beyond this military dimension, other activities associated with the war on terrorism have also drastically reduced the threat posed by al-Qaeda. Notably, a number of states beyond the US have worked actively to counter the organization's reach and appeal, with the pursuit and capture of thousands of alleged al-Qaeda operatives and sympathizers by intelligence agencies in countries including Malaysia, Thailand, Sudan, Syria, Yemen and even Iran (Gerges, 2005/2009: 232; also Bergen *et al.*, 2011: 83). Pakistan alone, for example, apprehended over 600 individuals believed to be members of al-Qaeda by 2006 (Mueller, 2006: 183). Importantly, these states and their leaderships have a genuine interest in reducing the capacities of al-Qaeda and related organizations, either because they are themselves potential targets of attacks, or because of a desire to ally with the US for financial or political reasons (Byman, 2005: 216; Mueller, 2005: 501–502). After the 9/11 attacks, therefore, al-Qaeda central suffered a resounding lack of political support, including, importantly, amongst regimes in the Muslim and Arab world.

A third factor limiting al-Qaeda's threat has been its inability to recruit new members to replace those killed or captured after 9/11. Where the Soviet campaign in Afghanistan of 1979 prompted an influx of foreign Muslims seeking to fight alongside the Afghan population, no such swelling of numbers occurred in the aftermath of the 2001 invasion. This lack of global assistance was likely a product of the Taliban's global unpopularity, including in the Muslim world (Sageman, 2008: 136). The regime was tainted by a notoriously poor human rights record, and lacked international credibility: only three states ever recognized it as Afghanistan's legitimate government. It also reflected a broader opposition to al-Qaeda amongst potential recruits from other jihadist groups. Indeed, many other organizations sharing a broadly Islamist ideology have publicly criticized bin Laden and his war against the 'far enemy', either on pragmatic grounds as a strategic error, or on moral and religious grounds due to his organization's killing of civilians and Muslims (Gerges, 2005/2009).

The lack of volunteers to assist al-Qaeda and the Taliban in their struggle points to a fourth important constraint on the group's activities. This concerns the widespread lack of support amongst Muslims worldwide for the movement's strategies, and perhaps even its ambitions. This rejection of al-Qaeda is pervasive amongst individuals living in states most directly – and devastatingly – affected by the aftermath of 9/11, with a 2007 poll in Iraq revealing 100 per cent opposition to al-Qaeda attacks on civilians there, and 98 per cent opposition to the group's efforts to recruit foreign fighters (Gerges, 2005/2009: 301). Elsewhere, in other predominantly Muslim countries such as Pakistan, Jordan, Indonesia and Saudi Arabia, a similar public backlash has occurred (Gerges, 2005/2009: 289–290; also Cronin, 2006: 45; Sageman, 2008: 161). This aversion towards al-Qaeda amongst potential constituents is crucial given that organizations engaging in terrorism rely heavily on public support for their activities, whether active, for example by the raising of finances, or passive, for example by refusing to cooperate with police and other authorities (Cronin, 2006: 27). Significant too, here, has been the number of individuals with credible religious standing who have repeatedly criticized not only al-Qaeda's targeting of civilians, but also bin Laden's theological credentials and capacity to speak for the world's Muslim populations (Bergen *et al.*, 2011: 83; English, 2009: 142).

A final factor concerns a series of internal fractures and weaknesses within al-Qaeda itself. As with most human organizations, al-Qaeda has never been immune from disagreement and rivalries, with endogenous tensions having dogged the organization from its establishment. These have included, inter alia, arguments over finances and pay received by its members (Gerges, 2005/2009: 103–107); internal tensions along national and other fault-lines, such as continuing complaints over the perceived over-representation of Egyptians in bin Laden's inner circle (Gerges, 2005/2009: 102–104; Byman, 2003: 159); and considerable strategic disagreement such as the admonishing of Abu Masab al Zarqawi for his group's brutalities against Muslims in Iraq (Neumann, 2009: 57). Much of this infighting continued and even increased amidst the international pressure heaped on al-Qaeda after the 9/11 attacks. With Ayman al-Zawahiri now widely viewed as bin Laden's likely successor, the movement's future will also depend on his ability, first, to contain such internal power struggles, and second, to prevent its further fracturing into a series of smaller organizations with their own local ambitions (see Cronin, 2009).

Al-Qaeda 2.0

As we have seen, the attacks of 11 September 2001 were followed by a sustained strategic, political, public and religious backlash that coincided with considerable internal tensions within al-Qaeda. As a coherent and functioning terrorist organization, al-Qaeda has been drastically weakened. Its capabilities to plan and organize attacks have been dramatically reduced, and its founder and figurehead now lies buried at sea. For many scholars, however, this does not necessarily mean al-Qaeda no longer exists as a potent force in global politics. Rather, they argue it has evolved into something quite different from the 1996–2001 period, with the threat it poses having similarly changed. In this argument, al-Qaeda Version 2.0 functions today more as an ideology (Post, 2007: 221), a social movement (Sageman, 2008: 31) or even a 'brand' (Gerges, 2005/2009: 40) than a specific, formal organization. It is a nebulous phenomenon in which operational control no longer resides in the hands of those such as al-Zawahiri and, prior to his assassination, Osama bin Laden (Cronin, 2006: 40).

Attacks attributed to it, in this argument, are conducted frequently by small cells of individuals with very limited connection to the inner circle, for example, the 7/7 bombings in London of 2005. Or by those simply inspired by their ideas and wishing to associate with al-Qaeda, for example, the Madrid bombings of March 2004. Driving this shift is both a sophisticated propaganda machine used to motivate sympathizers (Bergen *et al.*, 2011: 81), and a bottom-up process whereby groups of individuals 'buy in' to the brand within online and offline communities (Sageman, 2008). Although proponents of this argument frequently view this dispersed, decentralized network as a continuing and serious security threat, there are three important reasons to, again, maintain a sense of perspective here.

First, a large number of the plots associated with al-Qaeda in recent years have actually been the conduct of amateur 'wannabe' terrorists lacking the training, knowledge and resources required to carry out violence successfully (Jackson *et al.*, 2011: 135). Despite occasional, limited successes, many attempted attacks are intercepted either before or during their initiation because of their protagonists' ineptitude. These attempts range from semi-credible efforts to the frankly ludicrous, even pitiful. Recent examples include Colleen LaRose – the self-proclaimed 'Jihad Jane' – a middle-aged American woman arrested after allegedly meeting plotters planning to kill cartoonist Lars Vilks; the 2010 bombings in Stockholm that succeeded in killing only the attempted attacker; Umar Farouk Abdulmutallab's effort to blow up an airplane over Detroit on Christmas Day 2009 which left him severely burned and the aircraft intact (Bergen *et al.*, 2011: 92); and an earlier plot to bring down the Brooklyn Bridge with a blowtorch in March 2003! These best efforts of such 'wannabes' clearly demonstrate the chasm that frequently exists between their intent and capabilities.

The amateurism within al-Qaeda 2.0 poses another, broader, set of challenges to the long-term threat that it poses. For individuals to remain attracted to a movement such as this, a number of conditions must continue to be met (see Sageman, 2008). These include, first, the continuing resonance of al-Qaeda's struggle and ambitions, both in their own terms and relative to other sources of interest or distraction amongst potential recruits. Second, a continuation of the political grievances noted in this chapter's introduction. Third, the continued appeal of broader interpretive frameworks which give meaning to al-Qaeda's activities, such as the 'War against Islam' discourse that has achieved currency in recent years. And, fourth, a continuing belief in the viability and efficacy of violence as a tool for social, political and cultural change. Many, if not all, of these conditions are likely to change over time for reasons described above and, as the public opinion figures suggest, this may already be happening. What is more, this is also likely to have a greater impact upon individuals inspired by, yet not integrated within, an organization conducting terrorism. The history of terrorism is replete with examples of even well-organized, active, organizations later renouncing the use of violence, such as the Irish Republican Army and al-Jama'a al-Islamiya (the Egyptian Islamic Group) (see Gerges, 2005/2009: 200–210). Taking this history seriously, therefore, suggests the appeal of al-Qaeda, and global Islamist terrorism more generally, will continue to fade from its heyday in 2001.

Finally, and extending a point made above, the vastly enhanced range of counterterrorism powers introduced across the world after 11 September 2001 have made it increasingly difficult for amateur 'wannabes' to engage in al-Qaeda-inspired attacks. States such as the UK and US have invested huge amounts of money and resources in confronting the apparent threat of terrorism both at home and abroad (see Jackson *et al.*, 2011), with international cooperation over intelligence, policing and border control having also increased significantly. Although many of these measures are accompanied by deleterious side effects (see below), the chances of 'wannabe terrorists' evading suspicion and capture are now even slimmer (although see Mueller, 2006: 176–177). As such, while the pull factors attracting individuals to al-Qaeda have declined, the push factors prompting potential recruits away from terrorism have also increased.

Conclusion

This chapter has identified a number of strategic, political and public developments that have severely reduced the international threat posed by al-Qaeda, both as a coherent organization and as a broader social movement. In absolute terms – and certainly relative to other causes of harm – the threat posed by this entity (and terrorism more generally) is minimal; certainly, it is far short of existential. As John Mueller (2005: 488) notes, even if we include the outlier that was 9/11, the number of Americans killed by international terrorism since the 1960s is about the same as those killed by allergic reactions to peanuts. Indeed, the most hysterical and hyperbolic of fears around al-Qaeda – such as the existence of US-based sleeper cells or its likely deployment of weapons of mass destruction in mass casualty attacks – have failed to materialize (see Mueller, 2006: 180; Bergen *et al.*, 2011: 67). The existence of these fears, it seems, is instead simply a product of our 'contemporary cultural proclivity to speculate wildly as to the likelihood of adverse events and to demand high-profile responses and capabilities based on worst-case scenarios' (Durodié, 2007: 444).

Despite this, it is possible, indeed likely, that future years will witness further attacks or attempts by individuals inspired by al-Qaeda. Bin Laden's recent death in particular may be followed by plots against American, Western and other targets attributed to, or claimed by, al-Qaeda in the context of ongoing conflicts in areas of Pakistan, Afghanistan, Iraq and beyond. Many commentators here point to Muslim diasporas in Europe as the probable demographic source of further recruitment to the movement (Greenberg, 2005; Sageman, 2008). Yet, while all destruction of human life is to be regretted and condemned, these attacks will not constitute anything akin to a serious international threat – individually, or even collectively. The retreat and disintegration of other radical Islamist groups since the 1980s, indicates the difficulties of sustaining a campaign of terrorist violence indefinitely (Gerges, 2005/2009; Mueller, 2006: 175), an experience paralleled by the collapse of numerous earlier terrorist organizations (Cronin, 2009).

Finally, let us not forget that efforts to counter the perceived threat of al-Qaeda and related terrorist movements have themselves been extremely costly, both in economic terms, and in their impacts on civil liberties (Cole, 2003; Mueller, 2006: 181). At their most destructive, these efforts have resulted in the forms of harm (death and serious injury) associated with the threat itself, such as the July 2005 killing of Brazilian Jean Charles de Menezes by the UK's Metropolitan Police after London's 7/7 attacks. Moreover, aggressive counterterrorist policies may even exacerbate the threat posed by al-Qaeda (English, 2009: 130) in either its narrow or extended form by spreading further resentment amongst those potentially drawn to the movement. Earlier precedents include the aftermath of Clinton's 1998 cruise missile attacks which both strengthened the Taliban/al-Qaeda relationship (Byman, 2005: 202–203), and greatly enhanced the status of Osama bin Laden and his movement (Bergen, 2002: 122–129). Numerous analysts have pointed to the 2003 invasion of Iraq as a similarly counter-productive development, with the subsequent conflict there offering a rallying point for individuals attracted by ideas of jihad against the far enemy (Sageman, 2008; Gerges, 2005/2009). With these historical and contemporary examples in mind, it would be prudent – and far less costly – to recognize that the threat posed by al-Qaeda is actually extremely limited, even minimal, and respond to the movement accordingly.

Discussion questions

1 How should we conceptualize al-Qaeda and its multilayered structure? Is it an organization, an ideology, a social movement, or something else?
2 In what ways is al-Qaeda a 'unique' terrorist entity, if any?
3 What were the origins, aims and grievances of al-Qaeda?
4 What are some alternative ways to measure progress for non-state activists?
5 How might Western conceptions of al-Qaeda's 'success' differ from theirs?
6 What are the important distinctions separating grass-roots al-Qaeda-inspired militants
   and those linked to its formal networks?
7 How have strategic and political developments after 11 September 2001 reduced the
   threat posed by al-Qaeda?
8 What internal factors have contributed to the demise of al-Qaeda's central leadership?
9 What effect will the death of bin Laden have on the long-term survival of the group?
10 How significant is the threat posed by those inspired by the ideas and ideology of
   al-Qaeda today?

Further readings

Atwan, A., 2006. *The Secret History of al-Qa'ida*, London: Saqi Books.
Bergen, P., 2002. *Holy War, Inc.: Inside the Secret World of Osama bin Laden*, revised ed., London: Phoenix.
Byman, D., 2008. *The Five Front War*, Hoboken, NJ: John Wiley & Sons.
Gerges, F., 2009. *The Far Enemy: Why Jihad Went Global*, 2nd ed., Cambridge: Cambridge University
   Press.
Hellmich, C., 2011. *al-Qaeda: From Global Network to Local Franchise*, London: Zed.
Riedel, B., 2010. *The Search for Al Qaeda*, revised ed., Washington, DC: Brookings Institution Press.
Sageman, M., 2008. *Leaderless Jihad: Terror Networks in the Twenty-first Century*, Philadelphia, PA:
   Pennsylvania Press.
Stout, M., Huckabey, J., and Schindler, J., with Lacey, J., 2008. *The Terrorist Perspectives Project: Strategic
   and Operational Views of Al Qaida and Associated Movements*, Annapolis, MD: Naval Institute Press.
The 9/11 Commission Report, 2004. Available online at: http://www.9-11commission.gov/report/
   911Report.pdf.

Part IV
The causes of terrorism

7 Is terrorism the result of root causes such as poverty and exclusion?

YES: Do structural factors explain terrorism?

Dipak K. Gupta

Introduction

In the context of social sciences, it is a widely accepted assumption of human behavior that aggression is the outcome of frustration. When we do not obtain something to which we feel entitled, we feel anger and frustration, which, in turn, leads to violent actions aimed at removing the obstacle to our achievement. When we are horrified by acts of terrorism, by drawing this simple chain of causality we attempt to explain the motivations of those who carry these acts out. It is no wonder that millennia before psychologist John Dollard (1939) and his research team published their influential book linking frustration and anger resulting from social structural strains to aggressive behavior, Aristotle famously pronounced, 'poverty is the parent of revolution and crime'. Since the time of Aristotle, most of us have taken for granted the link between the gaps in the social fabric and political violence. In fact, looking at the numbing loss of non-combatant lives from attacks by sub-national groups, one can reach one of two conclusions: these are the work of insane minds, or that those who perpetrated the attacks have little to live for. These associations are reinforced when we come to the most puzzling of the attacks where the perpetrators willingly sacrifice their own lives to kill others.

Confusion about the motives of these actors was pervasive at the sight of the horrific attacks of 9/11. Reflecting the widespread view of the 'mad men of history', Senator John Warner (Atran, 2003a: 1), the then Chairman of the Senate Armed Services Committee commented: 'Those who would commit suicide in their assault on the free world are not rational'. The accusation of insanity, however, obviates the need of causal explanations of the violent actions. The argument that the terrorists suffer from psychological problems or some personality disorder has been put to rest by trained psychiatrists and psychologists from diverse parts of the world for nearly three decades (McCauley, 2007; Horgan, 2005a, b; Merari, 2005; Merari and Friedland, 1985; Post, 1984, 1990; Post, Sprinzak and Denny, 2003; Silke, 2003a; Taylor, 1988; Taylor and Quayle, 1994). None of the credible observations of terrorist personalities and behavior yields any reason to believe that the common foot soldiers fighting organized societies are psychologically different from the rest of the population. In fact, while there may be doubts about some of the leaders' states of mind, the followers, by and large, seem to be free of diagnosable maladies of the mind (Post, 2004).

With insanity eliminated as an explanation, the other often-cited reasons for terrorism and political violence are the various manifestations of social structural imbalance. The reasoning for this line of argument is simple. These structural imbalances, such as poverty, lack of education, blocked economic opportunities, income inequality, or lack of political freedom, prevent people from achieving their full potential. Inability to achieve what people believed to be their rightful entitlement creates frustration and anger, which leads to violent acts of political protest. Echoing this view, after the 9/11 attacks a number of prominent politicians and political decision makers almost reflexively pointed toward social structural imbalances of all sorts as generators of violence. Thus, Laura Tyson (2001), the former Chief of Presidential Council of the Economic Advisors under the Clinton Administration, called for a Marshall Plan as part of a frontal assault on terrorism. The former South Korean President and the Nobel Peace Prize winner, Kim Dae-Jung, in his acceptance speech, clearly stated (Malečková, 2005): 'At the bottom of terrorism is poverty'. While some sought the end of economic plight as a solution to the problems of sociopolitical violence, others pointed toward a 'freedom deficit'. President George W. Bush emphatically told the nation: 'They (the terrorists) hate us for our freedom', and proclaimed democracy as the antidote for terrorism. The purpose of this chapter is to examine the theoretical basis of these claims against actual evidence.

Theories linking social structure to terrorism and political violence

The long, circuitous path of scholarship that links Aristotle to Karl Marx to the sociologists of the 1960s had uniformly looked at the wrinkles in the social structure as the primary generators of political malevolence. Karl Marx saw a binary world divided between the rapacious bourgeoisie and the hapless proletariat who are alienated by the lack of control over their own fruits of labor. The rise of Communist and Socialist-led revolts around the world reinforced a belief in the direct causal connection between a shared feeling of deprivation resulting from structural imbalances and rebellion.

The social structural theory received a boost in the 1950s and early 1960s with contributions from a number of prominent sociologists, such as Coser (1956), Dahrendorf (1958), and Smelser (1963). Among these authors, Smelser perhaps offered the most comprehensive theory of mass movements. He argued, inter alia, that structural strains felt within a society add to the 'generalized belief' of protest, which brings about social upheavals. As examples, Smelser cited cases from prerevolutionary Russia, China, Cuba, Vietnam and many other third world countries. In this theoretical framework, political violence, however, was seen as an outcome of institutional and social structural imperfections found only in so-called 'third world' nations. In the democratic West, citizens were thought to be empowered by their ability to voluntarily form lobbying groups and to change the offending social order, thereby eliminating the need for violent revolutions. Yet in the 1960s and 1970s, reality stood in the way of this rosy requiem of social conflict in the West. Observing the absence of a systematic analysis of social conflict, the prominent political scientist Harry Eckstein lamented (1964: 1):

> When today's social science has become intellectual history, one question will certainly be asked about it: why did social science, which had produced so many studies on so many subjects, produce so few on violent political disorder?

The conundrum for social scientists arguing for structural factors as root causes of conflict in the 1960s and 1970s was that the fires of protest were burning brightly in the cities of North America and Western Europe, where the gradually rising tide of economic prosperity had made life easier for most. To solve this riddle, a group of political scientists offered the 'relative deprivation' theory. The proponents of this theory argued that violence was taking place in the affluent nations because aggressive behavior is not generated by the presence of absolute poverty but of its relative perception (Gurr, 1968, 1970). It is interesting to note that the concern for social science during this period involved mass movements. Social scientists, at this time in history, had precious little to say about terrorism.

Studying terrorism: the moral dilemma

In its early stages, terrorism studies had to overcome a deep ideological obstacle. At the end of the twentieth century, while social scientists were exploring the root causes of social movements, there was one area within the broad range of conflict studies where the literature was conspicuous in its near absence: terrorism. With the exception of a few noteworthy early efforts (Laqueur, 1977; Crenshaw, 1981; Rapoport, 1988), few noted scholars in the field of social sciences had contributed anything on terrorism. This conscious aversion can perhaps be traced directly to the ideological implication of the term: it is impossible to separate the political implications of the term 'terrorism.' Therefore, not surprisingly, most of the early contributors to the field were associated with think tanks, intelligence communities, or policy institutes than more ideologically sensitive educational institutions (Wilkinson, 1977; Jenkins, 1982; Freedman and Alexander, 1983; Hoffman, 1998/2006; Post, 1984).

However, this moral compunction disappeared after the devastating 1995 Oklahoma City bombing and then, of course, the 9/11 attacks. Facing the increasing menace, the ideological inhibitions quickly evaporated. The number of books published with 'terrorism' in the title in the decade that follows was many multiples of the total number of similar books in the previous half a century (Gupta, 2008: 3). Inevitably the authors, reflecting the demands of the general public, policy-makers and the members of the intelligence community, attempted to explore the root causes of terrorism. Their inquiry turned them toward the question of social and economic structural factors.

The structural factors

The accumulated macro and micro data on terrorism offered a new challenge to the social science theory builders. The possibility of a link between terrorism and factors of structural imbalances can be sought at the individual level (micro), or at the aggregate level (macro). The macro-level analyses hypothesize that those individuals who would be drawn to participate in acts of terrorism are personally deprived individuals with low levels of educational and economic achievements. The macro-level aggregate analyses, in contrast, would show a correlation between macro-economic and political data with observed acts of terrorism.

It was, however, quickly realized that the link between frustration and demonstration of anger felt at an either individual or societal level is a complex one (Krueger and Malečková, 2003). By casting a cursory look, we can clearly see that none of the 9/11 attackers came from an impoverished background. In fact, some came from the wealthiest segments of their countries of origin. Several, including the supposed leader of the group, Mohammed Atta, were highly educated individuals. Similarly, Umar Farouk Abdulmutallab, the so-called 'Underwear bomber', came from a highly privileged Nigerian family, as did Faisal Shahzad, the Pakistan-born US citizen, who attempted to plant a bomb in the middle of Times Square.

Those who examined the question of the individual participants' socioeconomic background in a systematic way have generally found that the participants tend to be better educated and from a higher economic class than the rest of the population (Hassan, 2001; Bueno de Mesquita, 2003). These findings may reflect two different arguments.

First, despite the fact that Marx saw history as an eternal struggle between the proletariats and the bourgeoisie, he believed that in reality, it would be extremely difficult to recruit the poor proletariats for revolution (Fernbach, 1974: 77). He saw the leadership for a violent overthrow of the system coming from the disaffected members of the upper class of society. Lenin similarly had a dim view of the proletariat participating in the revolution, particularly at leadership positions (Lenin, 1969: 40). This reluctance for the poor to be recruited in a revolutionary force can be accounted for by the high opportunity cost of their participation, because they are busy eking out an existence which may be threatened if they take time off for revolutionary activities (Popkin, 1979; Gupta, 1990).

In more recent days, some scholars have argued that the relative absence of participants in terrorism from the poorest segments of society might reflect a selection bias, particularly when a large pool of motivated volunteers is available for the group to choose from (Krueger and Leitin, 2008). In such cases, it is likely that the best-educated and the best-trained ones, who can fit in with the target population, will be chosen. In contrast, when the pool of volunteers is comprised of poor and uneducated and the target population is demographically similar to the groups', it is likely that the attackers are not going to be different from the rest of the population. Thus, in areas where there is domestic insurgency, such as in Iraq, Afghanistan, Yemen and Pakistan, the terrorists may be drawn from the poor and uneducated.

If the micro-level evidence points to a confusing pattern, so does the macro-level evidence. Krueger and Malečková (2003) and Piazza (2003) did not find any direct correlation between terrorism and structural factors, such as per capita GDP, education, or poverty. By using scatter plots and obtaining simple regression equations, Gupta (2008) corroborated the results of the previous studies. Even democracy and political freedom produced but a weak correlation with violent rebellion (Krueger and Laitin, 2008). Only the index of state failure showed a strong correlation with incidents of terrorism (Gupta, 2008). Thus, after an exhaustive examination, Krueger and Laitin (2008: 178) concluded that: 'To sum up, our data analysis up until now confirms . . . that the economic foundations of terrorism are at best only indirect'.

While in search for the root causes of terrorism, there is another factor that is worth remembering. When we consider cross-national terrorism data, we see that while many countries across the spectrum experience terrorism, it is the poorer ones that experience prolonged and widespread violence. Sambanis (2004) defines civil war as one that causes more than 1,000 deaths over a specific period. If we broaden our definition of terrorism to include such a wider spread of violence, there are convincing results of statistically significant correlation between terrorism and per capita income and unequal distribution of income (Collier and Hoeffler, 2004; Fearon and Leitin, 2003; Nafziger and Auvinen, 2002; Sambanis, 2008).

Conclusion

I began my discussion by arguing that there are two possible explanations of terrorism: insanity or factors of social structural imbalances, which create a widespread feeling of frustration and anger. We saw that there is no evidence that the followers in a violent dissident movement suffer from any mental illness or exhibit any specific personality type. From all the disparate observations it seems clear that in their psychological makeup they are indistinguishable from the rest of the community. Hence, it must be the economic and political grievances. Unfortunately, as we have seen in the above discussion, the data analyses paint a muddled picture. If the most potent generators of grievances, such as poverty, unemployment, income inequality and even lack of political freedom have but weak correlation with cross-national variations of terrorism, then how do we explain it? There are two sets of explanations: the first is methodological, the second conceptual.

In order to discern the effects of structural factors, researchers by and large use cross-national studies. This is because most of the structural factors are extremely slow-moving variables. For instance, factors such as measures of income inequality, poverty, literacy and educational attainments of nations do not change perceptively within a short period of time. Therefore, in order to detect their impact on violent political dissent we are forced to use cross-national data. Yet the comparability of such datasets is often in question. Hence it is possible that these measurement errors are casting some shadows on the accuracy of estimation.

Second, I have argued (Gupta, 2008) that in these analyses we are missing one important factor. When terrorists are interviewed, they all talk about their resentment toward the extant political system; they complain about factors of poverty and income inequality. They talk about the lack of economic opportunities, injustice, discrimination, repression and intolerance facing their communities. Even when they themselves are from a well-off background, they tell researchers that they have been moved by the plight of their fellow community members. Why then do these factors not show up in our empirical analyses? I posit that without grievances there can be no political movement. However, these grievances only serve as the necessary conditions. This is because none of these movements reflect spontaneous explosions of anger and frustration. The reason for this is that they come up against the irrefutable logic of the collective action problem, first demonstrated by Mancur Olson (1968). That is, all political movements, in the end, aim to attain public goods that are to be distributed within the community, regardless of participation by others. In a dissident movement, until it gains a certain amount of momentum or public support, the costs imposed by the organized society fall primarily on those who are the first to openly express their disaffection with the established system. Therefore, every 'rational' member of the community would wait for some people to stick their necks out. With everyone behaving rationally, no movement would ever start.

This collective action problem cannot be solved within the strict framework of economics. Olson (1968: 161–162) was clear in arguing that the reason someone would assume the risk of being a dissident is a matter of social psychology and not of economics. Therefore, I argue that in order to fully understand the motivations behind mass movement in general, and terrorism in particular, we must expand the fundamental assumption of economic rationality to include the group. That is, as social beings, we all strive to maximize not just the utility of our own selves, but also that of the group in which we claim our membership. Hoffman (1998/2006: 43) is therefore correct in stating that: 'The terrorist is fundamentally an altruist: he believes in serving a "good" cause designed to achieve a *greater good for a wider constituency*' (my emphasis). Because economics and 'rational choice' models cannot fully explain altruism (Rose-Ackerman, 1996), for an explanation of such behavior we must look outside the disciplines that equate rationality with selfishness.

Although evolutionary logic has imbued us with the inescapable need to belong to groups, our choice of groups is not automatic; it depends on the work of leaders we may call 'political entrepreneurs'. The economist Joseph Schumpeter pointed out in 1912 that market interactions alone do not explain long-term movements in the economy. He emphasized the work of entrepreneurs, who through their innovations cause economic evolution. Similarly, some scholars have emphasized the need to have 'political entrepreneurs' to provide a shape of collective identity for a movement to start and sustain. These are the leaders, the Mohandas Gandhis, the V. I. Lenins, the Maos, the Martin Luther King Jr's, and the bin Ladens of the world, who are able to channel the collective anger felt within their community to create a full-fledged political movement. Hence, the presence of grievances is only the necessary cause for political violence. For sufficient cause, we must look for leadership. Because of this intervening factor of leadership, when we examine the data we can only find a weak correlation between the structural factors and political violence.

Schumpeter (1912/1939) introduced the concept of entrepreneurs – those rare individuals who can take the existing innovations and advances in technologies and create large enterprises that can move an economy (or the global economy) along. However, what he did not address was the question of why these entrepreneurs arrive on the global stage from certain countries at specific periods of time? The noted economist William Baumol (1990) attempted to answer this by arguing that it is the incentive structure within the structure of an economy that creates what he calls 'productive', 'unproductive' or even 'destructive' entrepreneurs. Baumol, of course, does not examine the case of radical political leaders, but he argues (1990: 893) that:

> while the total supply of entrepreneurs varies among societies, the productive contribution of the society's entrepreneurial activities varies much more because of their allocation between productive activities such as innovation and largely unproductive activities such as rent seeking or organized crime.

He establishes his hypotheses by drawing historical examples from Ancient Rome and China, the Middle Ages in Europe and the Renaissance. Baumol points out that a society that provides incentives for creative activities which may go against the accepted norms, practices and ideologies help supply crops of creative entrepreneurs, while those that develop institutional restrictions on free ideas tend to produce unproductive or destructive entrepreneurs.

We can extend his logic to see that the Arab/Islamic nations have largely been non-democratic, where the only expression of even moderate dissent or expression of frustration can take place within the confines of religious discourse. As a result, these societies have channeled their frustration, anger and a perception of humiliation through religious fundamentalism. Even in the democratic societies in the West, the hysteria created by the 9/11 and other attacks and a prolonged involvement in warfare in Iraq and Afghanistan have isolated Muslim youths, particularly in the Western European nations, such as France, the UK, Spain and even in the US (Sageman, 2008). This has created conditions where the radicalization of youth can take place. It is therefore of little surprise that these countries have produced the leaders of the next generation of al-Qaeda.

Finally, I should mention that terrorism is not a separate form of political violence. If we define it as attacks on a non-combatant population, then we must view it as a strategy employed by the group leadership. The most obvious manifestation of this strategic use of violence can be seen in the orchestration of suicide attacks. Despite the apparent implication of extreme emotion, a number of studies have found that suicide attacks are exquisitely timed to achieve certain political goals for the dissident group (Kydd and Walter, 2002; Berrebi and Klor, 2003; Pape, 2003; Gupta and Mundra, 2005; Hafez, 2007).

Hence, we can conclude that factors of structural imbalances do cause terrorism and political violence. However, such movements require the rise of leaders, who can frame the economic and political issues, give a widespread feeling of deprivation the concrete shape of a movement, and take appropriate strategic actions.

NO: Poverty and exclusion are not the root causes of terrorism

L. Rowell Huesmann and Graham R. Huesmann

Introduction

The question of whether poverty and exclusion are 'root causes' of terrorism depends, of course, on the meaning of the words 'terrorism' and 'root cause'. What qualifies as terrorism has been discussed in other parts of this book and in many other essays (Marsella, 2004; Miller and File, 2001; Whittaker, 2001), and we don't need to repeat the discussion here. For the purposes of this chapter, we simply define a 'terroristic act' as violent behavior intended to harm or kill innocent persons who are not directly threatening the perpetrator in order to help achieve a political end for a group with whom the perpetrator identifies. For psychologists and neuroscientists, the general puzzle is to understand what convergence of predisposing personal characteristics and precipitating situational characteristics *causes* an individual to deliberately, intentionally and without significant remorse commit such acts. However, in this chapter we address the narrower question of whether poverty and exclusion are root causes of this kind of behavior. By 'are they root causes', we mean:

1 Are poverty and exclusion *necessary* for terrorism? We say no, and probably so does everyone else, so we won't dwell on this question;
2 Are poverty and exclusion *sufficient* to cause terrorism? We say no, but probably some would say yes, so we explicitly address this question and explain why we say no; and
3 Can poverty and exclusion *contribute partially* to causing terrorism? We say yes, but we believe this would not qualify them to be called 'root causes' because of the complex psychological process through which we believe they operate.

However, before we address these questions, we need to provide a synopsis of what the psychological and neurological research on aggression and violence has told us. A major advantage of bringing to bear the aggression and violence research is that it greatly expands the body of 'empirical' literature available. While scholars have ruminated on the causes of terrorism for centuries, only recently has much empirical work been done in interviewing or surveying terrorists (see Atran, 2010; Merari and Friedland, 1985). This is not surprising. Terrorists are hard to find, don't want to be studied, and are likely to deceive when studied. Additionally, there are the imagined or real ethical issues that lead misguided Institutional Review Boards to ban various empirical approaches (Atran, 2007).

The root causes of violence

The first lesson that almost a century of psychological and neurological research has taught us about aggressive and violent behavior is that every violent act is the product of the impact on the perpetrator of situational factors proximal in time to the act, and within-person factors that are innate or have developed over time within that individual. These within-person factors, in turn, are the products of innate predispositions and socialization experiences dependent on the environmental context in which the person grew up. Consequently, environmental factors such as poverty or perceptions of exclusion could play two quite different roles in stimulating violence or terrorism – one role as a precipitator of the moment, and another as a long-term socializing agent.

Cognitive/neurological perspectives on social behavior

In order to understand the perspective on terrorism that we are offering in this chapter, the reader must be aware of the perspective on social behaviors that has evolved in psychology and neurology in recent years. Briefly, the human mind is a neural network in which certain programs for social behavior become encoded through a combination of individual differences in biology and individual differences in experience. These programs are typically called social scripts (Huesmann, 1988, 1998). The activation of particular scripts is influenced by situational factors as they are interpreted through encoded cognitive schemas about the world. Emotional states influence these attributions about the meaning of what is perceived in the world and, in turn, emotional states are changed by the attributions. While scripts are often acquired through a 'controlled' (conscious) process, once acquired, they are often invoked automatically. Whether the scripts are followed or not, however, also depends on the normative/moral filters that have been encoded in the neural network of the mind. The activation of scripts, schemas about the world and moral beliefs and their interaction are, in turn, controlled by higher-level programs (typically encoded in the frontal lobe of the brain and the limbic system – see below) denoted as executive functioning programs. These programs co-ordinate the interpretation of situations, the activation of scripts for behavior, the 'look ahead' at expected outcomes and the filtering of scripts by normative and moral beliefs.

How do differences across individuals in these cognitive/neurological elements develop? Individuals differ in genetic and biological elements that influence executive functioning and emotional responses. These predispositions interact with early experiences to cause differential expression of certain genetic tendencies, including tendencies toward antisocial behavior (Caspi *et al.*, 2002). However, relatively independently of these predispositions, scripts for social behavior, schemas about the world and moral beliefs can be acquired and encoded in the neural network of the brain through learning processes as the child develops. Although conditioning by parents, peers and society plays an important role in every child's development, learning by observation (imitation) is undoubtedly a more important process in the acquisition of most of these cognitions that control social behavior (Bandura, 1977; Huesmann, 1998).

Given this model, let us discuss what kinds of environmental variables both precipitate violent behavior in the short run, and mold individuals in the long run to be prone to violent behavior.

Situational precipitators of violence and terrorism

Much of the work on situational factors precipitating violent behavior can be summarized in the statement, 'when we feel bad, we act bad' (Berkowitz, 1993). It does not matter much what makes us feel bad, and the bad feeling does not have to start out being anger. Any negative emotion – sadness, fear, anger – can increase the chances that we will behave aggressively. Of course, frustration is a classic cause of aggression and violence for this reason (Dollard *et al.*, 1939); however, even a vague sense of unhappiness with no obvious cause will suffice. Spreading activation in the neural network of the mind causes even remotely related concepts to be 'primed' (partially activated) by bad feelings. It follows that aversive situations, regardless of whether they are frustrating, depressing, or angering, make violent acts more likely. Why? Because the bad feelings 'prime' violent scripts and hostile world schemas. This increase in risk for violent behavior can coincide with increases in anxiety and dysphoria that are also activated by the aversive stimulation. Whether the behavioral outcome is anger and aggressive behavior, or fear and withdrawal, depends on each individual's repertoire of encoded scripts and the strength of the associations. For example, the daily environments of many young terrorists in which violent scripts can be easily observed and encoded and aversive stimulation is constant, are ideal situations for increasing the risk of violent behavior.

A second well-known fact about human aggression is that we 'enjoy' hurting others when we are sufficiently enraged at them (Baron, 1977). While people who are not angry will halt actions that they learn are hurting others, the very angry person will just increase the hurting when they learn that they are really hurting others. Thus, if one is sufficiently angry at an enemy group, hurting innocents that the group cares about becomes a way to hurt the enemy group. The terrorist whose 'mean world schema' is primed and who attributes hostile intent to innocent others, or more likely, to those who care deeply about those others, can 'enjoy' hurting the innocent others.

Another important situational factor involved in gang violence applies well to terrorism. Associations with other like-minded in-group peers and segregation from out-group peers promote sub-group cohesion and a desire to act for the sub-group and the larger in-group. If the leaders of the group create the appropriate organizational climate, they can channel the anger of youth into violent acts by attending to certain well developed psychological principles; for example, they can make participation appear to be highly selective and honorific, cement in-group cohesion, demand public commitment to act in front of the group which will make disengagement difficult, enhance self-beliefs in the cause and place the individual on a track with no choice points (Merari and Friedland, 1985).

Poverty and exclusion

What about poverty and exclusion acts as *situational* causes of violence or terrorism? Crime rates are significantly higher in poorer neighborhoods (Williams and Flewelling, 1988), and being poorer is clearly an aversive stimulus that theoretically should instigate violence (Berkowitz, 1993). However, an absolute level of poverty across countries and within countries is not strongly related to levels of violence or crime. Instead, what seems to be important is *perceived inequality*, including perceived economic inequality (Blau and Blau, 1982). The highest crime rates in the USA are not in the poorest states, but in the states with the most income inequality. While wars throughout history have been more frequent in impoverished areas, they usually involve a protagonist with lesser resources trying to take resources from a richer protagonist. The highest homicide rates in the world in recent years have not been in the most impoverished countries in Africa or Asia, but rather in countries that are experiencing social upheavals with large income inequality (such as Russia and South Africa). Individuals who ascribe their own relative economic deprivation as 'unjust' are more likely to feel angry about it and behave more aggressively (Berkowitz, 1993). Of course, such a perception of 'relative deprivation' (Huntington, 1968) is a type of 'economic exclusion' as well. In terms of the cognitive/neurological model, if one perceives economic deprivation and views the deprivation as unjust, negative affect will be activated which in turn primes aggressive scripts which can overcome any moral beliefs against the violent behavior. Thus, the violent behavior is due to perceptions of inequality not due to poverty per se. Also, consistent with this conclusion is research by Atran (2003b, 2008) and others which has shown that terrorists do not come from particularly impoverished backgrounds. So there is little support for the idea that absolute poverty is either a necessary or sufficient immediate cause of terrorism.

The same psychological research on aggression does suggest that perceived exclusion that is unrelated to economic deprivation could also be a contributing cause to terrorism. For example, individuals who are excluded from participation in a simple group activity (i.e., ostracized) are likely to react aggressively toward the group (Williams, 2007). A simple theoretical extension is that individuals who perceive that the in-group with whom they identify is being excluded – such as in cases of the political exclusion of a minority – would feel negative affect which would prime aggressive scripts. However, whether the script would be executed would again depend on within-person characteristics. Exclusion could neither be called a sufficient nor a necessary *immediate* cause of terrorism.

Longer-term predispositions toward violence and terrorism

In examining the within-person longer-term characteristics that increase or decrease a person's risk of engaging in terrorism, we need to consider neurological and psychological factors that result both from biological differences and from differences in experiences.

Decades of research have revealed a large number of factors that predispose youth to be more at risk for behaving violently (see Berkowitz, 1993; Bushman and Huesmann, 2010; Huesmann, 1998). For example, youth are more at risk for behaving violently who experience stronger rage when bad things happen to them, who have a bias toward perceiving more hostility in the world, who experience less negative affect when they see or think about violence, who have encoded in their minds a greater number of social scripts emphasizing violence and who are more accepting of violence as normative and moral. In addition, research has shown that youth in gangs who are more susceptible to being led by others and succumbing to peer pressure are more at risk for participating in gang violence. Lastly, research has shown that youth who identify more with an in-group and feel a stronger sense of prosocial responsibility for the group are more at risk to responding violently to attacks on the group.

Environmental conditions

So what are the environmental and biological conditions that create these individual differences in youth? We believe that the most important condition is childhoods that include overwhelming exposure to blood, gore and violence in the youths' communities, among their friends and family and in the mass media they see. Through observing this violence and sometimes being victimized by it, four important changes are likely to occur. First, during such childhoods, youth become emotionally habituated to violence through repeated exposures and these stimuli no longer produce the negative emotional reactions they once did. Consequently thinking about the unthinkable – the outcome of a bomb exploding among innocent women and children, for example – is not unpleasant any more, and such scripts are more likely to be evaluated positively. At the same time, particularly, if they are victimized, emotional dysregulation is likely to occur, resulting in the type of internalizing problems typically called post-traumatic stress symptoms.

Repeated exposure to violence around them has three other important cognitive consequences for the potential terrorist youth (Huesmann and Kirwil, 2007). First, it teaches them violent scripts. They encode the scripts they see others using and repeated observations make the scripts well encoded and highly accessible. Second, repeated observations of the violence and aggression around them reinforce their views that the world is a mean place. Their schemas about the world and others emphasize hostility and conflict. Such hostile world schemas make hostile attributions about others intentions more likely (Dodge *et al.*, 1990). Third, exposure to violence and aggression all around them makes violence seem normative and acceptable (Guerra *et al.*, 2003; Huesmann and Guerra, 1997). The normative beliefs they encode and later use to evaluate scripts are more likely to be accepting of violence and aggression.

If we want our budding terrorist to be even more likely to carry out a violent act against a specific population, another kind of exposure would also be valuable, according to our model. Constant exposure to derogatory stereotyping of the target population and derogatory nicknames for them ('gooks,' 'huns,' 'dinks') by those with whom the young terrorist identifies – his family, teachers, peers, media personalities and heroes – would lead to the encoding of negative-valenced attitudes toward the target population. This makes dehumanization of the target population easier. Dehumanization of the target prevents identification with the target and reduces empathy, so the value of the violent outcome is not reduced by the experience of vicarious pain. Additionally, normative beliefs about actions toward sub-humans can be employed in filtering potential scripts, rather than normative beliefs about humans.

This process has a very social aspect too. When a set of peers, in response to growing up in a violent world, all develop the same hostile world schemas, beliefs that violence is acceptable and scripts for carrying out violence, the common beliefs are likely to become a set of 'sacred values' (Atran, 2010) that bind the group and promote actions congruent with the values. A characteristic of many modern acts of terrorism carried out by groups of youths has been the commitment to the group and its values that the members display.

Biological factors

Just as differences in peoples' experiences influence differences in their behavior, so do differences in people's neurobiology. Some of the biological differences may be innate, and some may also be the product of different experiences. In both cases, there has been some very interesting research we will touch on here that hints at what some of the differences in the neurobiology of terrorists might be, how the differences occur and what their consequences might be.

In a simplistic view of the brain, behaviors can be localized to lobes and systems: frontal lobes for executive decisions, right parietal lobe for attention and motivation and the limbic system for emotions and memory formation. Physicians and researchers have learned about the function of these lobes and systems in large part by studying what has changed in patients after focal brain injury from stroke, trauma, tumor and the like. For example, patients with damage to one or both frontal lobes tend to become very impulsive, acting on their feelings (Harlow, 1868). From these studies, the inferred function of the frontal lobe has become generally to be one of an executive function able to bring together many aspects of a situation (such as make attributions), compare to past information (such as moral beliefs or normative beliefs), look forward and play out scenarios (activate scripts for behavior and evaluate impact of action) and incorporate the emotional context that is presumed to be at least partly supplied by connections into the frontal lobe from the underlying cingulate cortex (part of the limbic system).

While a bilateral frontal lobe injury would make someone impulsive enough to carry out a terrorist attack, they would not be disciplined enough to learn the skills needed or even likely to have the focus to carry out such an attack. So while lobar damage is too gross an injury to explain the neurobiological changes in the mind of a terrorist, the change in personality from frontal lobe damage does suggest that the environmental influences that make impulsive terrorist actions more likely may change the synaptic structures in the frontal lobe. Additionally, the research suggests that more subtle innate differences in frontal lobe neurobiology might predispose some people more than others toward violent behavior including terrorism. If the executive decision making was intact but not as heavily influenced by, say, the emotional context of a situation, then a person might carry out complex actions that, in a normal brain, would send up red flags and be inhibited.

Similarly, on the basis of prior research, it seems clear that serotonin is a primary neurotransmitter for behavioral inhibition, and those lower in central nervous system (CNS) serotonin will be more prone to responding to situational provocation or emotional distress by acting impulsively and violently towards others or themselves (suicide). At least some empirical research has seemed to confirm this theory (Linnoila and Virkunnen, 1992).

The literature on post-traumatic stress disorder (PTSD) provides some additional clues that exposure to stress and violence produce neurological changes that can make violence more likely. While the connection between PTSD and an increase in violent behavior has not conclusively been shown, there is a trend toward more impulsive and aggressive behavior in those with PTSD compared to those without. For example, Huesmann, Dubow and Boxer (2011) have reported that in Palestinian and Israeli children exposed to war violence, the amount of PTSD symptoms correlates significantly with how aggressive they are toward their peers. There are some very interesting clues about why this happens that can be drawn from animal models and human studies. The anterior cingulate cortex (ACC) is part of the limbic system. The ACC underlies the frontal lobes and sends projections into the medial-orbito-frontal lobes (Posner and DiGirolamo, 1998), thus forming a strong point of communication between emotional content and rational analysis. In rat models, this area is known to undergo significant change under chronic stress (restraint). Dendrites of the neurons in the medial prefrontal cortex, an area that connects to the anterior cingulate cortex, retract during stress (Goldwater *et al.*, 2009). Behavioral (fear conditioning) studies that require a functioning prefrontal cortex show a reduction in extinction recall after this retraction (Garcia *et al.*, 2008). While recovery from stress did allow for a functional recovery, the distal dendrites did not recover completely. Thus, while not evident in rat behavioral studies, there is evidence for lasting changes in the anatomy and connectivity between the anterior cingulate cortex and medial prefrontal cortex as a result of chronic stress.

There is also evidence from human studies that these same areas are affected in patients with PTSD. Magnetic resonance imagery analyses of the anterior cingulate cortex volume shows that there is decreased grey matter in patients with PTSD (Yamasue *et al.*, 2003). This is even true in twin studies, where one twin had combat exposure and one did not (Kasai *et al.*, 2008). Such changes could promote lasting effects from exposure to violence on either anxiety or anger reactions.

One aspect that is not addressed by these data is differences in outcome. Some people can have severe post-traumatic stress reactions from a relatively non-traumatic event by an outsider's perspective, while others can survive incredible trauma without suffering from PTSD. Some people react to severe trauma with anger and aggression while others do not. Many things can explain the differences in response from the genetics governing synapse resistance to stress and regrowth, to coping skills that are learned to deal with stress.

What is clearly suggested by this brief look at stress and brain anatomy is that there are anatomical changes that occur, and that these changes occur in areas at the interface between executive control and emotional impulse. The animal models suggest that repeated traumatic stress, such as exposure to violence, has a more pronounced impact on the connections resulting in permanent changes to the axons and connections. Such a structural change could be evolutionarily adaptive, to decrease the stress response over time. However, the consequences of such changes in a brain in modern society might have the outcome of fostering a personality that can separate emotion from action, and thus be capable of carrying out acts of violence and trauma. In particular, this analysis suggests that the likelihood of terrorism should be much greater in those societies which have had protracted violent conflict over a long period – such as Israel, Chechnya, Kashmir, Northern Ireland and elsewhere – and that it is not root causes like poverty but situations of violent conflict which are conducive to the emergence of terrorism.

Conclusion

In this chapter, we have argued that poverty and exclusion should not be called root causes of terrorism. They are neither necessary nor sufficient conditions for a person to commit a terroristic act. A person commits such an act when there is a convergence of situational precipitating factors (such as provocations and aversive situations), and predisposing psychological factors that have developed over time. These predisposing factors may result from innate individual differences in biology, but more likely they are due to biological and psychological changes produced by growing up in a violent environment (that is, at the cultural, community, family, or peer level). Youth in such environments become emotionally desensitized to violence, more accepting of violence and more easily directed into terroristic acts by those for whom such an act is instrumental. The neural structure of the frontal lobes and limbic system may change. While absolute poverty by itself seems to play no role in this process and most terrorists have not come from impoverished backgrounds, the perception of economic deprivation and political exclusion are clearly aversive stimuli that may have long-term and short-term effects in making terrorism more likely. However, the root causes are not the poverty and exclusion, but the psychological and neurological changes that are engendered through the complex processes we have described and that make some individuals embrace violence while others do not.

Discussion questions

1   What are the key social structural factors associated with political violence, and why have scholars and policy-makers always suspected them as being the primary causes of terrorism?
2   What does the evidence show about the correlation between terrorism and the structural causes of terrorism?
3   Why is it difficult to directly test the correlation between the two?
4   Explain why structural factors may be the necessary conditions, but not sufficient cause for generating terrorism?
5   How does leadership and wider social grievance at structural inequality interact in the causation of political violence?
6   From what kind of socioeconomic background do most terrorists seem to have come? What does this suggest about the role of poverty in terrorism?
7   Which do you think is more important in socializing youth about what are appropriate social behaviors – what they are told or what they see around them? Can you cite evidence to back up your answer?

8   Evidence suggests that youth who see a lot of political violence committed against their in-group behave more violently themselves against peers within their in-group. Can you explain this seemingly paradoxical finding? What psychological processes are involved?

9   Which areas of the brain seem to be most involved in inhibiting violent behavior? What does constant exposure to stress and violence seem to do to those areas?

Further readings

Atran, S., 2010. *Talking to the Enemy: Faith, Brotherhood, and the (Un)making of Terrorists*, New York: Harper Collins.

Bjorgo, T., 2005. *Root Causes of Terrorism: Myths, Reality and Ways Forward*, London: Routledge.

English, R., 2010. *Terrorism: How to Respond?* Oxford: Oxford University Press.

Guerra, N., Huesmann, L., and Spindler, A., 2003. 'Community Violence Exposure, Social Cognition, and Aggression Among Urban Elementary-School Children', *Child Development*, 74: 1507–1522.

Gupta, Dipak K., 2008. *Understanding Terrorism and Political Violence: The Life Cycle of Birth, Growth, Transformation, and Demise*, London: Routledge.

Huesmann, L., and Kirwil, L., 2007. 'Why Observing Violence Increases the Risk of Violent Behavior in the Observer', in Flannery, D., Vazsonyi, A., and Waldman, I., eds, *The Cambridge Handbook of Violent Behavior and Aggression*, Cambridge, UK: Cambridge University Press.

Krueger, A., 2008. *What Makes a Terrorist: Economics and the Roots of Terrorism*, Princeton, NJ: Princeton University Press.

Merari, A., and Friedland, N., 1985. 'Social Psychological Aspects of Political Terrorism', *Applied Social Psychology Annual*, 6: 185–205.

8 Is religious extremism a major cause of terrorism?

YES: Religious extremism as a major cause of terrorism

Amanda Munroe and Fathali M. Moghaddam

Introduction

> One day Mulla was walking near a house when someone fell from the roof and landed on him, breaking his neck, while the man falling was unhurt. Pondering over the accident, Mulla observed, 'One should not believe that the principle of cause and effect is inevitable. A stranger falls off the roof, and it is my neck that gets broken'.
>
> (Nakosteen, 1974: 112)

Sufi stories, such as the one above, have been used over many centuries to help students and teachers question and re-examine basic assumptions. The story above is about Mulla Nasreddin (known to Turks as Gogia NaserEddin Effendi, and to Arabs as Haja; Nakosteen 1974: xiv), who ends up questioning 'the principle of cause and effect' after an accident. We use this Sufi story as a point of departure to discuss the role of religious extremism 'as a major cause of terrorism', but our point of departure inevitably involves a questioning of the meaning of 'causation'.

As Aristotle and numerous others have discussed over the last 2,500 years or so, causation is complex and multifaceted. Using an invalid model of the natural sciences, traditional social scientists have narrowly interpreted causation to mean only what Aristotle discussed as *efficient causation*, where the cause precedes the effect it produces. But this is clearly wrong, because important aspects of the natural sciences are not compatible with efficient causation – think of quantum field theory, for example.

The relationship between complex aspects of human social behavior, such as 'religious extremism' and 'terrorism', are best understood in terms of what Aristotle called *formal causality*, referring to the structure of a process, and *final causation*, the purpose of a process. It is formal causality and final causation that allow us to understand meaning and purpose in social life, but these involve non-linear relationships.

Invalid assumptions about causation have resulted in incorrect assumptions about the relationship between religion and *terrorism*: politically motivated violence, perpetrated by individuals, groups, or state-sponsored agents, intended to instill feelings of terror and helplessness in a population in order to influence decision making and to change behavior. We propose that the relationship between religious extremism and terrorism has to be understood in the context of accelerating 'fractured globalization' (Moghaddam, 2008a), but in terms of formal and final causation, rather than efficient causation (for further discussion of causation fallacies and their relationship to religion, see Burns, 2008).

In this chapter, we adopt a macro approach in two ways. First, we consider the larger context of global trends. Second, we take an evolutionary perspective, giving particular attention to catastrophic evolution (Moghaddam, 2008b). We acknowledge that given the range of factors postulated by Stern (2004) and others as potentially influencing terrorist action, our analysis gives priority to macro processes and neglects the micro-level processes that, for example, Juergensmeyer (2003) has presented from a reductionist, psychoanalytic viewpoint. The reason for this 'neglect' is that reductionist accounts are invalid, whether applied specifically to terrorism (Moghaddam, 2006) or more broadly to human behavior (Moghaddam, 2005).

Situations and behavior

Our argument is that terrorism arises in certain contexts, and we must look to situational characteristics to explain terrorism. The larger context of our analysis is fractured globalization and the consequent process of sudden contact. Particular groups, including religious groups, are experiencing abrupt exposure to out-groups without pre-adaptation, and at faster rates and more often than ever before. Research with animals and plants shows that *sudden contact*, involving the coming together of groups with little or no previous history of contact between species with low pre-adaptation, can result in rapid decline or even extinction of one or both groups in contact. The history of human societies since industrialization and the colonization of large parts of Africa and Asia by Western powers reflect the same trend of sudden contact leading to declining diversity.

Under intense pressures associated with sudden contact in the twenty-first century, some groups and individuals feel seriously threatened. This threat is not only concerned with material resources, but also with cultural and identity characteristics. Groups and individuals faced with surviving in a globalized world are forced to deal with both macro- and micro-level changes that threaten their distinct identities. Individual worries and constructions of meaning are reflective of macro-level concerns for group extinction.

Indeed, our argument is that sudden contact poses threats and heightens group and personal perceptions of mortality. Violence is a meaningful response to this threat. Terrorism is therefore not an inevitable result of strict ideology, but rather a reaction to the perception of threatened extinction or decline and loss of status. Numerous studies have attempted to pinpoint factors that predispose certain types of individuals toward terrorism, but there are rarely extraordinary characteristics singling out individuals who perpetrate terrorist violence. On the contrary, it is extraordinary circumstance that results in radical and sometimes violent action. It has been shown that neither socio-economic status (Krueger and Malečová, 2002), high levels of psychopathology (Crenshaw, 1981; Ruby, 2002), nor level of education (Winthrop and Graff, 2010; Atran, 2003b) are directly linked to terrorist activity. On the contrary, terrorists are often recruited upon recognition of 'their technical skill and sophistication' (Winthrop and Graff, 2010: 32) and their ability to easily traverse cultures. It is rather the *kind* of education that terrorist recruits have undergone, which often favors unquestioning obedience to authority, fervent passion for a cause and a dichotomous belief in right and wrong, that make them ripe for recruitment across geographical boundaries (*cf.* Burns, 2008: 75; Winthrop and Graff, 2010: 32; Zimbardo, 2007: 292).

A very robust body of psychological evidence supports the view that people with normal psychological profiles can become extremely destructive and aggressive in certain conditions (Milgram, 1974; Zimbardo, 2007). In his famous studies on obedience to authority, Milgram (1974) demonstrated how psychologically normal individuals can be influenced by an authority figure to inflict (apparently) lethal levels of electric shock on innocent others. Zimbardo used a prison simulation to show how healthy individuals randomly assigned to play the role of prison guard seriously mistreated others who were randomly assigned to the role of prisoner. In discussing the behavior of American guards at Abu Ghraib prison, Zimbardo argued persuasively that the context created at Abu Ghraib, and not individual guards, determined behavior in the prison (Zimbardo 2006: 274) and illustrates how ideology is used to justify this fatal movement from good toward 'evil'. Ideology can show itself on the small scale (as in social psychology experiments, where a 'cover story' is used to encourage patients not to question certain orders) or on the large scale (as in the case of national or international movements, or in order to justify war).

Thus, from the social–psychological standpoint we know that particular situations can lead ordinary individuals to do extraordinary things. Determinate in this process are circumstances, guiding systems and dominant ideologies. Might forces of globalization, convergence and reaction have an effect on these circumstances?

With this body of social psychological research in mind, we turn to reassess terrorism arising out of Islamic communities. It has been argued that Islamic societies are experiencing an identity crisis in the global context, as Western values and lifestyles 'invade' Islamic societies and put pressure particularly on Islamic traditionalists and fundamentalists (Moghaddam, 2008a). These developments are resulting in a backlash against globalization on the part of Islamic fundamentalists, and a radicalization of even Islamic traditionalists. For example, the rapid modernization in the 1960s and 1970s in Iran resulted in a radical revolution spearheaded by Muslim fundamentalists, toppling the pro-American Shah. Similarly, funded by sources in Saudi Arabia, the rise of Wahabbism and Salafist traditions can be seen as a reaction to the threat of globalization. Because of a resurgent adherence to reactionary interpretations of religion, women's rights have been markedly compromised in some Islamic communities. These are examples of the power of globalization to influence religion, and the power of religion to influence social life. In the following section, we address the way in which the forces of globalization affect psychosocial processes, and how this expresses itself – sometimes through terrorist actions.

Global trends spurring fractured globalization

'Fractured globalization' is a process by which social–psychological needs on a personal, micro level prove incompatible with macro level global trends. There is now virtually no location on the planet that remains untouched by globalization trends. Technological, economic and political forces connect people inextricably. This can be seen in international media and entertainment, the evolution of transportation and the global exchange of ideas. Technological forces in turn affect the world's economic stability by shifting labor sources and moving people. Likewise, national companies have morphed into global monopolies and multinational corporations. Finally, the political scene is being altered, as nations ally in larger and more cohesive blocs of trade and defense. The most comprehensive example of this emergence recently is the growth of the European Union, although alliances such as NATO (North American Treaty Organization) and the AU (African Union) make equally supportive arguments for the case, showing that strength can be found in size and the unification of goals.

At the same time that these macro forces of technological, economic and political con-nectivity reflect global convergence, forcing individuals and entire cultural groups to confront dissimilar out-groups, individuals' personal psychological needs often result in reactions against international pressures that promote similarity instead of difference, and sameness instead of uniqueness. These individual needs, particularly the need for a positive and distinct identity, are highlighted by research on social identity theory (Tajfel, 1978) and subsequent developments in self-categorization and social identity research (Postmes and Jetten, 2006). As global forces promote similarity, psychological defense mechanisms act to protect individuality – one's positive and distinct identity. This can be observed on a social level in a resurgence of local, regional and religious identities that serve to differentiate individuals and their communities from the seemingly oppressive and foreign forces of globalization. In addition to the above examples of Iran and Saudi Arabia, consider the increasing strength of regional political parties who wish to return to local governance and leave the European Union, the example of the 'Tea Party' in the United States promoting 'traditional' American ideals in the face of unwanted outsiders, or the many examples of independence movements attempting to break away to form smaller units globally, such as Basque separatists, Quebec nationalists, French and Flemish separatists in Belgium, or the recent emergence of Southern Sudan. This trend toward the glorification of small, recognizable identity markers can be seen throughout the world.

The incompatibility of these simultaneous occurrences results in internal conflict, which sometimes manifests itself violently. We will investigate this conflict specifically in regard to religion. Combined with 'catastrophic evolution', global forces help explain a salient link between religion and terrorism, connecting the two through formal and final causation.

Catastrophic evolution: rapid and fatal

A final phenomenon which we believe noticeably impacts feelings of being threatened and the resultant resurgence of religious values linked to terrorism can be explained through the concept of *catastrophic evolution*, the process by which sudden contact between different cultures leads to a rapid decline in diversity, including religious diversity. In the same way that plant and animal species have begun to face extinction due to human destruction and the invasion of foreign species, unique languages, cultures and entire ways of life – including religions (particularly, fundamentalist communities) – are being lost in the process of globalization and cultural assimilation. This markedly began with the process of European colonization through the seventeenth, eighteenth and nineteenth centuries. Other examples include west-ward expansion through North America and the persecution of Native American peoples. Historically, migration of human groups was a gradual process that allowed both immigrating and receiving cultures the time to adapt to one another. With the onset of the industrial and technological revolutions and the enormous progress of rapid transportation over the last 200 years, the pattern of inter-group adaptation has changed dramatically.

Perhaps the most telling barometer for sudden contact today is the decline in the world's linguistic diversity. Catastrophic evolution is especially apparent in the vast expansion of world languages such as English, Mandarin Chinese and Spanish, daily gaining new adherents (languages which simultaneously diversify, developing distinct dialects), while at the same time contributing to the extinction of less-spoken languages. Hundreds of languages have only one or a few speakers still living, and by the twenty-second century, only 200 lan-guages are likely to remain, the majority of humanity's seven billion people speaking just ten of them (Crystal, 2000).

Highly relevant to our thesis is the fact that this same process of declining diversity can be observed first, in the worldwide spread of dominant religions, and second, in the impact of globalization and sudden contact on fundamentalist interpretations of major religions. It is thus a twofold process: on the one hand, the spread of major religions, and on the other, pressure on fundamentalist movements.

Western colonization, in particular, spread Christianity throughout Africa and the Americas. Today, many more adherents to Christianity exist in places where people formerly subscribed to local religious traditions. Islam is likewise growing rapidly. In January 2011, the Pew Forum on Religion and Public Life published a report stating: '[t]he world's Muslim population is expected to increase by about 35% in the next 20 years, continuing an extraordinary growth rate that began more than 10 years ago' (Pew Research Center, 2011). Although the world's major religions, like its major languages, have increased the diversity of their expressions through divergent sects and the emergence of new denominations and movements, it can simultaneously be observed that local, smaller religions have decreased in adherence as the major religions (such as Christianity, Islam, Hindu and Judaism) increase their global membership yearly (Moghaddam, 2008b: 107–108; Banchoff, 2008: 6–11).

At the same time that major religions gain influence, fractured globalization and sudden contact is seriously threatening the survival of communities based on fundamentalist interpretations of the major religions. This threat is centered on the changing role of women, motored by technological transformations which mean that 'brains' could now matter more than 'brawn'. Women have demonstrated that when given the opportunity, they can equal or outpace men in education and brains domains, laying a foundation for their progress in the employment market and in financial and political spheres. This is enormously threatening to Islamic fundamentalists, among others, who see their continued power as requiring that women remain restricted to their traditional domestic role. Thus, the line in the sand for fundamentalists in the Muslim world becomes symbols such as the hijab and other 'cultural carriers' that support and represent the homebound role for women.

Our contention, then, is that fractured globalization and sudden contact have created conditions in which Islamic fundamentalists, among others, see themselves under threat of extinction. Their reaction has been radicalization and revolution, as in Iran, as well as terrorism, arising out of a number of Muslim communities. However, as we demonstrate in the next section, this is by no means a unique experience.

Terrorism through space and time: examples of religious extremism and terrorist activity in history

In order to further illustrate the link between the perception of threatened extinction and terrorist action, it may be helpful to remove ourselves from our present de facto conceptions of terrorists and terrorist violence. In the following, we investigate three specific examples of groups who, under threat of impeding forces comparable to fractured globalization and catastrophic evolution, reacted violently with the intention of instilling terror in the opposing group.

Native American groups in 'The American Indian Wars', 1865–1891

One example that clearly illustrates our argument is the case of Native American ethnic communities in North America during the 'American Indian Wars'. Lasting from 1865 to 1891, the American Indian Wars were a slow process of minor battles between westward-moving 'Whites' (generally American citizens of European descent) and Native American 'Indians' defending their territory. In the same way that we witness catastrophic evolution today in the extinction of languages, cultures and species, so the Native Americans in the late 1800s were witnessing a threat to, and even the extinction of, their way of life. White soldiers and traders were ruthlessly killing buffalo herds that supported Native Americans and increasingly advancing on territory occupied by Native Americans. As these two groups encountered each other, conflict ensued.

At the same time that these processes of encroachment and defense took place, the native people clung fast to religion. Powerful religious leaders and medicine women and men in more than one of the ethnic communities had visions and prophecies. Leadership under these prophecies became an identifiable way out around which many people (feeling threatened) could rally. Indeed, it helped motivate Native American warriors for the numerous tragic battles occurring as Whites pressed their way West. In the Plains Indian tradition, a 'Ghost Dance' ritual became widely practiced. Sioux Indians in fact explicitly transformed one aspect of the Ghost Dance – a ceremony intended for peace – into war preparation: the Ghost Dance shirt (received at a Ghost Dance, embellished with designs reminiscent of sacred visions) was rumored to protect the warrior wearing it against bullets (Hook and Pegler, 2001: 107). Apache groups also witnessed a heightened amount of cultish adherence to prophetic religion, which became inextricable from war. Shamans would accompany warriors into battle, would pray before an assault and conducted rites and rituals during the battle, 'for war was a religious undertaking' (2001: 125).

Thus, we witness Native Americans fighting back against an overwhelming oppressor as they've encountered *sudden contact* through *fractured globalization* under threat of extinction (*catastrophic evolution*). The concentrated, deadly (and sometimes suicidal/sacrificial) attacks that Native Americans raged on American Whites during the American Indian Wars could be labeled as terrorism – for it was most certainly politically motivated violence with the intent to imbue feelings of terror and helplessness – and the Native Americans certainly wished to change the Whites' way of thinking about Western conquest and taking property. Under extreme circumstances, drastic changes and fervent religious ascription occurred within Native American communities.

Zionists and British soldiers in the negotiation of Palestine, 1946–47

It is often in the face of incredible odds, under cultural oppression and with few other visible ways out that terrorist-like activities can be observed. For instance, as the modern state of Israel was being negotiated, there were numerous attempts by insurgents (former colonial residents) to rebel against Great Britain during the breakdown of colonial rule. A most telling example is the fervent insurgency launched by Palestinian Zionists, the Yishuv, in the late 1940s. Buildings were bombed, bloody conflicts ensued, martial law was imposed by the British in Tel Aviv (Cesarani, 2009), and violence erupted continually in attacks and counter-attacks, not unlike what news media call terrorism today.

The Irish Republican Army, 1968–2000

Similar examples of insurgencies and counter-insurgencies at the end of British colonial rule were seen in Kenya, Malaya, the Middle East and most notably Northern Ireland, more well-known for its recent terrorist activity. J. Bowyer Bell (2000) illustrates the volunteer and recruitment process for the Irish Republican Army, generally made up of devout North Irish

Catholic Nationalists. Explaining the inseparable link between religion and political life, Bell names it ideology:

> In a real sense, structured ideology is a crucial component but has played only a limited role in the Provisionals' armed struggle . . . A volunteer does not so much learn right thinking as perform rites, acts of doctrine . . . that shape and deepen the faith.
>
> (2000: 71–72)

In Belfast, Palestine and the American West, what we have come to name 'terrorism' can arguably be observed throughout time. Without a doubt, these groups were suffering from the perception of a very real and overwhelming threat. And without a doubt, the ability to perpetrate such concerted, targeted terror was made possible through rigid adherence to an ideology. Psychologically, humans would find it far more difficult to commit such acts were it not so.

Conclusion

We have rejected the simplistic idea that religion causes terrorism and instead explored a more complex and subtle relationship between the macro processes of fractured globalization, sudden contact and catastrophic evolution. Terrorist violence is perpetrated by individuals facing a world of threats who often seek refuge in strict religious communities. These communities perceive themselves to be facing extinction. Islamic fundamentalists are fighting back by taking over entire countries (as in the case of Iran) or radicalizing and undertaking terrorist actions (as in Pakistan and many other parts of the world). From this perspective, 9/11 was part of an effort to weaken the forces that are threatening Islamic fundamentalism with extinction.

Under threat to their way of life, individuals who flock to strict religious communities are often socialized into a rigid ideology, one that thrives on authoritarian systems of governance and black-and-white definitions of right and wrong. This unquestioning acceptance of authority makes such individuals especially attractive to recruiting terrorist organizations today, the 'us-versus-them' mentality increasing the individual's capacity to dehumanize their opponent. Threatened by oppressive factors they cannot control, individuals have a need to displace aggression. Fundamentalist religion provides both a welcoming community and an expression for that aggression. Looking for a way out, the individual moves from religious fervor toward terrorism, finding what feels like a justified escape.

NO: 'Religious terrorism' as ideology

Jeff Goodwin

Many scholars assume that life-and-death conflicts arise over struggles for control of people, land and other valued resources like oil and water. We assume, that is, a materialist basis to violent conflicts. Yet the idea that religion is a principal cause of contemporary as well as past campaigns of terrorist violence is of course widespread. Textbooks and pundits tell us that 'religious terrorism' is one of the main types of political violence, alongside 'nationalist' and 'revolutionary' terrorism. The main piece of evidence for these claims seems to be the undeniable fact that a number of groups that have employed terrorism as a strategy have also spoken in highly religious terms, emphasized their religious identities, and even invoked a religious duty to kill their enemies. Certain Islamic discourses, in particular (e.g., Salafism), are widely cited as a principal cause of terrorism – hence, the widespread concept of 'Islamic terrorism' – although just as many argue that these discourses are a perversion or distortion of 'true' Islam, which they portray as inherently nonviolent. A better conclusion would be that religious discourse is a rather malleable tool that can be used to justify a wide range of behaviors.

The case against religious terrorism

Strong allegations about Islamic (or Islamist) terrorism and religious terrorism more generally rest upon a series of conceptual errors as well as empirical claims with remarkably little empirical support. The conceptual errors arise from a misunderstanding of what an explanation of terrorism requires, namely, an account of why certain states, political groups, or individuals would decide to employ a particular strategy – violence against certain groups of ordinary people or 'noncombatants.' Religion may be central to the goals and self-understanding of states, organizations, and individuals without in any way causing them to employ this or any other strategy.

States and nonstate political organizations have of course expressed a range of discourses and ideologies – religious and secular, civic and ethnic – while contending in violent ways with others. But it cannot be automatically inferred that such discourses and ideologies account for the use of violence (let alone specifically terrorist attacks against noncombatants) by such states or organizations. Instead, such discourses may be employed for any number of reasons that have absolutely nothing to do with the strategic decision to kill ordinary people. For example, states and political movements may employ ideologies (including religion) to recruit soldiers and other supporters; to build solidarity and commitment among those soldiers and supporters; or to signal the general righteousness and legitimacy of their political goals. A mix of nationalism, populism and religion is typically projected by states and oppositional movements alike as they do battle with one another. But these ideas do not necessarily account for the strategies and tactics of states and movements, which can change dramatically over time in response to changing circumstances.

Those who stress the primacy of religion obviously run into some problems when non-religious factors provide a perfectly sufficient explanation for terrorism. First, it is of course possible that religion is being used purposively to mask the real motivations for terrorism. Moreover, as Stephen Holmes (2007: 17) has suggested:

> The problem is not that individuals with secretly secular (personal or political) purposes may feign religious goals to burnish their reputations for purity. The problem, instead, is that one and the same decision could have been taken for either religious or secular reasons. In that case, it is often impossible to tell which motive played a preponderant role. For instance, emotions with a religious tinge, such as dread of contamination, might conceivably induce some individuals to face death without blinking; but so can non-religious emotions, such as the craving for blood revenge. Duty to God can desensitize a believer to ordinary costs and benefits; but so can boiling rage.

One could take this argument a step further. For even if it could be demonstrated conclusively that 'emotions with a religious tinge' did indeed facilitate a willingness to kill and be killed in a particular instance, those emotions do not necessarily explain the prior decision by a state or political group to employ a strategy of violence in the first place, let alone violence against particular noncombatants.

Sometimes, analysts infer that terrorism is motivated by religion without even examining the discourses or ideologies of the states or groups that have employed terrorist tactics. It is apparently enough to note that the two sides to a conflict (or some people on each side) practice different religions. For example, in his analysis of the 'deliberately exaggerated violence' allegedly perpetrated by religiously inspired organizations, Mark Juergensmeyer (2003: 123) cites the August 1998 bombing in the town of Omagh in Northern Ireland which killed 29 people and injured over 200. The bombing was carried out by a small group that calls itself the 'Real' Irish Republican Army (IRA), which consists in part of former members of the Provisional Irish Republican Army who oppose the political accords that were reached in Northern Ireland a few months prior to the bombing. The clear implication of Juergensmeyer's discussion is that the Real IRA is a religiously motivated group, presumably because the Nationalist community in Northern Ireland in whose interests the group claims to act is overwhelmingly Catholic. Alas, there is no evidence whatsoever for this inference. The motives and goals of the Real IRA – above all, the separation of Northern Ireland from Great Britain – are articulated and justified by the Real IRA in a completely secular language. The members of the Real IRA are no more religious (and probably less so) than Catholics who eschew violence.

The fact that the Real IRA is not religiously motivated does not mean that the carnage at Omagh is unusual in its viciousness. Research demonstrates that secular ethnonationalist groups like the Real IRA are just as likely as groups that define themselves as religious to carry out so-called mass-casualty terrorism (e.g., Asal and Blum 2005). Robert Pape (2005) has also shown the fallacy of attempts to explain suicide bombing as a product of religion. To begin with, much suicide bombing has been carried out by secular groups like the Tamil Tigers in Sri Lanka. And virtually all suicide bombing, Pape shows, has been part of broader campaigns to end military occupations or foreign support for dictators.

Even if religious promises of an afterlife may make it easier for some individuals to become suicide bombers, these promises do not explain why such individuals would seek to kill certain ordinary folk in the first place. Religious injunctions to kill designated enemies may similarly render it more likely that some individuals will kill, but these injunctions do not explain why specific groups are seen as enemies in the first place. Pape (2005) suggests that groups become the targets of terrorist violence for reasons (like military occupations) that have nothing to do with religion.

If it is so badly mistaken, what might account for the popularity of the idea that a great deal of terrorism is caused by religious beliefs? I would argue that the idea serves an important ideological function. That is, it fits well with the material interests of those who propound it. More specifically, an account of terrorism as fundamentally religious prevents any consideration of the material circumstances that lie at the heart of the conflicts that have generated so much terrorism. For example, if Hamas's suicide bombings against Israeli civilians are not generated by religious ideas but are part of an effort to end the Israeli occupation, then Israelis might need to consider more forthrightly the justice and efficacy of the occupation. If al-Qaeda's attacks on U.S. citizens are not generated by religion but are part of an effort to introduce fundamental change in U.S. government policies toward Muslim countries, then Americans might need to consider more carefully the justice of those policies. In sum, religious terrorism is a comforting ideological concept, one that mystifies and deflects attention from the actual reasons behind the use of terrorist tactics. This serves the partisan interests of some of the key actors in many contemporary conflicts.

A relational account of terrorism

Are those who argue that religion may be a primary cause of terrorism in certain instances *necessarily* wrong? Or have they simply exaggerated the importance of religion somewhat or failed to make their case as convincingly as they might? To answer these questions requires an account of how terrorism might in principle be explained, assuming that no single cause or set of causes is likely to provide an adequate explanation for all cases.

Explaining terrorism requires a determination of why and under what conditions armed actors (state or nonstate) regard the killing of ordinary people or noncombatants as a reasonable (although not necessarily exclusive) means to advance their political agenda. I will outline briefly here a 'relational' account of terrorism in which social relations and interactions among key actors – states, armed rebels, and civilians – carry the primary explanatory burden, as opposed to ideas and ideologies, including religion. The presence (or absence) and the nature of social ties (whether conflictual or cooperative) between armed actors (states or rebels), on the one hand, and different kinds of civilians, on the other, provide the main incentives or disincentives for terrorism.

We can begin to move toward a better understanding of terrorism by considering the precise kind of civilians or noncombatants which states and rebels (sometimes) target for violence. Clearly, states and rebels do not indiscriminately attack just *any* civilians or noncombatants. Indeed, both states and rebels are also usually interested in winning the active support or allegiance of certain civilians. So which are the 'bad' or enemy civilians whom they attack?

When they employ a strategy of terrorism, states and rebels generally attack or seek to harm civilians whose support or acquiescence is valuable to their armed enemies. These are civilians who support enemy armed actors and/or have some capacity to influence the actions of an enemy state or rebel movement. Attacking such civilians is a way to attack indirectly one's armed opponents. Indeed, the main strategic objective – the primary incentive – of terrorism is *to induce civilians to stop supporting, or to proactively demand changes in, certain government or rebel policies or to change or even destroy the government or rebel movement itself*. Terrorism, in other words, mainly aims to apply such intense pressure to civilians that they will either demand that 'their' government or movement change or abandon certain policies or, alternatively, cease supporting the government or rebels altogether. The religious beliefs of states and rebels are basically irrelevant to these considerations.

States' and rebels' calculations about whether they should employ terrorism as a strategy are strongly shaped by social and political contexts. An adequate account of terrorism needs to specify the key contextual factors that create incentives or disincentives for states or rebels to choose terrorism as a strategy. Most important in this regard is the incentive for states and rebels to employ terrorism against civilians who support violence by their states or rebels. By contrast, terrorism is discouraged when violence by armed enemies is opposed by significant numbers of civilians (or is limited or nonexistent). Rebel movements, for example, that have employed a strategy of terrorism have typically emerged from populations that have suffered extensive and often indiscriminate state repression (for example, in French Algeria, the West Bank and Gaza, Sri Lanka and Chechnya). In these contexts, moreover, there was also *substantial civilian support* for or acquiescence to that repression 'on the other side' (by European settlers, Jewish Israelis, Sinhalese and Russians, respectively). Indeed, the governments that carried out the repression in these cases had (or have) a substantial measure of democratic legitimacy among civilians. Democratic rights and institutions, in fact, are often effective at creating the impression (especially at some social distance) of substantial solidarity between the general citizenry and their states.

When extensive and indiscriminate state violence is supported by civilians and/or orchestrated by democratically elected governments, it is hardly surprising that rebel movements would tend to view both repressive states *and* the civilians who stand behind them as legitimate targets of counterviolence, which typically begins, and is justified, as 'self-defense.' Nor is it surprising that *retribution* for such violence would be directed at civilians as well as at the enemy state's armed forces. For it would also be reasonable under these circumstances for rebels to conclude that attacking civilians might cause the latter to put substantial pressure on 'their' states to change their ways. Extensive state terrorism seems to beget extensive oppositional terrorism, in other words, in contexts where there is *a citizenry with significant democratic rights*. The latter would appear to be a common if not necessary precondition for extensive terrorism by rebel movements.

This also helps us to understand why rebels who are facing an authoritarian or autocratic regime often carry out very little terrorism. Terrorism is much more likely when an entire ethnic group or nationality is supportive of a government as compared, for example, to a small economic elite or the cronies of a dictator. (In fact, all major cases of terrorism seem to have entailed the use of violence against or infliction of harm upon a large ethnic or national group.) For example, the Sandinista Front in Nicaragua carried out virtually no terrorism during their armed conflict with the personalistic Somoza dictatorship, an otherwise bloody insurgency during which some 30,000 people were killed. Civilians who supported the dictatorship consisted of a tiny number of Somoza cronies and a loyal elite opposition, both of which were drawn mainly from Nicaragua's small bourgeoisie. Virtually all other civilians in Nicaragua, from the poorest peasant to Somoza's bourgeois opponents, were viewed by the Sandinistas as potential allies, and indeed many would become such. Had the Somoza dictatorship been supported by more people – a larger social stratum, say, or a substantial ethnic group – then the Sandinistas (other things being equal) might very well have employed terrorism more frequently than they did.

Civilians may support the violence of their states and rebels, and thereby incentivize terrorism, in three main ways – politically, economically and militarily. First, terrorism is likely to be employed against noncombatants who *politically* support – or at least do not actively oppose – one's armed enemies. In this context, terrorism is a reasonable strategy (other things being equal) to weaken civilian political (or 'moral') support or tolerance for violence. By contrast, terrorism is much less likely to be employed against civilians who do not politically support – or are substantially divided in their support for – one's armed enemies.

Secondly, terrorism is likely to be employed against noncombatants who *economically* support armed enemies by, for example, supplying them with weapons, transportation (or the means thereof), food and other supplies needed to employ violence. In this context, terrorism is a reasonable strategy (other things being equal) to weaken civilian economic support for violence. By contrast, terrorism is much less likely when soldiers are supplied by foreign states or nonstate allies or through covert, black markets.

Thirdly, terrorism is likely to be employed, preemptively, against noncombatants who may *militarily* support armed enemies by, for example, being required to serve an obligatory tour of duty in a state or rebel movement's armed forces or by serving voluntarily in a state or rebel reserve force, militia, or paramilitary force. In this context, terrorism is a reasonable strategy (other things being equal) to preempt or weaken civilian participation in the armed forces of a state or rebel movement. By contrast, terrorism is much less likely when civilians are not required to serve as warriors for states or rebels or show little interest in doing so – and may be actively resisting such service.

It is important to note that terrorism is *less* likely to occur in contexts in which civilians have a history of politically supporting or cooperating with opposing states or rebels – which is another way of saying that some significant fraction of civilians has defected from their state or rebel movement to the other side. Such civilians are not simply opposing the violence of their state or rebels – which, as noted above, would itself make terrorism against them less likely – but are also actively supporting the warriors who are fighting their state or rebels. In this context, terrorism would clearly *not* be a reasonable strategy (other things being equal) for the warriors who are supported by the dissident fraction of such civilians. Such terrorism would not only put at risk the support that these warriors are receiving from the dissidents, but would also make it much less likely that additional civilians would defect from their state or rebels. By contrast, terrorism is much more likely (other things being equal) when civilians have not and do not support or cooperate with opposing states or rebels.

The existence of a significant fraction of dissident civilians explains why the African National Congress (ANC) – the leading antiapartheid organization in South Africa – rejected a strategy of terrorism against white South Africans. The ANC eschewed this strategy even though the apartheid regime that it sought to topple employed very extensive state violence against its opponents. This violence, moreover, was clearly supported (or tolerated) by large segments of the white, especially Afrikaner, population. The Nationalist Party governments that unleashed the security forces against the regime's enemies were elected by the white population. So why did the ANC adhere to an ideology of multiracialism and refuse to view whites as such as enemies? The answer lies in the ANC's long history of collaborating with white South Africans, especially of British background – as well as with South Asian and 'colored' (mixed race) South Africans – in the antiapartheid struggle. Especially important in this respect was the ANC's long collaboration with whites in the South African Communist Party. Tellingly, an important, long-time leader of MK, the ANC's armed wing, was Joe Slovo, a white Communist. For the ANC to have indiscriminately attacked South African whites would have soured this strategic relationship, which, among other things, was essential for securing substantial Soviet aid for the ANC. In sum, given the long-standing multiracial – including international – support for the antiapartheid movement, a strategy of terrorism against white civilians made little strategic sense to ANC leaders.

The case of al-Qaeda: religious terrorism?

Let me now try to demonstrate how the relational account of terrorism outlined here helps to explain why al-Qaeda and affiliated or similar Islamist groups have carried out extensive terrorism in recent years, including the attacks of September 11, 2001. Although the violence of al-Qaeda is typically depicted as an exemplary case of religious terrorism, a closer look reveals that religion is not the primary cause of Al-Qaeda's terrorist tactics.

To be sure, al-Qaeda's political project may certainly be described as religious. Al-Qaeda views itself as a defender of the transnational *umma* or Muslim community. In al-Qaeda's view, this multiethnic, transnational community is currently balkanized and violently oppressed by 'apostate' secular and 'hypocritical' pseudo-Islamic regimes, from Morocco to Mindanao, as well as by the 'Zionist entity' in Palestine. And standing behind these regimes – and occupying

Iraq and Afghanistan – is the powerful U.S. government (and, to a lesser extent, other Western governments, especially Britain). This understanding that the United States is the ultimate power which is propping up repressive, un-Islamic regimes in the Muslim world is the fundamental source of al-Qaeda's conflict with the United States. The problem as al-Qaeda sees it is not that the U.S. is a Christian nation, but that it is oppressing Muslims. Al-Qaeda believes that until the U.S. government (the 'far enemy') can be compelled to end its support for these regimes (the 'near enemy') and withdraw its troops and other agents from Muslim countries, local struggles against these regimes cannot succeed.

But why does al-Qaeda kill ordinary, 'innocent' Americans in addition to U.S. armed forces? Why would al-Qaeda target the World Trade Center, for example, in addition to U.S. political and military installations? Shortly after 9/11, Osama bin Laden described the rationale for the 9/11 attacks in an interview that first appeared in the Pakistani newspaper *Ausaf* on November 7, 2001:

> The United States and their allies are killing us in Palestine, Chechnya, Kashmir, Palestine and Iraq. That's why Muslims have the right to carry out revenge attacks on the U.S. . . . The American people should remember that they pay taxes to their government and that they voted for their president. Their government makes weapons and provides them to Israel, which they use to kill Palestinian Muslims. Given that the American Congress is a committee that represents the people, the fact that it agrees with the actions of the American government proves that America in its entirety is responsible for the atrocities that it is committing against Muslims. I demand the American people to take note of their government's policy against Muslims. They described their government's policy against Vietnam as wrong. They should now take the same stand that they did previously. The onus is on Americans to prevent Muslims from being killed at the hands of their government.
>
> (Quoted in Lawrence 2005: 140–141)

Bin Laden believes that it is reasonable to kill ordinary American citizens, then, not because they are Christian or Jewish, but because they pay taxes to and otherwise support an elected government, which makes Americans responsible for the violent actions of this government in Muslim countries (and, indirectly, of governments supported by the United States). Al-Qaeda views ordinary American citizens, in other words, not as 'innocents,' but as morally responsible for U.S.-sponsored 'massacres' and oppression of Muslims in a number of countries.

This idea has also been articulated by Mohammad Sidique Khan, one of the four suicide bombers who killed more than 50 people in London on July 7, 2005. In a videotape broadcast on *al-Jazeera* television in September 2005, Khan said:

> Your democratically-elected governments continuously perpetuate atrocities against my people all over the world. And your support of them makes you directly responsible, just as I am directly responsible for protecting and avenging my Muslim brothers and sisters. Until we feel security, you will be our targets.
>
> (quoted in Rai 2006: 131)

Again, civilian support for oppressive governments – not the religion of those civilians – is the factor that renders those civilians the targets of violence for Khan and his comrades.

Conclusion

We have seen that religion may matter in a number of ways for the states and political groups that employ terrorism, but that religion is not the primary cause of terrorism. That cause is civilian support for armed actors – usually oppressive governments – and the goal of terrorism is to induce civilians to stop supporting (politically, economically and militarily) those armed actors.

The idea that a great deal of terrorism today as well as in the past is fundamentally religious is ideological. That is, the conceptual framework of religious terrorism prevents consideration of the actual material circumstances that lie at the heart of the conflicts that have generated terrorist violence. By deflecting attention from the actual reasons behind the use of terrorist tactics, this framework serves the partisan interests of some of the key actors in these conflicts.

Discussion questions

1 How should we understand the causal relationship between religion and violence?
2 How might religion matter for terrorism without actually causing it?
3 What aspects of religious belief make it prone to violent exploitation?
4 Why might one assume that the 'Real' IRA in Northern Ireland practices religious terrorism? Why is this assumption mistaken?
5 Why do religious fundamentalists place so much importance on gender roles?
6 In what sense is the idea of religious terrorism ideological?
7 What aspects of globalization threaten the continued existence of religious and cultural groups?
8 Why would a state or political group attack ordinary people or noncombatants?
9 Given the thesis that fractured globalization and catastrophic evolution have resulted in terrorism arising out of communities threatened with extinction, from what sources should we expect terrorism to arise in the future?
10 Why did the Sandinista Front in Nicaragua and the African National Congress in South Africa largely reject a strategy of terrorism?

Further readings

Burns, C., 2008. *More Moral than God*, New York: Rowman and Littlefield.

Gerges, F., 2009. *The Far Enemy: Why Jihad went Global*, 2nd edn, Cambridge: Cambridge University Press.

Goodwin, J., 2006. 'A theory of categorical terrorism', *Social Forces*, 84, 4: 2027–2046.

Herman, E., and O'Sullivan, G., 1989. *The 'Terrorism' Industry: The Experts and Institutions that Shape our View of Terror*, New York: Pantheon.

Kurzman, C., 2011. *The Missing Martyrs: Why there are so few Muslim Terrorists*, Oxford: Oxford University Press.

Moghaddam, F., 2005. 'The Staircase to Terrorism: A Psychological Exploration', *American Psychologist*, 60(2): 161–169.

Moghaddam, F., 2006. *From the Terrorists' Point of View*, Westport, CT: Praeger.

Stern, J., 2004. *Terror in the Name of God*, New York: Harper Perennial.

Tilly, C., 2004. 'Terror, terrorism, terrorists', *Sociological Theory*, 22(1): 5–13.

Winthrop, R., and Graff, C., 2010. 'Beyond Madrasas: Assessing the Links Between Education and Militancy in Pakistan', Working Paper 2, Washington, DC: The Center for Universal Education at Brookings.

Zimbardo, P., 2007. *The Lucifer Effect: Understanding How Good People Turn Evil*, New York: Random House.

Part V
Dealing with terrorism

9 Are counterterrorism frameworks based on suppression and military force effective in responding to terrorism?

YES: The use of force to combat terrorism

Boaz Ganor

Introduction

The severity of modern terrorism and the casualties and damages it causes require the state to do all within its power to defend its citizens, including the use of military measures. The aim of this chapter is to demonstrate that offensive proactive military activities – the targeting of terrorist leaders and activists, striking military bases, weaponry, facilities and the like – can be an effective and legitimate response to terrorism. For the purpose of this chapter, modern terrorism is defined as a type of campaign in which a sub-national organization makes use of deliberate violence targeted at civilians to achieve its political goals, nationalist, socio-economic, religious, or ideological.

The terror equation: motivation and operational capabilities

Modern terrorism is the product of two variables: motivation and operational capabilities. When a group of people share similar political aspirations and when they calculate that the most effective path to fulfilling them is through acts of terrorism, they attempt to gain the operational capabilities necessary for attacks: armaments, operational knowledge and experience, special equipment and the like. An active terrorist organization is therefore a product of a motivated group with the means to perpetrate acts of terrorism. The terror equation is thus a function of two variables: motivation multiplied by capability (Ganor, 2005). The same equation can be used to understand the goals of counterterrorism. Terrorist attacks can be prevented by either reducing the organization's capabilities or by reducing the perpetrators' motivation. Reducing one of the variables to nil can seemingly prevent terrorist attacks from taking place altogether. Thus, even if a group is motivated, but lacks operational capabilities, terrorist attacks will not occur. The opposite is also true: when a terrorist organization has the capability but its members and leaders are unmotivated, an attack will not take place.

In this chapter, we will examine the question of whether counterterrorism frameworks based on proactive activity and military force, such as targeted killings, military strikes on the terrorist's bases, facilities weaponry and the like, are effective in responding to terrorism (Shultz and Vogt, 2003). This question deals with one of the two variables in the terror equation, namely, counterterrorism operations intended to reduce the terrorist organization's operational capabilities. The nature of such activities dictates they are operational and offensive activities (proactive or reactive operations of the state's military forces, security services and police) against terrorists, aimed to disrupt the organization, attack its leaders and commanders, its members, facilities, resources and its general ability to continue perpetrating attacks. Offensive operations of this kind are one of several components in the strategy of counterterrorism (Ganor, 2005). It should not be regarded as the single means of the state to confront terrorism, and in many cases, not even the primary tool of counterterrorism policy. A well-designed strategy to combat terrorism includes as its primary focus the intelligence effort – collecting and processing basic and tactical information on the terrorist organization (Charters, 1991). This information is used both defensively (through knowledge of the intentions and modi operandi of the terrorist organization), and offensively (knowledge of its bases and resources as well as its various organizational functions).

Another component of the state's counterterrorism strategy is deterrence – the body of actions and signals the state communicates to the terrorist organization in order to change its cost–benefit calculations and cause it to refrain from attacks for fear of harsh reprisals. The third component involves operational-offensive activities against the terrorist organization. These activities are designed to undermine the terrorist organization's ability to perpetrate attacks (Kilcullen, 2005). Together with these three components of combating terrorism, there is another component to countering terrorism, namely the attempt to reduce the motivation to perpetrate attacks and the instrumental motives for terrorism while systematically dealing with the root causes behind the activities of terrorists and terrorist organizations.

Proactive and reactive action

Operational offensive activity can be divided into two types: proactive and reactive action. Reactive action is an offensive operational action usually taken after brutal and deadly terrorist attacks in the state and constitutes an immediate or late response to terrorist attacks (Guiora, 2007). Proactive offensive activities are meant to disrupt future attacks through offensive operational means, usually based on prior intelligence or an educated estimation of a terrorist organization's intent. At times, it is difficult to tell these two types of operations apart due to lack of accurate information on the considerations facing decision makers prior to executing the operational activities, their tendency to claim their actions are preventative and proactive, and their reluctance to present it as a retaliatory act of reprisal. Decision makers avoid referring to their offensive actions as reactive action because of the negative connotations this type of activity raises and due to the perception that retaliatory action leads to a 'cycle of violence' in which a violent action by one side is then followed by a violent counter-action from the other, making both sides equally responsible for any escalation (Wilkinson, 2001/2006/2011). The reasons for proactive, pre-emptive offensive action are more easily accepted by global public opinion and the connotations it entails are naturally more positive. In other words, it is difficult for a casual observer to determine whether an offensive operation is a reactive-retaliatory action or a preventative pre-emptive action.

As for offensive reprisal actions, despite criticism against it, it is a necessity born of the characteristics and balance of power within modern democratic states. Paradoxically, democracies are more likely to be deterministically forced to take offensive retaliatory action in response to terrorist attacks on their territory than non-democratic countries. This process is part of the 'democratic dilemma' and is rooted in the democratic regime's dependence on the public will, its authority drawn from the 'social contract' with the people and its commitment to defend the life and limb of its citizens. The democratic government is therefore more sensitive to public opinion and strives to satisfy the people's expectations. For this reason, democratic governments find it difficult to turn the other cheek following severe terrorist attacks. The elected leadership is pushed to make retaliatory reprisals to prove to the public and constituency that it takes all possible measures to defend the population. Facing severe terrorist attacks with restraint might be viewed as a weakness. When accompanied by criticism from political opposition who present the lack of response as hesitation or as a failing policy, the government can do little but commit itself to reactive offensive actions. In a sense, the results of the offensive action are secondary (so long as it does not cause escalation) and its primary objective is to respond to public demand and, if possible, to deter the enemy. The government takes reactive offensive action following popular demand and sometimes following decision-makers' perception of what the public expects of them, a perception not necessarily grounded in reality.

However, offensive actions taken by the state are often not reactive and not meant to be a reprisal for attacks, but proactive pre-emptive activities meant to foil terrorist attacks before they come to fruition. A country under the threat of terrorism (any country and certainly democratic countries) can ill afford to passively rest on its laurels when confronting this phenomenon. As the severity of terrorism rises, with increasing numbers of potential victims, so does the need to foil attacks prior to their execution. The escalation of terrorist attacks requires a greater disruptive effort. When a series of attacks, such as 9/11, can cause the death of thousands and billions of dollars in financial damages, states can no longer afford the risk of suffering these attacks, and where the intelligence and operational capabilities are available they will strive to take proactive and disruptive action as early as possible.

Therefore, the question of whether counterterrorism frameworks based on proactive activity and military force are effective in responding to terrorism should be divided into two secondary questions: is there a need for proactive actions in combating terrorism? And is such action effective or does it constitute a false economy?

Proactive offensive activity takes place at one of the stages preceding the attack, from the initiative stage, through planning, recruiting, training, preparing and finally transporting to the intended destination. The offensive action in this case may be directed at the perpetrators of the planned attack or against any link in the chain of planning, preparing and executing the attack – intelligence gatherers, recruiters, leaders, commanders, operators who prepare the weapons and explosives and the like. Targeted disruptive operations intended to kill or apprehend one of these elements may prevent the execution of the attack. Disruptive proactive action is, therefore, vital to thwarting concrete terrorist attacks when based on tactical intelligence, but the importance of proactive disruptive action is multiplied when confronting suicide attacks.

The success of a suicide attack is assured once the suicide bomber leaves their base towards the target. Unlike other terrorist modi operandi which can be thwarted by increasing security measures, erecting checkpoints, increasing police and defensive activities, in the case of a suicide attack, even if security forces have detailed intelligence enabling the attacker's location and even if security personnel manages to reach them before they arrive at their intended target, once the suicide bomber realizes they have been compromised, they will detonate their explosive charge and harm innocent bystanders. It is very uncommon that a terrorist determined to commit suicide as part of the attack will turn themselves over to authorities or surrender. The only way to stop a suicide bomber and foil the attack is by arresting them or attacking them or another vital part of the terrorist network prior to their embarkation on the mission. Therefore, in cases of confronting suicide attacks, a proactive offensive activity is not only a vital or important tool in the arsenal of counterterrorism, but the exclusive means to thwart such attacks and save innocent lives.

The cost–benefit calculations of employing force

For offensive proactive operations to be effective and to benefit the state, it is important to pay attention to the following repercussions that one can expect while taking these measures.

Foiling the planned attack

The offensive operation should seriously damage a main link in the attack's chain of execution, such as by eliminating an operative with unique know-how on setting explosives, in possession of technological skills critical to the organization or having other unique operational capabilities, or by causing sufficient damage to the organization's bases or speciality armaments and equipment. The offensive operation aims to foil, disrupt or postpone the terrorist attack.

Disrupting the routine and operational activities of the organization

The offensive operation ought to deter the organization's members and leaders from continuing to commit acts of terrorism due to its boldness, modus operandi or by illustrating the state's intelligence, operational or technological superiority. The operation should not increase the organization members' motivation to avenge and should not motivate others to join a terrorist organization or to volunteer to take part in terrorist attacks.

The boomerang effect

The operation might create a boomerang effect leading to new terrorist initiatives, to escalation in the type and modus operandi of attacks or to rushing the planned attack to its execution. An example of a 'boomerang attack' is Hezbollah's bombing of the Israeli embassy in Buenos Aires a few weeks after Hezbollah's secretary general, Abass Musawi, was killed by Israel in 1992. The planners of the operation should take into consideration in their cost–benefit calculation the boomerang effect, but this possible effect is not a sufficient reason by itself to avoid proactive offensive actions, since reprisal attacks are not necessarily more severe in scope or cause greater mortality than the original foiled attack. It also should be noted that the boomerang effect will not take place if the limiting factor of the number of the terrorist attacks conducted by the organization is their operational capability. In that case, the raising of the motivation will not bring about a higher number of terrorist attacks (Ganor, 2008).

Entanglement with other terrorist organizations and with foreign military forces

In calculating the effectiveness of a proactive offensive attack, one should take into account at the planning stage the possibility that the operation will go awry and the military force in the field will find itself under fire, pinned down or captured. In addition, there is a possibility of the operation being uncovered at a certain stage which would lead to the armed intervention of other terrorist organizations, militias or paramilitary forces, as well as supportive states. An asymmetric conflict under these circumstances can quickly escalate into a full-scale war between armies and sovereign nations.

Repercussions of the operation in the local and international arena

It should be noted that even if the offensive proactive operation was successful and its execution flawless, exposing the state's involvement in the operation (especially if it trespassed on foreign territory), may bring about a deterioration of the state's international status and undermine its relations with its neighbours or with other nations. On the other hand, bold and successful offensive operations may whet the international public's imagination and strengthen the country's image.

Effect on the morale of the organization's members, their supporters and the state's own citizens

Modern terrorism is a form of psychological warfare in which a terrorist organization attempts to terrorize the country's population (Schmid, 2006). Proactive offensive action is meant, among other things, to demoralize the organization's operatives and supporters, while at the same time to strengthen the morale of the state's citizens and strengthen solidarity and psychological stamina against further attacks. However, if the offensive operation leads to boomerang attacks, it might deteriorate the public's morale.

Intelligence dilemmas

In the overall calculation of the cost of the operation, the possibility that the operation may expose the source of the information necessary for the planning and execution of the operation should be taken into account. Proactive offensive operations rely heavily on sensitive, specific and up-to-date intelligence. Such accurate information is available only through a small number of sensitive and closely guarded intelligence assets. In many cases following an effective offensive operation, terrorist organizations engage in an extensive attempt to expose informants and spies in their ranks. Sometimes this activity results in the death of alleged collaborators who, in hindsight, are revealed to have had no relation to the operation or to the state's intelligence services.

These are some of the main calculations to be made when examining the effectiveness of proactive offensive activity. However, it should be noted that operations that seem effective in the short term may prove to be ineffective or even damaging in the medium and long term. Effectiveness should always be evaluated in reference to the goals of the operation, both tactical and strategic. Put simply, the planned military operation should bring the attacking side closer to achieving its goals. Effectiveness is thus calculated on a scale which measures the achievement of the military goals of the perpetrator. It is therefore based on the rationality of the attacking side who calculate the costs and benefits of different alternatives and choose the alternative which maximizes the benefits whilst minimizing the costs. Moreover, the attempt to evaluate the effectiveness of a proactive offensive operation before its implementation is difficult and problematic, since such an evaluation relies on incomplete intelligence, suffering from many unknown variables and of uncertain credibility.

Legality and morality

Another issue relating to the undertaking of proactive offensive operations is the legality and morality of these operations. The issue of morality is the very heart of the definition of modern terrorism: does the modern terrorist battlefield fall within the legal or the military realm? Should the operational treatment of the terrorist phenomenon be attempted with military means or police measures? Treating terrorism as a criminal activity, requiring the use of policing measures, casts doubt on the legality and morality of using deadly force during an offensive operation, even when such action is pre-emptive in nature. In addition, as Brian Jenkins explains:

> if we look at terrorism as a crime, we will need to gather evidence, arrest the criminals, and put them on trial. This approach provokes problems of international cooperation and is not a suitable response for acts of terrorism perpetrated by a distant organization or a country involved in terrorism. In contrast, if we approach terrorism as warfare, we can be less concerned with the aspect of individual guilt, and an approximate assessment of guilt and intelligence is sufficient. The focus is not on a single perpetrator, but rather on proper identification of the enemy.
>
> (Quoted in Ganor, 2005)

However, treating the terrorist phenomenon as a military campaign legitimizes pre-emptive operations as a legitimate disruptive measure constituting an act of self-defence. The limitations and obligations which apply to the initiators of a military proactive offensive operation are markedly different from the limitations imposed on crime fighting. Even if the use of deadly force during a military counterterrorism campaign is sometimes legitimate, it is still not without limitations and obligations. A state making use of offensive operations (especially if the operation involves the use of deadly force such as in the case on targeted killings – the use of selective offensive strikes aimed against a leader or an activist of a terrorist organization) must observe the following principles: the target must be legitimate, that is to say, a terrorist involved in the execution of attacks (and not a political operative uninvolved in attacks) or an installation used by the terrorist organization in its military-terrorist activities. The offensive action should be aimed at thwarting concrete and future attacks or disrupting the organization's activities, making it difficult for it to organize attacks. The offensive operation must also be carried out using legal weapons and tactics within the framework of Humanitarian Law and the Geneva Conventions, and while attempting to reduce collateral damage to a minimum.

Finally, when performing specific offensive activity (such as targeted killings), the use of deadly force must be considered only as a last resort when lacking the alternative of capture. Despite this, it must be noted that a state facing the threat of terrorism has an inherent and legitimate right to self-defence when confronting terrorism and the right to take all necessary measures, including proactive offensive operations, in defending the lives, well-being and safety of its citizens. It should also be noted that the issue of the morality of the proactive offensive operation is dependent of the issue of effectiveness, since the more an offensive action is seen as illegitimate or illegal and generates international criticism, the more its effectiveness will be undermined by the cost the state will incur by it.

Conclusion

In conclusion, in answering the question of whether counterterrorism frameworks based on proactive activity and military force are effective in responding to terrorism, it can be determined that offensive military measures are an important part of the war on terror, and in some cases, such as the case of suicide attacks, the proactive offensive operation is a vital if not an exclusive component in thwarting these attacks. This becomes a duty, a moral obligation based on the right to self-defence of a society assaulted by terrorism. However, the right and duty to make use of proactive offensive measures in order to foil terrorist attacks does not exempt the state confronting terrorism from its obligation to deploy offensive military measures only as a last resort, in proportion with the threat and in accordance with humanitarian law. To ensure the effectiveness of the offensive operation it must be proactive and pre-emptive, rather than reactive and retaliatory. The action must be based on accurate, credible and up-to-date intelligence. Concrete goals must be set and targets must be carefully chosen. The most appropriate modus operandi must be adapted to the goals set and decision-making processes and rules of engagement must adhere to international humanitarian law. Above all, one should remember that despite the need and sometimes the urgency to make use of proactive offensive military measures to foil concrete terrorist attacks, when the offensive operation achieves its goals and reduces the scale of attacks, it only buys the state necessary time to attend to the motivation behind terrorism.

NO: Wars on terror – learning the lessons of failure

Paul Rogers

Introduction

This chapter examines the assertion that the primary means for countering terrorism are by suppression of the threat, especially using military force. In this context, the chapter places emphasis on sub-state terrorism. It does so while recognizing that the great majority of terrorist actions have been perpetrated by states against their own populations or against populations that they control (see Jackson *et al.*, 2010). Such actions may include prisoner abuse, torture, the use of death squads, direct military assaults on unarmed populations and many other forms of terror. The responsibility to protect may, in some circumstances, involve transnational action to prevent such state terrorism. This may involve the suppression of the state authorities responsible for such terror, and bringing to trial those held responsible for state terrorism. It may involve the use of military force in the pursuit of such aims. The analysis of such processes may be singularly important but is beyond the scope of this chapter.

The aim here is initially to examine the impact of the most significant recent example of the use of suppression and military force as a counterterrorism framework against a sub-state actor – the response to the 9/11 atrocities and the subsequent 'war on terror'. This critical perspective will then be extended to the more general argument against responding to terrorism with vigorous military force. Finally, some general conclusions will then be drawn in relation to the security issues that are likely to prove dominant in the coming decades.

Responding to 9/11

The destruction of the World Trade Center and the attack on the Pentagon were visceral in their impact on the United States. This was especially so under the Bush administration because it had embraced the concept of the *New American Century* in which America's values and its political and economic systems would serve as worldwide models for a peaceful twenty-first century.

In the immediate aftermath of the attacks there were some analysts who warned against a large-scale military response to the atrocities, especially in the form of intended regime termination in Afghanistan and Iraq (Elworthy and Rogers, 2001). Such views contended that elevating the response to a 'war on terror' would prove to be of lasting value to the al-Qaeda movement, because such action would suggest that al-Qaeda had the status of a major transnational terrorist endeavor that could be controlled only through robust and extensive military action. An alternative approach would see the movement as a transnational criminal endeavor intent on mass murder. Given that those directly involved in the attacks had killed themselves, the aim would therefore have been to bring the leadership of the movement to justice, preferably through an internationally established court.

Thus, al-Qaeda would not be seen as an enemy worth fighting by traditional military means but as a common criminal entity. This was in direct contrast to the al-Qaeda self-perception, with its origins in the 1980s war against the Soviet occupation of Afghanistan (Burke, 2007) which embraced the narrative that the Soviet Union had been crippled by that endeavor. Thus, antecedents of al-Qaeda had brought down a superpower, and could seek to do the same by attracting US and other western military forces into the region where, in due course, they would be worn down by guerrilla warfare. 'In due course' could mean a matter of decades, since al-Qaeda is an unusual transnational revolutionary movement in that it has an eschatological dimension – its leadership sees its ambitions to create a new kind of Islamist Caliphate as stretching beyond this life – over many decades, if not a century (Lawrence, 2005).

Nevertheless, the Bush administration and some close allies – especially Britain, Italy and Spain – were intent on pursuing a military campaign with great vigor, first, with the termination of the Taliban regime and the destruction of al-Qaeda in Afghanistan towards the end of 2001, and then the termination of the Saddam Hussein regime in Iraq in March/April 2003. Whether such a military response proved effective can be measured against the individual war aims in Afghanistan and Iraq and comparing them with the outcomes in both countries as well as the wider impact on the al-Qaeda movement.

War aims

The aims for the first phase of the war were the termination of the Taliban regime and destruction of the center of the al-Qaeda movement in its training camps and other centers in southern and eastern Afghanistan. The US avoided an immediate and large-scale occupation. It embarked instead on a short and intense military campaign that combined heavy use of air power and the deployment of Special Forces against the Taliban, combined with the rapid re-arming and re-supplying of the Northern Alliance of warlords that had previously been in retreat from the Taliban in the Afghan civil war.

By December 2001, the Taliban regime had melted away, albeit with most of its military forces and their weapons intact, and the al-Qaeda paramilitaries had largely dispersed from their camps, many of them crossing over into northwest Pakistan (Rashid, 2010). By the time of the 2002 State of the Union Address to both Houses of Congress, President George W.

Bush could point to a highly successful operation in Afghanistan, while extending the war on terror to an 'axis of evil' of which the main components were the rogue states of Iraq, Iran and Afghanistan.

By the early months of 2002, there was confidence within the administration that the Taliban problem was over and that the al-Qaeda movement had suffered a serious and potentially fatal blow. There was an expectation that as the United States moved towards regime termination in Iraq, the burden of supporting post-war peace-building in Afghanistan would be borne mainly by the Europeans. In due course, Afghanistan was confidently expected to make the transition to a pro-Western peaceful society. Furthermore, there would be two additional and valuable outcomes. One was that the United States and its coalition partners would maintain a valuable military presence in a geopolitically important state.

The second outcome is related to this, namely, the basing agreements concluded with Central Asian republics at the start of the war. Some of these could be maintained and would substantially increase US influence in Central Asia. Given the oil and gas reserves of the region, and the influence of Russia and China, this was an extraordinarily useful bonus to the war. In short, US political and military influence in a singularly important part of the world had been enhanced in a manner that was thoroughly useful in the pursuit of the New American Century, and it was in this context that the termination of the Saddam Hussein regime in Iraq was implemented in early 2003. Less than a month after that, President Bush made his 'mission accomplished' speech on the flight deck of the aircraft carrier *USS Abraham Lincoln*. While not claiming that the war was over, he was confident that Iraq would make a successful transition away from the status of a rogue state. The insurgency and complex set of intercommunal conflicts that subsequently developed have been put down to a serious lack of post-war expectations by the US Department of Defense, but this narrative does not fit with expectations at the time.

As the Coalition Provisional Authority (CPA) was established in Iraq during April and May 2003, there was actually a very clear idea of what would ensue. The CPA, under Paul Bremmer, envisaged an Iraq in which the extensive apparatus of state-run industries would be privatized and opened up to substantial foreign investment. The economy would rapidly evolve along true free market lines, with a flat-rate tax system and a minimum of financial regulation. In political terms, Iraq would evolve into a pro-Western democracy so that a free-market liberal entity would serve as a beacon for political change across the Middle East. While security might ultimately be ensured primarily by a reformed police and military, the United States would develop several major bases in the country and would retain very close diplomatic relations, including what would become the world's largest embassy in Baghdad.

These aims should be seen in the context of long-term US security concerns with the Islamic Republic of Iran. Such concerns go right back to the Iranian Revolution and the sudden loss of a major regional ally at the height of the Cold War, and were further exacerbated by the traumatic experience of the Iranian hostage crisis in 1980–81. For the United States in mid-2003, the war aims in Afghanistan and Iraq thus have to be seen also in terms of the impact on Iran. Put bluntly, a key outcome of the regime terminations in Afghanistan and Iraq would be the impact on the regime in Tehran. From an Iranian perspective, the post-war region would include an Afghanistan to the east which would be progressively pro-Western and have an enduring US military presence. To the west would be Iraq, also pro-Western and with an even stronger US military presence, while an expanded US Navy Fifth Fleet would be dominant in the waters of the Persian Gulf and the Arabian Sea. Furthermore, improved US relations with Central Asian republics would not just impact on China and Russia but would also limit any future attempt by Iran to increase its influence.

As to al-Qaeda, with the loss of its sponsor and protector, the Taliban regime in Kabul, the movement would lose much of its impetus, if indeed its leadership survived. Furthermore, Iraq would signal the start of a region-wide transformation to free-market democracy which would succeed in rendering the political ambitions of the al-Qaeda movement obsolete. The 9/11 atrocities had been appalling and had required an extremely forceful response, and by mid-2003 that response had proved to be singularly successful. Two deeply antagonistic regimes had been eliminated, a third was thoroughly constrained and there was every prospect that out of the trauma of 9/11 a better world might emerge; the New American Century looked once again to be a civilized and visionary prospect.

What is important to recognize here is that the response to a specific catastrophic attack by a transnational political movement went far beyond the requirement to counter that movement and formed part of a much wider security posture for the United States. Responding to terrorism with extreme force may have been exceptional, but it has implications for a much wider analysis of the means used to control terrorism and political violence. This is especially marked when the outcomes of the Afghan and Iraqi actions are examined.

Outcomes – Afghanistan

By the end of 2001, the Bush administration had as its main international security concern the issue of regime termination in Iraq. Afghanistan was far less significant and it was expected that much of the support for post-war stabilization and reconstruction would come from European partners. Within Afghanistan and in some circles in the United Nations there were concerns that a security vacuum might develop unless a very substantial stabilization force was established. However, no more than 5,000 personnel were deployed by late 2002 and over the period to early 2006, Taliban and other armed opposition groups (AOGs) successfully re-established a presence in many parts of Afghanistan. They were aided by four factors; endemic corruption and maladministration of the government in Kabul; substantial illicit revenues from opium and its refined products; an innate and deeply embedded opposition to the presence of foreign troops; and the informal support from Pakistan which saw links with the Taliban as a means of maintaining influence in Afghanistan.

The combined and somewhat synergistic impact of all of these four factors is an underlying reason for the protracted war in Afghanistan, and does much to explain the rise of the Taliban in the late 2000s and the resultant increase in foreign troops in the country from early 2006. Towards the end of his second term, in 2008, President George W. Bush was exploring a further surge in troop numbers in Afghanistan, and after almost a year of reflection, the Obama administration elected to follow a similar policy, ordering in additional force of some 30,000 troops into Afghanistan during the course of 2010. Taking into account an expansion of other NATO forces, this brought the total number of foreign troops in the country to about 140,000, not far short of the total in Iraq at the height of that war.

By mid-2011, it was too early to assess the impact of that surge, but Obama saw the troop surge not as a means of victory but as a basis for negotiating withdrawal from a position of strength, while tacitly acknowledging a role for Taliban elements in future Afghan governance. The Obama administration made it clear that there would be a declared timetable for withdrawal and handover to Afghan security forces, with this substantially in progress by early 2012, before the Presidential election campaign. Within Afghanistan, as the war headed towards its second decade, the Karzai administration was making it clear that there would be a need for a substantial foreign troop presence beyond 2014. A military operation that initially formed the basis of the overall war on terror and looked likely to be over in weeks, now had the prospect of lasting 15 years or more (Nordland, 2011).

Outcomes – Iraq

In Iraq, resistance to the coalition presence became obvious by August 2003, with the destruction of the UN headquarters in Baghdad and the killing of the admired Director of UN operations, Sergio Vieira de Mello, but armed opposition to coalition forces had started almost immediately after they entered the country five months earlier. By the end of 2003, the United States, which was providing the great majority of the combat forces, was facing a full-scale urban insurgency in circumstances for which it was simply not prepared. Over the following two years, the war evolved into a complex set of overlapping conflicts that included major elements of intercommunal violence between Sunni and Shi'a communities. There also developed an element of violent opposition stemming from paramilitary groups linked to the al-Qaeda movement. This so-called al-Qaeda in Mesopotamia (AQIM) operated partly against foreign troops, but also worked persistently to promote violence against the Shi'a majority.

In trying to control the insurgency, the United States experienced three major problems which together offer some explanation as to why the war became so entrenched. The first is that it proved impossible to increase the size of the coalition forces and the number of states involved, especially when, in mid-2003, India refused to commit a reinforced army division because of domestic opposition. The ensuing war became very largely a US operation rather than a genuinely multinational endeavor. The second problem was the lack of training and experience of US troops in confronting determined insurgents. Imbued with a narrative of an insurgency that was directly linked to the 9/11 atrocities, US forces saw their opponents as terrorists, making it fully legitimate to use firepower on a massive scale, even in dense urban environments, greatly increasing the level of collateral damage and civilian casualties.

Finally, as the US forces sought to learn from their experiences, they turned substantially to their associates in the Israeli Defence Force (IDF) with its extensive experience of urban counter-insurgency (Opall-Rome, 2004). A potent effect of this collaboration was to provide Islamist propagandists with a singularly powerful narrative of a Crusader-Zionist force taking control of one of the major states of the Islamic world. This was made even more potent by two further elements – that the true purpose was to control Iraq's oil reserves, which are four times larger than those of the United States, and that the Crusader-Zionists were now occupying the city, Baghdad, that had been the center of the great Abbasid Caliphate in the early years of Islam.

The termination of the Saddam Hussein regime led on to a war that lasted seven years and, even eight years later, left a country with deep instability. The direct consequences included well over 100,000 Iraqis killed, several hundred thousand seriously injured, at least 120,000 detained without trial, some for years, and four million people displaced from their homes. For the United States, over 4,400 military personnel were killed and well over 20,000 seriously injured, many of them maimed for life, and the final cost of the war, including lifetime support of those injured was estimated as high as $3 trillion (Stiglitz and Bilmes, 2008).

Two further factors should be recognized. The first is that the state that benefited most from the seven-year Iraq War was Iran, which, in the original war aims, was expected to be thoroughly constrained in the post-war environment, and the second is that during the conflict, some thousands of young foreign paramilitaries spent periods with insurgent forces in Iraq. The long-term impact of the existence of this cohort is not easy to predict, but may turn out to be one of the most grievous long-term consequences of the war.

Outcomes – al-Qaeda

Although there was an assumption in early 2002 that the termination of the Taliban regime had resulted in the crippling and dispersal of the al-Qaeda movement, over the following six years the movement and its various loose associates proved to be far more active than in the previous six years. Leaving aside the many attacks in Afghanistan, Iraq and Pakistan, there were frequent attacks across the world. These included quadruple bombings in Casablanca and Istanbul, triple bombings in Amman, double bombings in Djakarta, multiple attacks in Mumbai, Sinai and Mobassa, the attack on the Sari nightclub in Bali, the Djerba synagogue in northern Tunisia and the *Limburg* oil tanker off the coast of Oman, failed attempts in Rome and Paris and major attacks in Madrid and London. There were, in addition, numerous attempts that failed or had very limited effect.

The extent and frequency of actual attacks diminished after 2008, but numerous interceptions were made, especially in Western Europe, following massive increases in funding and resources for counterterrorism operations. By mid-2011, there was little confidence that the al-Qaeda movement had been properly constrained. Even the extensive use of armed drones in Pakistan, which appeared to be responsible for the deaths of many middle-ranking leaders in the movement, also had the effect of bringing younger and more radical jihadists to the fore, while causing increasing anger among significant sectors of the Pakistani political class. The death of Osama bin Laden in May 2011 was hugely welcomed as evidence of closure, and there were indications that the Obama administration might use this as a means of speeding the withdrawal from Afghanistan. It was also possible that the 'Arab Spring' stemming from a broad population base rather than part of an Islamist revolutionary fervor, was problematic for the al-Qaeda movement. At the same time, the movement had already evolved into a thoroughly dispersed entity, with initiatives evolving in Yemen, Somalia and parts of North Africa. Furthermore, if the Arab Spring was to fail to foster an era of emancipation and democracy, a more radical Islamist response could well emerge.

The use of force

The strongest argument in favor of the use of military force in responding to the 9/11 attacks is the requirement of a state to protect its own people. This can be said to apply to any state, with the US response being no more than a particularly tough one, albeit from the world's strongest military power and involving military actions that went well beyond suppressing the movement responsible for the attacks. As has been argued, much of this was concerned with regaining the impetus for the New American Century, including restricting Iran and effecting a transformation across the Middle East. The results have been radically different and will have consequences, especially for Iraq, Afghanistan and Pakistan, that may be measured in decades.

A more general consequence, in spite of these outcomes, is the presumption that methods of counterterrorism that became acceptable for the United States risk becoming more generally acceptable. These include forms of torture, long-term detention without trial, rendition, targeted assassination, remote warfare entailing collateral damage and the more ready targeting of civil infrastructure. If the United States can engage in such actions, then it is less easy to argue against some or all of them in other contexts, whether these are NATO's military campaign in Libya, Israeli actions in the occupied territories and Lebanon, suppression of the Naxalite rebellion in India, or responses to civil unrest in Russia or China.

Moreover, such developments run counter to a core trend towards greater cooperation over responding to transnational criminality, including the use of terror. This trend, demonstrated by the establishment of the International Criminal Court and a series of tribunals, and also by increasing cooperation between policing agencies, is damaged by major unilateral actions by a state either acting on its own or leading a limited coalition.

Furthermore, in addition to the value of sustained efforts to bring terror movements to justice, recent experience in a number of sub-state conflicts involving political violence indicates that responding to the deep-seated circumstances that give rise to paramilitary movements is essential to restoring stability. A 30-year conflict in Northern Ireland involved a wide range of military actions, as well as political processes such as internment. It was eventually eased in large measure by the progressive social and economic emancipation of the nationalist minority. Spain has responded to ETA by many policing and paramilitary actions, but has also embraced a range of political developments that have substantially limited support for the movement.

Elsewhere, though, the experience is different. Russia has not responded to the Chechen issue in this manner, and there are strong indications that the conflict will re-emerge. The Thai government's tough actions against the Islamist separatists in the south has failed to curtail the conflict, and while the Sri Lankan government believes that it has defeated the LTTE (Liberation Tigers of Tamil Eelam – the Tamil Tigers), there are strong arguments that the absence of serious post-conflict emancipation for the minority Tamils will lead to further violence.

Of all the countries that have found it appropriate to respond to paramilitary actions, and what they see as terrorism, with persistent force, Israel is one of the most determined. After 63 years of independence, however, the state remains in a condition of near-permanent war – impregnable in its insecurity – and facing new military problems from missile proliferation, and political challenges from the consequences of the Arab Spring.

The global context

As it approaches its second decade, the war on terror has produced outcomes that are radically different from those expected. Rapid regime change in Afghanistan and Iraq has been followed by protracted wars involving heavy civilian and military casualties, and the al-Qaeda movement remains active if much more dispersed than ten years ago. It is possible that Iraq will prove to be a stable and peaceful state, but the consequences of the conflict will take decades to heal. The worst excesses of the Afghan war may be over, provided moves towards negotiations with the Taliban and other groups are successful, but the overall costs of the past decade have been massive and continuing violence in Pakistan is one likely long-term consequence.

The use of high levels of military force to respond to paramilitary movements has substantial implications for the future. There are now very strong arguments that the key global security problems of the early and mid-twenty-first century will be determined by three trends (Abbott *et al.*, 2006). One is the increasing transnational socio-economic divide between about one fifth of the global population that has benefited hugely from a neo-liberal economic environment, and the majority of the world's people who are relatively marginalized. Well over 80 percent of income accrues to barely 20 percent of the world's population; there has been economic growth without economic justice. This is compounded by the second factor, the hugely welcome improvements in education, literacy and communications that also have the pronounced effect of increasing the awareness of the marginalized majorities of their predicament. There are numerous examples of 'revolts from the margins' (Rogers, 2010), especially in Latin America and South Asia, but the entrenched and radical Naxalite movement in India and sustained social unrest in China are two of the leading instances.

The third trend is the development of severe environmental constraints on human development, especially the likely effect of climate change. This is expected to have a particular impact on the tropical and subtropical regions, with a combination of extreme weather events and sustained changes of rainfall patterns expected to have a profound effect on the sustainability of the agro-ecosystems on which the majority of the world's population depends. In the context of this combination of a divided and constrained world, there is a strong probability that the richer and more powerful states, especially in Western Europe and North America, will deem it necessary to maintain control of an unstable global system by methods which include the ready use of military force – what might be termed a 'control paradigm' or a more crudely termed 'liddism' – keeping the lid on problems rather than addressing underlying causes of conflict (Rogers, 2010).

This is where the specific experience of the past decades, and the more general experience of forceful counterterrorism policies, is so relevant. Given the capacity for asymmetric and irregular warfare, and the likely evolution of transnational paramilitary groups, this may prove to be a thoroughly inappropriate approach. The notable failure of the current counterterrorism framework based on suppression and military force may prove to be an encouragement in the search for a new security paradigm that focuses on sustainable security rooted in emancipation and justice, not the maintenance of the status quo.

Discussion questions

1 What are the main aims of using military force against terrorists?
2 How should victory or effectiveness in counterterrorism be measured?
3 Can terrorism be eliminated through the use of military force? Is it possible to defeat al-Qaeda through the use of military force, for example?
4 Are democratic states bound to respond forcefully to acts of terror against their citizens?
5 Does the 'boomerang effect' exist? Can it be avoided?
6 How can security officials find a balance between the need to foil terrorist attacks and deter terrorists, and the likelihood of 'collateral damage'?
7 Has the war on terror been an effective response to terrorism?
8 Why did the Bush administration extend the war on terror to include the termination of the Saddam Hussein regime in Iraq?
9 What was the relationship between the Taliban movement and al-Qaeda?
10 What are the implications of the conduct of the war on terror for future responses to radical paramilitary movements?

Further readings

Burke, J., 2007. *Al-Qaeda: The True Story of Radical Islam*, London: Penguin Books.
Byman, D., 2006. 'Do Targeted Killings Work?', *Foreign Affairs*, 85(2): 95–111.
Dershowitz, A., 2006. *Preemption*, New York: W. W. Norton.
Ganor, B., 2005. *The Counter-Terrorism Puzzle*, New Brunswick, NJ: Transaction Publishers.

Ganor, B., 2008. 'Terrorist Organization Typologies and the Probability of a Boomerang Effect', *Studies in Conflict & Terrorism*, 31(4): 269–283.

Henriksen, T., 2007. 'Security Lessons from the Israeli Trenches', *Policy Review*, No. 141, Hoover Institution, Stanford University, available online at: http://www.hoover.org/publications/policy-review/article/5859.

Jenkins, B., 1985. 'Military Force May Not be Ruled Out', *The Rand Paper Series*, P-7103, Santa Monica: The Rand Corporation.

Lawrence, B., ed., 2005. *Messages to the World: The Statements of Osama bin Laden*, London and New York: Verso.

Rashid, A., 2010. *Taliban*, London: I.B. Tauris.

Rogers, P., 2010. *Losing Control: Global Security in the 21st Century*, London: Pluto Press.

10 Is the use of coercive interrogation or torture permissible and effective as a counterterrorism method?

YES: The truth about American state interrogation techniques, torture and the ticking time-bomb terrorist

Jeffrey Addicott

Introduction

> When I respond by describing the sterilized needle being shoved under the fingernails [torture], the reaction is visceral and often visible – a shudder coupled with a facial gesture of disgust.
>
> (Dershowitz, 2002)

Since the start of the 'War on Terror', the issue of interrogation and interrogation techniques for al-Qaeda, the Taliban and associated forces in American custody has been a constant source of legal and policy discussion. Unfortunately, both in the public square and in the political arena, rational discussion of the matter is often difficult to conduct. On one hand, the government's penchant for secrecy in protecting intelligence sources and methods is a source of great consternation, and on the other hand, the constant claims of torture as the American modus vivendi by various ideologues serves only to stifle the distinction between opinions based on the emotion versus those based on the actual rule of law.

After providing a brief chronological timeline associated with interrogations of unlawful enemy combatants by the military and by the Central Intelligence Agency (CIA), this chapter will then discuss the issue of torture to include its effectiveness and permissiveness. The bottom line is that torture does work, but the United States has never sanctioned the practice. Instead, America has employed lesser coercive methods short of torture and 'ill-treatment', that fully complied with the existing rule of law at the time.

Definitions

Interrogation techniques are only illegal if they violate an applicable rule of law. Thus, the matter of coercive interrogation must be distinguished from the matter of 'illegal' coercive interrogation. In other words, torture and other lesser forms of illegal coercive interrogation cannot be intelligently discussed without a firm understanding of the applicable rule of law.

By international law and customary practice, the prohibition on State torture is now universal in nature, as is the prohibition on lesser coercive interrogation techniques termed as 'other acts of cruel, inhuman, or degrading treatment or punishment', which is shortened simply to 'ill-treatment'.

Since the creation of the United Nations, the prohibition of torture and ill-treatment are now codified in a variety of international documents and treaties culminating in the 1984 United Nations Convention Against Torture, and Other Cruel, Inhuman or Degrading Treatment or Punishment (Torture Convention). Although the Torture Convention distinguishes between torture and the lesser acts of ill-treatment, the major emphasis is on torture. Thus, ill-treatment is not defined, but torture is set out as:

> [A]ny act by which severe pain or suffering, whether physical or mental, is intentionally inflicted on a person for such purposes as obtaining from him or a third person information or a confession, punishing him for an act he or a third person has committed or is suspected of having committed, or intimidating or coercing him or a third person, or for any reason based on discrimination of any kind, when such pain or suffering is inflicted by or at the instigation of . . . public official or other person acting in an official capacity. It does not include pain or suffering arising only from, inherent in or incidental to lawful sanctions.

In short, for torture to exist:

1 the act must be intentional;
2 the act must be performed by a State agent;
3 the act must cause severe pain or suffering to body or mind; and
4 the act must be accomplished with the intent to gain information.

At the outset, the Torture Convention explicitly excludes exceptional circumstances as a pretext to torture. Article 2 states: 'No exceptional circumstances whatsoever, whether a state of war or a threat of war, internal political instability or any other public emergency, may be invoked as a justification for torture' (United Nations, 1984).

As noted, the lesser acts of ill-treatment are not defined in the Torture Convention. Accordingly, coercive interrogation techniques that do not rise to the level of ill-treatment may be morally repugnant, but perfectly legal under international law. Only the basic legal framework associated with torture and ill-treatment is set out in the Torture Convention. In contrast to the firm requirements set out in the case of torture, the Torture Convention barely addresses ill-treatment. Article 16 contains all provisions related to ill-treatment. Ill-treatment need not be criminalized in domestic penal codes, there is no requirement for prosecution, victims of ill-treatment need not be compensated and statements obtained as the fruit of ill-treatment are not excluded from evidence at a criminal trial.

Having established the basic legal framework for torture and ill-treatment, one can now address the matter of what level of pain in a coercive interrogation scenario would qualify as torture or ill-treatment. In the Anglo-Saxon legal tradition, this is done by reference to the leading judicial decisions and extrapolating of the facts in those cases to a particular case at hand. Thus, while some often cavalierly brand the CIA's water-boarding of three al-Qaeda unlawful enemy combatants as torture, the question can only find resolution in a competent judicial ruling (which has not occurred in the United States) or by means of extrapolation from similar competent judicial rulings.

In the case of State coercive interrogation practices, the leading case comes from a decision rendered by the leading international court in Europe – the European Court of Human Rights. The European Court of Human Rights ruling in *Ireland v. United Kingdom* provides the absolute best international legal standard concerning what coercive interrogation acts would and would not amount to torture. The *Ireland* Court held certain coercive interrogation techniques employed by the British on suspected Irish Republican Army (IRA) detainees to be 'ill-treatment', under the European Convention on Human Rights, but not severe enough to rise to the level of torture. Stating that ill-treatment 'derives principally from a difference in the intensity of the suffering inflicted', the Court ruled by an overwhelming majority (13–4) that the use of coercive interrogation measures known as 'the five techniques' which were used for periods of 'four or five' days pending or during interrogation sessions, did not constitute torture:

- Wall-standing: forcing the detainee to stand for some period of hours in a stress position described as 'spread-eagled against the wall, with their fingers put high above their head against the wall, the legs spread apart and the feet back, causing them to stand on their toes with the weight of the body mainly on the fingers'. Wall-standing was practiced for up to 30 hours with occasional periods for rest.
- Hooding: placing a dark hood over the head of the detainee and keeping it on for prolonged periods of time except during interrogation.
- Subjection to noise: holding the detainee in a room where there was a continuous loud and hissing noise.
- Deprivation of sleep: depriving detainee of sleep for prolonged periods of time.
- Deprivation of food and drink.

Although *Ireland* was decided prior to the 1984 Torture Convention, the definitional language of torture and ill-treatment in the European Convention on Human Rights is identical to the Torture Convention's definition of torture and ill-treatment. To clear up all doubt on this issue, the European Court of Human Rights cited *Ireland* with approval in *Selmouni v. France* (1999).

A similar outcome related to illegal coercive interrogation was reached in the 1999 Israeli High Court decision entitled *Public Committee Against Torture v. State of Israel* (*Public Committee*). The High Court ruled that otherwise reasonable interrogation practices employed by the General Security Service of Israel (GSS) on suspected terrorists could become illegal if taken to an extreme point of intensity. For example, playing music to disorient a subject prior to questioning is not illegal per se, but could become illegal – that is, torture or ill-treatment – if taken to an extreme. Although the Supreme Court of Israel did not classify the interrogation techniques as torture, they did find, as in *Ireland*, that they were illegal, as ill-treatment and violated Israel's Basic Law – Human Dignity and Liberty.

United States domestic law

Currently, torture is criminalized at 18 U.S.C. § 2340 as:

[A]n act committed by a person acting under the color of the law specifically intended to inflict severe physical or mental pain or suffering (other than pain or suffering incidental to lawful sanctions) upon another person within his custody or physical control.

Long before the Torture Convention was adopted, the United States Supreme Court had already developed a string of case law which basically equated torture with actions that 'shocked the conscience'. In the 1952 case of *Rochin v. California*, police had a medical doctor force an emetic solution through a tube into a drug suspect's stomach in order to recover two capsules of illegal morphine. The Supreme Court overturned the drug conviction and held that obtaining evidence by methods that are 'so brutal and so offensive to human dignity' stands in violation of the Fourteenth Amendment's due process clause:

> [W]e are compelled to conclude that the proceedings by which this conviction was obtained do more than offend some fastidious squeamishness or private sentimentalism about combating crime too energetically. This is conduct that *shocks the conscience* . . . They are methods too close to the rack and screw to permit of constitutional differentiation. (Emphasis added).
>
> (Rochin v. California, 342 U.S. 165 (1952) at 172)

The very latest Supreme Court case regarding coercive interrogation questioning came in 2003, *Chavez v. Martinez*. During an altercation with police in Oxnard, California, drug suspect Martinez was shot five times in the face. Blinded and not expected to survive, Martinez was interrogated by police sergeant Chavez over a 45-minute timeframe. Further, Martinez was uncooperative. 'At one point, Martinez said, "I am not telling you anything until they treat me", yet Chavez continued the interview'. Chavez never read Martinez his Miranda warnings. At the end, Martinez finally admitted to pointing a gun at police.

While Justice Stevens lamented that the interrogation was clearly torture, a majority of the members did not view the interrogation as rising to the level of torture. Not only did the *Chavez* court leave in place the well-established, yet subjective 'shock the conscience' standard, they also recognized the parallel concept of measuring the actions of law enforcement in the light of exigent circumstances related to public safety issues. This means that the Court will provide greater deference if the government can demonstrate a justification for its conduct based on the totality of the circumstances. The stronger the justification, the greater the flexibility allowed.

False allegations of United States sanctioned torture in the war on terror

A central tool in antiterrorism efforts in the War on Terror is gaining information from suspected terrorists – unlawful enemy combatants or jihadists (those that do not qualify as enemy combatants) – in order to prevent future attacks. Since the advent of the War on Terror, almost all interrogation issues have centered on unlawful enemy combatants who would be members of al-Qaeda, the Taliban, or associated forces.

Many of these individuals have been captured in Afghanistan, but some like Hamdi, Al-Marri and Padilla, were captured in the United States. The vast majority of these individuals have been detained in the custody of the Department of Defense (DOD) at the Navy Base in Guantánamo Bay, Cuba (GITMO), or Bagram Air Force Base, Afghanistan. Until their transfer to GITMO in 2006, a small group of less than 20 were detained and interrogated by the CIA in 'undisclosed' locations. Currently, President Obama is detaining about 175 at GITMO and over 600 at Bagram Air Force Base. Since the detainees are not lawful enemy combatants, that is, prisoners of war (POW), Article 17 of the Third Geneva Convention does not apply. POWs are only required to give their 'surname, first names and rank, date of birth, and army regimental, personal or serial number, or failing this, equivalent information', but unlawful enemy combatants may be subjected to additional questioning.

The answer to the question of what interrogation techniques were used and whether they were lawful depends directly on the chronological timeframe and whether it involved the DOD or the CIA. Apart from the rule of law established in the Torture Convention, the United States has self-imposed other legal restrictions over the years since 2002. It was not until the passage of the Detainee Treatment Act of 2005 that additional uniform standards for interrogation of detainees in the custody of the DOD were set out. In the main, the Detainee Treatment Act prohibits ill-treatment of detainees. Then, in 2006, the Supreme Court in *Hamdan v. Rumsfeld* ruled that detainees must be given all the provisions set out in Common Article 3 of the Geneva Conventions, including (1)(c), which prohibits any conduct that 'outrages upon personal dignity, in particular humiliating and degrading treatment'. Since September 2006, the DOD interrogation program is now set out in DOD *Directive 2310.01E, entitled: The Department of Defense Detainee Program* (DOD, 2006). In addition, *Army Field Manual (FM) 2-22.3, Human Intelligence Collector Operations* (September 2006), absolutely prohibits the use of torture or ill-treatment in conducting interrogation.

With the 2006 public release of secret 2004 memorandums, it is now possible to establish the DOD interrogation program conducted from 2002–2005. Despite all the negative propaganda, it is clear that the DOD did not engage in torture or ill-treatment. The documents reveal that on October 11, 2002, Major General Michael Dunleavy, the Joint Task Force Commander for GITMO, submitted a formal request for approval to use non-standard interrogation techniques on certain detainees held at Guantánamo Bay. The requested interrogation techniques submitted for approval to the Secretary of Defense were divided into three categories:

Category I:

1 Yelling at the detainee;
2 Deceiving the detainee by:
   a   Using multiple interrogators; or
   b   posing as interrogators from a country with a reputation for harsh treatment of detainees;

Category II:

1 Placing the detainee in stress positions;
2 Using falsified documents or reports to deceive the detainee;
3 Placing the detainee in isolation;
4 Interrogating detainees in non-standard interrogation environments or booths;
5 Depriving detainee of light and auditory stimuli;
6 Hooding detainee during interrogation;
7 Interrogating detainee for twenty-hour sessions;
8 Removing all 'comfort items' (including religious items);
9 Switching detainee from hot food to cold rations;
10 Removing all clothing;
11 Forced grooming (shaving facial hair);
12 Exploiting individual phobias (such as fear of dogs) to induce stress;

Category III:

1 Convincing the detainee that death or severe pain is imminent for him or his family;
2 Exposing the detainee to cold weather or water (with medical monitoring);
3 Water boarding;
4 Using light physical contact, such as grabbing, pushing, or poking with a finger.

(Secretary of Defense 2002)

On December 2, 2002, Secretary of Defense Donald Rumsfeld authorized all Category I and II techniques, but only a single Category III approval was given for interrogators to use 'mild, noninjurious physical contact'. Six weeks later, on January 15, 2003, Rumsfeld rescinded the approval of the use of all Category II techniques and the one approved Category III technique.

The CIA interrogation program came to light shortly after President Bush also informed the public in 2006 that 14 'high value' terror suspects had been transferred from undisclosed CIA locations overseas to GITMO. The Bush Administration denied that any of the CIA detainees were subjected to interrogation techniques that violated international or domestic law. The harshest of the techniques was the 'water boarding' interrogation technique used on three detainees – Abu Zubaydah, Abd Al-Rahim Al-Nashiri (captured in November 2002), and Khalid Sheik Mohammed (captured in March 2003).

In 2002, the CIA psychologists requested approval from the Department of Justice's (DOJ) Office of Legal Counsel (OLC) for 12 'enhanced interrogation techniques' (EITs) which they had modeled entirely from practices used in the U.S. military's Survival, Evasion, Resistance, and Escape (SERE) training program (except for the use of non-poisonous insects). The DOJ reviewed the request and in August 2002, in a classified memorandum, concluded that the SERE techniques produced no prolonged mental harm that would violate the Torture Convention. In the so-called Bybee memorandum, the DOJ authorized the CIA to use 10 of the 12 proposed EITs. Each technique was carefully described in the legal memorandum, along with restrictions and safeguards which required, for instance, the presence of psychologists and medical personnel along with the interrogator.

Later, other OLC legal memorandums were issued in 2005 and 2007. No one has been water boarded (with the exception of US military personnel) since 2005. As noted, the CIA program shut down in 2006. President Obama's Executive Order 13491 issued in January 2009, directs the CIA and all federal agencies to proceed with interrogations 'strictly in accord with the principles, processes, conditions, and limitations [FM 2-22.3] prescribes'.

In summary, while individuals in the DOD and CIA may have engaged in violations of the law in their individual capacities (to include murder and torture), it is a false claim that the United States ever engaged in torture as a State policy. Even the worst of the CIA EITs, water boarding, is clearly not torture when measured against *Ireland* and given the fact that the technique is still used on American military personnel in SERE training courses.

Torture works

Amazingly, some hold the rather naive view that torture is not an effective interrogation technique because it does not produce reliable information. The argument is made that individuals will most likely say anything to stop the pain, making their statements worthless. Obviously, the best way to get reliable information is to treat the subject humanely. But what if humane treatment fails to work? Certainly, if the detainee does not know the information being sought, no useful purpose will result from torture. But what if the detainee has the information sought? Will torture break him? In the real world, except in rare cases where the detainee will not talk under any set of circumstances, the answer must be in the affirmative. The fact is that torture does work on someone who has information. Indeed, recognizing that our enemies in Korea and Vietnam engaged in torture, the very structure of the DOD's Code of Conduct for Members of the United States Armed Forces (see Army Regulation 350-30) realizes that our soldiers will most likely 'break' under torture. Accordingly, Americans in the military are only required to resist unlawful interrogation to the utmost of their ability. Article V of the Code states:

> When questioned, should I become a prisoner of war, I am required to give name, rank, service number, and date of birth. I will evade answering further questions to the utmost of my ability. I will make no oral or written statements disloyal to my country and its allies or harmful to their cause.
>
> (Executive Order 12633)

Ticking time-bomb scenario

If torture is effective, are there limited circumstances where it should be employed in interrogation, despite the absolute prohibition in both international and domestic law? Many influential commentators, including self-proclaimed civil liberty activist and Harvard law professor, Alan Dershowitz, have publicly advocated that torture does work and should be used in the case of a 'ticking time-bomb terrorist'. So strongly does Dershowitz believe in the effectiveness of torture, that he also advocates (2002) that a judicial warrant should be issued to engage in the conduct so as to immunize the official from subsequent prosecution for his acts.

The concept of the ticking time-bomb terrorist envisions a situation where a detainee terrorist has actionable information about an imminent terror attack that involves the loss of innocent lives. The detainee refuses to answer any questions and lawful interrogation techniques yield no results. Government officials are then faced with a Hobson's choice between the evil of torture or allowing the evil of imminent death to innocent civilians. In Dershowitz's view, this scenario poses one of the strongest arguments for the use of non-lethal torture. Of course, given the premise of the ticking time-bomb scenario, one cannot be a centrist – either you allow whatever means necessary to get the information or you allow the slaughter of innocent civilians.

In the Israeli *Public Committee* case, the Supreme Court of Israel recognized that torture does work. Further, if a ticking time-bomb terrorist was subjected to torture then the interrogator could raise the common law doctrine defense of necessity at their criminal trial. The Court stated that '[o]ur decision does not negate the possibility that the "necessity" defense be available to GSS investigators [in ticking time bomb scenarios] . . . if criminal charges are brought against them, as per the Court's discretion'. The Court noted, however, that the threat of the future terror attack must constitute a 'concrete level of imminent danger'. The defense of necessity is a doctrine well-known to the common law. It is a justification defense for a person who acts illegally in order to prevent a great imminent harm from occurring.

Conclusion

With the threat of weapons of mass destruction in the hands of terrorists, the discussion of interrogation is sure to continue. Since the enemies in the War on Terror do not wear uniforms or fight in traditional forms, it is imperative that governments obtain accurate information in order to prevent attacks from occurring. This means using coercive, but lawful, interrogation to get information.

Despite the fact that torture works as an interrogation technique, its practice is abhorrent to freedom-loving peoples. It is imperative that a government based on consent of the people conduct only lawful interrogations under the applicable rule of law as set out in the Torture Convention and as self-imposed by domestic law. Again, this does not mean that all interrogations are illegal, only that illegal interrogations are illegal. In other words, a nation need not overreact or buckle to the shrill cries of political correctness. For instance, when the Supreme Court ruled in 2006 that the Geneva Convention's Common Article 3 prohibited any conduct that was 'humiliating and degrading' to jihadist detainees, the DOD interpreted this to prohibit a non-Muslim official from handing a Koran to a detainee!

In the extreme case of a ticking time-bomb terrorist, torture may be the only tool available to save lives. Nevertheless, Dershowitz is clearly wrong in his desire to legitimize torture by obtaining a judicial warrant for the practice. No civilized nation can legitimize torture. A nation that follows the rule of law must place the interrogator who tortures on criminal trial for his crimes, no exceptions. The interrogator's defense of necessity is evaluated in the light of reasonableness. Whatever the outcome, the rule of law has been followed. Torture is wrong. The wrongdoer was prosecuted.

NO: Why torture is wrong

Robert Brecher

Introduction

Even people who think torture is justified in certain circumstances regard it – to say the least – as undesirable, however necessary they think it is. So I shall approach the issue by analyzing the extreme case where people such as Dershowitz (2002), Posner (2004) and Walzer (2003) think torture is justified, namely, the so-called ticking bomb scenario. And since the justification offered is always consequentialist – no one thinks that torture is in any way 'good in itself' – I shall confine myself to consequentialist arguments. That is to say, I shall take the argument on its own terms. And that is because any non-consequentialist objection to torture merely invites the response, 'So much the worse for non-consequentialism': if a moral theory insists that torture is wrong even if it would save thousands of lives that just shows how wrong the theory is (compare Kant, 1797, on lying).

I shall also focus only on the question of the *moral* justifiability of torture in the 'ticking bomb' case, and not ask whether, even if admittedly immoral, it should nonetheless be legalized (see Brecher, 2007).

My main argument is in two parts: (1) the 'ticking bomb' scenario falls apart when analyzed; and (2) even if it did not, the likely consequences of permitting torture would be worse than the bomb going off. Then (3) I shall briefly consider a genuine case. But before all that I need to say what is sufficient to be described as torture (see Brecher, 2007: 3–6, for why the demand for *definition* is a mistake). Christopher Tindale (1996: 355), adapting the 1994 United Nations General Assembly's Convention Against Torture, puts it particularly clearly:

> [torture is] any act by which severe pain or suffering, whether physical or mental, is . intentionally inflicted on a person for such purposes as obtaining from that person or a third person information or confession, punishing that person for an act committed or suspected to have been committed, or intimidating or dehumanizing that person or other persons.
>
> (United Nations, 1984)

So, suppose there is good reason to think that someone has planted a bomb somewhere in a city; and that it is going to go off pretty soon, maiming and killing hundreds, even thousands, of people. But no one knows where the bomb is – except one person who is already in custody but of course won't tell. Maybe they have planted it themselves; maybe not. Either way, they remain silent. Should they be tortured to force them to reveal where the bomb is? No. The scenario I have sketched is misleadingly simplistic. And even if it weren't, the consequences of torturing the suspect would be even worse than the carnage the bomb would cause.

Why the ticking bomb scenario does not work

The ticking bomb scenario presents no more than a set of highly questionable conjectures; moreover, the more likely some of its conditions, the less likely the others. First, it assumes that interrogators *know* that their captive has the information they need – otherwise we are being asked to approve torturing someone who *may* know where the bomb is; and so to approve torturing *anyone* who *may* know it (I shall return to this). How likely is it, then, that the authorities have 'the right person'? The most notorious proponent of interrogational torture, Alan Dershowitz, offers no more than an unreferenced claim that 'There is little doubt that some acts of terrorism – which could have killed many civilians – were prevented' (Dershowitz, 2002: 55; see also 150) in Israel. Michael Walzer speaks vaguely of 'a captured rebel leader who knows or probably knows the location of a number of bombs' (Walzer, 1973/2004: 60). Unsurprisingly, the literature (mostly citing Israel) offers only anecdote. But just how likely is it that the authorities would have the near-omniscience here that they clearly lack elsewhere, especially as determined terrorists are likely to be careful planners? And that is one reason why imaginary scenarios, however useful in thinking about philosophical problems, are useless as a basis for public policy.

Second, the same uncertainty surrounds the putative knowledge that time is running out. Unless we know (from the suspect?) that the bomb is about to go off, we cannot know what we need to know to justify torture. Furthermore, the shorter the time in question, the less time the suspect needs to hold out and the more effective their obvious recourse to lying about the bomb's whereabouts; especially as they know that the torture will cease as soon as they give the 'information' required and resume only once it becomes clear that they've been lying – unless the bomb goes off by then. And of course, this is a condition of the scenario, otherwise we are being asked to agree to torturing suspects as punishment, not for information.

Third, the upshot of these two uncertainties together shows that the sense of necessity the scenario is intended to engender is spurious. We cannot know that torture is necessary, but only that it *may be* necessary – in which case it also may *not* be. It is only after the event – in this case after the bomb has gone off – that anything can be known to have been necessary. Until and unless it does, it is only (more or less) probable that the suspect knows about the bomb and/or how pressing time really is. So what proponents of the ticking bomb justification of torture are actually talking about is cases where this person *might* know about a bomb and/or that it *might* be too late for subtler interrogation.

Fourth, the argument relies on the assumption that torture would actually work in such cases. As before, the evidence offered is often anecdotal. For example, some people have assured me that they have been assured that torture does elicit the information needed in urgent cases and others that it does not. But I know of no systematic empirical study that establishes its efficacy; while on the other hand, several investigations (see Rejali, 2007) conclude that torture produces information that is at best unreliable and often useless. Two points need to be made. First, torture is as a matter of fact very rarely used to elicit information compared to its standard use: to terrorize, to punish and so on (Crelinsten, 1995). Second, military manuals worldwide, including the US *Field Manual*, prohibit torture on grounds of its ineffectiveness in eliciting information (Rose, 2004: 95; see also Pachecco, 1999: 30; Casebeer, 2003). No wonder Dershowitz's most detailed example (2002: 37; see also 34–36) of 'effective' interrogational torture is this:

> The *Washington Post* has recounted a case from 1995 in which Philippine authorities tortured a terrorist into disclosing information that may have foiled plots to assassinate the pope and to crash eleven commercial airliners carrying approximately four thousand passengers into the Pacific ocean . . . For sixty-seven days, intelligence agents beat the suspect . . .

Sixty-seven days? So what on earth has this to do with any imminent catastrophe?

Finally, the ticking bomb scenario as presented in the literature almost always asks the reader, 'What would you do if . . . ?', and talks about what 'we' should do (see Dershowitz, 2002; Allhoff, 2003; Walzer, 2003). But that is at best silly, at worst deeply irresponsible. Why? Because 'you' would not have the slightest idea what to do – and especially given that the more urgent the case, the greater the level of expertise and precision that would be needed. The torture that its defenders argue is 'necessary' is something that requires professionals, not amateurs; and that is itself a crucial consideration, as we shall see below. These thinkers' blithe neglect of the obvious is an especially depressing instance of the tendency, in discussions of torture, no less than in other 'hard cases', to advocate public policy on the basis of individuals' visceral responses. Of course, if someone is threatening to kill your mother you might try to do all sorts of things to stop them. But that is why we have law, not vigilante (in)justice.

To sum up: the ticking bomb scenario remains radically under-determined.

The consequences of permitting torture

But even if the ticking bomb scenario were not radically under-determined, the appalling consequences of permitting interrogational torture would outweigh the immediate benefit claimed. Dershowitz's argument for legalizing interrogational torture is that 'it is better to legitimate and control a *specific* practice that will occur than to legitimate a *general* practice of tolerating extralegal actions so long as they operate . . . beneath the radar screen' (Dershowitz, 2002: 271–272). This view may be adapted to constitute an argument that such torture, whether legalized or not, is justifiable: because the practice is prevalent and will not go away, and because honest recognition is better than the hypocrisy of pretending otherwise, it is better to be realistic, permit interrogational torture and regulate it. This might be termed an argument about the institutional consequences of interrogational torture: not only will the ticking bomb at least sometimes be defused – a direct consequence – but torture, being carefully regulated, will decrease, an indirect consequence to do with the more general impact of the practice on some of society's institutions, such as truth-telling, non-interrogational torture and so on. These sorts of consequence are indeed important. But hypocrisy can be eliminated *either* by honesty *or* by giving up the hypocritical practice. And Dershowitz, like other proponents of interrogational torture, ignores other likely institutional consequences.

First, as we saw earlier, interrogational torture requires expertise; it requires professional torturers. And the profession of torturer, like other professions, tends to spread. It seeks to expand its own scope, protect its members and so on: 'the very process of routinization of torture involves a kind of continuous and dynamic distortion of facts and events which, in the end, amounts to the construction of a new reality' (Crelinsten, 1995: 75). The inculcation of obedience to authority, the creation of 'enemies', the need to achieve 'results' to justify resources, leading to finding ever more such enemies and the expansion of what counts as information, all lead to the creation of a particular social reality. What a Brazilian torturer is reported to have told a prisoner would cease to appear bizarre: 'I'm a serious professional. After the revolution, I will be at your disposal to torture whom you like' (Langguth, 1978). Once torture was normalized in so-called ticking bomb cases, once it had been made morally thinkable, its use would spread. Here is what the *Economist* – hardly a radical publication – thinks:

> How will the counterterrorist program uphold a monopoly on the use of torture? Investigators of many other crimes – narcotics trafficking, serial murder, sabotage of information systems, espionage, financial scams – will consider their own pursuits compelling . . . Both U.S. and British judiciaries have struggled for decades with the overwhelming ill consequences of coercive interrogation of suspects. . . .
>
> (*Economist*, 2003)

Quite so: Dershowitz has been invoked in *entirely different* circumstances from 'ticking bombs':

> The brief for the petitioner, seeking to exonerate the police officer who persisted in questioning the wounded and screaming suspect, invoked the image of an official questioning a 'suspect [who] has been arrested for kidnaping [*sic*] a small child who cannot survive without immediate adult intervention. The child is being hidden some-where, and time is running out on his life', and invited the Court to refer to Professor Dershowitz's analysis.
>
> (Kreimer, 2003: 291)

In Israel, interrogational torture was quasi-legal from 1987–1999: while formally illegal, a retrospective defense of 'necessity' was available to exculpate torturers who were held to have acted justifiably. All the evidence suggests that in those 12 years, torture increased considerably, which is why the defense was withdrawn in 1999 (see, for example, Biletzki, 2001; Allen, 2005; Parry and White, 2002: 757–760). Why would the consequences of permitting interrogational torture be different anywhere else?

Second, we need to reflect on how potential 'terrorists' would react to the use of interrogational torture. Are there likely to be more or fewer 'ticking bombs'? It seems at least as plausible to suppose that 'martyrdom to torture' would lead to more, not fewer, volunteers. What is known of volunteers for so-called suicide bombing certainly suggests that many feel themselves compelled to volunteer on account of what they perceive (rightly or wrongly) as the enormity of what the target regime has done: Hany Abu-Assad's 2005 film, *Paradise Now*, and Louise Richardson's (2006) analysis both make the point brilliantly. Those responsible for the London bombings of July 2005, for instance, cited the UK government's role in the bombing and occupation of Iraq, with its attendant atrocities, as their motivation. For the same reason, sympathy for all sorts of terrorist causes would be likely to increase: no country that tortures can lay claim to the moral high ground. As a 'senior Pentagon intelligence analyst' puts it, 'Quite frankly I'd have thought that if they weren't terrorists before they went to Gitmo [Guantánamo Bay], they would have been by the time they came out' (Rose, 2004: 72), while even a recent British Foreign Secretary 'warned that the camp was as much a "radicalising and destabilising influence" as it was an aid in the "war on terror"' (*Independent*, 2006).

Nor is that all. Torturers require training. On whom should they practice? And on what grounds can 'we' ask that they 'get their hands dirty' in a way 'we' would not, that they attend, and give, 'Special classes . . . where new torturers are shown what torture looks like, either in filmed demonstrations or even live demonstrations on actual prisoners' (Crelinsten, 1995: 49), on colleagues or on people 'picked up' from the street (Haritos-Fatouros, 1995)? To admit the profession of torturer to the range of recognized professions would require that we recognize torture training in the same way that we recognize, for example, legal, medical and teacher education and training (see Gray's 2003 satire).

And what about the doctors and medical researchers whose expertise would also be required? If interrogational torture is necessary in a particular case, and thus justified, on what good grounds could these professionals decline to use their expertise? After all, given consequentialism, they would be morally wrong to refuse to act for the sake of the greatest happiness of the greatest number. The impact on the medical, nursing, psychiatric and psychological professions would be disastrous, implicating their members in torture and thus undermining public confidence in them: imagine being treated by a medical professional who only yesterday was 'assisting' in torture. Nor is this at all exaggerated, as the recent row in the American Psychological Association shows (Welch, 2008).

If it proved anything, the argument would prove too much. Since doing what has the best consequences is to do what is right, such participation would not be merely permissible, but required. It would become 'our' or 'our surrogates'' *duty* to torture. And since not many members of the public are trained torturers, we have to ask on what grounds we would be justified in urging a moral *duty* upon others which we ourselves are not prepared to accept by undergoing the training required – including 'moral training' – provided, of course, that we do not lack the necessary abilities through no fault of our own. Posner's insistence that 'No one who doubts' that interrogational torture is in certain circumstances justified 'should be in a position of public responsibility' (Posner, 2004: 295) can be turned back against the advocates of torture. Is it not hypocritical – or worse – to expect public officials to torture people if you are not prepared to do it yourself?

Of course, we all of us expect others to do things we ourselves would shy away from: doctors, nurses, dentists, mortuary attendants and a host of others. But it is one thing to shy away from doing what you expect other people to do for you, or on your behalf, and quite another not to be prepared in principle to undergo the requisite training for what you think is a morally *required* job, rather than one which is morally merely permissible. If you really think that capital punishment is morally necessary, that it is society's moral duty to impose the death penalty for certain crimes, then if you would not under any circumstances be prepared to learn to act as executioner, you are being hypocritical. If you think that assisted suicide is a moral right, so that someone or other has a concomitant moral duty to assist in certain circumstances, then, provided you are able, you have to be willing to do so yourself. In that light I offer the words of a professional torturer:

> Finally, I went forward to look at his face and closely examined his condition. I realized that he had lost his mental balance. We removed him from the torture bench and instead hung him from special handcuffs installed on the wall.
>
> (Kooijmans, 1995: 13)

The argument proves too much in another direction too. If consequences justify actions, then why not torture other people beside suspects? Ironically, Dershowitz inadvertently makes the point himself (2002: 36): 'There can be no doubt that torture sometimes works. Jordan apparently broke the most notorious terrorist of the 1980s, Abu Nidal, *by threatening his mother.*' Nor will it do to counter the point in the way Dershowitz does: an act-utilitarian 'justification [of the use of interrogational torture] is simple-minded' because 'it has no inherent limiting principle', so that 'anything goes as long as the number of people tortured or killed does not exceed the number that would be saved'. We therefore need 'other constraints on what we can properly do', which 'can come from rule utilitarianisms [*sic*] or other principles of morality' (Dershowitz, 2002: 8). If rule utilitarianism rules out torturing the innocent because following the rule 'Torture even innocents if need be' has overall negative consequences, then it rules out torturing suspects on the same grounds. As for 'other principles of morality': consequentialism allows for none. That is its point: only the consequences decide what is right and wrong.

A real example

Thinking about a real case allows us to focus on the central issue without falling foul of the entanglements of fantasy. In Germany, in 2002, the police – having collected conclusive evidence from his flat and watched him collect the ransom – knew that it was Magnus Gäfgen who had kidnapped Jakob von Metzler, the 11-year-old son of a banker. He refused to say where the boy was. Knowing that he might be slowly dying, the police president 'ordered his men to threaten Gäfgen with violence to force a statement' (Schroeder, 2006: 188). That was enough to elicit what he knew. Unhappily, however, the boy was already dead. The case provoked an impassioned debate about torture in Germany. There was no consensus. So: assuming a professional torturer could be found, should Gäfgen have been tortured to force him to reveal the boy's whereabouts? My answer, even here, is no; no, because – to keep within the consequentialist framework – the consequences of doing so would be even worse than the boy's dying, as I have argued above. Why?

In addition to what I argued previously, because torture is the breaking of a human being. It is the worst thing a person can do to another, worse – much worse – even than killing them:

> The subject of judicial or interrogational torture is 'broken' when, and only when, he has become so distraught, so unable to bear any more suffering, that he can no longer resist any request the torturer might make. The tortured then 'pours out his guts'.
>
> (Davis, 2005: 165)

The tortured person's capacity to act is broken. And since it is our capacity to act which makes us persons, rather than just instances of a particular biological species – however heavily circumscribed that capacity might be under certain circumstances – the tortured 'subject' is no longer a person. Jean Améry, speaking as a person who temporarily survived torture (he eventually committed suicide), makes the point better than I ever could:

> Only in torture does the transformation of the person into flesh become complete. Frail in the face of violence, yelling out in pain, awaiting no help, capable of no resistance, the tortured person is only a body, and nothing else besides that.
>
> (Améry, 1980: 6)

A society that thinks it has to torture will become, as it tortures, something no longer recognizable as a human society. Sometimes it really is too late to avert a catastrophe: the cost of doing so is too high. And if the response is that politicians or others acting on our behalf sometimes have to get their hands dirty, as Walzer famously argues (1973/2004; 2003), the reply must be this. Yes, you're right: but they have to get their hands dirty by doing nothing.

Discussion questions

1 Why is it so difficult to discuss torture and interrogation rationally?
2 In the case of a ticking time-bomb terrorist, should the authorities be provided with a warrant from a judge that authorizes torture?
3 Is the ticking bomb scenario just a fantasy, and does that matter?
4 What are some of the main criticisms of the ticking bomb scenario?
5 Does torture work?
6 If interrogational torture resulted in saving lives, would it be justified? Or, does the case of torture show that consequentialism is wrong?
7 Should the concept of 'ill-treatment' in the Torture Convention have legal penalties attached? Why?
8 If government agents commit torture must they be prosecuted? Why? What legal defense might be asserted at their criminal trial?
9 Is torture worse than killing?
10 What would be the likely consequences of permitting interrogational torture?

Further readings

Addicott, J., 2011. *Terrorism Law: Materials, Cases, and Comments*, 6th ed., Tuscon, AZ: Lawyer and Judges Publishing Co.

Brecher, B., 2007. *Torture and the Ticking Bomb*, Oxford: Wiley-Blackwell.

Card, C., 2010. *Confronting Evils: Terrorism, Torture, Genocide*, Cambridge: Cambridge University Press.

Dershowitz, A., 2002. *Why Terrorism Works*, New Haven, CT and London: Yale University Press.

Ginbar, Y., 2008. *Why Not Torture Terrorists?*, Oxford: Oxford University Press.

Levinson, S., ed., 2006. *Torture: A Collection*, Oxford: Oxford University Press.

Ohlin, J., 2010. 'The Torture Lawyers', *Harvard International Law Journal*, 51(1): 193–256.

Rejali D., 2007. *Torture and Democracy*, Princeton, NJ: Princeton University Press.

11 Is the targeted assassination of terrorist suspects an effective response to terrorism?

YES: A viable and vital policy option

Stephanie Carvin

Introduction

There can be little doubt that over the last decade there has been a substantial increase in states targeting individuals engaged in terrorist activities. Israel, Russia and the United States have included targeted strikes as a weapon in their counterterrorism arsenal: Israel during the Second Intifada, Russia in its struggle against the Chechen fighters and the United States in the War on Terror. That the latter had begun to openly engage in the practice was made dramatically clear in 2002 when it used a Predator Drone in Yemen to kill Qaed Salim Sinan al-Harethi – an al-Qaeda operative suspected of masterminding the attack on the *USS Cole* in October 2000. Since then, the US has continued to use drone strikes in the Afghanistan–Pakistan region and resorted to targeting and killing Osama bin Laden with a highly trained Navy SEAL team in May 2011.

The issue of targeted killing is one that generates an impassioned and emotional response from commentators, no doubt due to a perceived link with 'assassination' – a term for which there is no universally accepted definition, but which is normally associated with 'the killing of a specific individual who is politically prominent and who is targeted because of that prominence' and also customarily involves the use of treacherous means to carry out the killing (David, 2003a: 112).

Although both involve the killing of individuals, the two notions must be considered separately. In fact, a conflation of the two is what often leads to considerable confusion about policies of targeted killing as a counterterrorism tactic. In seeking to explain and clarify much of this confusion, this chapter will argue that targeted killing of terrorists is an effective and legitimate policy, particularly when utilized with several other tactics as part of a larger counterterrorism strategy.

The problem of definition

The term 'targeted killing' is often used inconsistently, with many authors using the same or similar terms to mean very different practices. Some, as mentioned above, directly link targeted killing to 'assassination' (Stein, 2003), or 'named killing' (Gross, 2003, 2006). Others use the term specifically to refer to a particular tactic of the Israeli government's counter-terrorism strategy during the second intifada after November 2000 (David, 2003a). And while Audrey Kurth Cronin (2009) links the term to 'decapitation' (directly targeting the top leadership of a terrorist organization), Nils Melzer uses the term to refer to the 'use of lethal force attributable to a subject of international law with the intent, premeditation and delib-eration to kill individually selected persons who are not in the custody of those targeting them' (2008: 5) – a situation which covers everything from CIA activities in Vietnam, through to US policies to target Gaddafi in the 1980s, to the policy of the Israeli government discussed above.

In other words, there is no consensus as to what the term means. As such, 'targeted killing' has been used to describe radically different policies which further confuse discussions of the topic. While decapitation strikes aim at the leadership of an organization, the Israeli policy is much broader, targeting mid-ranking members of terrorist organizations. Further, the US drone strikes in Afghanistan target 'militants' within the context of an armed conflict, whereas its May 2011 raid against Osama bin Laden clearly targeted just him. All of these activities have been referred to as targeted killing.

For the purpose of this article, targeted killing will be understood broadly as the *planned direct killing of an individual because of their role in the leadership of a terrorist movement*. However, as there is no consensus as to what targeted killing actually is, it will frequently make references to literature which uses other definitions that are more narrow or wide to make various points or to describe certain arguments.

The problem of comparison

A second issue (related to the problem of definition) is that of comparison. If we cannot agree upon a definition of the concept, it becomes almost impossible to compare and contrast studies on the subject that have essentially measured different things. This is evident in a number of ways.

First, most of the extensive studies on targeted killing seem to be based upon Israeli policies in Palestine and there are several reasons why this is problematic. By almost any measure, the Israeli–Palestinian situation is *sui generis*. Effectively, it is a long-standing state of hostilities between two immediate neighbors: a small yet powerful democracy and a movement fighting for its rights and territory (with branches that resort to political violence) that alternates between a state of armed conflict and uneasy peace. In this sense, it is difficult to draw conclusions for liberal democracies that may have some problems with threats from abroad and what might be called home-grown terrorism, but few of the immediate problems that characterize the Israeli–Palestinian conflict.

Second, as argued above, it is clear that the policy of targeted killing carried out by the Israelis is more comprehensive than simply 'decapitation': 'Most of those killed . . . were mid-level fighters, important enough to disrupt a terrorist cell but not so important as to provoke retaliation' (David, 2003a: 118). Thus, the Israeli program has been very ambitious in its scope, probably far more so than other examples of targeted killing by other states.

How similar is this to the US policy? It is reasonable to suppose that with the reported scale of the US program in Afghanistan–Pakistan that it also targets mid-level combatants. This has led some scholars such as Daniel Byman to argue that the US 'seems to have adopted the [Israeli] policy in recent years' (Byman, 2006: 96). On this basis, advocates of the Israeli program such as Alan Dershowitz have concluded that targeted killing has been 'vindicated' by the American adoption of the tactic (Dershowitz, 2011).

Yet there are crucial differences between the two programs that even advocates of targeted killing must acknowledge when making a comparison between them. With the American drone strikes, the fact that they are taking place within the context of an armed conflict (at least in Afghanistan), the lack of proximity to the origin of the threat and the fact that such activities are done remotely by drones, suggest that this is a very different policy from that engaged in by the Israelis. Additionally, that the latter tend to use various tactics such as booby-traps, helicopters and sending in highly trained Special Forces to carry out these killings also suggests there are substantial differences between the two policies.

This is not to say that comparisons cannot be made or that general points cannot be addressed. However, it is imperative to acknowledge from the beginning that any discussion of the issue will have to be careful about how evidence and studies are used. A significant amount of caution should be employed when it comes to extending the lessons or results of studies (particularly those based upon the targeted killing scenario in Israel/Palestine) without giving thought to the context of other cases.

Evaluating the evidence

So, armed with the knowledge that there is no consensus as to what targeted killing actually is, and that caution must be applied when trying to compare different cases, or extend lessons from one case to another, what have studies on targeted killing been suggesting? Our starting point, as proposed above, is that most of the recent and scholarly studies have been on the Israeli response to the Second Intifada post-November 2000. Many of these studies (Kaplan *et al.*, 2004; Hafez and Hatfield, 2006) conclude that there is no evidence which suggests that targeted killing is an effective counter-terrorism policy. As Kaplan *et al.* argue, 'Although Israeli actions have reduced the rate of suicide bombings over time, it is preventative arrests rather than targeted killings that seem more responsible for this outcome' (2004: 225).

An exception to the above trend is the work of Cronin (2009) who looks at cases where states have engaged in policies of 'decapitation', including targeted killing such as the Philippines and Abu Sayyaf, Russia and Chechen Leaders, as well as the Israeli policy. Additionally, Jenna Jordan looks at 298 cases of 'decapitation' – or strikes against 'the top leader of an organization or any member of the upper echelon who holds a position of authority within [an] organization' (2009: 733; although Jordan's approach seems to be looking at individual strikes rather than overall campaigns). Both agree that the evidence that such strikes work is mixed at best, but are very suspect of the practice in general.

Thus, from the outset it would seem that many (if not most) of the studies on targeted killing suggest that there is little to no evidence which suggests that it is an effective counterterrorism strategy, and may in fact cause greater problems as individuals become radicalized and recruited by terrorist organizations as their leaders are 'martyred'. Additionally, any drop in the number of attacks carried out by targeted organizations or perceived successes with terrorism are attributed to other strategies such as preventative arrests.

But is this really the case? If most of the arguments made about targeted killing have been based on one single situation – Israel–Palestine – this suggests there are substantial problems with drawing general conclusions. The duration of the Israeli policy, frequency of its use, as well as the fact it targets mid-level individuals, suggests that it is exceptional rather than exemplary. As Jordan acknowledges, 'a core problem with the current literature and a primary reason for discrepancy over the effectiveness of decapitation is a lack of solid empirical foundations' (Jordan, 2009: 721).

Cronin's study which looks at several cases besides Israel–Palestine suggests that the evidence might be more mixed. Although Cronin has serious doubts as to whether targeted killing is effective, she concedes that the decapitation of the leaders of Abu Sayyaf in the Philippines 'contributed to a shift in the group's mission' (2009: 27) from terrorism to crime. Perhaps this is not an ideal solution, but one that at least led to a decrease in political violence. Additionally, in her assessment of the Israeli policy, she argues that 'targeted killings have probably prevented specific strikes and saved Israeli lives' (2009: 30). Similarly, while Mannes argues that it is hard to demonstrate whether or not decapitation strikes are effective, 'The general decline in incidents when groups are subject to decapitation strikes indicates that this strategy may be useful in certain circumstances' (2008: 43).

Second, if all of these cases have one thing in common, it is impossible to say what would or would not have happened if the policy of targeted killing had not been carried out. Essentially, trying to speculate is to engage in an impossible counter-factual history; it is impossible to know whether, without targeted killings, these various situations would have ended up differently. For example, would there have been more civilian deaths in the Philippines, Russia or Israel if the policy of targeted killing had *not* been carried out? Who could possibly say?

Yet, even if we take the case studies on Israel–Palestine as a base for deciding upon the efficacy of targeted killing, it is clear that few of them argue that the policy has led to a significant *increase* in overall civilian deaths in terrorist attacks. For example, Hafez and Hatfield argue: 'Targeted assassinations do not quell violence, but they do not increase violence either' (2006: 377–378). While they argue that the policy has not led to an increase in suicide attacks in Israel, they also argue that there is no evidence that such killings have led to any form of 'backlash' (2006: 378).

So would there have been more attacks if these policies were not in place? As mentioned, Cronin reluctantly seems to think that at least some Israeli lives have been saved. And if there have been no demonstrable increases in violent activity, then it stands to reason that some of the dire effects that have been predicted for societies have not come to pass. As Byman (2006) argues, the costs of engaging in a policy of targeted killing may not be as high as some critics argue. He notes that in the wake of the Israeli policy, 'it is not clear that the popularity of groups such as Hamas has increased as a result' (2006: 101–102).

Finally, and perhaps most importantly, many of the studies which have been conducted tend to have an exceptionally high criteria for deeming any policy a 'success'. As Patrick B. Johnston (2010: 2) notes,

> previous research has set the bar unrealistically high for decapitation to be considered a success. Leadership removals have generally been coded as failures unless they led to quick victories or the immediate collapse of insurgent or terrorist organizations.

For example, in her study on decapitation, Jenna Jordan defines success as a situation where 'an organization was inactive for two years following the incident of decapitation, the case was coded as a success' (2009: 731). As Jordan herself notes, 'this is fairly restrictive criteria for success' (2009: 732). However, this leaves Johnston (2010: 2) to conclude:

> While this may be a reasonable way of assessing the proximate impact of leadership removals, it threatens to lead scholars to neglect leadership decapitation's impact on key factors such as militant organization cohesion, capacity and morale and strategy.

Targeted killing can be effective

In the previous section, we looked at studies which conclude that targeted killing has no demonstrable effect on terrorist attacks (at least in the Israeli–Palestinian context). However, if there has been no *decrease*, there certainly has not been any *increase* either. Additionally, these studies neglect other factors which should be taken into consideration, particularly the extent to which targeted killing may disrupt terrorist organizations and their plans.

As Byman (2006) argues, 'Contrary to popular myth, the number of skilled terrorists is quite limited. Bomb makers, terrorism trainers, forgers, recruiters and terrorist leaders are scarce'. Once these individuals are eliminated, it is hard for terrorist organizations to find new recruits with the same level of expertise. As such, 'these same recruits will not pose the same kind of threat' (2006: 104). Additionally, Byman (2006: 104) argues, targeted killings force terrorists to spend less time plotting and more time protecting themselves:

> To avoid elimination, the terrorists must constantly change locations, keep those locations secret, and keep their heads down, all of which reduces the flow of information in their organisation and makes internal communications problematic and dangerous.

Obviously, time spent ensuring ones' survival, is time *not* spent working on terrorist activities.

Similarly, David argues that there is some evidence that 'targeted killings have reduced the performance of terrorist operations' (2003a: 120):

> Israelis estimate they stop over 80 percent of attempts, and the incidence of poorly planned attacks, such as suicide bombers who appear with wires sticking out of their bags or detonations that occur with little loss of life, indicates that there have been problems either with the organization of the operation or with those available to carry them out. There are individual leaders whose charisma and organizational skills keep a group together. If they are eliminated, they are not easily replaced.

And, as Byman (2009) points out, even if targeted killing does not eliminate threats entirely:

> Killing terrorist operatives is one way to dismantle [terrorist safe] havens. Plans are disrupted when individuals die or are wounded, as new people must be recruited and less experienced leaders take over day-to-day operations. Perhaps most importantly, organizations fearing a strike must devote increased attention to their own security because any time they communicate with other cells or issue propaganda, they may be exposing themselves to a targeted attack.

Moreover, that the targeted killing of bin Laden (and the gathering of intelligence at his compound) led to subsequent deadly and devastating attacks on al-Qaeda is clear. Within six weeks of the operation there were further successful targeted strikes on Ilyas Kashmiri – an al-Qaeda operative described as 'the most dangerous al-Qaeda operative to emerge in years' (Yousafzai *et al.*, 2010), and Fazul Abdullah Mohammed, al-Qaeda's leader in East Africa, responsible for the 1998 US embassy bombings in Kenya and Tanzania (Sehgal, 2011). While removing deadly threats to the West, these strikes also help to convey the valuable impression that al-Qaeda is an organization that is on the run and looking for cover, rather than an organization of brave and competent warriors.

Certainly, it is true that targeted killing is not a solution in and of itself; killing the leadership will not necessarily end terrorism or the foundations of its existence. However, as part of a broader strategy, targeted killings seem to be an effective tool. For example, used in conjunction with the wall/security fence as well as other counterterrorist tactics, the number of terrorist attacks (and their lethality) in Israel dropped dramatically by 2003. As Byman notes, 'In combination with the border fence, aggressive intelligence collection, and other tough security measures, [Israelis] say the killings have caused the number of Israeli deaths from terrorism to decline precipitously over the last few years' (2006: 96). In this sense, although targeted killings may have certain flaws (particularly if they are solely relied upon by states), used as part of an aggressive package, they can have an impressive effect.

Targeted killing is legitimate

A second way of approaching the targeted killing issue is the question of legitimacy. Many against targeted killing not only argue that the policy is ineffective, but that it is also illegal under international and domestic law. Stein (2003: 131), for example, raises questions over the Israeli policy where in her view:

> the state kills human beings without legal sanction, the legal opinion that allegedly permits such a policy is not made public, the decision to take such action is made in the back rooms of the security services, and the assassination is carried out without judicial process.

Stein's use of the term 'assassination' here is deliberate. Almost all scholars, including those who support targeted killing, agree that assassination is illegal. And given the confusion over the term 'targeted killing' above, and the fact that it involves the killing of an individual/ individuals by a state, many seek to exploit this confusion by conflating the two different programs.

It is true that assassination is illegal under both international and the domestic law of many countries. In particular, President Ronald Reagan issued a ban on assassination in 1981 – Executive Order 12333 (United States Government, 1981). Section 2.11 of the order states that: 'No person employed by or acting on behalf of the United States Government shall engage in, or conspire to engage in, assassination.' Section 2.12 also prohibits indirect participation (Bazan, 2002: 1). However, as Bazan points out, even with this direct prohibition of assassination, the term has never been defined and 'the scope of the term seems to be the subject of differing interpretations both generally, and depending upon whether the killing took place in a time of war or time of peace' (2002: 2). Additionally, as David notes, 'Assassination typically refers to the killing of politically prominent officials because of their political prominence, usually takes place in times of peace and employs deception' (David, 2003b: 138). No matter how the activities in Palestine and Afghanistan are categorized, they do not meet this description.

Some opponents raise concerns over the number of innocent civilians killed in targeted killing operations (Stein, 2003; Gross, 2003). Yet the reality is that such operations are probably more proportional than the alternatives. Would sending in a ground invasion and subsequent invasion into harsh and mountainous regions of Afghanistan to root out terrorists truly be a more proportional response than the use of drone strikes in Afghanistan? Or is the use of targeted killing by Israel in Palestine worse than its invasion of Jenin in 2002? If anything, the wars that the West has engaged in during the past decade demonstrate that counter-insurgency operations (opposed to counterterrorist operations) tend to be far more bloody and disproportionate as a whole, resulting in many thousands of civilian dead. No one is disputing that sometimes civilians die in targeted killing operations, but compared to other kinds of operations, they may actually be the most humane.

The point here is that while many opponents of targeted killing see it as a clear-cut issue, the context in which many of these activities are taking place is simply not clear – or certainly not as clear as those ready to invoke international law claim it is. Yet the idea that targeted killing is some kind of lawless, ungoverned activity is also wrong. The policies carried out by the United States and Israel are highly organized activities, carried out by state apparatus and subject to control. As David notes:

> Within Israel, targeted killing is not a secret extralegal policy. There is a body of case law within the Israeli courts concerning the policy, and the general finding has been that it can be carried out in a legal way.
>
> (2003a: 114)

Finally, perhaps the most important point regarding legitimacy is that principle underlying the international order is that of a state's right of self-defense. The idea that a state may not respond to a threat to its existence or the lives of its people simply does not exist in international law. Today, this right is acknowledged in Article 51 of the UN Charter which states that, 'Nothing in the present Charter shall impair the inherent right of individual or collective self-defence' (United Nations, 1945). Defending itself and its population is the most fundamental task a state must perform, and targeted killing conducted by governments against terrorist organizations must be understood in this context.

Targeted killing: best of a bad lot?

There is no question that targeted killing as a counterterrorism strategy has its flaws; it is an imperfect solution. Targeted killings may result in civilian casualties, such as those which have been the source of a great amount of anger from the Afghan government towards NATO. Frustration with casualties may inhibit future cooperation. Additionally, targeted killing is a second-best solution when the aim of a counterterrorism policy is to gather intelligence. As the old saying would have it, 'Dead men tell no tales'; an operative captured alive will quite often be a source of valuable intelligence for further counterterrorist activities.

But does this mean that it is ineffective? Quite simply, the answer is no – and for several good reasons. First, as we have seen, any evidence that targeted killing does not work is flawed and incomplete. Perhaps there is no better indication of this than the fact that no one can agree upon a definition of what 'targeted killing' actually is. Additionally, comparisons between different strategies are problematic given the differences between them. Second, the definition of 'success' in many of these studies has simply been too high. There are many other things that targeted killing can accomplish as a part of a broader counterterrorism strategy that these studies ignore in their codifications and quantifications. Third, it is a legitimate tactic under a nation's inherent right of self-defense which is enshrined in international law. Finally, targeted killing is arguably far more proportionate than other counterterrorism strategies or invasions and occupations conducted in COIN operations. Such operations throw into jeopardy the lives of soldiers, but more importantly, civilians who are on the ground.

In the end, as Daniel Byman (2009) argues, while the policy is imperfect, 'it is one of the United States' few options for managing the threat posed by al-Qaeda from its base in tribal Pakistan'. It is almost impossible to actually deter terrorists, especially those aiming to engage in suicide attacks. Additionally, it is quite often impossible to carry out arrests and/or capture terrorists, such as those who live in the mountainous, ungoverned territory of the Afghan-Pakistan border. As such, given the risks,

> each strike needs to be carefully weighed, with the value of the target and the potential for innocent deaths factored into the equation . . . But equally important is the risk of not striking – and inadvertently allowing al Qaeda leaders free reign to plot terrorist mayhem.
>
> (Byman, 2009)

It is far too soon to say that the numbers on targeted killing do not add up.

NO: The case against targeted assassination

Andrew Silke

Introduction

The killing of Osama bin Laden by American Special Forces in May 2011 was heralded as an event of massive symbolic importance. Within the US, news of the killing led to impromptu street celebrations and pushed approval ratings for President Obama up six points. Yet well before the dust settled, many voices were already warning that bin Laden's death did not mean the end of the threat from al-Qaeda, and indeed, some warned that it was quite possible for the movement to actually emerge stronger and even more dangerous from the loss of its leader.

Bin Laden's death did, however, reignite the debate over whether the targeted assassination of suspected terrorists is an effective strategy to follow. For some, targeted assassination is one of the most potent tools a state can deploy in countering a terrorist group. For others, it is a deeply flawed approach which creates at least as many problems as it solves. The targeted assassination of suspected terrorists has certainly become a significant feature of the overall counterterrorism strategy of many countries, and has been used at different times by a wide range of states including Israel, the United Kingdom, Spain, the USA and many others. The key question facing this chapter is: does this policy work?

Assessing the evidence

In fairness, no state has used targeted assassination as its sole response to terrorism or indeed has identified such assassination as its primary solution. All instead have tried to respond with a variety of measures focused on a range of different issues. For advocates of hard-line policies like targeted assassinations, the loss of assassinated members deals a steady stream of serious blows to the terrorist groups. The death of an experienced bomb-maker, for example, can disrupt planned attacks which must be postponed or abandoned until alternative sources of weaponry can be acquired. The reliability and quality of these alternative suppliers may be uncertain, resulting in less effective and more risky operations for the terrorists. The loss of senior leaders also necessitates internal reorganization and again, a period of adjustment for the group. Thus, at a minimum level the assassination results in a negative impact on the terrorist group, disrupting its activities and reducing its effectiveness. It is also generally argued by proponents that assassinations will have a deterrent impact on the terrorist group – that it will encourage current members to 'retire' from the organization and will make potential recruits think twice before they join up. Over the long term, such a deterrent impact could seriously weaken the terrorist organization and reduce the overall level of violence it engages in and perhaps make it more amenable to non-violent solutions to the conflict.

Some potential support for this theory came from research by Cronin (2009) which highlighted how terrorist campaigns are ended. Cronin examined the life cycles of 450 terrorist groups and identified six scenarios in which the campaigns were finally halted:

- The terrorists leaders are captured or killed
- The terrorists are crushed by state repression
- The terrorists win (which happened in 6 percent of cases)
- The terrorist group moves away from politics and into criminality
- The terrorists negotiate and accept a compromise settlement
- The terrorists lose popular support.

Proponents of targeted assassination can argue that the policy would fit comfortably into the first two categories and should be encouraged on those grounds. However, there are significant problems with taking Cronin's findings as a green light for a particular strategy. Indeed, Cronin explicitly warns in her analysis that the findings are not measures of effectiveness: the data do not reveal which policies are the most effective in dealing with terrorism. Rather, they describe some major events in the immediate closing stage of the conflict. Cronin also warns that there is evidence that arresting terrorist leaders is more effective than killing them. Jordan (2009) also adds a cautionary note after her findings examining 298 cases of leadership decapitation in terrorist groups. Jordan found that larger and older terrorist groups – as well as those motivated by nationalist or religious agendas – were effectively immune from the effects of leadership decapitation. Overall, she concluded that decapitation 'was not an effective counter-terrorism policy' and should not be encouraged. Indeed, the results suggested that groups who occasionally lost their leaders in this way were actually *more* robust and endured for *longer* than groups who never suffered decapitation. In other words, there is scant encouragement here for those who harbored hopes that Osama bin Laden's death might herald the demise of al-Qaeda.

In assessing whether targeted assassination works it is vital to consider the evidence dealing with the impact of the policy (Silke, 2011). Unfortunately, good evidence is often difficult to find in terrorism research. In a review of the impact of a wide range of different counter-terrorism strategies, Lum, Leslie and Sherley (2006b) found that out of over 20,000 studies considered, only seven contained moderately rigorous evaluations of counterterrorism programs. One of the main findings of the review was that:

> Retaliatory attacks (for example, the U.S. attack on Libya in 1986 or attacks by Israel on the PLO) have significantly increased the number of terrorist attacks in the short run, particularly against the United States, the United Kingdom, and Israel.

In itself, this conclusion should give pause for thought about the use of targeted assassination, though Lum, Leslie and Sherley (2006b) did not include any research specifically on targeted assassination in their analysis. Fortunately, there are now some studies which can shed further light on this particular issue and the following sections will focus on what the best of the available evidence reveals about the impact of targeted assassinations.

The Israeli experience

Israel has a deserved reputation for using aggressive tactics as a key component of its counter-terrorism strategy. These elements can include large-scale military interventions – up to and including the invasion of neighboring regions – as well as a consistent favoring of targeted assassination of suspected terrorists. In the period running from 2000 to 2011, Israeli forces have killed 242 suspected Palestinian militants using targeted assassination (B'Tselem, 2011). Some of these attacks have been extremely high profile, such as the killing of Salah Shehada, a senior Hamas leader who died when an Israeli jet deliberately dropped a 2,000-pound bomb on his apartment building. The attack killed Shehada, but also caused the deaths of at least 14 bystanders, including 9 children (Byman, 2006). One of the most controversial aspects of Israeli targeted killings is the high number of bystanders who are also killed or injured in these attacks. Statistics collected by B'Tselem suggest that while 242 individuals were deliberately killed as part of this policy, a further 170 Palestinians also died in the attacks. For roughly every three suspected militants who are killed, two bystanders will also die.

Within the Israeli context, the targeted assassination of suspected terrorists fulfills a number of objectives, including retribution for previous terrorist attacks against Israeli targets, disruption of current terrorist activity and deterrence of future terrorist activity. Targeted assassination as an explicit Israeli policy came to light in the aftermath of the terrorist attack against the Israeli squad at the 1972 Munich Olympic Games. Eleven Israelis were killed in the attack carried out by the Palestinian group Black September. Five terrorists were also killed during the incident, but three survived and these were all released by the West German authorities a few months later in response to the Palestinian hijacking of a Lufthansa passenger jet. Outraged by the deaths of the eleven team members and later no doubt goaded even further by the release of the three surviving terrorists, the Israeli government secretly authorized Operation *Wrath of God*. This was a deliberate and systematic campaign of assassination targeting all the individuals believed to be involved in the planning and carrying-out of the Munich attack. *Wrath of God* was not about capturing or imprisoning those responsible. It was purely and simply about killing those the Israelis could find and terrorizing those they could not. In order to accomplish this task, a specialist assassination unit known as the *kidon* was activated, comprising just under 40 highly trained members of the Israeli security forces (Silke, 2003b).

Death warrants were issued for 35 people believed to have been involved in or connected to the Munich attack, and the *kidon* members were allowed enormous latitude in their operations. Less than five weeks after Munich, the first of the targets, Wael Zaitter, a cousin of Yasser Arafat and a principle organizer of PLO terrorism in Europe, was gunned down at his apartment near Rome. Over the following months, the assassination squads killed several more people on the list, and the following year in a major operation on April 10, 1973, a large commando raid was launched against Palestinians based in Beirut. Over 100 people were killed in the attack, including a number on the *Wrath of God* death list. In time, two of the three terrorists released by West Germany were tracked down and killed, though one managed to survive and is believed to still be in hiding (Reeve, 2001).

Despite the mistaken assassination of at least one innocent victim in Norway – and a growing perception that many on the death list probably had no involvement with Munich – *Wrath of God* continued until 1979, when assassins finally managed to kill the elusive Ali

Hassan Salameh with a car bomb in Beirut. One hundred thousand people came to his funeral, while the widow of one of the murdered Munich athletes publicly thanked the assassins for what they had done. Though *Wrath of God* itself was wound down, targeted assassination as a policy has remained a key element in Israeli counterterrorism efforts in the following decades.

While targeted assassination has many strong supporters within Israel, evidence regarding its impact in terms of diminishing or deterring Palestinian terrorism has not been compelling. Evaluations of large-scale military retaliations in response to terrorism have not found a significant impact in terms of reducing future terrorist attacks. On the contrary, research such as that by Brophy-Baermann and Conybeare (1994) found that major retaliations either led to a dramatic short-term *increase* in terrorist attacks against Israel, or else had no impact whatsoever (that is, the number of terrorist attacks neither increased or decreased in the aftermath). In cases where an increase occurred, this dissipated within nine months and then returned to pre-retaliation levels. The explanation for the lack of impact in most cases was that the terrorists expected the retaliations and planned for them accordingly. They were built in as a given into how they operated and had no discernible long-term effect.

Further evaluations have attempted to explore the impact of the much smaller scale targeted assassinations. Hafez and Hatfield (2006) carried out an impact of assessment of Israeli targeted assassinations which were carried out between November 2000 and June 2004. In this time period, Israel conducted approximately 151 targeted assassinations. The research found that there was no significant impact on Palestinian terrorism as a result of the assassinations. The overall level of attacks remained the same in the aftermath of the killings; there was neither an increase in violence nor a decrease. Similarly, there was no significant evidence of a reduction in the quality of Palestinian attacks as a result of the assassinations. In other words, the Palestinian attacks overall did not become less lethal or less sophisticated.

Hafez and Hatfield did highlight that where positive impacts were seen in the reduction of Palestinian attacks, it was in the context of different strategies adopted by the Israelis and in particular, to enhanced target hardening approaches such as the creation of new security checkpoints in Palestinian areas, the construction of the extensive defense barrier, as well as increasingly sophisticated intelligence operations. Ultimately, Hafez and Hatfield (2006) concluded that:

> Our analysis raises doubts about the effectiveness of targeted assassinations as a tactic in the arsenal of counter-terrorism measures. Targeted assassinations may signal a determination to fight back the terrorists and exhibit commitment not to succumb to their demands. They may also placate an angry public demanding tough measures to stop the terrorists . . . Targeted assassinations, however, should not be presented as a proven solution to patterns of political violence and rebellion.

The Northern Ireland experience

While the Israeli approach to targeted assassinations has been explicit and officially openly acknowledged, other countries have often been much more circumspect in admitting that targeted assassination is a part of the state's counterterrorism arsenal. This was certainly the case with the United Kingdom which during the 1980s and early 1990s operated a 'shoot-to-kill' policy in Northern Ireland which was primarily targeted against members of the Provisional IRA (Murray, 2004). In practice, this was a somewhat more nuanced form of targeted assassination, as the security forces tried to only kill militants who had either just carried out an attack or were in the process of doing so. The result was that scores of IRA members were killed in ambushes prepared by security special forces. Several of these ambushes were high profile. In 1987, eight IRA members were killed in an ambush in Loughgall. An innocent passer-by was also killed by the ambushers. In 1988, the SAS shot dead three unarmed IRA members in Gibraltar in another high-profile case.

In most cases, the security forces had detailed intelligence in advance of the terrorist attack and knew when and where the terrorists were planning to attack, what methods the terrorists were planning to use, where their staging areas were and even the identities of most or all of the terrorists involved. Even though this intelligence would have allowed the security forces to intercept and arrest the terrorist teams before they could carry out the planned attack, the ambushes were normally carried out immediately *after* the IRA members had carried out an attack rather than before (the Gibraltar killings were an exception to this general rule). By waiting until the IRA teams had carried out an attack, the ambushes took on increased apparent legitimacy. At Loughgall, the security forces knew that the IRA intended to bomb a police station and this was surrounded with a team of highly trained security personnel in hidden positions. The team allowed the IRA team to drive a bomb up to a police building and detonate it. It was only as the IRA team were fleeing the scene that the ambushers opened fire killing them all. Such premeditated ambushes continued and were also accompanied by the passing of intelligence files on suspected IRA members to elements within the loyalist paramilitary groups.

What impact did the shoot-to-kill policy have on terrorist violence in Northern Ireland? For some, the shoot-to-kill campaign was a significant factor in driving the IRA to the negotiation table in the early 1990s, though even at that time some analysts were warning that the positive impact of the policy was probably being greatly overestimated (see Urban, 1992). More recent research evidence continues to cast doubt on the view that shoot-to-kill was an effective policy. Finnegan (2009) for example, conducted interviews with both former members of the IRA and members of the British Security Forces to gain an insight into the impact of shoot-to-kill from the perspective of both sides.

A former member of the SAS warned that while the military would have liked to think the killings were having an impact, in reality they probably made little difference:

> we'd (SAS) like to think so, but probably not, in the longer term . . . there will always be punters at a lower level willing to yield a gun in most situations, chasing after them is relatively pointless in the overall scheme of things.
>
> (Finnegan, 2009: 31)

Overall, the former SAS member concluded that the killings had 'no direct effect' on the overall levels of violence. Similarly, a former IRA member reported that the killings did not deter existing members or future recruits:

> the Volunteers kept coming forward (after Loughgall), but the British hoped that through a campaign of attrition, they would take out our most experienced and serious activists . . . [The deaths] only had a short term effect on morale, people felt down that volunteers were killed, but were very easily rallied by the funerals.
>
> (Finnegan, 2009: 31)

Finnegan's overall conclusion was that the targeted assassinations had no impact on the level of violence in Northern Ireland. Whatever positive impacts were gained from the shootings were cancelled out by negative effects and the overall level of violence remained unchanged. In the views of his interviewees from both sides, the policy had no significant impact on the conflict and other factors were identified as being more important in terms of affecting the course of campaigns.

Finnegan's qualitative findings are also supported by more recent quantitative work. Lafree, Dugan and Korte (2009) carried out a time series analysis of attacks in Northern Ireland and plotted these against a range of counterterrorism initiatives and events. Included in the assessment were two high-profile shoot-to-kill incidents: the 1987 Loughgall shooting and the 1988 Gibraltar shooting. The research found that there was no significant impact from the Loughgall deaths: the deaths of the IRA members there neither increased nor decreased the overall level of violence in the Province. In contrast, however, the Gibraltar shooting did lead to a significant increase in violence. This increase was long-lasting and was still detectable three years after the event. Thus, the research suggested that targeted assassinations in a Northern Ireland context failed to decrease the level of violence taking place; on the contrary, attacks either increased or else remained at the same level.

Experiences from other conflicts

Targeted assassination played a role in Spanish efforts to combat ETA, particularly in the period running from the late 1970s to the late 1980s. During this time over 40 individuals were killed initially by relatively loosely organized death squads and later by a more formalized organization, Grupos Antiterroristas de Liberacion (GAL) (Heiberg, 2007). As well as killing suspected terrorists in Spain, GAL operatives also crossed the border into France to kill suspected ETA members based there.

In assessing the impact of these killings, Perkoski (2010) analyzed ETA violence over two periods: the first running from 1983 to 1987, the second from 1988 to 1992. He found that killings of ETA members had no impact on ETA violence in the initial period; the killings neither increased nor decreased the overall level of violence in the conflict. He did find a difference however, in the second period. The killing of ETA members in this period did produce a short-term decrease in ETA attacks. This lasted no more than one month. At first glance, this would seem to support the argument that targeted assassinations do work, but Perkoski then found that there was a rebound effect: in the second month after the killing, ETA attacks *increased* significantly. Overall, looking across the whole two months the number of attacks carried out by ETA remained at the same level. In assessing the value of the killings as counterterrorism strategy, Perkoski concluded:

> Overall, violent counterterrorism either was insignificant, or it ended up increasing terrorism by the same amount that it initially decreased terrorist incidents. Overall, repression neither had a net increase nor decrease on the frequency of terrorist events . . . Therefore, this study suggests that violent tactics to deter terrorism should be avoided.

In contrast to the lack of lasting impact through killings, Perkoski did find that arresting ETA members (as opposed to shooting them dead) was correlated with a significant reduction in violence. He also identified that Spanish prison programs which dispersed rather than concentrated prisoners and offered early release for reformed prisoners also led to significant reductions in violence. His general finding was that it was non-violent and unambiguously legal policies which had the most impact in terms of reducing ETA violence. Similar results come from Monroe's (2008) research which examined counterterrorism across Western Europe in the second half of the twentieth century and also found that arrests had a very significant positive impact in decreasing terrorism, whereas the use of repressive force was more likely to be associated with a slight increase in terrorism.

Targeted assassination has become a major feature of US counterterrorism operations in and around Pakistan. This was obviously demonstrated with the high-profile killing of Osama bin Laden in May 2011, but the policy had already become a major feature of US efforts in the region for some time before that. In assessing the impact of this policy, Wilner (2010) analyzed the impact of four targeted killings and compares the 2–3 week period before each killing with a similar period afterwards. Wilner argues that there is evidence that the quality of the attacks degraded in the aftermath, though the figures presented do show that the number of attacks overall *increased* after the killings – rising from 332 before to 352 afterwards. As Wilner does not present data on the casualties caused by these attacks (before or after), it is difficult to judge to what extent the quality was affected.

Conclusions

Ultimately, there is no simple and single solution to terrorism, just as there is no simple and single cause. Responding effectively to terrorism is a complex matter: a considerable array of responses is available to any regime facing a terrorist threat. As with many things in life, the easy and popular options are often also the most useless and unhelpful. Terrorism – itself the extreme use of violence and force – encourages a view that forceful and violent responses are not simply justified in combating it, but are also obligatory. Such reactions are understandable, but they can show a poor awareness of human psychology.

For advocates of hard-line policies like targeted assassinations, the loss of assassinated members deals a steady stream of serious blows to the terrorist groups. The death of an experienced bomb-maker, for example, can disrupt planned attacks which must be postponed or abandoned until alternative sources of weaponry can be acquired. The reliability and quality of these alternative suppliers may be uncertain, resulting in less effective and more risky operations for the terrorists. The loss of senior leaders also necessitates internal reorganization and again, a period of adjustment for the group.

However, the evidence available to date has found that targeted killings fail on the key element of decreasing the number of attacks taking place. Indeed, the research findings from Israel, Spain, Northern Ireland, Afghanistan and elsewhere, point to targeted killings either having no impact on the level of violence or else leading to an increase in the number of attacks taking place. Despite whatever damage or losses the assassinations inflict on terrorist groups, the organizations are clearly able to endure and are not significantly weakened. If anything, some targeted killings appear to make groups (slightly) more aggressive and more robust.

Given that research has also identified that other strategies and tactics do seem to have powerful positive impacts (arresting terrorist leaders has a major positive impact compared to killing them), any evidence-based policy should naturally shy away from adopting targeted killing as a preferred solution to terrorism. While it might be an attractive policy to some for a range of different reasons, claims that it works in terms of reducing the threat do not bear up to close scrutiny.

In the end, what are good counterterrorism policies? One answer to this question – but not necessarily the one which always carries the most importance for policy-makers – are processes which lead to a sustained reduction in the level of terrorist violence and ultimately to a de facto end to the terrorist campaign. Policy which can achieve such ends needs to be holistic in nature and needs to consider carefully the question, what is it that will sustain a terrorist campaign? Targeted assassinations simply fail in this regard.

Discussion questions

1　What are the difficulties in trying to compare different cases of targeted killing?
2　According to targeted-killing advocates, what are the advantages of a strike against an organization's leader?
3　Are terrorists legitimate targets?
4　What are the main ethical issues raised by opponents of targeted killing?
5　Is targeted killing more proportionate than other counterterrorism strategies?
6　Identify three reasons why targeted assassination has such a limited impact.
7　Given its obvious limitations, why do states use targeted assassination?
8　Is targeted assassination more about revenge or deterrence?
9　Is the US making a sensible decision to incorporate targeted assassination as part of its overall counterterrorism strategy?
10　Does it make a difference if a policy of targeted assassination is openly declared (such as Israel) or officially denied (such as Northern Ireland)?

Further readings

Bazan, E., 2002. 'Assassination Band and E. O. 12333: A Brief Summary', *Congressional Research Service*, updated 4 January 2002, available at: http://opencrs.com/document/RS21037/2002-01-04/.
Byman, D., 2006. 'Do Targeted Killings Work?', *Foreign Affairs*, 85(2): 95–111.
Cronin A., 2009. *How Terrorism Ends: Understanding the Decline and Demise of Terrorist Campaigns*, Princeton, NJ: Princeton University Press.
David, S., 2003. 'Israeli's Policy of Targeted Killing', *Ethics and International Affairs*, 17(1): 111–126.
Hafez, M., and Hatfield, J., 2006. 'Do Targeted Assassinations Work? A Multivariate Analysis of Israel's Controversial Tactic during Al-Aqsa Uprising', *Studies in Conflict and Terrorism*, 29(4): 359–382.
Jordan, J., 2009. 'When Heads Roll: Assessing the Effectiveness of Leadership Decapitation', *Security Studies*, 18: 719–755.
Silke, A., 2005. 'Fire of Iolus: The Role of State Countermeasures in Causing Terrorism and What Needs to be Done', in Bjorgo, T., ed., *Root Causes of Terrorism*, London: Routledge.

12 Have global efforts to reduce terrorism and political violence been effective in the past decade?

YES: 'Looking for a needle in a stack of needles'

Mark Cochrane

Introduction

'Today we were unlucky, but remember, we only have to be lucky once. You will have to be lucky always' (quoted in Bishop and Mallie, 1988: 426). These are the words of the Provisional Irish Republican Army (PIRA) claiming responsibility following its attempt to murder British Prime Minister Margaret Thatcher and her government in a bombing at the Grand Hotel, Brighton in 1984. The law of probability dictates that the state cannot be lucky always and thereby presents the challenge of reducing the threat posed by terrorism. The post 9/11 declaration by President Bush of America's intent to wage a 'War on Terror' was not only an unfortunate choice of language, it was as unhelpful as it was inaccurate – a point acknowledged by Richardson (2006) who considers the futility of such a statement and comments that such a war can never be won. Despite the merit of such criticism, it is a perspective that does little to accept that governments must react immediately to terrorist attacks or incidents in order to mitigate fear and the feeling of citizen vulnerability.

The 'War on Terrorism' did not occur in a vacuum and those environmental factors prevalent at the time largely determined the reaction. It was understandable that the response, which Walt (2001–2) deemed to be the most rapid and dramatic change in United States' foreign policy, would attempt to make those considered responsible accountable for their acts. This was unsurprising, as to many in the United States, the concept of terrorism did not exist prior to 9/11, despite events such as the first New York City World Trade Center attack in 1993 and the Alfred Murrah federal building bombing in Oklahoma City in 1995.

In the aftermath of 9/11, the immediate kinetic response directed towards the al-Qaeda powerbase in Afghanistan was a success and had the desired effect in dismantling the organisation in their previously secure base in that region and the resultant defeat of the Taliban. Since that time, successful kill and capture operations, such as that of Osama Bin Laden on 1 May 2011, have further weakened the leadership of enemies of the West. As the dust settled post 9/11 however, it became evident that America was ill-prepared to respond to the threat facing them, illustrated by an observation by Cronin (2004) who viewed the nation as being impatient, litigious, intolerant of risk and accustomed to 'fixing' problems using superior technologies to defeat enemies and responding with military force.

Britain, unlike the United States, had a bitter learning experience in dealing with Irish terrorism in terms of intelligence gathering infrastructure, internal security measures and terrorist legislation, but the threat both now face from international terrorism poses a different problem. The implementation of any response is difficult due to the nature of a threat that is international in nature, from a variety of group networks and individuals, and intent to cause mass casualties (Mottram, 2007). Responses since 9/11 have forced our adversaries to change, and they have proven themselves to be capable and able to do so (Hoffman, 2005).

Despite the ongoing and complex nature of the threat, much of the media and academia take every available opportunity to critique and highlight supposed intelligence failures, but do little to acknowledge the numerous successes and progress made. Claims of such short-comings and ineptitude following incidents such as the Madrid bombing in 2004, the London attacks in 2005 on 7/7, the attempted bombing on 21/7 of the same year, and subsequent attempts to attack the United States and the United Kingdom, are events that viewed with hindsight, could have been handled more effectively. Therein lies the problem: hindsight is always 20/20 and errors made are easy to spot after the fact. For those charged with the challenge of countering terrorism, it is not a case of looking for a needle in a haystack; it is a case of looking for a needle in a stack of needles. However, even the harshest critic must grudgingly accept that terrorists have not experienced anything comparable to the 9/11 attacks due largely to the professionalism of the response.

A new level of threat

When one considers what the then Head of MI5 (the agency charged with protecting the United Kingdom against threats to national security) said in 2006, when she stated that the Security Service and police in the United Kingdom were working to contend with some 200 groupings or networks totalling over 1,600 identified individuals who at that time were actively engaged in plotting, or facilitating terrorist acts in the United Kingdom and overseas (cited in Hennessy, 2007), it is remarkable that there have been so few successful attacks. The decade would go on to demonstrate, particularly within the United Kingdom, the emergence of the home-grown terrorist, mostly first- or second-generation immigrants with an appetite to wreak havoc in their homeland (Hewitt, 2008), coming about as the direct result of what critics would declare to be Britain's neglect and ignorance in addressing the threat posed by Islamist terrorist activity in an appeasement of multiculturalism – a reference to the acceptance or promotion of multiple ethnic cultures rather than one national culture that Joppke (1996) deems to be one of the most pervasive and controversial intellectual and political movements in contemporary Western society (Phillips, 2006). The West has found that the 'enemy within' posed the greatest challenge to deal with, as demonstrated by those involved in terrorist attacks and others arrested prior to doing so.

In attempting to determine whether the response to terrorism has been effective since 9/11, one is immediately faced with what effectiveness or success looks like. Is it no attacks, one attack or a handful of attacks? Furthermore what does terrorism look like in the twenty-first century? Is it the same animal that it has always been?

When one reflects on the changing nature of the threat faced by the West and contemplates whether responses have been effective, one must recognise that military commitments in dealing with ongoing conflict in Iraq and Afghanistan within the period have presented an option for those seeking to attack Western interests. The attraction for those so inclined within the environment of the 'near war' enables them to participate in kinetic attacks against what they consider to be enemy forces as part of an insurgent campaign. The conflict in both Iraq and Afghanistan has arguably had the net result of fewer attacks mounted in the West. Despite a proven lust for martyrdom operations by those opposed to Western states embroiled the conflict, the fact remains that these are considerably easier to mount in-theatre in a 'near war' target-rich environment than to carry out in the securitised 'far war' arena of the West. That said, both arenas form separate and different components in the alleged War on Terror. The threat of attack today is more complex and diverse than at any time since 9/11 (Bergen and Hoffman, 2010). It is no longer the case that the threat remains solely from al-Qaeda, but from a plethora of affiliated groups, almost franchised in nature, assisted by a seemingly growing number of sympathisers.

Traditional counter-measures to the threat of terrorism have fallen into two broad categories: defensive and proactive (Rosendorff and Sandler, 2004). Drilling down further, these divisions are most commonly cited in the form of political measures, legislative and judicial measures and security measures (Art and Richardson, 2007). Global efforts adopted have seen a myriad of interventions in terms of both depth and scope. Strategic direction has fallen equally between the defensive and proactive measures, and a noticeable feature of these interventions has been the increased appetite for new technology, tools and partnerships resulting in an increase in personal, commercial and governmental expenditure in this field (Lum *et al.*, 2006a). Despite a significant move in this direction, British, French and Israeli experts share a degree of scepticism about technology as a 'solution' in counterterrorism (Lesser, 1999b).

Technology

Levels of airport screening, the increased use of closed circuit television (CCTV) monitoring and improvements in structural protection and design are representative of physical security measures utilised with increasing regularity in an attempt to reassure and protect the public at large. This is only to be expected, as these measures are both tangible and visible, albeit to a begrudging population who are resentful about the delay and disruption incurred but comforted nonetheless by their presence. The provision of these measures demonstrate a growth industry that has increased significantly since the events of 9/11, but has undoubtedly frustrated attempts by those intent on carrying out terrorist attacks or acts of political violence to alter their plans and therefore saved lives in the process. It is also regrettably the easy option. Physical protective measures in themselves cannot and will not prevent a would-be attacker with sufficient commitment, intent and capability. The ' shoe-bomber' Richard Reid in 2003, the 'Airlines' plot in 2006, the Glasgow Airport bombing of 2007, and the 'under-wear bomber' Umer Farouk Abdulmutallab in 2009, all demonstrate the continuance of targeting mass transit, particularly air travel, regardless of the initiatives introduced to combat such actions. Critics level the charge that such attacks demonstrate the incompetence and the amateurish calibre of today's terrorists, but seldom make reference to the fact that success-ful CT strategy, initiatives and target-hardening have pushed them down the road of desperation.

Creation of an appropriate counterterrorism strategy

The inaugural United States' *National Strategy for Combating Terrorism 2003* articulated an inclusive vision of partnership to protect the United States and sought to instil public confidence and acquire public support. The strands of this policy sought to 'Defeat, Deny, Diminish and Defend' America against terrorist threat with an acknowledgement that success will only come through sustained, steadfast and systematic application of national power: diplomatic, economic, information, financial, law enforcement, intelligence and military simultaneously across four fronts. Many criticisms have been made of the legislation and how a balancing act needs to take place between separate but important issues of freedom and security (Donohue, 2002). This is an important issue, and since the events of 9/11 there has been a need to tilt the fulcrum towards security with a potential loss of freedom, but once, and if, the threat is deemed to have diminished it is likely to return to a more acceptable balance (Golden, 2006).

Publication of the United Kingdom's counterterrorism strategy, '*Contest*' made the general public aware of the government's intent to reduce the risk from international terrorism (HM Government, 2006). In existence since 2003, the strategy remained 'secret' until 2006. Following the incidents in London on 7/7 and 21/7, the document was published in order to provide the public with additional information. The European Union's *Counter-Terrorism Action Plan*, updated in December 2004, looks impressive on paper. It contains over 150 measures, covering a broad range of counterterrorism co-operation, from emergency response to curbing terrorist funding. But the European Union does not have the powers, such as investigation and prosecution, to tackle terrorism like a national government. The European Union can help governments to identify, extradite and prosecute terrorists, but it is only slowly developing its own anti-terrorism policies (Keohane, 2005). Counterterrorism strategy to date has had an emphasis on counter-radicalization, as this is deemed to be one of the most important areas to address.

Targeting of European nations by terrorists has largely been confined to those playing roles in the coalition forces in Iraq and Afghanistan, in addition to singular attacks on a number of individuals who are perceived to have insulted Islam. Relative freedom of movement within the European Union, save for checks at seaports and airports, affords a great opportunity for terrorists to move with little chance of being apprehended. A case in point is that of Abbas Boutrab, arrested in Belfast in what was the first prosecution of a member of al-Qaeda in the United Kingdom in 2005 (BBC News, 2005).

Public awareness of counterterrorism strategy

The publication of national and regional counterterrorism strategies following 9/11 instilled awareness in the public consciousness that terrorism was a potential threat to each and every member of society in their everyday lives, but sought to provide reassurance that steps were being taken by the state in an attempt to safeguard them and protect citizens. Clear messages were highlighted of the need for multi-agency participation and an acknowledgement that law enforcement and intelligence agencies were reliant on other strands for support. The placement of counterterrorism strategy in the public domain provides a sense of ownership and responsibility for all to embrace.

Public involvement in counterterrorism strategy

Public awareness had the net effect of leading to public involvement. Steps taken to protect various elements critical to national infrastructure are seen in nearly all of the major counterterrorism initiatives introduced, as evidenced by the Federal Bureau of Investigation's (FBI) *Infraguard* initiative, the New York Police Department's (NYPD) *Operation Nexus* (Cochrane,

2008), and the United Kingdom's Centre for the Protection of National Infrastructure. *Infraguard* is a collaborative effort between federal law enforcement and private sector volunteers who represent critical infrastructure bodies, and the initiative has spread across each of the FBI's 56 field offices. *Infraguard* has grown significantly since the events of 9/11, and has seen an expansion, not only between the private sector and the FBI, but also the Department of Homeland Security, the National Institute of Standards and Technology and the Small Business Administration. The NYPD's *Operation Nexus* sees members committed to reporting suspicious business encounters that they believe may be linked to terrorism through the utilisation of their business and industry knowledge. New members to the initiative are supplied with a list of indicators specifically relevant to their business area as a reference point, and liaison visits by detectives to business premises are conducted on a frequent basis and not confined to the New York area.

Professionalisation of counterterrorism structures

On 1 October 2002, George Tenet, the then Director of Intelligence and the head of the Central Intelligence Agency (CIA), sought to explain the CIA's apparent failure to anticipate the events of 9/11 by reminding a congressional committee that the previous decade had seen the CIA budget cut by 18 per cent, leading to a 16 per cent reduction of employees across the board (Kessler, 2004: 261). This comment is indicative of both how the United States had failed to appreciate the nature and scope of threat that it faced, and to properly prepare itself for such an event (Gill and Pythian, 2006). This has largely been addressed by the overhaul of intelligence agencies, and greater global co-operation.

The Department of Homeland Security (DHS) was established in December 2002 to fulfil three objectives: (1) prevent terrorist attacks in the United States; (2) reduce America's vulnerability to terrorism; and (3) respond to any terrorist attacks and natural disasters that occur. Creation of the body resulted in a struggle for power with the FBI and CIA (and many other areas of US government, particularly the Defense Intelligence Agency), both of whom have increased rather than decreased their homeland security functions, and developments in intelligence sharing have come mostly in spite of, rather than because of, DHS actions (Jones, 2006). Organisationally, the FBI made the greatest internal changes, moving a significant number of personnel from criminal investigations to counterterrorism duties. In addition, an increase in the number of Joint Terrorism Task Forces and the creation of Field Intelligence Groups seek to enhance the function of each field office in counterterrorism work. The FBI has some way to go to become a fully fledged intelligence organisation, but has stated its willingness to do so and acquire the human intelligence expertise of its European counterparts. The battle for supremacy regarding the counterterrorism lead has continued within the United States, no better exemplified than in New York where an uneasy relationship is said to exist between the FBI and the New York Police Department. Knowledge is undoubtedly power and it will take time for this trust to be further developed.

Changes in legislation

Within days of the 9/11 attack, the Bush administration presented proposals to expand prosecutorial and police powers, and Congress introduced 323 bills and resolutions and 21 laws and resolutions relating to the attacks and the war on terror. Six weeks later, an overwhelming majority in Congress voted for the United and Strengthening America by Providing the Appropriate Tools Required to Intercept and Obstruct Terrorism Act, better known by its acronym, the PATRIOT Act (Nacos, 2008/2011). The Act permits wide-ranging powers that critics have said challenge balancing security, liberty and human rights.

In the United States, introduction of counterterrorist finance legislation has been a positive measure, but it is unclear as to how successful the initiative has been in disrupting the movement of terrorist money. The much-publicised freezing of assets totalling $142 million does not appear to have changed much since 2002. Such measures inevitably lead to increased bureaucracy and the tougher reporting measures created by the Patriot Act is said to have led to a flood of data for government agencies. The Financial Crimes Enforcement Network (FinCEN) and the Internal Revenue Service (IRS) have both reported difficulties in handling an increased workload (Giraldo and Trinkunas, 2007).

In Britain, the Terrorism Act 2006, the use of Control Orders, enforcement of the Immigration, Asylum and Nationality Act 2006, and the Border Management programme, have all played a part in strengthening areas of security weakness and improving border security with minimal disruption to law-abiding citizens. Britain, unlike the United States, was familiar with the use of terrorist and emergency legislation and sought to build new legislation around their past experience of terrorism in the UK and the emergence of the new threat.

Counterterrorist initiatives, which are commonly of a military and security nature, are often considered by detractors to escalate rather than alleviate levels of perceived threat, actual violence and alienation of the base population. Experience has taught us that military and physical force interventions are largely ineffective, and this is the reason that many post 9/11 initiatives have seen significant progress made towards a 'hearts and minds' based approach (Breen Smyth, 2007). Therein can lie the problem: there is a temptation to reinvent the wheel and a refusal to learn from the past. Thankfully, this is not always the case and an impressive example of harnessing lessons learned from the past exists in the *Legacy* programme in Afghanistan. A United States-funded initiative, whose budget is listed at $45 million for 2010–11, and administered by the British company New Century, seeks to use the experiences of the Royal Ulster Constabulary's Special Branch in order to train personnel and provide the foundations for a more effective response to terrorism in Afghanistan, while building capacity and sustainability for the Afghan police and military.

Conclusion

Both English (2009) and Kilcullen (2009) suggest frameworks for how efforts to respond to terrorism must be directed. Of the two, English is the more expansive. He suggests we should:

- learn to live with it;
- where possible, address underlying root problems and causes;
- avoid over-militarisation of the response;
- acknowledge that intelligence is the most vital element in successful counterterrorism;
- respect orthodox legal frameworks and adhere to the democratically established rule of law;
- co-ordinate security-related, financial and technological preventative measures; and
- maintain strong credibility in the counterterrorist public argument.

Many of the points raised by English have been widely accepted and adopted as counterterrorism strategy across the globe and it is timely to draw reference to a few.

Through the creation and publication of counterterrorism strategies and initiatives, the state has moved from the shadows into the public arena and acknowledgement of the danger we all face and must learn to live with. Such an announcement is designed to share responsibility in countering terrorism and charges society with a duty to assist in this regard. Law enforcement and intelligence agencies alone cannot and will not succeed in this battle. Military might has been erroneously used in the past and using a sledgehammer to crack a nut is counter-productive and plays into the hands of those who seek to provoke repressive acts or kinetic actions by the state. A multifaceted response geared towards addressing legitimate grievances and seeking to engage in dialogue with our enemies is preferable to a knee jerk security response. The importance of adhering to a criminal justice model also cannot be over-emphasised, and the necessity of putting suspected offenders before a court, even at the risk of them being acquitted, is a price worth paying in any democracy. Military courts and tribunals cannot be sustained or approved. The existence of Guantánamo Bay, Cuba, 2011, like Long Kesh, in Northern Ireland in 1971, ultimately serves only the interests of terrorists who obtain significant propaganda value and claims for legitimacy for their cause.

Recognition of the importance of intelligence in this struggle, particularly of human sources, must be developed and pursued as a matter of urgency. Human sources are the strongest and most adaptable weapon in the armoury of the state in its efforts to counter the threat of terrorism, and a heavy investment in their continued use should be encouraged. The protean capability of terrorism to morph and adapt as a living entity will undoubtedly continue to frustrate attempts to thwart and reduce activity, but the use of human intelligence has the potential to tip the balance in our favour. Counterterrorism efforts should continue to be directed not at focusing on attempting to defeat the terrorists, but attempting to have the terrorists defeat themselves (Geltzer and Forest, 2009). It is important to recognise that the response to the threat we face is complex, multifaceted and a living entity. There is no one-size-fits-all solution, no silver bullet to aid us in what lies ahead. As Gouré (2004: 272) aptly notes:

> Victory cannot be defined in terms of eradicating terrorism or eliminating risk. This war must be defined in more limited terms. It will consist of reducing the threat of terrorism to acceptable levels – levels that allow us to go on with our lives in spite of the fact that new attacks are possible and that we may well see further and more serious tragedies.

NO: 'Using a sledgehammer to crack a nut'

Rachel Monaghan

Introduction

There is little doubt that since the events of 9/11, the threat posed by al-Qaeda and al-Qaeda-inspired terrorists remains a considerable one. The current threat level (March 2011) in the United Kingdom in terms of international terrorism is severe, indicating that the Home Office considers the possibility of an attack as highly likely. In the United States, the Homeland Security Advisory System says that the government's national threat level is 'elevated' (yellow), indicating a significant risk of terrorist attacks, whilst the threat level for domestic and international flights is at 'high' (orange), suggesting a high risk of terrorist attacks. At a regional level, New York City is considered to be at 'high risk' (orange) of a terrorist attack.

This chapter considers the question of whether global efforts to reduce terrorism and political violence have been effective in the post-9/11 era. To this end, it will provide an examination of some of the policies and strategies that have been utilized and consider whether or not they have resulted in a reduction in terrorist activity.

Counterterrorism approaches

Within the literature, efforts to reduce terrorism and political violence have been divided into two broad categories – counterterrorism and anti-terrorism. Counterterrorism involves proactive policies designed to remove either the terrorist environment and/or the groups willing to utilize political violence to achieve their goal(s). Within counterterrorism, we can further identify two approaches in dealing with terrorism. The first are often labelled hard-line responses bereft of compromise or negotiation. Such responses often involve the use of the military and other repressive measures to eliminate the threat of terrorism. The second approach is that of soft-line responses. These involve measures aimed at reducing the terrorist environment through the use of diplomacy or negotiation, the addressing of grievances through social reform and other concessions (see Martin, 2010; Rees and Aldrich, 2005; Wardlaw, 1990). In contrast, anti-terrorism refers to defensive measures, which are designed to prevent terrorist attacks and would include enhanced security and target hardening (Lum *et al.*, 2006a; Martin, 2011).

Following the events of 9/11, a range of hard-line options have been pursued by the United States and its allies, the most obvious of which is the 'war on terror' initiated by the Bush Administration. Nine days after the attacks on the World Trade Center and the Pentagon, President Bush stated in a joint session of Congress:

> Our war on terror begins with al Qaeda, but it does not end there. It will not end until every terrorist group of global reach has been found, stopped and defeated . . . Every nation, in every region, now has a decision to make. Either you are with us, or you are with the terrorists. From this day forward, any nation that continues to harbor or support terrorism will be regarded by the United States as a hostile regime.
>
> (Bush, 2001)

In early October 2001, Operation Enduring Freedom began with the invasion of Afghanistan and a military campaign against the Taliban regime which had provided a safe haven to al-Qaeda. Whilst in the short term Operation Enduring Freedom succeeded in removing the Taliban from power and dispersing al-Qaeda and its leadership, the reality is that ten years after its inception more than 140,000 foreign troops remain in Afghanistan. In addition, since 2005, coalition military fatalities have risen with 711 fatalities recorded for 2010 (BBC News, 2010; icasualities.org, 2011). Furthermore, 2010 also saw an increase in the numbers of civilians (2,777) killed as a result of the armed conflict (United Nations Assistance Mission in Afghanistan, 2011).

In addition to the operation in Afghanistan, the United States and its allies launched Operation Iraqi Freedom in March 2003, which was designed 'to disarm Iraq of weapons of mass destruction, to end Saddam Hussein's support for terrorism, and to free the Iraqi people'

(Bush, 2003). Although Saddam Hussein was removed from power and the Iraqi Armed Forces and Republican Guard defeated in 2003, the allies were met with an insurgency from Iraqis opposed to the occupation of their country and a campaign of terrorism waged by 'foreign fighters', including al-Qaeda affiliates (Robben, 2010; Wilkinson, 2001/2006/2011). Political violence in Iraq continues today and estimates of the number of civilians killed vary depending upon the source. For example, leaked Pentagon files contain records of some 66,000 civilian deaths between 2005 and 2009, other sources such as the Iraqi Body Count suggest nearly 110,000 since the 2003 invasion, whilst a study published in *The Lancet*, a leading medical journal, estimates over 600,000 Iraqi post-invasion deaths as of July 2006 (Burnham *et al.*, 2006; Iraqi Body Count, 2011; Leigh, 2010).

In tangent with the military operations noted above, other repressive measures were employed to eliminate terrorism. The core leadership of al-Qaeda was targeted and in the first two years after 9/11, the United States had killed or captured some 20 core members. By 2007, the United States government was able to claim to have removed 75 per cent of al-Qaeda's old leadership, although this did not include Bin Laden at the time (Gregg, 2009). Since 2002, the United States has employed unmanned aerial vehicles or drones to target suspected al-Qaeda members. While such attacks have succeeded in killing al-Qaeda militants, they are also credited with causing civilian casualties and deaths (BBC News, 2011a).

A hard-line approach can also be observed in relation to the treatment of suspected insurgents and terrorists. The use of extraordinary rendition, whereby suspects are abducted and held in secret jails or 'ghost prisons' located in third countries such as Syria and Egypt, has been used by the United States in its 'war on terror' (Amnesty International, 2010a; Rees and Aldrich, 2005). Rogers (2008: 199) suggests that:

> since 9/11, around 100,000 people have been detained for varying lengths of time. Some have been detained without trial for close to five years and fewer than a thousand have been tried in court and then sentenced. At any one time, at least 15,000 people are detained without trial, mainly in Iraq and Afghanistan.

In terms of Iraq, Amnesty International (2010b) estimates some 30,000 people are held untried, despite the provisions of the 2008 Amnesty Law which stipulates that uncharged prisoners should be released after a period of between six to twelve months.

The initial decision by President Bush in 2002 to not recognize Taliban detainees and suspected al-Qaeda members as prisoners of war and also to deny them the legal provisions of the Third Geneva Convention meant that 'the decision to replace well established military doctrine, i.e., legal compliance with the Geneva Conventions, with a policy subject to interpretation, impacted the treatment of detainees in U.S. custody' (Senate Armed Services Committee, 2008: xiii). The Fay Report found evidence that military intelligence personnel were involved in the abuse of Iraqi prisoners at Baghdad's Abu Ghraib jail, but concluded that the behavior was confined to 'a small number of soldiers' (BBC News, 2004). However, it has since been found that detainees in American military custody in Afghanistan, Iraq and at Guantánamo Bay have been subject not only to mistreatment, but also to the use of aggressive interrogation techniques such as enforced nudity, stress positions and water-boarding (Robben, 2010; Senate Armed Services Committee, 2008).

In addition to these hard-line approaches involving the military overseas, the domestic arena in both the United States and the United Kingdom has experienced changes in terms of terrorism legislation. In the United States, the PATRIOT Act was passed in October 2001. This enabled greater surveillance by the state, including the use of roving wiretaps on telephones and enhanced electronic surveillance such as tapping into e-mail, electronic address books and computers. Additionally, the Act allowed for the deportation of immigrants who engaged in fundraising activities on behalf of terrorist groups and their detention without charge for seven days on suspicion of supporting terrorism (Martin, 2011). In the United Kingdom, amendments to the Terrorism Act 2000 have expanded both the police's powers and the definition of terrorism. Thus, the government has increased the length of time that suspected terrorists could be held without charge (this has recently decreased from 28 days to 14) and curtailed the movement of people deemed to be a threat to national security through the use of control orders (BBC News, 2011b). Furthermore, it is now an offense to incite and/or glorify terrorism, provide assistance to terrorists or provide training in the use of explosives and/or firearms (Klausen, 2009).

The United Kingdom's counterterrorism strategy, known as *Contest*, embodies elements of both hard-line and soft-line approaches aimed at reducing terrorism. *Contest* stresses a four-pronged response for dealing with terrorism, namely, Pursue, Prevent, Protect and Prepare (HM Government, 2006, 2010; Klausen, 2009). The Prevent strand aims to dissuade individuals from becoming involved in terrorism through 'addressing "structural problems" such as inequality and discrimination, changing "the environment" to deter radicalisation and "engaging in the battle of ideas"' (Klausen, 2009: 406).

The second broad category of efforts to reduce terrorism and political violence involves anti-terrorism measures. Such measures are designed to prevent or deter terrorist attacks. For example, key political locations such as the White House in Washington, DC and Downing Street in London have restricted vehicular access. As Martin (2011: 275) notes, 'these measures are not long-term solutions for ending terrorist environments but do serve to provide short-term protection for specific sites'.

Despite the combination of hard-line and soft-line approaches to terrorism and the continued use and development of anti-terrorism measures, terrorism has not gone away over the past ten years. Indeed, the world has witnessed a number of high profile attacks in Bali (2002), Madrid (2004), London (2005), Mumbai (2008) and the recent bombing of Moscow's Domodedovo International Airport (2011). The National Counterterrorism Center's report for 2009 records nearly 11,000 terrorist attacks in some 83 countries around the world, which saw 58,000 persons injured including 15,000 deaths (National Counterterrorism Center, 2010: 9). The report also suggests that 60 percent of all terrorist attacks occur in Afghanistan, Iraq and Pakistan and 'as has been the case since 2005, substantial numbers of victims of terrorist attacks in 2009 were Muslim' (National Counterterrorism Center, 2010: 11).

Whilst the hard-line approaches adopted by the United States have resulted in no more 9/11s, some argue that the invasion of Iraq actually saved the organization from imploding (Bergen, 2006; Hewitt, 2008). Subsequently, al-Qaeda continues to exist and has morphed to cope with the hostile environment created by the United States and its allies' 'war on terror' (Cronin, 2010; Jenkins, 2011; Keen, 2006). As Hoffman (2009a: 362) notes:

> The al-Qaeda of 2008 . . . is in fact a mere shadow of its pre-9/11 self. It does not have the freedom of movement, massive personnel numbers, robust network of training camps and operational bases, functioning international infrastructure, and considerable largesse that is possessed eight years ago when it was located in Taliban-ruled Afghanistan.

The United States' kinetic approach to counterterrorism has been criticized by many because it has failed to learn from previous counterterrorism and counterinsurgency operations. For such measures to work the support and trust of the civilian population must be won, restraint must be exercised with regard to the use of military force directed at the enemy and care taken not to injure and kill civilians (Benjamin, 2008; Wilkinson, 2001/2006/2011). Indeed, there are strong arguments that the use of the military in counterterrorism does not result in a reduction in terrorism but has the opposite effect in that it encourages it (Duyvesteyn, 2008; Keen 2006). For example, the use of targeted killings results 'always [in] an upsurge in terrorist or other violent activity. There is a cycle of violence and counter-violence' (Duyvesteyn, 2008: 338).

Additionally, the use of the military in counterterrorism fulfills the terrorist aims of ensuring an over-reaction by the state to their violence. Gregg (2009) further believes that the ongoing hard-line strategy involving the military is playing into the hands of al-Qaeda's ideology, especially in relation to its claim that Islam is under attack and therefore requires Muslims to wage *jihad* in defense of their faith. Thus, Operation Iraqi Freedom 'has significantly deepened the anger that is fuelling terrorism among Islamist militants in particular. Iraq has become to some extent a magnet and a cause célèbre for these militants' (Keen, 2006: 88). This view is further echoed by Stella Rimington, the ex-head of MI5 (British domestic security service):

> Look at what those people who've been arrested or have left suicide videos say about their motivation. And most of them, as far as I'm aware, say that the war in Iraq played a significant part in persuading them that this is the right course of action to take.
>
> (Quoted in Aitkenhead, 2008)

In addition, the treatment of detainees held in United States custody at Abu Ghraib and at Guantánamo Bay has also 'generated considerable opprobrium throughout the Muslim world and has become a rallying cry for terrorist recruitment and incitement of further anti-U.S. violence' (Hoffman, 2009a: 361). In 2003, young British Muslims started to become involved in Islamist terrorism, for example, the unsuccessful 'Shoe-bomber' Richard Reid, and Omar Sharif and Asif Hanif who launched a suicide attack in Tel Aviv, Israel (Pantucci, 2010).

It is argued that the treatment of Muslims in Britain has resulted in the 'cultivation [of] frustration and resentment that can translate into tacit support for acts of violence, despite the moderate and tolerant nature of the much larger majority' (Kirby, 2007: 422). Their experience of racism, domestic social inequalities, suspicion following 9/11, the generational gap between parents and their children together with radical preachers and the external events in Afghanistan and Iraq have all contributed to disaffected and detached Muslims being drawn into the global Islam cause (Kirby, 2007; Pantucci, 2010; Spalek and McDonald, 2009).

The events of 7/7 in London were the result of the radicalization of four young British Muslims: Hasib Hussain, Mohammad Sidique Khan, Germaine Linsday and Shehzad Tanweer (English, 2009; Hewitt, 2008). In his martyrdom video Khan explains the reason behind his decision to become a suicide bomber:

> Our driving motivation doesn't come from tangible commodities that this world has to offer . . . Your democratically elected governments continuously perpetuate atrocities against my people all over the world. And your support of them makes you directly responsible . . . Until we feel security, you will be our targets. And until you stop the bombing, gassing, imprisonment and torture of my people we will not stop this fight.
>
> (Quoted in Hoffman, 2009b: 1103)

Martin (2010) argues that growing anti-American and Western sentiment is linked to the foreign policies of the West and this is clearly articulated by Khan's quote. As Lawrence notes 'they hate us because of what we do, and it seems to contradict who we say we are . . . the major issue is that our policy seems to contradict our own basic values' (cited in Martin, 2010: 80).

The United States has also experienced domestic radicalization cases. According to Jenkins (2010: vii), between 9/11 and the end of 2009, there have been 46 such cases involving 125 individuals living in the United States who have either plotted to carry out terrorist attacks on American soil, engaged in 'providing material support to foreign terrorist organizations' or left America to join up with jihadi groups abroad. Of concern to Jenkins is both the increase in individuals involved (42) and the number of cases (13) discovered in 2009. Although 'overt expressions of [American] Muslim militancy are muted and rare', he argues, 'recruitment and self-recruitment to jihadist terrorism are, however, likely to continue' (Jenkins, 2010: 12).

According to the then Director-General (head) of MI5, Dame Eliza Manningham-Buller, in 2006 there were some 200 groups/networks involving around 1,600 known individuals who were plotting or facilitating terrorist acts both in the United Kingdom and abroad (Cronin, 2010). In August 2006, a planned airline bomb plot was foiled in London, and in June 2007, two car bombs failed to explode in central London. The bombers subsequently drove a suicide car bomb into the departure lounge of Glasgow International Airport. These incidents together with incidents in the United States, namely, the unsuccessful 'underwear bomber' Umer Farouk Abdulmatallab in 2009, the case of Najibullah Zazi (who planned to target the New York subway with a suicide bomb in 2009) and the car bomb left at Times Square by Faisal Shahzad in 2010, indicate that the number and frequency of attacks (successful and unsuccessful) have increased (Cronin, 2010).

The hard-line and soft-line approaches discussed have also resulted in additional costs far beyond their initial targets. The Report of the Eminent Jurists Panel on Terrorism, Counter-Terrorism and Human Rights (2009) argues that there has been both an 'erosion' of international humanitarian law and international human rights law. The treatment of suspected insurgents and terrorists, including secret detentions, detention without charge or trial, extraordinary rendition and their mistreatment by their captors, they argue, is not a legitimate counterterrorism response. Indeed, they state that:

> Such practices are not only inconsistent with established principles of international law, and undermine the values on which free and democratic societies are based, but as the lessons of history show, they put the possibility of short term gains from illegal actions, above the more enduring long term harm that they cause.
> (Report of the Eminent Jurists Panel on Terrorism, Counter-Terrorism and Human Rights, 2009: 160)

This view is echoed by Amnesty International (2011) who examined the record of the American administration and Congress in relation to human rights failures in respect of Guantánamo Bay detentions. They concluded that America 'had violated its obligations under international law, and betrayed the principles of human rights and rule of law it had previously professed to the world' (Amnesty International, 2011: 1).

At a national level, research has suggested that some legislation enacted in the aftermath of 9/11 has been used against 'ordinary' criminals, political opponents, dissenters, and members of minority communities (Report of the Eminent Jurists Panel on Terrorism,

Counter-Terrorism and Human Rights, 2009; Whitaker, 2007). Indeed, newspaper reports in the United Kingdom found that local councils were using anti-terror laws to 'spy' on local residents, tackle dog fouling, prevent the unlawful selling of pizza and deal with noisy children (Hastings, 2008; Mostrous, 2008). Such behavior undermines the criminal justice system in that the legislation is used arbitrarily and not for its intended purposes, namely, countering terrorism. In some cases, it has resulted in greater state oppression. For example, Mertus and Sajjad (2008) note that the Indian government's Prevention of Terrorism Act (POTA) of 2001 led to human rights violations and politically motivated detentions, whereas China justified a crackdown on Uighur separatists in its 'war on terror'.

Conclusion

Much of the global effort to reduce terrorism and political violence in the past decade has not been effective in either removing the terrorist environment or the groups willing to utilize political violence to achieve their goals. In some instances, the counterterrorism strategy employed has been akin to 'using a sledgehammer to crack a nut' and the hard-line approaches utilized, especially those measures involving the military and treatment of detainees, have inadvertently provided al-Qaeda with propaganda coups, boosted their recruitment and inspired others to undertake terrorism. Anti-terrorism measures in themselves cannot and will not prevent a would-be attacker with sufficient commitment, intent and capability, and may lead to the displacement of terrorist attacks on softer, less secure targets such as night-clubs. To quote the ex-head of MI5 (Baroness Manningham-Buller): 'You cannot guarantee security, however many resources, however clever you are, however much you work with other people. You will not stop all terror and it's a delusion to think you will' (quoted on Taylor, 2011).

Discussion questions

1   How should we evaluate the success or failure of counterterrorism since 9/11? What measures or standards should we use in that evaluation?
2   What successes and failures have there been in counterterrorism since 9/11?
3   Is the nature of the terrorist threat faced since 9/11 significantly different from the past? Does it require a new approach?
4   Which should take priority when attempting to counterterrorism – human rights or national security?
5   How should states address the threat of home-grown terrorists?
6   Do you consider hard-line or soft-line options to be the most appropriate for countering terrorism?
7   Can anti-terrorism measures alone prevent terrorism?
8   Should we consider 'talking to' al-Qaeda, and if so, under what circumstances?
9   How can counterterrorism measures be made to be more effective?

Further readings

Art, R., and Richardson, L., eds, 2007. *Democracy and Counter-terrorism: Lessons from the Past*, Washington, DC: United States Institute of Peace Press.
Cochrane, M., 2008. *Countering Terrorism through Intelligence-led Policing*, London: Fulbright Commission.
Crelinsten, R., 2009. *Counterterrorism*, Cambridge: Polity.
English, R., 2009. *Terrorism: How to Respond*, Oxford: Oxford University Press.

Hewitt, S., 2008. *The British War on Terror*, London: Continuum.

Nacos, B., 2008. *Terrorism and Counter-terrorism: Understanding Threats and Responses in the Post-9/11 World*, 2nd ed., New York: Penguin Academics.

Wilkinson, P., 2011. *Terrorism versus Democracy*, Abingdon: Routledge.

References

Abbott, C., Rogers, P., and Sloboda, J., 2006. *Global Responses to Global Challenges: Sustainable Security for the 21st Century*, Oxford: Oxford Research Group.

Abrams, M., 2006. 'Why Terrorism Does Not Work', *International Security*, 31(2): 42–78.

Abrahms, M., 2011. 'Fear of "Lone Wolf" Misplaced', *Baltimore Sun*, 5 January, 2011.

Ackerman, G., 2009. 'The Future of Jihadists and WMD', in Ackerman, G., and Tamsett, J., eds, *Jihadists and Weapons of Mass Destruction*, Boca Raton, FL: CRC Press.

Addicott, J., 2011. *Terrorism Law: Materials, Cases, and Comments*, 6th ed., Tuscon, AZ: Lawyers and Judges Publishing Co.

Aitkenhead, D., 2008. 'Free Agent', *The Guardian*, 18 October 2008, available online at: http://www.guardian.co.uk/commentisfree/2008/oct/18/iraq-britainand911?intcmp=239, accessed 15 February 2011.

al-Banna, Shaykh Ibrahim, 2010. 'Tawaghit Exposed', *Inspire*, 3 (November): 11.

al-Hindi, E. (aka Dhiren Barot), 1999. *The Army of Madinah in Kashmir*, Birmingham, UK: Maktabah Al Ansaar Publications.

al-Qirshi, A., 2002. 'The 11 September Raid: The Impossible Becomes Possible', in Majallat al-Ansar, ed., 'Book commemorates September 11 "raid"' (FBIS, Trans.; par. 114–193).

al-Uyayree, Y. (As-Sabeel, trans.), n.d., 'Meanings of Victory and Loss in Jihaad', available online at: http://www.maktabah.net/store/images/35/Meanings%20of%20Victory%20and%20Loss%20in%20Jihaad.pdf.

Albright, D., and Hygins, H., 2003. 'A Bomb for the Ummah', *Bulletin of Atomic Scientists*, March/April, 59(2): 49–55.

Alexander, Y., ed., 2010. *Combating Terrorism: Strategies of Ten Countries*, Ann Arbor, MI: University of Michigan Press.

Alibek, K., 1999. *Biohazard*, with Stephen Handelman, New York. Dell Publishing.

Allen, J., 2005. 'Warrant to Torture? A Critique of Dershowitz and Levinson', *ACDIS Occasional Paper, Program in Arms Control, Disarmament, and International Security*, University of Illinois at Urbana-Champaign, available online at: http://www.acdis.uiuc.edu, accessed 31 January 2011.

Allhoff, F., 2003. 'Terrorism and Torture', *International Journal of Applied Philosophy*, 17: 121–134.

Allison, G., 2004. *Nuclear Terrorism: The Ultimate Preventable Catastrophe*, New York: Times Books.

Alonso, R., 2001. 'The Modernization in Irish Republican Thinking toward the Utility of Violence', *Studies in Conflict and Terrorism*, 24(2): 131–144.

Améry, J., 1980. 'Torture', in Améry, J., ed., *At the Mind's Limit*, translated by S. and S. Rosenfeld, Bloomington, IN: Indiana University Press.

Amnesty International, 2010a. *Open Secret: Mounting Evidence of Europe's Complicity in Rendition and Secret Detention*, London: Amnesty International.

Amnesty International, 2010b. *New Order, Same Abuses: Unlawful Detentions and Torture in Iraq*, London: Amnesty International.

Amnesty International, 2011. *USA: Digging a Deeper Hole*, available online at: http://www.amnesty.org/en/library/asset/AMR51/016/2011/en/2c6adc7b-f362-4120-b934-a6a0d4d17c6c/amr510162011en.pdf, accessed 13 March 2011.

Arce, D., and Sandler, T., 2005. 'Counterterrorism; A Game-Theoretic Analysis', *Journal of Conflict Resolution*, 49(2): 183–200.

Arendt, H., 1967/1968. *The Origins of Totalitarianism*, 3rd ed., London: Allen and Unwin.

Arendt, H., 1973. 'On Violence', in Arendt, H., *Crises of the Republic*, Harmondsworth: Penguin.

Aristotle, 2000. *The Politics*, Dover Thrift Edition, Mineola, NY, reprint of the 1885 edition, translated by Benjamin Jowett, Oxford: The Clarendon Press.

Army Field Manual, 2006. *Army Field Manual (FM) 2-22.3, Human Intelligence Collector Operations*, available online at: http://www.army.mil/institution/armypublicaffairs/pdf/fm2-22-3.pdf.

Army Regulation 350-30, Code of Conduct, Survival, Evasion, Resistance, and Escape (SERE) Training, available online at: http://www.fas.org/irp/doddir/army/ar350-30.pdf.

Arquilla, J., and Ronfeldt, D., eds, 2001. *Networks and Netwars: The Future of Terror, Crime and Militancy*, Santa Monica, CA: RAND.

Arquilla, J., Ronfeldt, D., and Zanini, M., 1999. 'Networks, Netwar and Information-Age Terrorism', in Lesser, I., *et al.*, eds, *Countering the New Terrorism*, Santa Monica, CA: RAND.

Art, R., and Richardson, L., eds, 2007. *Democracy and Counter-terrorism: Lessons From the Past*, Washington, DC: United States Institute of Peace Press.

Asal, V., and Blum, A., 2005, 'Holy terror and mass killings? Reexamining the motivations and methods of mass casualty terrorists', *International Studies Review*, 7(1): 153–155.

Askenazi, A., 2005. 'On Islamic Websites: A Guide for Preparing Nuclear Weapons', *Sharvit Unconventional Solutions*, 12 October 2005, 1004.

Atran, S., 2003a. *In Gods We Trust: The Evolutionary Landscape of Religion*, Oxford: Oxford University Press.

Atran, S., 2003b. 'Genesis of Suicide Terrorism', *Science*, 299: 1534–1539.

Atran, S., 2007. 'Research Police: How a University IRB Thwarts Understanding of Terrorism', *Institutional Review Blog*, 28 May 2007, available online at: www.institutionalreviewblog.com/2007/05/scott-atran-research-police-how.html.

Atran, S., 2008. 'Who Becomes a Terrorist Today?', *Perspectives on Terrorism: A Journal of the Terrorism Research Initiative*, II(5): 3–10.

Atran, S., 2010. *Talking to the Enemy: Faith, Brotherhood, and the (Un)making of Terrorists*, New York: Harper Collins.

Bach Jensen, R., 2004. 'Daggers, Rifles and Dynamite: Anarchist Terrorism in Nineteenth Century Europe', *Terrorism and Political Violence*, 16(1): 116–153.

Banchoff, T., ed., 2008. *Religious Pluralism, Globalization, and World Politics*, Oxford: Oxford University Press.

Bandura, A., 1977. *Social Learning Theory*, Englewood Cliffs: Prentice Hall.

Barnhurst, K., 1991. 'Contemporary Terrorism in Peru: Sendero Luminoso and the Media', *Journal of Communication*, 41(4): 75–89.

Baron, R., 1977. *Human Aggression*, New York: Plenum Press.

Baumol, W., 1990. 'Entrepreneurship: Productive, Unproductive, Destructive', *Journal of Political Economy*, 98(5): 893–921.

Bazan, E., 2002. 'Assassination Band and E. O. 12333: A Brief Summary', *Congressional Research Service*, updated 4 January 2002, available online at: http://opencrs.com/document/RS21037/2002-01-04/.

BBC News, 2004. *Blame Widens for Abu Ghraib Abuse*, 26 August 2004, available online at: http://news.bbc.co.uk/1/hi/world/americas/3596686.stm, accessed 17 March 2011.

BBC News, 2005. 'Al-Qaeda Terror Suspect Convicted', 24 November 2005, available online at: http://news.bbc.co.uk/1/hi/northern_ireland/4467640.stm, accessed 26 February 2011.

BBC News, 2010. *Q & A: Foreign Forces in Afghanistan*, 18 November 2010, available online at: http://www.bbc.co.uk/news/world-south-asia-11371138, accessed 28 February 2011.

BBC News, 2011a. *US Drone Strike 'kills 40' in Pakistani Tribal Region*, 17 March 2011, available online at: http://www.bbc.co.uk/news/world-south-asia-12769209, accessed 18 March 2011.

BBC News, 2011b. *UK Counter-Terror Review Explained*, 26 January 2011, available online at: http://www.bbc.co.uk/news/uk-12289294?print=true, accessed 24 February 2011.

Beam, L., 1992. 'Leaderless Resistance', *The Seditionist*, 12, available online at: http://www.louisbeam.com/leaderless.htm.

Becker, S., 1963. *Outsiders: Studies in the Sociology of Deviance*, London: Simon and Schuster.

Beckett, I., 2001. *Modern Insurgencies and Counter-Insurgencies: Guerrillas and their Opponents since 1750*, London: Routledge.

Begin, M., 1951. *The Revolt: The Story of Irgun*, trans. Shmuel Katz, New York: Henry Schuman.

Bell, J., 2000. *The IRA 1968–2000: Analysis of a Secret Army*, London: Frank Cass.

Benjamin, A., and Simon, S., 2000a. 'The New Face of Terrorism', *The New York Times*, 4 January, 2000.

Benjamin, A., and Simon, S., 2000b. 'America and the New Terrorism', *Survival*, 42(1): 59–75.

Benjamin, D., 2008. 'Using Hard Power in the Fight against Terrorism', in The International Centre for the Study of Radicalisation and Political Violence, eds, *Perspectives on Radicalisation and Political Violence: Papers from the First International Conference on Radicalisation and Political Violence*, London: ICSR.

Benjamin, D., and Simon, S., 2005. *The Next Attack: The Failure of the War on Terror and a Strategy for Getting It Right*, New York: Henry Holt and Co.

Bergen, P., 2002. *Holy War, Inc.: Inside the Secret World of Osama bin Laden*, revised ed., London: Phoenix.

Bergen, P., 2006. *The Osama Bin Laden I Know: An Oral History of Al Qaeda's Leader*, New York: Free Press.

Bergen, P., 2010. 'Reevaluating Al-Qa'ida's Weapons of Mass Destruction Capabilities', *CTC Sentinel*, September: 1–4.

Bergen, P., and Hoffman, B., 2010. *Assessing the Terrorist Threat: A Report of the Bipartisan Policy Centre's National Security Preparedness Group*, Washington, DC: Bipartisan Policy Centre.

Bergen, P., Hoffman, B., and Tiedemann, K., 2011. 'Assessing the Jihadist Terrorist Threat to America and American Interests', *Studies in Conflict & Terrorism*, 34(2): 65–101.

Bergen, P., and Tiedemann, K., 2010. 'The Almanac of Al Qaeda', *Foreign Policy*, (May/June), available online at: http://www.foreignpolicy.com/articles/2010/04/26/the_almanac_of_al_qaeda.

Berkowitz, L., 1993. *Aggression: Its Causes, Consequences, and Control*, New York: McGraw-Hill.

Berrebi, C., and Klor, E., 2003. 'On Terrorism and Electoral Outcomes: Theory and Evidence from Israel-Palestinian Conflict', Mimeo: Princeton University.

Bianchi, A., and Keller, A., eds, 2008. *Counterterrorism: Democracy's Challenge, Studies in International Law, 19*, Oxford and Portland, OR: Hart Publishing.

Bienvenu, R., 1970. *The Ninth of Thermidor*, Oxford: Oxford University Press, Inc..

Biletzki, A., 2001. 'The Judicial Rhetoric of Morality: Israel's High Court of Justice on the Legality of Torture', unpublished paper, available online at: http://www.sss.ias.edu/publications/papers/papernine/pdf, accessed 31 January 2011.

Bilmes, L., and Stiglitz, J., 2008. 'The Iraq War Will Cost us $3 Trillion, and Much More', *Washington Post*, 9 March 2008, available online at: http://www.washingtonpost.com/wp-dyn/content/article/2008/03/07/AR2008030702846.html.

Bingham, T., 2010. *The Rule of Law*, London: Allen Lane.

Bishop, P., and Mallie, E., 1988. *The Provisional IRA*, London: Corgi Books.

Bissell, R., Haignere, C., McCamant, J., and Picklo, M., 1978. Varieties of Political Repression, Unpublished paper presented to the U.S. Department of State.

Blakeley, R., 2009. *State Terrorism and Neoliberalism: The North in the South*, Abingdon: Routledge.

Blau, J., and Blau, P., 1982. 'The Cost of Inequality: Metropolitan Structure and Violent Crime', *American Sociological Review*, 47: 114–129.

Blitz, J., 2010. 'A Threat Transformed', *Financial Times*, 10 January 2010, available online at: http://www.ft.com/cms/s/0/af31e344-0499-11df-8603-00144feabdc0.html#axzz1HGk5gWSr.

Blok, A., 2000. 'The Enigma of Senseless Violence', in Aijmer, G., and Abbink, J., eds, *Meanings of Violence: A Cross Cultural Perspective*, Oxford: Berg.

Bowman, S., and Barel, H., 1999. *Weapons of Mass Destruction – the Terrorist Threat. CRS Report for Congress*, December 9, 1999, Congressional Research Service, The Library of Congress, available online at: www.cnie.org, accessed 22 April 2011.

Brecher, B., 2007. *Torture and the Ticking Bomb*, Oxford: Wiley-Blackwell.

Breen Smyth, M., 2007. 'Symposium: The Case for Terrorism Studies – A Critical Research Agenda for the Study of Political Terror', *European Political Science*, 6(3): 260–267.

Brinkbäumer, K., and Goetz, J., 2010. 'Obama's Shadowy Drone War: Taking out the Terrorists by Remote Control', *Der Spiegel online*, 10 October 2010, available online at: http://www.spiegel.de/international/world/0,1518,722583-4,00.html.

Brodsky, B., 2007. 'Industrial Chemicals as Weapons: Chlorine', *James Martin Center for Nonproliferation Studies*, 31 July 2007, available online at: www.nti.org, accessed 22 April 2011.

Brophy-Baermann, B., and Conybeare, J., 1994. 'Retaliating Against Terrorism: Rational Expectations and the Optimality of Rules Versus Discretion', *American Journal of Political Science*, 38(1): 209.

Broszat, M., 1981. *The Hitler State*, London: Longman.

Bryan, D., Kelly, L., and Templer, S., 2011. 'The Failed Paradigm of "Terrorism"', *Behavioral Sciences of Terrorism and Political Aggression*, 3(2): 80–96.

B'Tselem, 2011. 'Statistics', available online at: http://www.btselem.org/english/statistics/casualties.asp, accessed 20 May 2011.

Bueno de Mesquita, E., 2003. 'The Quality of Terror', Mimeo: Department of Political Science, Washington University, St. Louis.

Bullock, A., 1962. *Hitler: A Study in Tyranny*, Harmondsworth: Pelican.

Burke, J., 2003. *Al-Qaeda: Casting a Shadow of Terror*, London: I.B. Tauris.

Burke, J., 2007. *Al-Qaeda: The True Story of Radical Islam*, London: Penguin Books.

Burnham, G., Lafta, R., Doocy, S., and Roberts, L., 2006. 'Mortality after the 2003 Invasion of Iraq: A Cross-Sectional Cluster Sample Survey', *The Lancet*, 368(545): 1421–1428.

Burns, C., 2008. *More Moral Than God*, New York: Rowman and Littlefield.

Burns, W., and Slovic, P., 2006. *Predicting Public Response to a Terrorist Strike*, Report No. 06–02, Eugene, OR: Decision Research.

Bush, G., 2001. *Address to a Joint Session of Congress and the American People*, 20 September 2001, available online at: http://georgewbush-whitehouse.archives.gov/news/releases/2001/09/20010920-8.html, accessed 28 February 2011.

Bush, G., 2003. *Radio Address: Beginning of Operation Iraqi Freedom*, 22 March 2003, available online at: http://georgewbush-whitehouse.archives.gov/news/releases/2003/03/20030322.html, accessed 25 March 2011.

Bushman, B., and Huesmann, L., 2010. 'Aggression', in Fiske, S., Gilbert, D., and Lindzey, G., eds, *Handbook of Social Psychology*, 5th ed., New York: Wiley.

Butterworth, A., 2010. *The World that Never Was*, London: The Bodley Head.

Byman, D., 2003. 'Al-Qaeda as an Adversary: Do We Understand Our Enemy?', *World Politics*, 56(1): 139–163.

Byman, D., 2005/2007. *Deadly Connections: States That Sponsor Terrorism*, Cambridge: Cambridge University Press.

Byman, D., 2006. 'Do Targeted Killings Work?', *Foreign Affairs*, 85(2): 95–111.

Byman, D., 2009. 'Do Targeted Killings Work?', *Foreign Policy*, 14 July 2009, available online at: http://www.foreignpolicy.com/articles/2009/07/14/do_targeted_killings_work.

Carpintero-Santamaría, N., 2010. 'The Incidence of Illegal Nuclear Trafficking in Proliferation and International Security', *Behavioral Sciences of Terrorism and Political Aggression*, DOI: 10.1080/19434472.2010.512156.

Carus, W., 2006. *Defining 'Weapons of Mass Destruction'*, Washington, DC: National Defense University Press.

Casebeer, Major (USAF) W., 2003. 'Torture Interrogation of Terrorists: A Theory of Exceptions (with notes, cautions, and warnings)', available at www.atlas.usafa.af.mil/jscope/JSCOPE03/Casebeer03.html, accessed 20 January 2011.

Caspi, A., McClay, J., Moffitt, T., Mill, J., Martin, J., Craig, I., Taylor, A., and Poulton, R., 2002. 'Role of Genotype in the Cycle of Violence in Maltreated Children', *Science*, 297: 851–854.

CBSNEWS, 2010. 'FBI Terror Stings: Entrapment or Prevention?', 30 November 2010, available online at: http://www.cbsnews.com/stories/2010/11/30/national/main7103284.shtml.

Cesarani, D., 2009. 'The Farran Affair', *History Today*, 59(3): 35–39.

Chaliand, G., and Blin, A., 2007. *The History of Terrorism: From Antiquity to al Qaeda*, Berkeley, CA: University of California Press.

Charters, D., ed., 1991. *Democratic Responses to International Terrorism*, New York: Transnational Publishers.

Chase, A., 2004. *Mind for Murder: The Education of the Unabomber and the Origins of Modern Terrorism*, New York: Norton.

Chomsky, N., 1991. 'International Terrorism: Image and Reality', in George, A., ed., *Western State Terrorism*, Cambridge: Polity Press.

Chossudovsky, M., 2005. 'Tom Ridge's Mea Culpa: The Code Orange Terror Alerts were based on Fake Intelligence', Center for Research on Globalization, 12 May 2005, available online at: http://www.globalresearch.ca/articles/CH0505D.html.

Cilluffo, F., Cozzens, J., and Ranstorp, M., 2010. 'Foreign Fighters: Trends, Trajectories and Conflict Zones', George Washington University (October 2010), available online at: www.gwumc.edu/hspi/policy/report_foreignfighters501.pdf.

Claridge, D., 1996. 'State Terrorism? Applying a Definitional Model', *Terrorism and Political Violence*, 8(3): 47–63.

Cline, R., and Alexander, Y., 1986. *Terrorism as State-Sponsored Covert Warfare*, Fairfax, VA: Hero Books.

CNN Special Investigations Unit Classroom Edition, 2007. CNN, 12 June 2007, available online at: http://www.cnn.com/2007/EDUCATION/05/31/cnnpce.edge.of.disaster/index.html?iref=newssearch.

Cochrane, M., 2008. *Countering Terrorism Through Intelligence-led Policing*, London: Fulbright Commission.

Cohen, S., 1972/1987. *Folk Devils and Moral Panics: The Creation of the Mods and Rockers*, London: MacGibbon and Key, various editions.

Cole, D., 2003. *Enemy Aliens: Double Standards and Constitutional Freedoms in the War on Terrorism*, New York: The New Press.

Collier, P., and Hoeffler, A., 2004. 'Greed and Grievances in Civil War', *Oxford Economic Papers*, 56: 563–595.

Conquest, R., 1968. *The Great Terror: Stalin's Purge of the Thirties*, London: Macmillan.

Coogan, T., 1993. *The IRA: A History*, Niwot, CO: Roberts Rinehart.

Copeland, T., 2000. 'Is the "New Terrorism" Really New?: An Analysis of the New Paradigm for Terrorism', *Journal of Conflict Studies*, 21(2): 7–27.

Coser, L., 1956. *The Functions of Social Conflict*, Glencoe, IL: Free Press.

Cozzens, J., 2006. 'Approaching al-Qaida's Warfare: Function, Culture and Grand Strategy', in Ranstorp, M., ed., *Mapping Terrorism Research*, London: Routledge.

Cozzens, J., 2009a. 'Victory – from the Prism of Jihadi Culture', *Joint Force Quarterly*, January.

Cozzens, J., 2009b. 'The Culture of Global Jihad: Character, Future Challenges and Recommendations', *Future Actions Series*, International Centre for the Study of Radicalisation, King's College London (April 2009), available online at: www.icsr.info/publications/.../1238519802 ICSRJeffCozzensReport.pdf.

Crawford, C., 2003. *Inside the UDA: Volunteers and Violence*, London: Pluto Press.

Crelinsten, R., 1987. 'Power and Meaning: Terrorism as a struggle over access to the Communication Structure', in Wilkinson, P., and Stewart, A., eds, *Contemporary Research on Terrorism*, Aberdeen: Aberdeen University Press.

Crelinsten, R., 1995. 'In their Own Words: The World of the Torturer', in Crelinsten, R., and Schmid, A., eds, *The Politics of Pain: Torturers and their Masters*, Boulder, CO: Westview Press.

Crenshaw, M., 1981. 'The Causes of Terrorism', *Contemporary Politics*, 13(4): 379–399.

Crenshaw, M., ed., 1995. *Terrorism in Context*, University Park, PA: Pennsylvania State University Press.

Crenshaw, M., 2009. 'The Debate over "New" vs. "Old" Terrorism', in Karawan, I., McCormack, W., and Reynolds, S., eds, *Values and Violence: Intangible Aspects of Terrorism, Studies in Global Justice Vol. 4*, Dordrecht, The Netherlands: Springer.

Cronin, A., 2004. 'Introduction: Meeting and Managing the Threat', in Cronin, A., and Ludes, J., eds, *Attacking Terrorism: Elements of a Grand Strategy*, Washington, DC: Georgetown University Press.

Cronin, A., 2006. 'How al-Qaida Ends: The Decline and Demise of Terrorist Groups', *International Security*, 31(1): 7–48.

Cronin, A., 2009. *How Terrorism Ends: Understanding the Decline and Demise of Terrorist Campaigns*, Princeton, NJ: Princeton University Press.

Cronin, A., 2010. 'The Evolution of Counterterrorism: Will Tactics Trump Strategy?', *International Affairs*, 86(4): 837–856.

Cruickshank, P., 2010. 'The Militant Pipeline: Between the Afghanistan–Pakistan Border Region and the West', New America Foundation, February 2010, available online at: http://newamerica.net/publications/policy/the_militant_pipeline_o.

Crystal, D., 2000. *Language Death*, Cambridge, UK: Cambridge University Press.

Daalder, I., and Lindsay, J., 2005. *America Unbound: The Bush Revolution in Foreign Policy*, Hoboken, NJ: Wiley.

Dahrendorf, R., 1958. 'Toward a Theory of Conflict', *Journal of Conflict Resolution*, 2: 69–105.

Dallin, A., and Breslauer, G., 1970. *Political Terror in Communist Systems*, Stanford, CA: Stanford University Press.

David, S., 2003a. 'Israeli's Policy of Targeted Killing', *Ethics and International Affairs*, 17(1): 111–126.

David, S., 2003b. 'If Not Combatants, Certainly Not Civilians', *Ethics and International Affairs*, 17(1): 138–140.

Davis, M., 2005. 'The Moral Justifiability of Torture and Other Cruel, Inhuman, or Degrading Treatment', *International Journal of Applied Philosophy*, 19: 161–178.

Dershowitz, A., 2002. *Why Terrorism Works: Understanding the Threat, Responding to the Challenge*, New Haven, CT: Yale University Press.

Dershowitz, A., 2011. 'Targeted Killing Vindicated', *Huffington Post*, 2 May 2011, available online at: http://www.huffingtonpost.com/alan-dershowitz/targeted-killing-vindicat_b_856538.html.

Dingley, J., 2001. 'The Bombing of Omagh, 15 August 1998: The Bombers, their Tactics, Strategy and Purpose Behind the Incident', *Studies in Conflict and Terrorism*, 24(6): 451–466.

DoD., 2006. *Directive 2310.01E, The Department of Defense Detainee Program*, available online at: http://www.defense.gov/pubs/pdfs/Detainee_Prgm_Dir_2310_9-5-06.pdf.

Dodd, V., 2011. 'British Airways Worker Rajib Karim Convicted of Terrorist Plot', *The Guardian*, 28 February 2011, available online at: http://www.guardian.co.uk/uk/2011/feb/28/british-airways-bomb-guilty-karim.

Dodge, K., Price, J., Bachorowski, J., and Newman, J., 1990. 'Hostile Attributional Biases in Severely Aggressive Adolescents', *Journal of Abnormal Psychology*, 99: 385–392.

Dollard, J., Doob, L., Miller, N., and Mowrer, O., 1939. *On Frustration and Aggression*, New Haven, CT: Yale University Press.

Donohue, L., 2002. 'Fear Itself – Counter-terrorism, Individual Rights, and U.S. Foreign Relations Post 9/11', in Howard, R., and Sawyer, R., eds, *Terrorism and Counter-terrorism: Understanding the New Security Environment*, New York: McGraw-Hill.

Durodié, B., 2007. 'Fear and Terror in a Post-Political Age', *Government & Opposition*, 42 (3): 427–450.

Duvall, R., and Stohl, M., 1983. 'Governance by Terror', in Stohl, M., ed., *The Politics of Terrorism*, 2nd ed., New York: Marcel Dekker.

Duyvesteyn, I., 2004. 'How New is the New Terrorism?', *Studies in Conflict & Terrorism*, 27(5): 439–454.

Duyvesteyn, I., 2008. 'Great Expectations: The Use of Armed Force to Combat Terrorism', *Small Wars & Insurgencies*, 19(3): 328–351.

Duyvesteyn, I., and Angstrom, J., eds, 2005. *Rethinking the Nature of War*, London: Frank Cass.

Duyvesteyn, I., and Fumerton, M., 2009. 'Insurgency and Terrorism: Is There a Difference?', in Holmqvist-Jonsater, C., and Coker, C., eds, *The Character of War in the 21st Century*, London: Routledge.

Eckstein, H., ed., 1964. *Internal War: Problems and Approaches*, New York: The Free Press.

Economist, 2003. 'Editorial: Is Torture Ever Justified?', 9 January 2003: 10–11.

Elworthy, S., and Rogers, P., 2001. *The United States, Europe and the Majority World After the 11 September Attacks, Oxford Research Group Briefing*, Oxford: Oxford Research Group.

Enders, W., and Sandler, T., 2005. 'After 9/11; Is it All Different Now?', *Journal of Conflict Resolution*, 49(2): 259–277.

English, R., 2003. *Armed Struggle: The History of the IRA*, London: Pan Macmillan/New York: Oxford University Press.

English, R., 2009. *Terrorism: How to Respond*, Oxford: Oxford University Press.

Executive Order No. 12,633, *Amending the Code of Conduct for Members of the Armed Forces of the United States*, 28 March 1988, available online at: http://en.wikisource.org/wiki/Executive_Order_12633.

Fazul, A., 2009. *War Against Islam: The Story of Fadil Harun*, vol. 2, as translated and quoted by Vahid Brown, available online at: http://www.jihadica.com/sayf-al-adl-and-al-qaidas-historical-leadership/.

Fearon, J., and Laitin, D., 2003. 'Ethnicity, Insurgency, and Civil War', *American Political Science Review*, 97: 75–90.

Felter, J., and Fishman, B., 2007. 'Al-Qa'ida's Foreign Fighters in Iraq: A First Look at the Sinjar Records', West Point CTC (December 2007), available online at: http://www.ctc.usma.edu/harmony/pdf/CTCForeignFighter.19.Dec07.pdf.

Fernbach, D., ed., 1974. *Karl Marx: The Revolution of 1848*, New York: Anchor Books.

Finnegan, R., 2009. *Perpetual War for Perpetual Peace: Pre-Emptive Strikes: A Critical Analysis of the Effectiveness and Implications for Counter-Terrorism Policies*, unpublished Masters manuscript, National University of Ireland, Maynooth.

Fisk, R., 1990. *Pity the Nation; Lebanon at War*, London: Deutsch.

Freedman, Z., and Alexander, Y., eds, 1983. *Perspectives on Terrorism*, Wilmington, DL: Scholarly Resources.

Frost, R., 2005. *Nuclear Terrorism After 9/11*, London: International Institute for Strategic Studies, Adelphi Paper 378.

Ganor, B., 2005. *The Counter-Terrorism Puzzle*, New Brunswick, NJ: Transaction Publishers.

Ganor, B., 2008. 'Terrorist Organization Typologies and the Probability of a Boomerang Effect', *Studies in Conflict & Terrorism*, 31(4): 269–283.

Garcia, R., Spennato, G., Nilsson-Todd, L., Moreau, J., Deschaux, O., 2008. 'Hippocampal Low Frequency Stimulation and Chronic Mild Stress Similarly Disrupt Fear Extinction Memory in Rats', *Neurobiol Learn Mem*, 89(4): 560–566.

Gareau, F., 2004. *State Terrorism and the United States: From Counterinsurgency to the War on Terrorism*, Atlanta, GA: Clarity Press.

Gearty, C., 1991. *Terror*, London: Faber and Faber.

Geltzer, A., and Forest, J., 2009. 'Assessing the Conceptual Battlespace', in Forest, J., ed., *Influence Warfare: How Terrorists and Governments Fight to Shape Perceptions in a War of Ideas*, Westport, CT: Praeger Security International.

George, A., ed., 1991. *Western State Terrorism*, Cambridge: Polity Press.

Gerges, F., 2005/2009. *The Far Enemy: Why Jihad Went Global*, New York: Cambridge University Press, various editions.

Gerlach, L., 2001. 'The Structure of Social Movements: Environmental Activism and Its Opponents', in Arquilla, J., and Ronfeldt, D., eds, *Networks and Netwars: The Future of Terror, Crime and Militancy*, Santa Monica, CA: RAND.

Gill, P., and Phythian, M., 2006. *Intelligence in an Insecure World*, Cambridge: Polity.

Gilmore Commission (Advisory Panel to Assess Domestic Response Capabilities for Terrorism Involving Weapons of Mass Destruction), 1999. *First Annual Report: Assessing the Threat*, 15 December 1999, Washington, DC: US Government Printer.

Giraldo, J., and Trinkunas, H., 2007. 'Terrorist Financing: Explaining Government Responses', in Giraldo, J., and Trinkunas, H., eds, *Terrorism Financing and State Responses: A Comparative Perspective*, Stanford, CA: Stanford University Press.

Golden, R., 2006. 'What Price Security? The USA PATRIOT Act and America's Balance Between Freedom and Security', in Howard, R., Forest, J., and Moore, J., eds, *Homeland Security and Terrorism: Readings and Interpretations*, New York: McGraw-Hill.

Goldwater, S., Pavlides, C., Hunter, R., Bloss, E., Hof, P., McEwen, B., and Morrison, J., 2009. 'Structural and Functional Alterations to Rat Medial Prefrontal Cortex Following Chronic Restraint Stress and Recovery', *Neuroscience*, 164(2): 798–808.

Goodin, R., 2006. *What's Wrong with Terrorism?*, Cambridge: Polity.

Gordon, A., 2010. 'Can Terrorism Become a Scientific Discipline? A Diagnostic Study', *Critical Studies on Terrorism*, 3(3): 437–458.

Gottron, F., and Shea, D., 2010. *Federal Efforts to Address the Threat of Bioterrorism*, CRS. 5-5700, available online at: www.fas.org/sgp/CRS/terror/R41123.pdf, accessed 29 May 2010.

Gouré, D., 2004. 'Homeland Security', in Cronin, A., and Ludes, J., eds, *Attacking Terrorism: Elements of a Grand Strategy*, Washington, DC: Georgetown University Press.

Graham, A., 2005. *Nuclear Terrorism*, New York: Henry Holt.

Gray, J., 2003. 'A Modest Proposal: For Preventing Torturers in Liberal Democracies from Being Abused, and for Recognising their Benefit to the Public', *New Statesman*, 17 February: 22–25.

Green, J., 1995. 'Terrorism and Politics in Iran', in Crenshaw, M., ed., *Terrorism in Context*, University Park, PA: Pennsylvania State University Press.

Greenberg, K., ed., 2005. *Al Qaeda Now: Understanding Today's Terrorists*, Cambridge: Cambridge University Press.

Gregg, H., 2009. 'Fighting Cosmic Warriors: Lessons from the First Seven Years of the Global War on Terror', *Studies in Conflict & Terrorism*, 32(3): 188–208.

Gross, M., 2003. 'Fighting by Other Means in the Mideast: A Critical Analysis of Israel's Assassination Policy', *Political Studies*, 51: 350–368.

Guiora, A., 2007. *Global Perspectives on Counterterrorism*, New York: Aspen Publishers.

Gunning, J., 2007. *Hamas in Politics; Democracy, Religion, Violence*, London: Columbia University Press.

Gupta, D., 1990. *The Economics of Political Violence: The Effects of Political Instability on Economic Growth*, New York: Praeger.

Gupta, D., 2001. *Path to Collective Madness: A Study of Social Order and Political Pathology*, Westport, CT: Praeger.

Gupta, D., 2008. *Understanding Terrorism and Political Violence: The Life Cycle of Birth, Growth, Transformation, and Demise*, London: Routledge.

Gupta, D., and Mundra, K., 2005. 'Suicide Bombing as a Strategic Instrument of Protest: An Empirical Investigation', *Terrorism and Political Violence*, 17(4): 573–598.

Gurr, N., and Cole, B., 2002/2005. *The New Face of Terrorism: Threats from Weapons of Mass Destruction*, London: I.B. Tauris, various editions.

Gurr, T., 1968. 'A Causal Model of Civil Strife: A Comparative Analysis Using A New Indices', *American Political Science Review*, 62: 1104–1124.

Gurr, T., 1970. *Why Men Rebel*, New Haven, CT: Yale University Press.

Gurr, T., 1986. 'The Political Origins of State Violence and Terror: A Theoretical Analysis', in Stohl, M., and Lopez, G., eds, *Government Violence and Repression: An Agenda for Research*, New York: Greenwood Press.

Gutteridge, W., 1986. *The New Terrorism*, London: Mansell Publishing Limited.

Hafez, M., 2007. *Suicide Bombers in Iraq: The Strategy and Ideology of Martyrdom*, Washington, DC: US Institute of Peace.

Hafez, M., and Hatfield, J., 2006. 'Do Targeted Assassinations Work? A Multivariate Analysis of Israeli Counter-Terrorism Effectiveness during Al-Aqsa Uprising', *Studies in Conflict & Terrorism*, 29(4): 359–382.

Hanlon, Q., 2008. 'Globalization and the Transformation of Armed Groups', in Horowitz, J., ed., *Armed Groups*, Newport, RI: US Naval War College.

Hardy, R., 2006. Lecture at St Anthony's College, Oxford University in December 2006.

Haritos-Fatouros, M., 1995. 'The Official Torturer', in Crelinsten, R., and Schmid, A., eds, *The Politics of Pain: Torturers and their Masters*, Boulder, CO: Westview Press.

Harlow, J., 1868. 'Recovery from the Passage of an Iron Bar Through the Head', *Publications of the Massachusetts Medical Society*, 2: 327–347.

Harris, J., 1983. *The New Terrorism: The Politics of Violence*, New York: Julian Messner Press.

Hassan, N., 2001. 'An Arsenal of Believers: Talking to the Human Bombs', *The New Yorker*, 19 November 2001.

Hastings, C., 2008. 'Anti-terrorism Laws Used to Spy on Noisy Children', *The Telegraph*, 6 September 2008, available online at: http://www.telegraph.co.uk/news/uknews/2696031/Anti-terrorism-laws-used-to-spy-on-noisy-children.html, accessed 25 March 2011.

Heiberg, M., 2007. 'ETA: Euskadi 'ta Askatasuna', in Heiberg, M., O'Leary, B., and Tirman, J., eds, *Terror, Insurgencies and States: Breaking the Cycle of Protracted Conflict*, Philadelphia, PA: University of Pennsylvania Press.

Hellmich, C., 2011. *Al-Qaeda: From Global Network to Local Franchise*, London: Zed.

Hennessy, P., ed., *The New Protective State: Government, Intelligence and Terrorism*, London: Continuum Books.

Her Majesty's Government, 2006. *Countering International Terrorism: The United Kingdom's Strategy*, London: Foreign and Commonwealth Office, Cm 68888, available online at: http://www.official-documents.gov.uk/document/cm68/6888/6888.pdf.

Her Majesty's Government, 2010. *Pursue Prevent Protect Prepare: The United Kingdom's Strategy for Countering International Terrorism*, Annual Report, March, London: HM Government.

Hewitt, S., 2008. *The British War on Terror*, London: Continuum.

Hoffman, B., 1998/2006. *Inside Terrorism*, New York: Columbia University Press, various editions.

Hoffman, B., 2001. 'Change and Continuity in Terrorism', *Studies in Conflict and Terrorism*, 24: 417–428.

Hoffman, B., 2003. 'Al Qaeda, Trends in Terrorism, and Future Potentialities: An Assessment', *Studies in Conflict & Terrorism*, 26(6): 429–442.

Hoffman, B., 2005. *Does Our Counter-terrorism Strategy Match the Threat?*, testimony presented before the House International Relations Committee, Subcommittee on International Terrorism and Nonproliferation, 29 September , Santa Monica, CA: RAND.

Hoffman, B., 2009a. 'A Counterterrorism Strategy for the Obama Administration', *Terrorism & Political Violence*, 21(3): 359–377.

Hoffman, B., 2009b. 'Radicalization and Subversion: Al Qaeda and the 7 July 2005 Bombings and the 2006 Airline Bombing Plot', *Studies in Conflict & Terrorism*, 32(12): 1100–1116.

Hoffmann, B., 2010. 'Al-Qaeda has a New Strategy: Obama Needs One, Too', *Washington Post*, 10 January 2010, available online at: http://www.washingtonpost.com/wp-dyn/content/article/2010/01/08/AR2010010803555.html?sid=ST2010031703003.

Holmes, S., 2007. 'Did religious extremism cause 9/11?' in *The Matador's Cape: America's Reckless Response to Terror*, Cambridge University Press, Cambridge, pp. 13–68.

Hook, J., and Pegler, M., 2001. *To Live and Die in the West: The American Indian Wars*, Chicago: Fitzroy Dearborn.

Horgan, J., 2005a. 'The Social and Psychological Characteristics of Terrorism and Terrorists', in Bjorgo, T., ed., *Root Causes of Terrorism: Myths, Reality and Ways Forward*, London: Routledge.

Horgan, J., 2005b. *The Psychology of Terrorism*, London: Routledge.

Huesmann, L., 1988. 'An Information Processing Model for the Development of Aggression', *Aggressive Behavior*, 14: 13–24.

Huesmann, L., 1998. 'The Role of Social Information Processing and Cognitive Schemas in the Acquisition and Maintenance of Habitual Aggressive Behavior', in Geen, R., and Donnerstein, E., eds, *Human Aggression: Theories, Research, and Implications for Policy*, New York: Academic Press.

Huesmann, L., and Guerra, N., 1997. 'Children's Normative Beliefs about Aggression and Aggressive Behavior', *Journal of Personality and Social Psychology*, 72: 408–419.

Huesmann, L., and Kirwil, L., 2007. 'Why Observing Violence Increases the Risk of Violent Behavior in the Observer', in Flannery, D., Vazsonyi, A., and Waldman, I., eds, *The Cambridge Handbook of Violent Behavior and Aggression*, Cambridge, UK: Cambridge University Press.

Huesmann, L., Dubow, E., and Boxer, P., 2009. *The Psychological Scars of Ethno-political Conflict: Aggressive and Anxious Children – Overview of Findings from Research on Children Exposed to Political Violence, Part I: Effects on Palestinian and Israeli Children of Exposure to Extreme Political Violence*. Invited address at Promoting Resilience and Protecting Children from the Psychological Consequences of Violence: NICHD Research on Children Exposed to Violence. Washington, DC: State Department.

Huntington, S., 1968. *Political Order in Changing Societies*, New Haven, CT: Yale University Press.

IAEA ITDB Factsheet, 2009. Available online at: www.ns.iaea.org, accessed 10 April 2010.

Ibrahim, Y., 2010. Commentary in *Inspire*, 3rd ed., November 2010; in author's possession.

icasualties.org, n.d. Available online at: http://icasualties.org/; http://icasualties.org/Iraq/US CasualtiesByState.aspx.

icasualties.org, 2011. *Operation Enduring Freedom*, available online at: http://icasualties.org/oef/, accessed 17 March 2011.

Independent, 2006. 'Beckett Admits Guantanamo Bay Camp Should be Shut Down', 13 October 2006, available online at: http://news.independent.co.uk/uk/politics/article/1868066.ece, accessed 3 February 2011.

Innes, M., ed., 2007. *Denial of Sanctuary: Understanding Terrorist Safe Havens*, Westport, CT: Praeger.

Inspire, 2010. 'Interview with Shaykh Abu Basir', *Inspire*, 1 (July): 17.

Iraqi Body Count, 2011. *Documented Civilian Deaths from Violence*, available online at: http://www.iraq bodycount.org/database/, accessed 25 March 2011.

Jackson, R., 2005. *Writing the War on Terrorism: Language, Politics, and Counter-terrorism*, Manchester: Manchester University Press.

Jackson, R., 2008. 'The Ghosts of State Terror: Knowledge, Politics and Terrorism Studies', paper prepared for the International Studies Association (ISA) Annual Conference, 26–28 March 2008, San Francisco, USA.

Jackson, R., 2009. 'Critical Terrorism Studies: An Explanation, a Defence and a Way Forward', paper prepared for the BISA Annual Conference, 14–16 December, 2009, University of Leicester, UK.

Jackson, R., 2011. 'In Defence of "Terrorism": Finding a Way Through a Forest of Misconceptions', *Behavioural Sciences of Terrorism and Political Aggression*, 3(2): 116–130.

Jackson, R., Jarvis, L., Gunning, J., and Breen Smyth, M., 2011. *Terrorism: A Critical Introduction*, Basingstoke: Palgrave-Macmillan.

Jackson, R., Murphy, E., and Poynting, S., eds, 2010. *Contemporary State Terrorism: Theory and Cases*, Abingdon: Routledge.

Jarman, N., 1997. *Material Conflicts: Parades and Visual Displays in Northern Ireland*, Oxford: Berg.

Jarvis, L., 2009. *Times of Terror: Discourse, Temporality and the War on Terror*, Basingstoke: Palgrave.

Jenkins, B., 1975. *International Terrorism: A New Mode of Conflict?*, London: Croom Helm.

Jenkins, B., 1982. *Terrorism and Beyond*, Santa Monica, CA: RAND.

Jenkins, B., 2008. *Will Terrorists Go Nuclear?* Amherst, NY: Prometheus.

Jenkins, B., 2010. *Would-Be Warriors: Incidents of Jihadist Terrorist Radicalization in the United States Since September 11, 2001*, Santa Monica, CA: RAND.

Jenkins, B., 2011. *The Tenth Year: A Briefing on Terrorism Issues to New Members of the 112th Congress*, Santa Monica, CA: RAND.

Johnston, P., 2010. 'Assessing the Effectiveness of Leadership Decapitation in Counterinsurgency Campaigns', Working paper and presentation at 11th Annual Triangle Institute for Security Studies New Faces Conference, Chapel Hill, NC, 2010, available online at: http://patrickjohnston. info/materials/decapitation.pdf.

Jones, D., and Smith, M., 2010. 'Whose Hearts and Whose Minds? The Curious Case of Global Counter-Insurgency', *Journal of Strategic Studies*, 33(1): 81–121.

Jones, S., 2006. 'Terrorism and the Battle for Homeland Security', in Howard, R., Forest, J., and Moore, J., eds, *Homeland Security and Terrorism: Readings and Interpretations*, New York: McGraw-Hill.

Joppke, C., 1996. 'Multiculturalism and Immigration: A Comparison of the United States, Germany, and Great Britain', *Theory and Society*, 25(4): 449–500.

Jordan, J., 2009. '"When Heads Roll": Assessing the Effectiveness of Leadership Decapitation', *Security Studies*, 18: 719–755.

Juergensmeyer, M., 2001/2003. *Terror in the Mind of God: The Global Rise of Religious Violence*, Berkeley, CA: University of California Press.

Jurgensmeyer, M., 2003. 'The Religious Roots of Contemporary Terrorism', in Kegley, C., ed., *The New Global Terrorism*, Englewood Cliffs, NJ: Prentice Hall.

Jurkowitz, M., 2010. 'Terrorism Tops Disasters', Pew Research Center's Project for Excellence in Journalism, 11 May 2010, available online at: http://pewresearch.org/pubs/1589/media-coverage-times-square-bomb-faisal-shahzad-bp-oil-tennessee-flooding.

Kakutani, M., 2006. 'Personality, Ideology, and Bush's Terror Wars', *New York Times*, 20 June 2006, available online at: http://www.nytimes.com/2006/06/20/books/20kaku.html.

Kaldor, M., 1999. *New and Old Wars: Organized Violence in a Global Era*, Cambridge: Polity.

Kant, I., 1797. 'On a Supposed Right to Lie From Philanthropy', available online at: http://www.philosophyblog.com.au/immanuel-kant-and-the-supposed-right-to-lie-to-murderers-from-benevolence/, accessed 22 January 2011.

Kaplan, E., Mintz, M., and Mishal, S., 2004. 'What Happened to Suicide bombings in Israel: Insights from a Terror Stock Model', *Studies in Conflict and Terrorism*, 28: 225–235.

Kaplan, J., 1997. 'Leaderless Resistance', *Terrorism and Political Violence*, 9(3); 80–95.

Kasai, K., Yamasu, H., Gilbertso, M., Shenton, M., Rauch, S., and Pitman, R., 2008. 'Evidence for Acquired Pregenual Anterior Cingulate Gray Matter Loss from a Twin Study of Combat-Related Post-Traumatic Stress Disorder', *Biological Psychiatry*, 63(6): 550–556.

Keen, D., 2006. 'War without End? Magic, Propaganda and the Hidden Functions of Counter-Terror', *Journal of International Development*, 18(1): 87–104.

Kenney, M., 2010a. 'Beyond the Internet: *Metis, Techne,* and the Limitations of Online Artifacts for Islamist Terrorists', *Terrorism and Political Violence*, 22(2): 177–197.

Kenney, M., 2010b. '"Dumb" Yet Deadly: Local Knowledge and Poor Tradecraft Among Islamist Militants in Britain and Spain', *Studies in Conflict & Terrorism*, 33(10): 911–922.

Keohane, D., 2005. *The EU and Counter-Terrorism: Centre for European Reform Working Paper*, May 2005, London: Centre for European Reform.

Kepel, G., and Milelli, J., eds, 2008. *Al Qaeda in its Own Words*, Cambrige, MA and London: The Belknap Press of Harvard University.

Kessler, R., 2004. *The CIA at War*, New York: St Martin's Griffin.

Khan, A., 2010. 'Strategic Response to Suicide Terrorism in Pakistan', PAK Institute for Peace Studies, available online at: http://www.san-pips.com, accessed 6 January 2011.

Khrushchev, N.K., 1956. 'The Secret Speech – On the Cult of Personality, 1956', available online at: http://www.fordham.edu/halsall/mod/1956khrushchev-secret1.html.

Kilcullen, D., 2005. 'Countering Global Insurgency', *Journal of Strategic Studies*, 28(4): 597–617.

Kilcullen, D., 2009. *The Accidental Guerilla: Fighting Small Wars in the Midst of a Big One*, London: Hurst.

Kilcullen, D., 2010. *Counterinsurgency*, London: Hurst and Company.

Kirby, A., 2007. 'The London Bombers as "Self-Starters": A Case Study in Indigenous Radicalization and the Emergence of Autonomous Cliques', *Studies in Conflict & Terrorism*, 30(5): 415–428.

Klausen, J., 2009. 'British Counter-terrorism After 7/7: Adapting Community Policing to the Fight Against Domestic Terrorism', *Journal of Ethnic and Migration Studies*, 35(3): 403–420.

Kooijmans, P., 1995. 'Torturers and Their Masters', in Crelinsten, R., and Schmid, A., eds, *The Politics of Pain: Torturers and their Masters*, Boulder, CO: Westview Press.

Korotzer, F., 2010. 'Pre-emptive Prosecution', *Next Left Notes*, 15 April 2010, available online at: http://nextleftnotes.wordpress.com/2010/04/15/pre-emptive-prosecution-by-fran-korotzer/.

Korsching, P., Besser, T., Miller, N., Hofstedt, B., Welch, B., and Orr, R., 2004. 'Transforming an Informal Group into a Formal Network', Iowa State University Department of Sociology, available online at: http://www.soc.iastate.edu/ruralnetworks/transforminformal_6.pdf.

Krauthammer, Charles, 2004. 'Blixful Amnesia', *Washington Post*, 9 July.

Kreimer, S., 2003. 'Too Close to the Rack and Screw', *University of Pennsylvania Journal of Constitutional Law*, 6: 278–325.

Kropotkin, P., 1927. *The Great French Revolution, 1789–1793*, N. F. Dryhurst, trans., New York: Vanguard Printings, original work published 1909, available online at: http://dwardmac.pitzer.edu/anarchist_archives/kropotkin/frenchrev/lxv.html, accessed 15 March 2011.

Krueger, A., and Malečková, J., 2002. 'Does Poverty Cause Terrorism?', *The New Republic*, June 24, 2002: 27–33.

Krueger, A., and Laitin, D., 2008. 'Kto Kogo?: A Cross-Country Study of the Origins and Targets of Terrorism', in Keefer, P., and Loayza, N., eds, *Terrorism, Economic Development, and Political Openness*, Cambridge: Cambridge University Press.

Krueger, A., and Malečková, J., 2003. 'Education, Poverty, and Terrorism: Is There A Causal Connection?', *Journal of Economic Perspective*, 17: 119–144.

Kurtulus, E., 2011. 'The "New" Terrorism and its Critics', *Studies in Conflict and Terrorism*, 34(6): 476–500.

Kydd, A., and Walter, B., 2002. 'Sabotaging the Peace: The Politics of Extremist Violence', *International Organization*, 56(2): 263–296.

LaFree, G., Dugan, L., and Korte, R., 2009. 'The Impact of British Counterterrorist Strategies on Political Violence in Northern Ireland: Comparing Deterrence and Backlash Models', *Criminology*, 47: 17–45.

Langguth, A., 1978. *Hidden Terrors: The Truth about U.S. Police Operations in Latin America*, New York: Pantheon.

Laqueur, W., 1977. *Terrorism*, Boston, MA: Little Brown.

Laqueur, W., 1996. 'Postmodern Terrorism: New Rules for an Old Game', *Foreign Affairs*, 75(5): 24–36.

Laqueur, W., 1999/2001. *The New Terrorism: Fanaticism and the Arms of Mass Destruction*, New York: Oxford University Press, various editions.

Laqueur, W., 2001. *A History of Terrorism*, New Jersey: Transaction Publishers.

Laqueur, W., 2003. *No End to War: Terrorism in the Twenty-First Century*, New York: Continuum.

Lawrence, B., ed., 2005, *Messages to the World: The Statements of Osama bin Laden*, London and New York: Verso.

Leigh, D., 2010. 'Iraq War Logs Reveal 15,000 Previously Unlisted Civilian Deaths', *The Guardian*, 22 October 2010, available online at: http://www.guardian.co.uk/world/2010/oct/22/true-civilian-body-count-iraq/print, accessed 25 March 2011.

Leitenberg, M., 2005. *Assessing the Biological Weapons and Bioterrorism Threat*, Carlisle, PA: Strategic Studies Institute, U.S. Army War College.

Lenin, V., 1969. *What Is To Be Done?*, originally published 1902, New York: International Books.

Lesser, I., 1999a. 'Introduction' in Lesser, I., *et al.*, eds, *Countering the New Terrorism*, Santa Monica, CA: RAND.

Lesser, I., 1999b. 'Countering New Terrorism: Implications for Strategy', in Lesser, I., Hoffman, B., Arquilla, J., Ronfelt, D., and Zanini, M., eds, *Countering the New Terrorism*, Santa Monica, CA: RAND.

Lesser, I., Arquilla, J., Ronfeldt, D., Hoffman, B., Zanini, M., and Jenkins, B., 1999, *Countering the New Terrorism*, Santa Monica, CA: RAND.

Levi, M., 2007. *On Nuclear Terrorism*, Cambridge, MA: Harvard University Press.

Levi, M., and Kelly, H., 2002. 'Weapons of Mass Disruption', *Scientific American*, 1 November: 77–81.

Lifton, R., 1999. *Destroying the World to Save It: Aum Shinrikyō, Apocalyptic Violence, and the New Global Terrorism*, New York: Henry Holt.

Linnoila, V., and Virkunnen, M., 1992. 'Aggression, Suicidality, and Serotonin', *Journal of Clinical Psychology*, 53(10): 46–51.

Lum, C., Kennedy, L., and Sherley, A., 2006a. 'Are Counter-terrorism Strategies Effective? The Results of the Campbell Systematic Review on Counter-terrorism Evaluation Research', *Journal of Experimental Criminology*, 2(4): 489–516.

Lum, C., Kennedy, L., and Sherley, A., 2006b. *The Effectiveness of Counter-Terrorism Strategies: A Campbell Systematic Review*, available online at: http://db.c2admin.org/doc-pdf/Lum_Terrorism_Review.pdf.

Lustick, I., 2006. *Trapped in the War on Terror*, Philadelphia, PA: University of Pennsylvania Press.

Lustick, I., 2008. *Our Own Strength Against Us: The War on Terror as a Self-Inflicted Disaster*, 4 April, Washington, DC: Independent Institute, Policy Report.

Lutz, J., and Lutz, B., 2011. *Terrorism: The Basics*, London: Routledge.

MacKinlay, J., 2009. *The Insurgent Archipelago; From Mao to Bin Laden*, London: Hurst and Company.

Malečková, J., 2005. 'Impoverished Terrorists: Stereotype or Reality?', in Bjorgo, T., ed., *Root Causes of Terrorism: Myths, Reality, and Ways Forward*, London: Routledge.

Malkki, L., 2010. *How Terrorist Campaigns End: The Cases of the Rode Jeugd in the Netherlands and the Symbionese Liberation Army in the United States*, Ph.D. dissertation, Acta Politica 41, Department of Political and Economic Studies, University of Helsinki.

Malkki, L., 2011. 'Radicalisation and Terrorism in History: Lessons from the Radical Left Terrorist Campaigns in Europe and the United States', in Coosaet, R., ed., *Jihadi Terrorism and the Radicalisation Challenge: European and American Experiences*, Farnham: Ashgate.

Mann, J., 2004. *The Rise of the Vulcans: The History of Bush's War Cabinet*, London: Penguin.

Mannes, A., 2008. 'Testing The Snake Head Strategy: Does Killing or Capturing its Leaders Reduce a Terrorist Group's Activity?', *Journal of International Policy Solutions*, 9: 40–49.

Marchak, P., 1999. *God's Assassins: State Terrorism in Argentina in the 1970s*, Montreal: McGill-Queen's University Press.

Marsella, A., 2004. 'Reflections on International Terrorism: Issues, Concepts, and Directions', in Moghaddam, F., and Marsella, A., eds, *Understanding Terrorism*, Washington, DC: American Psychological Association.

Martin, G., 2010. *Understanding Terrorism*, London: Sage.

Martin, G., 2011. *Essentials of Terrorism*, London: Sage.

McCauley, C., 2007. 'Psychological Issues in Understanding Terrorism and Response to Terrorism', in Bongar, B., *et al.*, eds, *Psychology of Terrorism*, New York: Oxford University Press.

McNermey, E., and Rhodes, M., 2009. 'Al-Qaʿida's CBRN Activities', in Ackerman, G., and Tamsett, J., eds, *Jihadists and Weapons of Mass Destruction*, Boca Raton, FL: CRC Press.

McPhee, J., 1974. *The Curve of Binding Energy*, New York: Farrar, Straus and Giroux.

Melzer, N., 2008. *Targeted Killing in International Law*, Oxford: Oxford University Press.

Merari, A., 2005. 'Palestinian Resistance and "Suicide Bombing": Causes and Consequences', in Bjorgo, T., ed., *Root Causes of Terrorism: Myths, Reality and Ways Forward*, London: Routledge.

Merari, A., and Friedland, N., 1985. 'Social Psychological Aspects of Political Terrorism', *Applied Social Psychology Annual*, 6: 185–205.

Mertus, J., and Sajjad, T., 2008. 'Human Rights and Human Insecurity: The Contributions of US Counterterrorism', *Journal of Human Rights*, 7(1): 2–24.

Meselson, M., 1991. 'The Myth of Chemical Superweapons', *Bulletin of the Atomic Scientists*, April: 12–15.

Michael, G., and Wahba, K., 2001. 'Transcript of Usama Bin Laden Video Tape', 13 December 2001, available online at: http://www.defense.gov/news/Dec2001/d20011213ubl.pdf.

Milgram, S., 1974. *Obedience to Authority: An Experimental View*, New York: Harper & Row.

Miller, M., 1995. 'The Intellectual Origins of Modern Terrorism in Europe', in Crenshaw, M., ed., *Terrorism in Context*, University Park, PA: Pennsylvania State University Press.

Miller, M., and File, J., 2001. *Terrorism Factbook*, Peoria, IL: Bollix Press.

Mockaitis, T., 2007. *The 'New' Terrorism Myths and Reality*, Westport, CT: Praeger Security International.

Moghaddam, F., 2005. *Great Ideas in Psychology*, Oxford: Oneworld.

Moghaddam, F., 2006. *From the Terrorists' Point of View*, Westport, CT: Praeger.

Moghaddam, F., 2008a. *Multiculturalism and Intergroup Relations: Psychological Implications for Democracy in Global Context*, Washington, DC: American Psychological Association.

Moghaddam, F., 2008b. *How Globalization Spurs Terrorism: The Lopsided Benefits of "One World" and Why That Fuels Violence*, Westport, CT: Praeger.

Moghaddam, A., and Fishman, B., eds, 2010. *Self-Inflicted Wounds: Debates and Division within Al-Qaʿida and its Periphery*, West Point, NY: USMA Combating Terrorism Center.

Monroe, H., 2008. *Does Violence Beget Violence? A Quantitative Analysis of Terrorism and Counter-terrorism in*

Western Europe, 1950–2004, available online at: http://www.cda-cdai.ca/cdai/uploads/cdai/2009/04/munroe08.pdf, accessed 10 April 2011.

Moore, B., 1966. *Terror and Progress – USSR*, Cambridge, MA: Harvard University Press.

Morenkov, O., 2002. 'Bioterrorism: A View from the Side', High-Impact Terrorism, Proceedings of a Russian–American Workshop, *National Research Council*, Washington, DC: National Academy Press.

Mostrous, A., 2008. 'Terror Law Turns Thousands of Council Officials into Spies', *The Times*, 31 May 2008, available online at: http://business.timesonline.co.uk/tol/business/law/article4036231.ece, accessed 26 March 2011.

Mottram, R., 2007. 'Protecting Citizens in the Twenty-first century: Issues and Challenges', in Hennessy, P., ed., *The New Protective State: Government, Intelligence and Terrorism*, London: Continuum Books.

MSNBC, 2009. 'Ridge Says he was Pressured to Raise Terror Alert', 20 August 2009, available online at: http://www.msnbc.msn.com/id/32501273/ns/us_news-security/.

Mueller, J., 2005. 'Six Rather Unusual Propositions about Terrorism', *Terrorism and Political Violence*, 17(4): 487–505.

Mueller, J., 2006. *Overblown: How Politicians and the Terrorism Industry Inflate National Security Threats, and We Believe Them*, New York: Free Press.

Mueller, J., 2010. *Atomic Obsession: Nuclear Alarmism from Hiroshima to Al Qaeda*, New York: Oxford University Press.

Mueller, J., and Mueller, K., 2009. 'The Rockets' Red Glare: Just what are "Weapons of Mass Destruction", Anyway?', *foreignpolicy.com*, 7 July.

Murray, R., 2004. *The SAS in Ireland*, Cork: Mercier Press.

Nacos, B., 2008/2011. *Terrorism and Counter-terrorism: Understanding Threats and Responses in the Post-9/11 World*, 4th ed., New York/Boston: Penguin Academics/Longman, various editions.

Nafziger, W., and Auvinen, J., 2002. 'Economic Development, Inequality, War, and State Violence', *World Development*, 30: 153–163.

Nakosteen, M., 1974. *Mulla's Donkey and Other Friends*, Boulder, CO: Estes Press.

National Counterterrorism Center, 2010. *2009 Report on Terrorism*, Washington, DC: NCTC.

Neumann, P., 2009. *Old and New Terrorism*, Cambridge, UK: Polity.

New York Times, 'Chertoff Warns of Higher Risk of Terrorism', 11 July 2007, available online at: http://www.nytimes.com/2007/07/11/us/nationalspecial3/11terror.html.

Ní Aoláin, F., 2000. *The Politics of Force: Conflict Management and State Violence in Northern Ireland*, Belfast: Blackstaff Press.

Nordland, R., 2011. 'Afghan Talks Focus on Long Term Strategy', *International Herald Tribune*, 19 April.

Norris, P., Kern, M., and Just, M., eds, 2003. *Framing Terrorism; The News Media, The Government and The Public*, London: Routledge.

Olson, Mancur, 1968. *The Logic of Collective Action*, Cambridge, MA: Harvard University Press.

Oommen, T., 2005. *Crisis and Contention in Indian Society*, New Delhi: Sage.

Opall-Rome, B., 2004. 'Israeli Arms, Gear Aid U.S. Troops', *Defense News*, 30 March.

Pachecco, A., 1999. *The Case Against Torture in Israel: A Compilation of Petitions, Briefs and Other Documents Submitted to the Israeli High Court of Justice*, Jerusalem: Public Committee Against Torture in Israel, available at www.stoptorture.org.il/eng/publications.asp?menu=7&submenu=2, accessed 30 January 2011.

Packer, G., 2005. *The Assassins' Gate*, New York: Farrar, Straus and Giroux.

Pakistan Defence, 2009. *Pakistani Nuclear Safety: Queries*. (2008). Retrieved 7 January 2011 from www.defence.pk.

Pantucci, R., 2010. 'A Contest to Democracy? How the UK has Responded to the Current Terrorist Threat', *Democratization*, 17(2): 251–271.

Pape, R., 2003. 'The Strategic Logic of Suicide Terrorism', *American Political Science Review*, 97(3): 343–361.

Pape, R., 2005. *Dying to Win: The Strategic Logic of Suicide Terrorism*, Random House: New York.

Pape, R., 2009. 'What is New about Research on Terrorism', *Security Studies*, 18(4): 643–650.

Parachini, J., 2001. 'Comparing Motives and Outcomes of Mass Casualty Terrorism Involving Conventional and Unconventional Weapons', *Studies in Conflict and Terrorism*, 24: 389–406.

Parry, J., 2010. *Understanding Torture: Law, Violence, and Political Identity*, Ann Arbor, MI: University of Michigan Press.

Parry, J., and White, W., 2002. 'Interrogating Suspected Terrorists: Should Torture be an Option?', *University of Pittsburgh Law Review*, 63: 743–766.

Pearsall, J., and Trumble, B., eds, 2006. *Oxford Referencing Dictionary*, 2nd ed., revised, Oxford: Oxford University Press.

Perdue, W., 1989. *Terrorism and the State: A Critique of Domination through Fear*, London: Praeger.

Perkoski, E., 2010. *Rethinking Repression: Exploring the Effectiveness of Counterterrorism in Spain*, unpublished thesis, Wesleyan University.

Pew Center for the People and the Press, 2003. 'Views of a Changing World, 2003', 3 June 2003, available online at: http://peoplepress.org/reports/print.php3?PageID=712.

Pew Research Center's Project for Excellence in Journalism, 2010. 'Despite Years of Terror Scares, Public's Concerns Remain Fairly Steady', PEW News Release, 2 December.

Phillips, M., 2006. *Londonistan: How Britain is Creating a Terror State Within*, London: Gibson Square.

Piazza, J.A., 2003. *Rooted in Poverty? Terrorism, Poor Economic Development, and Social Change*. Mimeo, Meredith College, Raleigh, NC.

Pilch, R., 2006. 'The Bioterrorism Threat in the United States', in Howard, R., and Sawyer, R., eds, *Terrorism and Counterterrorism: Understanding the New Security Environment*, Chicago, IL: McGraw Hill.

Popkin, S., 1979. *The Rational Peasant*, Berkeley, CA: University of California Press.

Posner, R., 2004. 'Torture, Terrorism, and Interrogation', in Levinson, S., ed., *Torture: A Collection*, Oxford: Oxford University Press.

Posner, M., and DiGirolamo, G., 1998. 'Executive Attention: Conflict, Target Detection, and Cognitive Control', in Parasuraman, R., ed., *The Attentive Brain*, Cambridge, MA: MIT Press.

Post, J., 1984. 'Notes on a Psychodynamic Theory of Terrorist Behavior', *Terrorism*, 7: 241–56.

Post, J., 1990. 'Terrorist Psycho-Logic: Terrorist Behavior as a Product of Psychological Forces', in Reich, W., ed., *Origins of Terrorism: Psychologies, Ideologies, Theologies, States of Mind*, New York: Cambridge University Press.

Post, J., 2004. *Leaders and Their Followers in a Dangerous World: The Psychology of Political Behavior*, Ithaca, NY: Cornell University Press.

Post, J., 2007. *The Mind of the Terrorist: The Psychology of Terrorism from the IRA to Al-Qaeda*, Basingstoke: Palgrave.

Post, J., Sprinzak, E., and Denny, L., 2003. 'The Terrorists in Their own Words: Interviews with 35 Incarcerated Middle Eastern Terrorists', *Terrorism and Political Violence*, 15: 171–184.

Postmes, T., and Jetten, J., eds, 2006. *Individuality and the Group: Advances in Social Identity*, London: Sage.

Rai, M., 2006. *7/7: The London Bombings, Islam and the Iraq War*, Pluto Press: London and Ann Arbor, MI.

Ranstorp, M., 1996. 'Terrorism in the Name of Religion', *Journal of International Affairs*, 50(1): 41–62.

Ranstorp, M., ed., 2006. *Mapping Terrorism Research*, London: Routledge.

Ranstorp, M., 2007. 'The Virtual Sanctuary of Al–Qaeda and Terrorism in an Age of Globalisation', in Eriksson and Giacomello, G., eds, *International Relations and Security in the Digital Age*, London: Routledge.

Ranstorp, M., 2008. 'Perspectives on Terrorism: What Will It Look Like 2018 and Beyond?', Centre for Asymmetric Threat Studies, Stockholm: Swedish National Defence College.

Ranstorp, M., and Wilkinson, P., eds, 2008. *Terrorism and Human Rights*, London: Routledge.

Rapoport, D., 1984. 'Fear and Trembling; Terrorism in Three Religious Traditions', *American Political Science Review*, 78(3): 658–677.

Rapoport, D., 1988. 'Messianic Sanctions for Terror', *Comparative Politics*, 20(2): 195–213.

Rapoport, D., 1999. 'Terrorists and Weapons of the Apocalypse', *National Security Studies Quarterly*, 5(1): 49–67.

Rapoport, D., 2003. 'The Four Waves of Rebel Terror and September 11', in Kegley, C., ed., *The New Global Terrorism*, Englewood Cliffs: NJ: Prentice Hall.

Rashid, A., 2010. *Taliban*, London: I.B.Tauris.

Rees, W., and Aldrich, R., 2005. 'Contending Cultures of Counterterrorism: Transatlantic Divergence or Convergence', *International Affairs*, 81(5): 905–923.

Reeve, S., 2001. *One Day in September*, New York: Seaver Books.

Reinares, F., 2009. 'Global Terrorism: A Polymorphous Phenomenon', published by the Real Instituto Elcano, 21 April 2009, available online at: http://www.realinstitutoelcano.org/wps/portal/rielcano_eng/Content?WCM_GLOBAL_CONTEXT=elcano/elcano_in/zonas_in/ari65-2009.

Rejali D., 2007. *Torture and Democracy*, Princeton, NJ: Princeton University Press.

Report of the Eminent Jurists Panel on Terrorism, Counter-terrorism and Human Rights, 2009. *Assessing Damage, Urging Action*, Geneva: International Commission of Jurists.

Richardson, L., 2006. *What Terrorists Want: Understanding the Enemy, Containing the Threat*, New York: Random House.

Robben, A., 2010. 'Chaos, Mimesis and Dehumanisation in Iraq: American Counterinsurgency in the Global War on Terror', *Social Anthropology*, 1892: 138–154.

Robespierre, M., 1794. *Sur les principes de morale politique*, available online at: http://www.royet.org/nea1789-1794/archives/discours/robespierre_principes_morale_politique_05_02_94.htm, accessed 5 March 2011.

Rogers, P., 2008. *Global Security and the War on Terror*, London: Routledge.

Rogers, P., 2010. *Losing Control: Global Security in the 21st Century*, London: Pluto Press.

Ronfeldt, D., 2007. 'Al-Qaeda and Its Affiliates: A Global Tribe Waging Segmental Warfare', in Arquilla, J., and Borer, B., eds, *Information Strategy and Warfare: A Guide to Theory and Practice*, London: Routledge.

Rose D., 2004. *Guantanamo: America's War on Human Rights*, London: Faber and Faber.

Rose-Ackerman, S., 1996. 'Altruism, Nonprofits, and Economic Theory', *Journal of Economic Literature*, 36 (June): 701–728.

Rosendorff, P., and Sandler, T., 2004. 'Too Much of a Good Thing?; The Pro-active Response Dilemma', *Journal of Conflict Resolution*, 48(5): 657–671.

Ruby, C., 2002. 'Are Terrorists Mentally Deranged?', *Analysis of Social Issues and Public Policy*, 2: 15–26.

Ryan, J., and Glarum, J., 2008. *Biosecurity and Bioterrorism*, Burlington, MA: BH Elsevier.

Sageman, M., 2008. *Leaderless Jihad: Terror Networks in the Twenty-first Century*, Philadelphia, PA: University of Pennsylvania Press.

Saito, T., 2010. 'Tokyo drift?', *CBRNe World*, Autumn, available online at: http://biopreparedness.jp, accessed 26 January 2011.

Salama, S., 2006. 'Special Report: Manual for Producing Chemical Weapon to Be Used in New York Subway Plot Available on Al-Qaeda Websites since late 2005. An Analysis for WMD Insights', James Martin Center for Nonproliferation Studies, available online at: http://cns.miis.edu/other/Salama-060720.htm, accessed 8 April 2011.

Sambanis, N., 2004. 'Expanding Economic Models of Civil War Using Case Studies', *Perspectives on Politics*, 2: 259–280.

Sambanis, N., 2008. 'Terrorism and Civil War', in Keefer, P. and Loyaza, N. eds, *Terrorism, Economic Development, and Political Openness*, Cambridge: Cambridge University Press.

Saul, B., 2008. *Defining Terrorism in International Law*, Oxford: Oxford University Press.

Sayari, S., and Hoffman, B., 1994. 'Urbanisation and Insurgency: The Turkish Case, 1976–1980', *Small Wars and Insurgencies*, 5(2): 162–179.

Schmid, A., 1997. 'The Problems of Defining Terrorism', in *International Encyclopedia of Terrorism*, Chicago, IL: Fitzroy Dearborn Publishers.

Schmid, A., 2005. 'Terrorism as Psychological Warfare', *Democracy and Security*, 1: 137–146.

Schmid, A., ed., 2009/2011. *Handbook of Terrorism Research*, London: Routledge.

Schmid, A., and de Graaf, J., 1982. *Violence as Communication: Insurgent Terrorism and Western News Media*, Beverly Hills, CA: Sage.

Schmid, A., and Jongman, A., 1997. 'Violent Conflicts and Human Rights Violations in the mid-1990s', *Terrorism and Political Violence*, 9: 166–192.

Schmid, A., and Jongman, A., 1988. *Political Terrorism: A New Guide To Actors, Authors, Concepts, Databases, Theories And Literature*, Amsterdam: North Holland Publishing Company.

Schroeder, D., 2006. 'A Child's Life or a "Little Bit of Torture"? State-sanctioned Violence and Dignity', *Cambridge Quarterly of Healthcare Ethics*, 15: 188–201.

Schumpeter, J., 1912/1939. *The Theory of Economic Development: An Inquiry into Profits, Capital, Credit, Interest, and the Business Cycle*, trans. R. Opie, Oxford: Oxford University Press, 1912, New York.

Sedgwick, M., 2004. 'Al-Qaeda and the Nature of Religious Terrorism', *Terrorism and Political Violence*, 16(4): 795–814.

Sehgal, U., 2011. 'Al-Qaeda Continues to Crack as Embassy Bomber is Killed', *The Atlantic Wire*, 11 June 2011, available online at: http://www.theatlanticwire.com/global/2011/06/al-qaeda-continues/38737/.

Senate Armed Services Committee, 2008. *Inquiry into the Treatment of Detainees in U.S. Custody*, 11 December 2008, available online at: http://levin.senate.gov/newsroom/supporting/2008/Detainees.121108.pdf, accessed 19 March 2011.

Senate Select Committee on Foreign Relations, 2009. *Tora Bora Revisited: How We Failed To Get Bin Laden And Why It Matters Today*, Report, available online at: http://foreign.senate.gov/reports/.

Serrano, R., 2011. 'U.S. Faces "Heightened" Threat Level', *Los Angeles Times*, 10 February.

Shabad, G., and Ramo, F., 1995. 'Political Violence in a Democratic State: Basque Terrorism in Spain', in Crenshaw, M., ed., *Terrorism in Context*, University Park, PA: Pennsylvania State University Press.

Sharon, A., Kutsher, Y., Yaar, I., Shlomo, M., and Schwartz, J., 2008. 'A 3-Monte Carlo Based Dispersion Model for an RDD or a Nuclear Terror Scenario', in Apikyan, S., Diamond, D., and Ralph, R., eds, *Prevention, Detection and Response to Nuclear and Radiological Threats*, Dordrecht: Springer.

Secretary of Defense, 2002. *Memorandum from the Secretary of Defense*, 2 December 2002.

Shultz, R., 2008. *Global Insurgency Strategy and the Salafi Jihad Movement*, INSS Occasional Papers, 66, available online at: http://www.usafa.edu/df/inss/docs/OCP%2066%20Global%20Insurgency%20and%20Salafi%20Jihad%20Movement.pdf.

Shultz, R., and Vogt, A., 2003. 'It's war! Fighting Post-11 September Global Terrorism Through a Doctrine of Pre-emption', *Terrorism and Political Violence*, 15(1): 1–30.

Silke, A., 1996. 'Terrorism and the Blind Men's Elephant', *Terrorism and Political Violence*, 8(3): 12–28.

Silke, A., 2003a. 'Becoming a Terrorist', in Silke, A., ed., *Terrorists, Victims and Society: Psychological Perspectives on Terrorism and Its Consequences*, London: Wiley.

Silke, A., 2003b. 'Retaliating Against Terrorism', in Silke, A., ed., *Terrorists, Victims and Society: Psychological Perspectives on Terrorism and Its Consequences*, Chichester: Wiley.

Silke, A., 2008. 'Research on Terrorism: A Review of the Impact of 9/11 and the Global War on Terrorism', in Chem, H., Reid, E., Sinai, J., Silke, A., and Ganor, B., eds, *Terrorism Informatics: Knowledge Management and Data Mining for Homeland Security*, New York: Springer Verlag.

Silke, A., 2011. *The Psychology of Counter-Terrorism*, London: Routledge.

Simon, S., and Benjamin, D., 2000. 'America and the New Terrorism', *Survival*, 42(1): 59–75.

Sinclair, S., 2010. 'Fears of Terrorism and Future Threat: Theoretical and Empirical Considerations', in Antonius, D., Brown, A., Walters, T., Martín Ramirez, J., and Sinclair S. J., eds, *Interdisciplinary Analyses of Terrorism and Political Aggression*, Newcastle upon Tyne: Cambridge Scholars Publishing.

SITE Intelligence Group, 2009. 'INSITE Newsletter', January.

Smelser, N., 1963. *Theory of Collective Behavior*, New York: Free Press.

Snow, D., and Byrd, S., 2007. "Ideology, Framing Processes, and Islamist Terrorist Movements", *Mobilization: An International Quarterly Review*, 12(1): 119–136.

Spaaij, R., 2010. 'The Enigma of Lone Wolf Terrorism: An Assessment', *Studies in Conflict and Terrorism*, 33(9): 854–870.

Spalek, B., and McDonald, L., 2009. 'Terror Crime Prevention: Constructing Muslim Practices and Beliefs as "Anti-Social" and "Extreme" through CONTEST 2', *Social Policy & Society*, 9(1): 123–132.

Spencer, A., 2006. 'Questioning the Concept of New Terrorism', *Peace, Conflict & Development*, 8: 1–33.

Stein, Y., 2003. 'By Any Name Illegal and Immoral', *Ethics and International Affairs*, 17(1): 127–137.

Stenersen, A., 2008. *Al-Qaida's Quest for Weapons of Mass Destruction: The History Behind the Hype*, Saarbrücken, Germany: VDM Verlag Dr. Müller.

Stenersen, A., 2009. 'Al-Qaeda's Thinking on CBRN: A Case Study', in Ranstorp, M., and Normark, M., eds, *Unconventional Weapons and International Terrorism: Challenges and New Approaches*, London and New York: Routledge.

Stern, J., 2004. *Terror in the Name of God*, New York: Harper Perennial.

Stewart, S., and Burton, F., 2008. 'The "Lone Wolf" Disconnect', *Stratfor*, 30 January 2008, available online at: http://www.stratfor.com/weekly/lone_wolf_disconnect.

Stiglitz, J., and Bilmes, L., 2008. *The Three Trillion Dollar War*, London: Allen Lane.

Stohl, M., 1979. 'Myths and Realities of Political Terrorism', in M. Stohl, ed., *The Politics of Terrorism*, New York: Marcel Dekker.

Stohl, M., 1988. 'Demystifying Terrorism: the Myths and Realities of Contemporary Political Terrorism', in M. Stohl, ed., *The Politics of Terrorism*, 3rd ed., New York: Marcel Dekker.

Stohl, M., 2008. 'Old Myths, New Fantasies and the Enduring Realities of Terrorism', *Critical Studies in Terrorism*, 1(1): 5–16.

Stohl, M., and Lopez, G., eds, 1984. *The State as Terrorist: The Dynamics of Governmental Violence and Repression*, Westport, CT: Greenwood Press.

Stohl, M., and Lopez, eds, 1986. *Government Violence and Repression: An Agenda for Research*, Westport, CT: Greenwood Press.

Sude, B., 2010. 'Al-Qaeda Central: An Assessment of the Threat Posed by the Terrorist Group Headquartered on the Afghanistan-Pakistan Border', New America Foundation, February 2010, available online at: http://counterterrorism.newamerica.net/publications/policy/al_qaeda_central.

Tajfel, H., ed., 1978. *Differentiation Between Social Groups*, Cambridge, UK: Cambridge University Press.

Taleb, N., 2007. *The Black Swan: How the Improbable Rules the World and Why we Don't Know it*, New York: Random House.

Tan, H., ed., 2006. *The Politics of Terrorism: A Survey*, London: Routledge.

Taylor, M., 1988. *The Terrorist*, London: Brassey's Defence.

Taylor, M., and Quayle, E., 1994. *Terrorist Lives*, London: Brassey's.

Taylor, P., 1999. *Loyalists*, London: Bloomsbury.

Taylor, P., 2011. *The Secret War on Terror: Part One*, BBC2, broadcast 14 March 2011.

Teichman, J., 1989. 'How to Define Terrorism', *Philosophy*, 64: 505–517.

Thayer, C., 2009. 'Terrorism Studies: The Dismal Science?', in Brawley, S., ed., *Doomed to Repeat? Terrorism and the Lessons of History*, Washington, DC: New Academia Publishing.

Thornton, T., 1966. 'Terror as a Weapon of Political Agitation', in Eckstein, H., ed., *Internal War*, New York: Free Press.

Tilly, C., 2004. 'Terror, Terrorism, Terrorists', *Sociological Theory*, 22(1): 5–13.

Tindale, C., 1996. 'The Logic of Torture', *Social Theory and Practice*, 22: 349–374.

Townsend, C., 2002. *Terrorism: A Very Short Introduction*, Oxford: Oxford University Press.

Transactional Records Clearing House, 2009. 'Who Is A Terrorist? Government Failure to Define Terrorism Undermines Enforcement, Puts Civil Liberties at Risk', 28 September 2009, available online at: http://trac.syr.edu/tracreports/terrorism/215/.

Trotsky, L., 1920. *Terrorism and Communism*, 1961 edition, Ann Arbor, MI: University of Michigan Press.

Tucker, D., 2001. 'What's New about the New Terrorism and How Dangerous is it?', *Terrorism and Political Violence*, 13: 1–14.

Tucker, J., 1996. 'Chemical/Biological Terrorism: Coping with a New Threat', *Politics and the Life Sciences*, 15(2): 167–183.

Tucker, J., 2006. *Chemical Warfare from World War I to Al-Qaeda*, New York: Anchor Books.

Tucker, J., and Sands, A., 1999. 'An Unlikely Threat', *Bulletin of Atomic Scientists*, July/August: 46–52.

Tyson, L., 2001. 'It's Time to Step up the Global War on Poverty', *Business Week*, 3 December.

United Nations, 1945. Charter of the United Nations, available at: http://www.un.org/en/documents/charter/index.shtml.

United Nations, 1984. *Convention Against Torture and Other Cruel, Inhuman or Degrading Treatment or Punishment, G. A. Reg. 39146*, U.N. GOAR, 39th Sess., Supp. No. 51, at 197, U.N. Doc. A/39/51/Annex, New York: United Nations.

United Nations Assistance Mission in Afghanistan, 2011. *Annual Report 2010 Protection of Civilians in Armed Conflict*, March 2011, available online at: http://unama.unmissions.org/Portals/UNAMA/human%20rights/March%20PoC%20Annual%20Report%20Final.pdf, accessed 25 March 2011.

United Nations Human Rights Council, 2010. *Report of the International Fact-finding Mission to Investigate Violations of International Law, Including International Humanitarian and Human Rights Law, Resulting from the Israeli Attacks on the Flotilla of Ships Carrying Humanitarian Assistance*, New York: United Nations Human Rights Council, available online at: http://www2.ohchr.org/english/bodies/hrcouncil/docs/15session/A.HRC.15.21_en.pdf, accessed 12 May 2011.

United States Department of State, 2004. *Patterns of Global Terrorism 2003*, Washington, DC: US Department of State.

United States Department of State, 2011. *United States Code Title 22 – Foreign Relations and Intercourse, Chapter 38*, http://uscode.house.gov/download/pls/22C38.txt.

United States Department of Justice, 2010. *Amerithrax Investigative Summary*. Release Pursuant to the Freedom of Information Act, Friday, 19 February 2010, available online at: www.justice.gov/amerithrax/docs/ans-investigative-summary.pdf, accessed 11 April 2011.

United States Government, 1981. Executive Order 12333, available at: http://www/archives.gov/federal-register/codification/executive-order/12333.html.

Urban, M., 1992. *Big Boys Rules: The SAS and the Secret Struggle against the IRA*, London: Faber & Faber.

Usmani, Zeeshan Ul Hassan, 2010. http://pakistanbodycount.org/bla.php, cited in Khan, A. 'Strategic Response to Suicide Terrorism in Pakistan', PAK Institute for Peace Studies, available online at: http://www.san-pips.com, accessed 6 January 2011.

Van Creveld, M., 1991. *The Transformation of War*, New York: Free Press.

Varon, J., 2008. 'Refusing to be "Good Germans": New Left Violence as a Global Phenomenon', *GHI Bulletin*, 43 (Fall): 21–43.

Velarde, G., 2011. Personal Communications, 27 January.

Velarde, G., and Carpintero-Santamaría, N., 2010. 'Global Terrorism: An Assessment of Biological, Chemical and Nuclear Threat', in Antonius, D., Brown, A., Walters, T., Martín Ramirez, J., and Sinclair S. J., eds, *Interdisciplinary Analyses of Terrorism and Political Aggression*, Newcastle upon Tyne: Cambridge Scholars Publishing.

Waldman, A., 2006. 'Prophetic Justice', *The Atlantic Monthly*, October.

Walt, S., 2001–2. 'Beyond bin Laden: Reshaping U.S. Foreign Policy', *International Security*, 26(3): 56–78.

Walter, E. V., 1969. *Terror and Resistance*, London: Oxford University Press.

Walzer, M., 1973/2004. 'Political Action: The Problem of Dirty Hands', reprinted in Levinson, S., ed., *Torture: A Collection*, Oxford: Oxford University Press, various editions.

Walzer, M., 2003. 'Interview', *Imprints*, 7(4), available online at: http://eis.bris.ac.uk/~plcdib/imprints/michaelwalzerinterview.html, accessed 3 February 2011.

Wardlaw, G., 1990. *Political Terrorism: Theory, Tactics, and Counter-measures*, Cambridge: Cambridge University Press.

Weapons of Mass Destruction Commission, 2006. *Weapons of Terror: Freeing the World of Nuclear, Biological and Chemical Arms*, Final Report, Stockholm, Sweden, 1 June 2006, available online at: www.wmdcmomission.org, accessed 10 March 2010.

Weber, M., 1958. 'Politics as a Vocation', in Gerth, H., and Mills, C., *From Max Weber*, Oxford: Oxford University Press.

Weinberg, L., Pedahzur, A., and Hirsch-Hoefler, S., 2004. 'The Challenges of Conceptualizing Terrorism', *Terrorism and Political Violence*, 16(4): 777–794.

Welch, B., 2008. 'Torture, Political Manipulation and the American Psychological Association',

Counterpunch, 28 July 2008, available online at: www.counterpunch.org/welch07282008.html, accessed 31 January 2011.

Whitaker, B., 2007. 'Exporting the Patriot Act? Democracy and the "War on Terror" in the Third World', *Third World Quarterly*, 28(5): 1017–1032.

Whitlock, C., 2007. 'Homemade, Cheap and Dangerous: Terror Cells Favor Simple Ingredients In Building Bombs', *Washington Post*, 5 July: A1.

Whittaker, D., 2001. *The Terrorism Reader*, New York: Routledge.

Wight, C., 2009. 'Theorising Terrorism: The State, Structure and History', *International Relations*, 23: 99–106.

Wiktorowicz, Q., and Kaltenthaler, K., 2006. 'The Rationality of Radical Islam', *Political Science Quarterly*, 121(2): 295–319.

Wilkinson, P., 1977. *Terrorism and the Liberal State*, London: Macmillan.

Wilkinson, P., 2001/2006/2011. *Terrorism versus Democracy: The Liberal State Response*, London: Routledge, various editions.

Williams, K., 2007. 'Ostracism', *Annual Review of Psychology*, 58: 425–452.

Williams, K., and Flewelling, R., 1988. 'The Social Production of Criminal Homicide: A Comparative Study of Disaggregated Rates in American Cities', *American Sociological Review*, 53: 421–431.

Wilner, A., 2010. 'Targeted Killings in Afghanistan: Measuring Coercion and Deterrence in Counterterrorism and Counterinsurgency', *Studies in Conflict and Terrorism*, 33: 307–329.

Winthrop, R., and Graff, C., 2010. *Beyond Madrasas: Assessing the Links Between Education and Militancy in Pakistan*, Working Paper 2, Washington, DC: The Center for Universal Education at Brookings.

Wirz, C., and Egger, E., 2005. 'Use of Nuclear and Radiological Weapons by Terrorists?', *International Review of the Red Cross*, 87(859): 497–510.

Woodworth, P., 2001. *Dirty Wars, Clean Hands: ETA, the GAL, and Spanish Democracy*, Cork: Cork University Press.

Yamasue, H., Kasai, K., Iwanami, A., Ohtani, T., Yamada, H., Abe, O., Kuroki, N., Fukuda, R., Tochigi, M., Furukawa, S., Sadamatsu, M., Sasaki, T., Aoki, S., Ohtomo, K., Asukai, N., and Kato, N., 2003. 'Voxel-based Analysis of MRI Reveals Anterior Cingulate Gray-matter Volume Reduction in Posttraumatic Stress Disorder Due to Terrorism', *PNAS*, 100(15): 9039–9043.

Younger, S., 2009. *The Bomb: A New History*, New York: Ecco.

Yousafzai, S., and Moreau, R., 2010. 'Inside Al Qaeda', *Newsweek*, 4 September.

Yousafzai, S., Moreau, R., and Dickey, C., 2010. 'The New Bin Laden', *Newsweek* 23 October 2010, available online at: http://www.newsweek.com/2010/10/23/is-ilyas-kashmiri-the-new-bin-laden.html#.

Zimbardo, P., 2007. *The Lucifer Effect: Understanding How Good People Turn Evil*, New York: Random House.

Zimmerman, P., and Loeb, C., 2004. 'Dirty Bombs: The Threat Revisited', *Defense Horizons*, January: 1–11.

Index

Abdulmutallab, Umar Farouk 101, 109, 183; *see also* Detroit
Abu Ghraib 123, 189, 191
Abu Sayyaf 168–9
Afghanistan 5–6, 21, 30–9, 62–3, 73–8, 94–9, 102, 110, 112, 133, 144–9, 155, 166–8, 171, 179, 181–4, 186–91
African National Congress (ANC) 22, 132, 134
aggression 5, 7, 12, 77–8, 83, 107, 113–18, 120, 127
Algeria 38, 45, 61–2, 76, 94, 130
Al-Qaeda 3–6, 13, 15–16, 20, 30–4, 37, 39, 62, 67, 73, 76–8, 81–103, 112, 129, 132–3, 144–55, 166, 170–4, 181–93
al-Jama'a al-Islamiya 101
amateur(s) 4, 32, 38, 101, 161, 183
American Indian Wars 125–6
Amnesty International 189, 192
anarchism/anarchists 13, 16, 18, 37–9
anthropology 18–19
Arab Awakening/Spring 12, 14, 148–9
Aristotle 44, 107–8, 121
Aum Shinrikyo 40–1, 64, 77, 79, 84, 87
Ayman al-Zawahiri 90, 97–8, 100

Baader-Meinhof gang 20
Bahrain 18, 34
Bali bombing 41, 148, 190
Beirut 175–6
Black September 175
Black Swans 96
Bombay 76
boomerang effect 140–1
Bosnia 15, 66
Bremmer, Paul 145
Brighton 181
Burundi 14–15

capital punishment 21, 164
Casablanca 76, 148
catastrophic evolution 122, 124–7
CBRN weapons 31–2, 40, 64, 76–89; *see also* WMD

CCTV 183
Central Intelligence Agency (CIA) 88, 91, 152–7, 167, 185
Chechnya 14, 62, 65, 92, 95, 119, 130, 133
China 14, 39, 44, 71, 73, 108, 112, 145, 149–50, 193
Christian 30, 125, 133
Coalition Provisional Authority (CPA) 145
coercive interrogation 5–7, 152–5, 162
cognitive schemas 114
Cold war 1, 12–14, 21, 30, 34, 40, 74, 94, 98, 145
collateral damage 22, 142, 147–8
collective action problem 111
Colombia 63
Contest 184, 190
counter-insurgency 35, 126, 147, 171
critical terrorism studies 17, 21, 24, 51
Cuba 108, 155, 187
culture 1, 3, 16, 93, 96, 122, 124, 126, 182
Cyprus 39, 61–2

De Menezes, Jean Charles 102
Department of Homeland Security 67, 185
Deprivation of sleep 154
Dershowitz, Alan 152, 158–62, 164, 167
Detroit 62, 101; *see also* Abdulmutallab Umar Farouk
Diplock Courts 65
drone(s) 148, 166–8, 171, 189

Egypt 34, 76, 92, 97, 189
enhanced interrogation techniques (EITs) 157
European Convention on Human Rights 154
European Court of Human Rights 154
European Union (EU) 96, 123–4, 184
Euskadi ta Askatasuna (ETA) 16, 20, 36, 64, 77, 149, 178
ethnic cleansing 15, 46, 53
ethno-separatist terrorists 15
extra-judicial killings 12, 48
extraordinary rendition 55–6, 189, 192

fascists 44, 61–2, 66
First World War *see* World War One
fractured globalization 5, 122–3, 125–7
freedom fighters 16, 18, 20, 22, 45,
French republican revolutionaries 18
French revolution 13, 44
Front de Libération Nationale (FLN) 32, 38

Gaddafi, Muammar 12, 15, 167
Gavrilo Princip 18
Gaza 22, 64, 130
Geneva Convention 142, 155–6, 159, 189
George W. Bush 20, 25, 41, 69–71, 108, 144–6, 157, 181, 185, 188–9
German Red Army *see* Red Army Faction
Germany 12, 15, 44, 61, 74, 164, 175
Gibraltar 177–8
Gilmore Commission 84–7
globalization 5, 34, 36, 94, 122–7
Grupos Antiterroristas de Liberacion (GAL) 48, 178
Guantanamo Bay (GITMO) 155–7, 163, 187, 189, 191–2

Hamas 39, 41, 129, 169, 175
Hezbollah 33, 37, 39, 46, 140
highly enriched uranium (HEU) 80–1
Hindu 63, 125
Hiroshima 20–1
home-grown terrorists 6, 167, 182
hooding 154
human rights 12, 14–16, 48, 55–6, 99, 186, 192; law 6; violations 14, 193
humanitarian law 5, 142–3, 192

improvised explosive devices (IEDs) 12, 79, 94
improvised nuclear devices (INDs) 80, 82–3, 86
India 5, 13, 62–3, 76, 82, 85, 147, 149–50, 193
Indonesia 14, 98, 100
insurgency 12, 35–6, 49, 62–3, 110, 126, 131, 145, 147, 189–90
International Atomic Energy Agency (IAEA) 82–3
internet 1, 4, 34, 38, 78, 81, 88, 92, 94
interrogation 5–7, 19, 56, 65, 152–65
Iran 62, 99, 123–5, 127, 145, 147–8
Iranian Revolution 30, 145
Iraq war 5–6, 14–15, 22–3, 34, 36, 62, 69–102, 110, 112, 133, 144–50, 163, 182–4, 188–91
Irgun 39
Irish Republican Army (IRA) 16–22, 33–9, 63, 101, 126, 129, 154, 177–8, 181; Real IRA 129
Islamic fundamentalists 5, 123, 125, 127
Israel 5–6, 22, 37, 64, 76, 97, 119, 126–33, 140, 149, 154, 158, 160, 162, 166–76, 183, 191
Israeli Defence Force (IDF) 147
Italy 12, 44, 61, 144

Japan 64, 77–8
Japanese Red Army *see* Red Army Faction
Jewish 39, 46, 62, 94, 97, 131, 133
Jihad Jane 101
Jihad/Jihadists 34, 62, 71, 77, 81, 92–7, 99, 102, 148, 155, 159, 191–2; leaderless jihad 37
Jordan 98
Judaism 125

Kashmir 62–3, 119, 133
Kenya 30, 45, 97, 126, 170
Khalid Sheikh Mohammed 88, 157
Khan, Mohammad Sidique 133, 191–2
Kosovo 15, 66
Kurdistan Workers Party 32

Lebanon 34, 41, 46, 63, 149
Lehi group 18
Liberation Tigers of Tamil Elaam (LTTE) 16, 32, 62, 65, 129, 149
Libya 12, 15, 34, 149, 174
liddism 150
London bombings (7/7) 41, 76, 95, 101–2, 133, 148, 163, 182, 184, 190–2
lone wolf terrorism/lone wolves 37–8, 88

Madrid bombing 41, 76, 101, 141, 148, 182, 190
Malaya/Malaysia 99, 126
media 1, 4, 17, 31, 38, 46, 51–2, 68, 70–2, 76, 78, 83, 95, 116–17, 123, 126, 182
MI5 182, 191–3
Milgram experiment 123
moral panic 20
Mujahideen 78, 92, 95
Mumbai 63, 148, 190
Munich 175–6
Muslim 4, 6, 39, 62–3, 92, 94, 97, 99–102, 112, 123, 125, 129, 132–3, 159, 190–2
Myanmar 14

National Liberation Front of Algeria (FLN) 32, 38
National Organization of Cypriot Fighters (EOKA) 32, 39
Native Americans 5, 126
NATO 123, 146, 148, 172
naxalite(s) 63, 149–50
NAZIs 13, 15, 44, 46, 61, 74
Nelson Mandela 18
network 3–4, 13, 24, 31–5, 37, 39, 41, 64, 90–6, 99, 101, 140, 182, 190, 192
neurological 113–16, 118–19
New American Century 73, 144–6, 148
North Korea 14–15
Northern Ireland 6–7, 18–19, 22–4, 38, 63–5, 119, 126, 149, 176–9, 187

Obama, Barack 84, 146, 148, 155, 157, 173

Oklahoma City 30, 35, 67, 109, 181
Omagh 41, 129
one percent doctrine 69
Operation Enduring Freedom 188
Operation Iraqi Freedom 188, 191
Operation Nexus 184–5
Operation Wrath of God 175
Osama bin Laden 4, 76, 81, 87–91, 97–102,
    112, 133, 148, 166–74, 179, 181, 189
Oslo Accords 64

Pakistan 5, 39, 62–3, 76, 81–2, 85, 89–90, 95–6,
    99–100, 102, 109–10, 127, 133, 144, 146,
    148–9, 166–7, 172–3, 179, 190
Palestine 18, 33, 39, 45, 61–2, 64, 99, 118,
    126–7, 132–3, 167–71, 175–6; occupation of
    33, 64, 129, 149, 167–71, 175–6
Palestinian Liberation Organisation (PLO) 20,
    22, 33, 37, 174–5
PATRIOT Act 186, 189
Pentagon 17, 22, 144, 188–9
political entrepreneurs 5, 111
political violence 3, 5–6, 11–12, 17–18, 20–2,
    24, 44, 46, 50, 53, 61, 63, 107–8, 112, 128,
    146, 149, 167, 169, 176, 181, 183,188–90,
    193
Post Traumatic Stress Disorder (PTSD) 5, 72,
    116, 118
poverty 2, 5, 56, 107–16, 119
Project for a New American Century 73
propaganda 12, 16, 94–5, 101, 156, 170, 187,
    193,
Provisional Irish Republican Army (PIRA) 129,
    176, 181

radioactive bomb 81–2, 87–8
Red Army Faction (RAF) 20, 33, 36–7, 40;
    German 39; Japanese 33
Red Brigade 20
Reid, Richard 183, 191
reign of terror 13, 43–4, 50
relative deprivation 5, 115
religious extremism 2, 5, 77, 121–2, 125
risk 4, 6, 21, 24, 38, 40, 63, 72–87, 98, 111,
    115–6, 132, 139, 148, 173, 179– 188
Robespierre 13, 43–4, 49
Royal Ulster Constabulary (RUC) 186
Russia 5, 13, 16, 62, 65, 76, 79, 85, 108, 115,
    145, 149, 166, 168–9; *see also* Soviet Union
Rwanda 14–15, 46

Salafism 94, 123, 128
Saudi Arabia 30, 34, 97, 100, 123–4
Scheuer, Michael 85
segmented, polycentric, ideologically integrated
    network (SPIN) 92
September 11, 2001 (9/11/2001, 9/11) 1, 3–7,
    13, 17–22, 30, 35, 40, 46, 50–1, 56, 66–76,

84, 88, 93–102, 107–9, 112, 127, 132–3, 139,
    143–8, 181–93
Serbia 14
Shining Path 65
Shock and Awe 23
Singapore 71
single-issue terrorists 15
social identity theory 124
social scripts 114, 116
Somalia 32, 92, 96, 148
South Africa 21, 115, 132
Soviet Union 14–15, 20–1, 44, 65, 74, 94, 97,
    144; *see also* Russia
Spain 6, 12, 48, 77, 112, 144, 149, 173, 178–9
state sponsorship (of terrorism) 12, 14, 31–2, 34,
    50, 121
Stern Gang 18
subjection to noise 154
Sudan 32, 39, 97–9, 124
suicide bombing 12–13, 23, 46, 81, 97, 107, 112,
    129, 133, 139–40, 143, 163, 168–70, 173,
    191–2
suicide terrorism 5
suppression 5, 12, 14, 143, 149–50
Symbionese Liberation Army 37
Syria 14, 34, 99, 189

Taliban 63, 88, 94, 97–100, 102, 144–55, 181,
    188–90
Tamil Tigers *see* Liberation Tigers of Tamil
    Elaam (LTTE)
Tanzania 30, 97, 170
targeted assassination 6, 148, 169, 173–80
Tea Party 124
terrorism Studies 1–2, 13, 15–18, 33, 51–2, 56,
    84, 109
Thailand 99, 149
The Troubles 19–20
Tiananmen Square massacre 14
ticking bomb scenario 6, 158–63
Times Square 71, 192
Tora Bora 34, 90
Torture Convention 153–7, 159
Trotsky 13, 44, 49
Tunisia 34, 92, 98, 148
Turkey 62, 76, 98
Tutsis 46

Ulster Defence Association (UDA) 19–20
Ulster Freedom Fighters (UFF) 20
Ulster Volunteer Force (UVF) 19
UNA bomber 38
United Kingdom (UK) 12, 18, 65, 98, 173–4,
    176, 182, 184–93
United Nations (UN) 13–15, 22, 34, 87, 146–7,
    153, 160, 172, 188; Human Rights Council
    22
US State Department 22

USS Cole 97, 166
Uzbekistan 76

Vietnam 39, 45, 108, 133, 158, 167

wall-standing 154, 165
Walzer, Michael 159–61, 165
war on terror(ism)/global war on terror 5, 24,
    41, 56–7, 67, 69, 73, 98–9, 143–55, 159, 163,
    166, 181, 183, 188–90, 193
water-boarding 153, 157, 189

weapons of mass destruction (WMD) 3–4, 35,
    40–1, 64, 69, 73, 77–89, 102, 159, 188
Weather Underground 39–40
World Trade Center 1993 bombing 17, 30, 67,
    133, 144, 181, 188
World War I 18, 44, 61, 66, 86
World War II 12, 23, 66, 74

Yemen 34, 39, 62, 95, 98–9, 110, 148, 166

Zimbabwe 21